Immigrant Narratives

Immigrant Narratives

ORIENTALISM AND CULTURAL TRANSLATION IN ARAB AMERICAN AND ARAB BRITISH LITERATURE

Waïl S. Hassan

Oxford University Press is a department of the University of Oxford.
It furthers the University's objective of excellence in research, scholarship,
and education by publishing worldwide.

Oxford New York
Auckland Cape Town Dar es Salaam Hong Kong Karachi
Kuala Lumpur Madrid Melbourne Mexico City Nairobi
New Delhi Shanghai Taipei Toronto

With offices in
Argentina Austria Brazil Chile Czech Republic France Greece
Guatemala Hungary Italy Japan Poland Portugal Singapore
South Korea Switzerland Thailand Turkey Ukraine Vietnam

Oxford is a registered trade mark of Oxford University Press
in the UK and certain other countries.

Published in the United States of America by
Oxford University Press
198 Madison Avenue, New York, NY 10016

© Oxford University Press 2011

First issued as an Oxford University Press paperback, 2014.

All rights reserved. No part of this publication may be reproduced, stored in a retrieval system, or transmitted, in any form or by any means, without the prior permission in writing of Oxford University Press, or as expressly permitted by law, by license, or under terms agreed with the appropriate reproduction rights organization. Inquiries concerning reproduction outside the scope of the above should be sent to the Rights Department, Oxford University Press, at the address above.

You must not circulate this work in any other form
and you must impose this same condition on any acquirer.

Library of Congress Cataloging-in-Publication Data
Hassan, Waïl S.
Immigrant narratives : orientalism and cultural translation in Arab American and Arab British literature /
Waïl S. Hassan.
p. cm.
Includes bibliographical references and index.
ISBN 978-0-19-979206-1 (cloth : alk. paper); 978-0-19-935497-9 (paperback)
1. American literature—Arab American authors—History and criticism.
2. English literature—Arab authors—History and criticism. 3. Immigration in literature.
4. Arab Americans—Ethnic identity. 5. Arab Americans in literature. 6. Arabs in literature. I. Title.
PS153.A73H37 2011
820.9′8927—dc22 2010054543

For Stephanie

No one today is purely *one* thing. Labels like Indian, or woman, or Muslim, or American are not more than starting-points, which if followed into actual experience for a moment are quickly left behind. Imperialism consolidated the mixture of cultures and identities on a global scale. But its worst and most paradoxical gift was to allow people to believe that they were only, mainly, exclusively, white, or Black, or Western, or Oriental.

—EDWARD W. SAID

CONTENTS

PREFACE

The idea of writing a book on Arab American and Arab British literature came to me nearly a decade ago, when, surveying publishers' catalogues, I came across several new Arab novelists who wrote in English. I was aware of a handful of such writers, but the new names and titles, as well as the variety of themes and authors' backgrounds, suggested to me that one could teach a whole course on Anglophone Arab writers. One reason for the appeal of that idea was the relative dearth, at that time, of good English translations of Arabic literary texts. The award of the Nobel Prize to Naguib Mahfouz in 1988 had generated interest in Arabic literature, but with the exception of the iconic figures of Mahfouz, Nawal el-Saadawi, Tayeb Salih, and a few others, the enormous breadth and variety of one of the world's great literatures was still woefully under-represented in English translation. The few writers who filtered through were, with few exceptions, subjected to unsatisfactory and sometimes even prejudicial translations that did more to reinforce than to dispel Orientalist stereotypes. The idea of Arab writers who communicated directly in English was, therefore, exhilarating. Another reason for my interest in those works was that I had for some years been working on Tayeb Salih, a Sudanese novelist who had immigrated to England in the early 1950s, where he wrote some of the most important works of modern Arabic fiction, works that were profoundly marked by his immigrant perspective. The question that the increasing number of Anglophone Arab novels suggested to me was, how would Salih's works have been different had he written in English (and his English was flawless) instead of Arabic? While that question may be impossible to answer, this book examines how other Arab immigrants who have written in English weave their narratives.

As I began to research the field, I was struck by the sheer number of writers and works that have gone unnoticed and passed quietly out of print—an entire tradition of Arab American literature, in fact, stretching back to the early years of the twentieth century. That tradition was rarely mentioned in the by-then thriving fields of ethnic American, minority, and postcolonial studies, and outside the bounds of Arabic studies, which understandably focuses only on the vast field of literature written in the Arabic language. In other words, a whole tradition had simply fallen between the disciplinary cracks. And while the history of Arab immigration to the United States was well documented, the genesis of Arab American literature remained to be adequately charted. A few general overviews, studies of individual authors, and anthologies provided useful entry points into the subject, but no systematic account of the birth and development of a literature that was entering its second century had been attempted on any large scale. Given the exponential increase in the amount of literature published by Arab American, Arab British, Arab Canadian, and Arab Australian writers since the early 1990s, the time seemed ripe for a critical framework and assessment.

As I read through those works, I came to realize that, first, a distinction needs to be made between the work of immigrants and that of U.S.- and British-born writers, that the biculturalism of immigrants and exiles needs to be distinguished from what may be described, following W. E. B. Du Bois, as the "double-consciousness" of U.S.- and British-born Arab writers. Although immigrants and immigrants' children are easy to homogenize under the aegis of minority, their experiences, adjustments, and perspectives require careful differentiation that continues to be lacking in the relatively slight body of literary scholarship produced thus far. Second, I realized that the Arab minority experience in countries that have played a major imperial role in the Arab world—the U.K. and the U.S.—is distinctive and must, both for practical reasons as well as for the sake of methodological coherence, and despite important similarities, be distinguished from Anglophone Arab writing in the Arab world or in other English-speaking immigrant destinations such as Canada and Australia. The writer's conception of the homeland and the land of immigration or exile is over-determined by the relationship between the two countries, and imperial interests and ventures make that relationship particularly vexed. Therefore, this book focuses on immigrant Arab American and Arab British narratives, as well as political and cultural commentary by the novelists and autobiographers under consideration. I argue that the predominant stance of those writers has been that of a cultural translator who claims a privileged position to interpret the Arab world to American or British readers. Such interpretation is always conducted through the prism of Orientalism, a hegemonic frame of reference that cannot be avoided, and is always framed, whether explicitly or implicitly, by the politics of empire. The strategies of Arab immigrants' confrontation with Orientalism have evolved in step with the changing ideological functions of that discourse from the late nineteenth century to the post-9/11 period.

This book is not a literary history. Although I have organized it chronologically, my aim has not been to discuss every writer of note or even every stage of development. Indeed, readers will find that several important authors and texts, including the great majority of Arab American poetry and drama, are simply left out.[1] Rather, my aim is to investigate how key authors and texts help us discern the main features of Arab immigrant narrative in the U.S. and Britain, and to draw from that a critical framework for reading that tradition. The Introduction unpacks the three key terms of the title: immigrant literature, Orientalism, and cultural translation. I argue that Arab immigrant literature can be usefully read in light of Gilles Deleuze and Félix Guattari's theory of minor literature, but that that theory must be supplemented by considerations, first, of the Orientalist framework which shapes both the production and the reception of Arab immigrants' work in the U.S. and Britain, and second, of the translational role that Arab immigrant writers play as interpreters and mediators between their homeland and adoptive countries. That is to say, the theory of minor literature needs to be nuanced by recourse to postcolonial and translation theory. Each of the subsequent chapters focuses on one, two, or three writers who represent different periods, orientations, or national backgrounds.

Evelyn Shakir, a pioneer of Arab American literary studies, divides the tradition into "three distinct stages—early, middle, and recent—each of them responsive to the political currents of its day" (Shakir 1996, 3). The major writers of the early period (1900–1920s) are Ameen Rihani, Kahlil Gibran, and Abraham Mitrie Rihbany. Chapter 1 focuses on Ameen Rihani, the first major Arab American author and a prolific novelist, poet, playwright, travelogue writer, political commentator, and literary critic who wrote in Arabic and English. The chapter places Rihani in relation to the two traditions that he tries to fuse in his work: Arabic literature, particularly its intellectual context of the nineteenth and early twentieth century, and the Euro-American literary tradition. Chapter 2 deals with the extraordinary fame of Kahlil Gibran, which was possible, I argue, because he embodied the stereotype of the Oriental sage. Poet, short-story writer, visionary, and self-styled guru, Gibran's model of cultural translation parallels but also differs from that of his senior contemporary, Rihani. The Gibran phenomenon is unavoidable in any consideration of the conditions of possibility of Anglophone Arab writing. Chapter 3 turns to the works of Abraham Rihbany, a Protestant preacher who wrote the first Arab American autobiography and several books on politics, culture, and theology, in which he assumed the role of Orientalist expert; his contemporary, George Haddad, the only pack peddler to write an autobiography, is also considered.

The middle period of Arab American literature, according to Shakir, spans the 1930s to the 1960s. It saw the publication of relatively few works by immigrants like Salom Rizk and George Hamid, and by second-generation writers like Vance Bourjaily and William Blatty, who either did not identify themselves as Arab American or felt highly conflicted about their heritage (see also Shakir 1982 and 1991). The early immigrants' emphasis on Americanization and integration, the drastic reduction of Arab immigration as a result of the 1924 National Origins Act, the prevalent hostility to foreigners, and the growing anti-Arab racism as a result of the political situation in the Middle East, all combined to force Arab Americans underground. Belonging to a nonvisible and largely Christian minority officially classified as white, many of them tried to pass, changing names and church affiliations and "costum[ing] themselves as regular Americans" (Shakir 1996, 6). Chapter 4 is devoted to the two immigrants from this period, Rizk and Hamid, whose narratives register the changing mood in the U.S. during the Depression and World War II and the effects of those conditions on the perception of immigrants. All of the writers discussed in the first four chapters are Lebanese immigrants.

The third phase of Arab American literature, according to Shakir's periodization, began in the 1970s and witnessed the emergence of scores of poets, novelists, memoirists, and playwrights—both immigrants who came after the immigration reforms of 1952 and 1965, and U.S.-born writers who have asserted their presence and Arab identity with great force. In the post-Civil Rights era, when minorities began to affirm and celebrate their ethnicity, and with the influx of immigrants from across the Arab world, "Arab American" became the new moniker used by Arab immigrants and those of Arab descent. Broader in coverage than the earlier term "Syrian," "Arab American" refers to anyone who hails from Arabic-speaking countries, predominantly Algerians, Egyptians, Iraqis, Libyans, Moroccans, Sudanese, Tunisians, and Yemenis, in addition to more immigrants from Greater Syria who now identify themselves as Lebanese, Palestinians, Syrians, or Jordanians. Unlike the immigrants of the late nineteenth and early twentieth century, the newcomers have been mostly Muslims, highly educated, and middle-class. They have also been politicized as a result of the events in the Middle East. Chapter 5 surveys Palestinian American autobiography in general, before focusing on the narratives of three 1948 refugees: Aziz Shihab, Edward Said, and Fawaz Turki. Chapter 6 registers the generational gap as well as the shift in discursive conditions discernible in the autobiographies of two Egyptian American academics, Ihab Hassan and Leila Ahmed, the one drawing upon American Orientalism within a postmodern mode, the other on Muslim feminist discourse. British-educated Ahmed also represents a bridge between Arab American and the emergent Arab British writing (Geoffrey Nash, for instance, discusses her work in his *The Anglo-Arab Encounter*, which focuses on Arab British literature). After briefly describing the beginnings of Arab British literature, chapter 7 turns to Egyptian-born novelist Ahdaf Soueif, whose work best illustrates what I call translational literature, works that foreground the processes of cultural translation. In this respect, Soueif's work completes the project initiated by Ameen Rihani and builds upon Edward Said's critique of Orientalism. Like Ahmed's memoir, Soueif's novels unfold in Egypt, England, and the U.S., focusing on the politics of empire throughout the twentieth century. Chapter 8 examines the fictional project of Sudanese Scottish novelist Leila Aboulela, who, like Soueif, emphasizes the translational nature of cultural exchange. However, Aboulela's fiction belongs to a new trend that has been called "Muslim immigrant literature," and her overarching concern is with expounding the Islamic worldview of the growing Muslim minority in Britain. Chapter 9 focuses on the queer fiction of Jordanian American Ramzi Salti and Lebanese American Rabih Alameddine, whose texts reveal their preoccupation with homosexuality, the problematic nature of storytelling, and the epistemology and politics of cultural translation. The conclusion draws out some of the implications of this book for the fields of American, Arabic, and British literary studies and for the college curriculum more generally.

I have benefited in countless ways from the insights, help, suggestions, and encouragement of an embarrassingly large number of people, something that is no less true for being a formulaic confession. It will become immediately clear to the reader that the main source of inspiration for this book has been the work of the late Edward Said, whose influence on literary and cultural studies is immeasurable. It may be that, according to Abdelfattah Kilito, Arabists working in European languages are almost always comparatists, and not always in the best sense, but I have learned the best practices of comparative literature from Michael Palencia-Roth. It is practically impossible to list by name hundreds of students who have given me the benefit of their insights and helped me see how the books I asked them to read worked on readers other than myself; impossible also to name countless patient and indulging audience members at lectures and conferences around the country and abroad, whose questions challenged me to think through many of the ideas presented here while they were still at various stages of ferment. Ferial Ghazoul gave me a deadline that made me write the very first portion of this book at a time when the task seemed almost impossible; it was a welcome and propitious push forward. Susan Andrade, Gordon Hutner, Elie Shalala, and Layla Al Maleh—astute, generous, and judicious editors—graciously invited me to their forums, furnished the motivation and encouragement, and gave me the benefit of their editorial acumen. Jonathan Arac, Nancy Armstrong, Marilyn Booth, Paul Bové, Christopher Breu, Gaurav Desai, Nouri Gana, Stephanie Hilger, Ronald Judy, Jeoffrey Nash, Mohamed-Salah Omri, Bruce Robbins, Steven Salaita, along with anonymous reviewers, all read and shared their immensely useful insights into various parts of the book. Roger Allen, Aida Bamia, Barbara Harlow, Anouar Majid, and Muhammad Siddiq in many ways helped make it possible. Some of the principal ideas in this book began to take shape during a uniquely productive year spent as a Sawyer/Mellon Postdoctoral Fellow at the University of Virginia's English Department in 2003–04, where I enjoyed the hospitality, friendship, support, and stimulating conversation of Alison Booth, Karen Chase, Rita Felski, Susan Fraiman, Eleanor Kaufman, Michael Levenson, Jahan Ramazani, Caroline Rody, and Jennifer Wicke. I was also the beneficiary of two summer research grants from Illinois State University in 2002 and 2003. At the University of Illinois at Urbana-Champaign, a Mellon Faculty Fellowship in 2004, a Research Board Award in 2007, and a Center for Advanced Study fellowship in 2008 allowed me to complete the book, and discussions with colleagues and friends at that wonderful institution found myriad paths into the book: Nancy Blake, Stephen Jaeger, Brett Kaplan, Lilya Kaganovsky, Jean-Philippe Mathy, Robert Parker, Junaid Rana, Robert Rushing, Zohreh Sullivan, and Mara Wade. Lectures based on material included here were presented at Illinois State University, New York University, the University of Colorado at Boulder, the University of Illinois at Urbana-Champaign, the University of Michigan-Dearborn, the University of Minnesota-Twin Cities, the University of Pennsylvania, the University of Virginia, and in keynote addresses at the Tenth Annual Red River Conference on World Literature, held at North Dakota State University in April 2007, and the *Jil Jadid* conference on Arabic studies, convened at the University of Texas at Austin in February 2011. For those unique opportunities, my gratitude to Emily Apter, Hani Bawardi, Hala Halim, R.S. Krishnan, Alex Magidow, John Mowitt, Issam Nassar, Maggie Nassif, Carol Pearson, Thomas Pepper, Michael Rothberg, Jochen Schulte-Sasse, John Stevenson, and Eric White. Junjie Luo was a phenomenally able, conscientious, meticulous, and judicious research assistant in 2005–06. At Oxford University Press, the enthusiasm, support, efficiency, and expert handling of the manuscript on the part of Shannon McLachlan, Brendan O'Neill, Jenny Wolkowicki, Susan Vunderink, Preetha Baskaran, Theresa Stockton, along with their capable editorial, production, and marketing teams, have been all that an author could possibly wish for. Throughout the time that I have worked on this book, Stephanie Hilger has been a thoughtful interlocutor, an incisive reader, a dependable companion, and an inexhaustible source of stimulation and support.

Earlier versions of some of the material in this book previously appeared in *Alif: Journal of Comparative Poetics* 22 (2002): 7–35; *Aljadid: A Review & Record of Arab Culture and Arts* 10:46/47 (Winter-Spring 2004): 36–37; *PMLA* 121:3 (May 2006): 753–68; *American Literary History* 20: 1/2 (Spring/Summer 2008), 245–75; *Novel: A Forum on Fiction* 41:2/3(Spring/Summer 2008): 298–319; and *Arab Voices in Diaspora: Critical Perspectives on Anglophone Arab Literature*, edited by Layla Al Maleh (Amsterdam: Rodopi, 2009): 65–92.

Immigrant Narratives

Introduction

How do Arab writers address English readers? Do they write differently in English than they do in Arabic, when addressing Arab readers? And how has such writing been shaped by immigration and the authors' minority status in the United States and Britain? How do those writers negotiate their position between two cultures? In what ways is that negotiation overdetermined by historical circumstances, cultural worldviews, ideological projects, political climates, discursive conditions, readers' expectations, editors' strictures, and publishers' marketing strategies? Those questions guide my investigation into Arab American literature, a substantial tradition that emerged in the early days of the twentieth century, and its Arab British counterpart, much smaller and more recent. Like other minority literatures, Arab immigrant writing is never free of such contextual considerations.

Over three decades ago, Edward Said argued that "because of Orientalism the Orient was not (and is not) a free subject of thought and action." This is because "no one writing, thinking, or acting on the Orient could do so without taking account of the limitations on thought or action imposed by Orientalism," and because a "whole network of interests [is] inevitably brought to bear on . . . any occasion when that peculiar entity . . . is in question" (Said 1978, 3). Following Said, postcolonial studies has investigated the pervasiveness of Orientalism and the myriad ways in which countless European and American writers have been marked by it. This book is about how Orientalism has also profoundly influenced immigrant Arab writers, how they have reacted to it, and how their position as cultural translators has shaped their discourses. According to Said, no European or American writer could approach the Arab world from a vantage point untainted by Orientalism; I argue here that Arab authors who use the medium of English, especially if they live in a country with a powerful tradition of Orientalist scholarship that serves imperial interests in the Arab world, could not ignore Orientalism, either.

Since the early nineteenth century, Arab modernity, politics, and the very sense of Arab identity have been profoundly impacted by the history of European, and later U.S., imperialism in the Arab world, in which Orientalism has played a central role. British and French colonialism drew the current political map of the Middle East; even the naming of the region, which dates back only to 1903, indexes the Eurocentrism of geopolitical discourse.[1] Following World War II, the U.S. replaced the British and the French as the major power broker in the region, and its imperial ventures there have intensified since the Soviet Union's demise, and especially since September 11, 2001. Arab immigrant writers have not responded uniformly to that history or to the cultural, racial, religious, and political discourses that shape their readers' views of Arabs. The chapters that follow examine how individual writers have negotiated historical, ideological, and discursive conditions in ways that vary according to education, profession, gender, national origin, political ideology, and personal temperament, as well as family, class, and religious background. Those writers are as heterogeneous as any other group: socioeconomically they include members of the peasantry, working class, lower to upper middle class, and the aristocracy; politically they include conservatives, liberals, and leftists; religiously they are Maronites, Catholics, Protestants, Anglicans, Sunnis, Shiites, Druze, agnostics, and atheists; and they include bohemians, feminists, gays, and lesbians. They have ranged in their ideological beliefs from racialists and Orientalists to multiculturalists, from Islamophobes to Islamists, and from Zionists to anti-Zionists. Their diversity is reflected in their widely divergent approaches to the problems of Orientalism and cultural translation. Yet despite that diversity, Arab immigrant writers since the late nineteenth century have all had to contend with Orientalist stereotypes and prejudices that surface in step with changes in domestic climate and political developments abroad. Indeed, what those writers have in common is the existential fact of being immigrants who write in English, whose relationship to their readers is mediated by the dominant discourse of Orientalism that defines them in their adoptive countries, and who have found that their position imposes limits on what they can say and how they say it, but also affords them a unique opportunity to act as cultural translators. Those three concepts—immigrant minority, Orientalism, and cultural translation—guide my reading of the tradition. In the first of the following four sections, I elucidate my use of the theory of minor literature; the two following sections focus on Orientalism in theory and in its American context; and in the final section I take up the question of cultural translation in relation to Orientalism and to translation theory.

Immigrants and Minor Literature

Immigrant writing is a minor literature, or a subset of minor literature, as defined by Gilles Deleuze and Félix Guattari in *Kafka: Toward a Minor Literature*. The French theorists argue that "a minor literature does not come from a minor language; it is rather that which a minority constructs within a major language" (Deleuze and Guattari 16). Such a literature has three characteristics: "the deterritorialization of language, the connection of the individual to a political immediacy, and the collective assemblage of enunciation" (18). First, a major language in the hands of a minority writer is defamiliarized through its infusion with words, expressions, rhetorical figures, speech patterns, ideological intentions, and the worldview of the author's minority group, which differentiate the writer's language from that of the mainstream culture, producing all sorts of estranging effects. The second characteristic—that, because of the marginal status of minor literatures, "everything in them is political"—means that there is little distance between individual concerns and the political status of the minority group. "The cramped space" of a minor literature "forces each individual intrigue to connect immediately to politics. The individual concern thus becomes all the more necessary, indispensable, magnified, because a whole other story [the story of the minority group] is vibrating within it" (17). Closely related to that is the third feature of minor literature, namely that "in it everything takes on a collective value," that is to say, "there are no possibilities for an individuated enunciation . . . that could be separated from a collective enunciation. . . . [W]hat each author says individually already constitutes a common action, and what he or she does is necessarily political, even if others aren't in agreement" (17). The personal is always collective, and the concerns of the individual are shared by other members of the minority, again because of social pressures from the majority. Deleuze and Guattari suggest that attention be paid to "the functions of language" and to "bilingualism or even multilingualism" (23) and stress the revolutionary potential of the minor (26), citing the example of Kafka, Joyce, Beckett, and Céline as novelists who deterritorialized the language of the (German, English, and French) majority.

Deleuze and Guattari's theory is immensely useful to understanding the dynamics at work in Arab immigrant literature, although, like all theories, it has its limitations. As the following chapters illustrate, the three features they describe are discernible to various degrees and in different combinations in the works under consideration. In fact, the three characteristics of minor literature are also evident in English-language works of Arab and Arab-descended writers beyond the scope of this book, which examines only the English-language texts of immigrants. It traces the figure of the immigrant who stands between the culture of origin and that of the adoptive country and, equipped with first-hand knowledge of both, assumes the role of mediator, interpreter, or cultural translator. Such is not the case with non-immigrant Arab minorities. Descendants of Arab immigrants are in a similar predicament to that of the children of immigrants from other parts of the world, who, growing up American or British, have various degrees of exposure to their parents' culture and language. Immigrants bring with them their own cultural background and worldview, and their transition into the U.S. or Britain involves a kind of negotiation and adjustment that is quite distinct from the cultural predicament of their children.

Deleuze and Guattari's theory does not make that distinction between immigrant and non-immigrant minorities, a limitation that restricts its usefulness not only to Arab but also to other ethnic immigrant literatures. Designed on the model of a single writer (Kafka) who belongs to a specific minority (the Jews of Prague) with a unique linguistic situation (German vis-à-vis Czech and Yiddish), that theory does not account for the differences between first generation (or immigrant) writers and those born as second, third, or fourth generation minorities. Furthermore, because they generalize the model of a single writer, Deleuze and Guattari posit the minor as always being an ideological antagonist. As the whole range of translational stances explored in the following chapters demonstrates, some Arab American and Arab British writers have, indeed, taken an oppositional stance toward dominant discourses, while others have been rather accommodating and have, in fact, promoted political and cultural ideas hostile to their countries and cultures of origin. Such aspects of immigrant writing as the rejection of (or rebellion against) the homeland, the desire to be accepted by the majority, and what may be diplomatically called ideological flexibility, go unnoticed in Deleuze and Guattari, as does the whole spectrum of discursive negotiations and ideological stances of immigrants.

This wide range of stances explains why the three characteristics of minor literature as described by Deleuze and Guattari (the deterritorialization of language, the alignment of individual and collective intrigue, and the political nature of individual enunciation and action) are not always fully or uniformly present in Arab American and Arab British texts. Sometimes they are found in different combinations, and many texts are often characterized by unresolved tension rather than seamless continuity between the individual and the community, the personal and the political. For instance, the fact that many writers accepted the basic tenets of Orientalism has had different consequences. Some accepted the hierarchical valuations based on the East/West dichotomy (e.g., Abraham Rihbany), while others rejected the implications of superiority and inferiority, opting instead for a dichotomy of equals (e.g., Ameen Rihani and the later Rihbany). Some of those who acquiesced to the notion of Oriental inferiority tried to distance themselves from the homeland, even voicing hostility toward it, and proclaiming an exclusive claim to Americanness; such writers tend to refuse to be seen as representatives of an Arab American collectivity, embracing instead the collectivity of the American majority (e.g., Salom Rizk), or the ideology of individualism (e.g. Ihab Hassan). Other immigrants who rejected the stigma of Orientalness resorted to passing as white and to the ultimate form of literary silence: abstaining from writing. Other forms of rejection of the stamp of Oriental inferiority are more assertive, identifying with and championing an immigrant and a broader Arab collectivity, itself imagined in multiple and sometimes irreconcilable ways (e.g., Rihani, Kahlil Gibran, Fawaz Turki, Edward Said, Ahdaf Soueif, Leila Aboulela). Such writers accept the kind of representational burden implied in Deleuze and Guattari's second and third features of minor literature. There are also writers who reject the Orientalist dichotomy altogether, and some of them embrace the representational burden of the second and third features of minor literature with the urgency of committed activism (e.g., Turki's first two memoirs, Said's scholarship, the later Soueif, Aboulela, Ramzi Salti, Rabih Alameddine). In the work of other writers who are more concerned with individual self-expression, there is a discernible tension between the demands of the personal and the political, the private and the collective (e.g., Turki's third memoir, the early Soueif, Alameddine's first novel). In such cases, while the writer accepts the burden of being a representative for the collectivity, he or she wrestles with and tries to change the terms of cultural discourse. All of this, in turn, has had different implications for the first characteristic, with some writers deliberately deterritorializing English through Arabic (e.g. Rihani), others foregoing linguistic and stylistic deterritorialization in favor of formal experimentation (Alameddine), another group writing in a fluent and idiomatic English meant to "prove" that they are worthy of American citizenship (Rihbany, Rizk), and still others combining formal and linguistic experimentation (Soueif). Despite such variations, and in fact because of them, Deleuze and Guattari's theory is a useful starting point for the interpretation of Arab immigrant writing; however, given that Orientalism is the reigning episteme within which that literature is produced and that cultural translation is its mode of being, Deleuze's and Guattari's theory must be supplemented by postcolonial and translation theory.

East/West

At the outset of his classic study of the subject, Edward Said states that by Orientalism he means three things: first, an academic discipline; second, "a style of thought based upon an ontological and epistemological distinction made between 'the Orient' and (most of the time) 'the Occident'"; and third, "a Western style for dominating, restructuring, and having authority over the Orient" (1978, 2–3). Though "interdependent" (2), those meanings of the term are nonetheless distinct, although their overlapping generated part of the controversy that swirled around *Orientalism*. The reasons have to do with the discrepant temporal and epistemological scope of each, despite the use of one word to designate all three of them, not to mention Said's own occasional slippage from one to the other throughout the book. The first meaning is perhaps the least problematic, referring to those who study and teach about the Orient in academic settings, some of which have continued to bear names such as "The Oriental Institute" and "The School of Oriental and African Studies." The second meaning is more open-ended, broader, and, as Said puts it, "more general" (2): simply "a style of thought" based on a dichotomy or a "basic distinction" accepted by many writers who have developed "elaborate theories, epics, social descriptions, and political accounts concerning the Orient, its people, customs, 'mind,' destiny, and so on. *This* Orientalism can accommodate Aeschylus, say, and Victor Hugo, Dante and Karl Marx" (2–3). The third meaning is "more historically and materially defined than either of the other two. Taking the later eighteenth century as a very roughly defined starting point, Orientalism can be discussed and analyzed as the corporate institution for dealing with the Orient . . . by making statements about it, authorizing views of it, describing it, by teaching it, settling it, ruling over it: in short, Orientalism as a Western style of dominating, restructuring, and having authority over the Orient" (3).

At this point, Said introduces Michel Foucault's concept of discourse: "without examining Orientalism as a discourse, one cannot possibly understand the enormously systematic discipline by which European culture was able to manage—and even produce—the Orient politically, sociologically, militarily, ideologically, scientifically, and imaginatively during the post-Enlightenment period" (3). However, it is not clear whether for Said the term "discourse" covers all three types of Orientalism or only the third, as suggested by the paragraph division in his text and by the fact that mention of the third type immediately precedes the sentence in which he brings in Foucault. After all, if, as Said himself points out, "the interchange between the academic [i.e., the first] and the more or less imaginative [the second] meanings of Orientalism is a constant one, and since the late eighteenth century there has been a considerable, quite disciplined—perhaps even regulated—traffic between the two" (3), then the same traffic must also exist between those two meanings and the third, administrative or colonial one, the beginning of which he also dates in the late eighteenth century. If that is indeed the case, then all three types of Orientalism are covered by the concept of discourse.

While this interpretation seems to be what Said had in mind, it creates a categorical difficulty. Much has been written on the problems posed by Said's inclusion of Aeschylus, Dante, and Hugo in one seemingly trans-historical discourse, something that is irreconcilable with Foucault's notions of the episteme and of rupture, which limit the temporal scope of discourse, as he uses it, to discrete historical periods, such as the Renaissance or the Enlightenment. Also problematic is Said's seemingly reductive and homogenizing treatment of Orientalists and his depiction of a passive Orient that could not resist Orientalist representation.[2] I have no desire to revisit those well-rehearsed controversies here, but I mention them in order to contextualize my analysis of the ways in which Arab immigrant writers have engaged with what I want to suggest are multiple Orientalist discourses, or "Orientalisms" as Malini Johar Schueller aptly puts it. As Said himself explains, Orientalism has American, British, French, German, Russian, and Spanish branches, which are not identical to one another; indeed, he decides to focus only on British and French Orientalisms from the late eighteenth to the mid-twentieth centuries, and on American Orientalism in the second half of the twentieth century, which he differentiates in important ways from the British and the French. Moreover, as Fu'ad Shaaban's work demonstrates, nineteenth-century American Orientalism was, in turn, rather different from, on the one hand, European Orientalisms of the same period, being based largely on biblical mythology and *Arabian Nights* fantasy, and, on the other hand, the American Orientalism of the second half of the twentieth century, which Said describes as being heavily weighted by Cold War politics and the Arab–Israeli conflict.

Yet at the same time, and despite this multiplicity, there is no doubt that Orientalist discourses share some fundamental principles, not only among themselves, but also with earlier discursive formations going back at least to the Crusades, as evidenced, for instance, by the Bush administration's rhetoric of "the War on Terror" and "the Axis of Evil," which gave many in the Arab and Muslim worlds the impression that the U.S. was declaring a new Crusade against Islam. Nor was the Bush rhetoric new. Nearly a century earlier, when the British army advanced on Palestine in October 1917, the campaign was portrayed in the British and American press as the "Last Crusade," and its leader was quite readily eulogized as "Allenby of

Armageddon."[3] By the same token, the scene of a victorious Allenby standing at the tomb of Saladin in Damascus to vaunt Europe's triumphant "return" remains quite vivid in Arab consciousness even today (Abu Zayd, *Al-Nass* 23). We could certainly, in the interest of theoretical accuracy, speak of a medieval discourse of the Crusades as distinct from, though sharing much with, modern Orientalist discourses, but clearly such academic distinctions are irrelevant in popular imagination and in the discourses of those policy makers, politicians, religious leaders, journalists, and writers who subscribe to Rudyard Kipling's doctrine that "East is East and West is West, and never the twain shall meet." Thus while it would be a mistake to posit a trans-historical discourse of Orientalism, it would also be naïve to deny that many of the cultural representations produced throughout that long history did not, in fact, pass on from one age to another, informing, and being assimilated into different modes of discourse, all based on "an ontological and epistemological distinction made between 'the Orient' and . . . 'the Occident'" (Said 1978, 2)—a distinction which falsely appears to many people to be intuitive and self-evident. Ultimately, it is on this dichotomy that all the various modes of Orientalism depend.

What demands emphasis here, though, is the interesting fact that, whereas Said's critique succeeded in dismantling the concept of the Orient or the East once and for all, its discursive twin and polar opposite, "the West," has proved to be astonishingly resilient. A product of early nineteenth-century colonial ideology, the construct of "the West" continues to inform political discourse, college curricula, academic research, and creative writing even by postcolonial and minority novelists, memoirists, poets, and activists. "The West" is made to appear unproblematic, self-evident, unitary, and trans-historical not only by writers who see themselves as Western or as champions of the West, but also by many who would not countenance its discursive and ideological counterpart, "the East" or "the Orient." At the end of the introduction to *Orientalism*, Said writes that if his book "stimulates a new kind of dealing with the Orient, indeed if it eliminates 'the Orient' and 'Occident' altogether, then we shall have advanced a little in the process of what Raymond Williams has called the 'unlearning' of 'the inherent dominative mode'" (28). Such progress would, indeed, be significant, but as the structure of the sentence suggests, Said's primary objective was to alter the way the "Orient" is treated, while the elimination of the dichotomy seems to have been an afterthought, a secondary and from his viewpoint optimistic goal, even though it is the logical consequence of his critique of the concept of "the Orient." That he did not develop that potential is perhaps understandable in view of the enormity of the task of undermining Orientalism's regime of truth, but his continued use of the term "the West" did not help, either—especially the homogenized, trans-historical "West" that prompted critics to fault him for relying on the same essentialism he criticized.

In any event, many scholars working in such diverse fields as classical studies, medieval studies, geography, history, economic theory, and anthropology have demonstrated how the concept of "the West" is "inherently dominative" and that it is a product of nineteenth-century racialist and colonial ideologies. "The West" constitutes not only a sense of cultural or civilizational identity, but, more fundamentally, an ideology of exceptionalism: the idea of the West as an autonomous (and above all superior) tradition that is radically distinct from other civilizations. Those civilizations are believed to have had no influence on its march from ancient Greece (which is supposed to have created itself *ex nihilo*) down to modern Europe and North America. Martin Bernal's monumental *Black Athena: The Afroasiatic Roots of Classical Civilization*, especially its first volume on *The Fabrication of Ancient Greece 1785–1985* (1986), argued that Eurocentric scholarship of the late eighteenth and early nineteenth century purged Greek history of formative African and Eastern Mediterranean influences in order to establish a purely Aryan origin for Greek civilization, which was construed as the cradle of "Western" civilization. This account of ancient Greece, which Bernal calls the "Aryan model" (Bernal 1986, 1) was consonant with colonial ideology, Romantic racialism, and anti-Semitism (2).[4] Two subsequent volumes of *Black Athena* (1991 and 2006) presented further archaeological, documentary, and linguistic evidence for his thesis.

Working on a similarly controversial topic related to a subsequent period of European cultural history, María Rosa Menocal's research in medieval studies uncovered the same impulse to construct a homogenous Western identity through the erasure of Semitic—Arab and Jewish—influences during seven centuries of Muslim rule in Spain. That period of Spanish history is often regarded as a hiatus or lacuna in the continuity of its Western identity from the Greco-Roman antiquity to the Renaissance, despite the tremendous role that Muslim Spain played in developing the Greek heritage. In "The Myth of Westerness," the first chapter of her path-breaking book, *The Arabic Role in Medieval Literary History: A Forgotten Heritage* (1987), Menocal argues that the concept of "the Western self" depends on "the essential continuity and unity of Western civilization from the Greeks through fifteenth-century Italy, having survived the lull of the Dark Ages. . . . It is a notion of history formulated as much to deny the medieval past and its heritage as to establish a new and more worthy ancestry" (Menocal 5). The denial of the medieval past is a denial of Arab and Jewish contributions to European culture. While the idea of "the Dark Ages" is a product of the Renaissance, "the Myth of Westerness" was created

> in the nineteenth century and it played a critical role at this moment of high-pitched awareness of the particularity and superiority of Europe that came with the imperial and colonial experience and the post-Romantic experience with the Orient. This experience certainly helped sharpen the perception not only of European community and continuity but also its difference from others, or from the Other. It was an Other (and the Arab world was one of its principal manifestations) that Europe was by its own standards bringing out of the darkness and civilizing, at least as far as that was possible for those who were not European in the first place.
>
> Thus was eliminated the possibility that the Middle Ages might be portrayed as a historical period in which a substantial part of culture and learning was based in a radically different foreign culture. To view an Arab-Islamic component, even in its European manifestations, as positive

> and essential would have been unimaginable. . . . The proposition that the Arab world had played a critical role in the making of the modern West, from the vantage point of the late nineteenth century and the better part of this century, is in clear and flagrant contradiction of cultural ideology. It is unimaginable in the context of the readily observable phenomenon that was institutionalized as an essential element of European ideology and that has remained so in many instances to this day: cultural supremacy over the Arab world. (6)

Menocal's project in this and later books (2002, 2008) has been to confront the reigning critical consensus of medievalists who ignore the Arabic role in medieval literary history despite copious evidence and marginalize scholarly work that emphasizes it (1987, vii–viii). This resistance, she argues, lies

> not so much in the difficulty of revising our view of an earlier period of history. In and of itself, that is relatively easy to do, and historical revisionism is one of the most popular of academic pastimes. The key to the unimaginability of this particular bit of revisionism is that it would have challenged and ultimately belied the regnant worldview, requiring the reversal of an ideologically conditioned sense of the communal Western self. It requires the ability not only to imagine but to accept as plausible and admissible an image of our own civilization, at one of its formative moments, as critically indebted to and dependent on a culture that was for some time generally regarded as inferior and, by some lights, as the quintessence of the foreign and the Other. (9)

That is precisely what "the myth of Westerness" guards against; it encapsulates a "cultural ideology" that "may often remain unarticulated—its very unconsciousness being one of its essential traits," but which is "no less powerful for being unspoken" (8).

While Bernal and Menocal have revealed the ideological underpinnings of that myth, J.M. Blaut, Johannes Fabian, Samir Amin, and Andre Gunder Frank have analyzed its projection into history, geography, anthropology, and economic theory. For these scholars, Eurocentrism is the ideological content of the concept of "the West." Blaut challenged "Eurocentric diffusionism," which consists, first, of "the notion that European civilization—'The West'—has had some unique historical advantage, some special quality of race or culture or environment or mind or spirit, which gives this human community a permanent superiority over all other communities, at all times in history and down to the present." Second, according to Blaut,

> that belief is both historical and geographical. Europeans are seen as the "makers of history." Europe eternally advances, progresses, modernizes. The rest of the world advances more sluggishly, or stagnates: it is "traditional society." Therefore, the world has a permanent geographical center and a permanent periphery: an Inside and an Outside. Inside leads, Outside lags. Inside innovates, Outside imitates. (Blaut 1993, 1)

Eurocentric diffusionism further spawns "the theory of the autonomous rise of Europe," the idea that "the economic and social modernization of Europe is fundamentally a result of Europe's *internal* qualities, not of interaction with the societies of Africa, Asia, and America after 1492" (1–2). Frank carries this critique of diffusionism and exceptionalism further in *ReOrient: Global Economy in the Asian Age* (1998), arguing that, contrary to the claims of Eurocentric social theory and economic historians, Europe before 1800 was marginal to the economic world system, which was dominated by Asia. Citing Bernal and Amin, in particular (though slightly disagreeing with Bernal), Frank argues that "the roots of Athens were much more in Asia Minor, Persia, Central Asia, and other parts of Asia than in Egypt and Nubia. . . . The roots of Europe extended into all of Afro-Eurasia since time immemorial. Moreover, . . . Europe was still dependent on Asia during early modern times, before the nineteenth-century invention and propagation of the 'Eurocentric idea'" (Frank 8).

Along similar lines, Amin's *Eurocentrism* (1989) emphasizes the erasure of the influence of Arab-Islamic civilization. In Amin's reading, Eurocentrism is the ideology of capitalism that emerged in the Renaissance and was consolidated in the nineteenth century (thus roughly aligning his periodization with that of Said, Bernal, and Blaut). Eurocentrism rests on "mythical foundations, whose function is to blur the extent of [its] rupture with the past through an affirmation of a nonexistent historical continuity. This false continuity constitutes the core of the Eurocentric dimension of capitalist culture" and is predicated on erasing the fact that "precapitalist Europe in its cultural dimensions [was] part of a broader 'peripheral tributary' ideological construct" (Amin xi). That "false continuity" is the posited unitary, autonomous, trans-historical, and essentialist character which the concept of the "West" often implies, along with the denial of any significant influence on its development by (inferior) non-Western cultures. In fact, as Fabian argues in *Time and the Other: How Anthropology Makes its Object* (1983), anthropology has produced the concept of the primitive in order to consolidate that of "the West." Much like the Orient of Orientalism, anthropology's notion of the primitive occupies a different temporality from the dynamic and constantly evolving West.

Despite the monumental evidence presented by those and other scholars, the concept of the "West" has proven to be surprisingly resilient, partly of course because it is invested with emotive, economic, geopolitical, and ideological interests—notions of who "we" are as opposed to "them"—but partly also out of convenience and intellectual laziness. A single word is used to designate, variously and vaguely, any of the following: one of the countries of Western Europe, all of Western Europe, all of Europe, the United States, North America, Europe and North America, NATO, the First (or "developed") World, "the coalition of the willing," capitalism, Christianity, Judeo-Christianity, and so on. Almost invariably, the "West" is used in contexts in which any of the entities designated by it is posited in implicit or explicit opposition to its Other, which may be constituted by any configuration of political, economic, religious, racial, or cultural ideas that almost always homogenize extremely varied phenomena associated with Africa, Asia, and (sometimes) Latin America—for example, Islam, "Eastern philosophy," fundamentalism, tradition, poverty, foreign debt, underdevelopment, political instability, dictatorship, and so on. Such oppositions constitute a hierarchical sense of identity that justifies foreign and domestic policies, economic exploitation, unjust social orders, and military campaigns. As Said observed, "European culture gained in strength and identity by setting itself off against the Orient as a sort of surrogate and even underground self" (3); the concept of "the West" is the epistemological product of that process of combative self-identification.

Of course, the Eurocentric distinction between "East" and "West" took root in much of the colonial world, where by a perverse logic it became instrumental in resisting the European, and later the American, cultural, political, and military onslaught. In that context, the "East" would typically be invested with positive values and become the privileged party, while the "West" would often acquire ambivalent or negative valuations: powerful militarily but materialistic, technologically advanced but morally depraved, Enlightened but hypocritical, to be emulated and at the same time rejected. The discourse of the *Nahda*, the Arab "revival" or "renaissance" of the nineteenth century, about which I will say more in chapter 1, exhibited that tendency, and so has the work of numerous Arab writers since then. Throughout the imperialized world, in fact, many indigenist discourses and ideologies (from Négritude to anti-colonial nationalism and Third Worldism to myriad sorts of religious fundamentalism and cultural nativism) appropriated that polarity in their oppositional constructions of resistant identities. Frantz Fanon's theory of decolonization as a Manichean conflict between two opposed forces is one well-known example. Rooted in colonial ideology, the East/West dichotomy was hardened and normalized by the colonized themselves, who often retooled it in defense of cultural identities forged in struggle. But the effect has been the same: the homogenization of complex and varied phenomena, which leads to simplistic and predictable interpretations, the foreclosure of nuanced analysis, and the continuation of ancient conflicts as a substitute for self-examination.

As the following chapters explain, immigrant writers have had to contend with the various Orientalist discourses prevalent in their day. They have also often found it difficult to oppose Orientalism, especially when their own intellectual formation was either in colonial schools that ingrained it, or in indigenous traditions that appropriated the East/West distinction as ontological and self-evident. Moreover, immigrant writers have often been expected to validate Orientalism or risk being ignored by publishers, reviewers, and readers. Many such writers have accepted its basic principle of opposition and strove to fulfill that role; others have tried with various degrees of success to redefine the relationship between the antithetical constructs, but no serious epistemological challenge to the intellectual foundation of Orientalism was mounted before Said. Arab immigrant writers have included academic Orientalists, most prominently distinguished historians Philip Hitti (1886–1978), who chaired the Department of Oriental Languages at Princeton University and pioneered Arab American studies in the U.S.; Albert Hourani (1915–93) of Oxford University; and more recently, neoconservative political scientist Fouad Ajami (b. 1945), of Johns Hopkins University. This book does not focus on those and other scholars who fit in Said's first definition of Orientalism. Neither am I concerned with the third definition, since before Said few immigrant Arab writers directly critiqued Orientalism as a colonial discourse. My focus is on the ways in which Arab immigrants negotiated Orientalism in Said's second sense, namely as "an ontological and epistemological distinction made between 'the Orient' and . . . 'the Occident'" (2) and its various deployments since the beginning of the twentieth century. The ambivalence, discursive maneuvers, and contradictions involved in such a position are the concern of this book.

Race and American Orientalism

Needless to say, there are significant differences between the conditions and history of Arab immigration in the U.S. and in Britain. In Britain, immigration is a post-imperial phenomenon and the total immigrant population is relatively small compared to indigenes. While immigrants have, of course, expanded the definition of British identity in recent decades, they have not impacted it the way U.S. immigrants have been transforming American identity since the mid-nineteenth century. Immigrants in Britain are mostly people from former British colonies in South Asia, Africa, and the Caribbean, with Arabs forming a tiny minority within the immigrant population.[5] What I call here Arab British identity is rather provisional and tentative, not an established or widely used term; in fact, it is often overshadowed by the pan-ethnic British Muslim identity, as we shall see in chapter 8. By contrast, that it is a country of immigrants is central to the identity of the U.S., which has always absorbed and been profoundly shaped by waves of immigration.[6] Arab American identity has been in the making since Arabic-speaking immigrants began to arrive in the United States in substantial numbers in the 1870s.[7] This first wave came to a near halt with the passage of the 1924 immigration laws, which imposed a quota system based on national origin. Another wave of mainly Palestinians dispossessed by Israel arrived after the passage of the Immigration and Nationality Act of 1952, which exempted refugees from the national origins restrictions imposed in 1924. A third wave of immigrants from all over the Arab world was made possible by the immigration reform of 1965, which lifted ethnic restrictions altogether.[8]

Arab American literature began around the turn of the twentieth century and is the work of dozens of novelists, memoirists, poets, and playwrights, whereas Arab British literature made a tentative debut in the 1940s then reemerged in the 1980s, but it remains the province of very few writers who, like other writers from former British colonies, are more readily identifiable as postcolonial.[9] Clearly, as a category, "Arab British" is a subset of the "postcolonial," but what interests me here are the parallels and continuities between Arab American and Arab British literature, which result from the historical challenges facing the Arab world and its English-speaking émigrés who settle in Britain and the U.S. In both countries, they constitute a minority within an Anglo-Saxon country that has defined its imperial interests in the Arab world in Orientalist terms. Their literary responses have, therefore, been quite similar. But while postcolonial studies has elucidated the situation in Britain, the American situation for Arab immigrants requires elaboration, especially in view of the nearly one-and-a-half centuries of their presence there.

In the U.S., Orientalism has been thoroughly racialized, something that was central to the early Arab immigrant experience since the late nineteenth century, when race had cultural, political, and legal implications. In fact, American Orientalism is indelibly marked by race and the history of racial thought in the U.S., where questions of citizenship and immigration were formulated in racialist terms. The vast majority of those who came to the U.S. during the first wave of Arab immigration (the 1870s through 1924) were Christians from what is now Lebanon, part of the then Ottoman province of Syria. They were, of course, seen as Orientals, but that designation was not useful from a legal perspective because it referred to Asians in general, including the Chinese, who were considered an undesirable race and banned from immigration in the 1882 Chinese Exclusion Act. The Arabic-speaking immigrants were racially ambiguous to U.S. customs officials and immigration courts, their official classification as white often contradicting how they were popularly perceived, and they themselves had no sense of racial or national identity. Race and nationality, the two paradigms of identity and citizenship used to determine the legal status of immigrants, were not the operative ones in the Arab newcomers' culture of origin, where they identified by family, clan, sect, and region. As for nationality, those immigrants came to the U.S. with Ottoman passports, but they did not identify with the Ottomans, whom they considered oppressors and who were ethnically, culturally, linguistically, and religiously different. As Michael Suleiman points out,

> the immigrants objected to being identified as "Turks" or "Other Asians," as the U.S. immigration and census records referred to them up to the 1920s. In fact, much of the time they left their native lands specifically to escape the tyranny, persecution, corruption, and military service of the Ottoman overlords. Besides, most early immigrants were Christian, whereas to Americans the term "Turk" was synonymous with Islam and Muslims—which were generally viewed negatively in the United States. In the end, some identification had to be made, so they were called, and they called themselves, Syrians, that is, the people who came from geographic or greater Syria. (Suleiman 1987, 42)

"Syrians" was, therefore, a default label that the immigrants had to accept because the alternatives ("Turks," "Other Asians") were objectionable. A new cultural identity, determined by their minority status, began to override (although without obliterating) the immigrants' original modes of identification, which the early Arabic press in the United States reflected during the 1890s–1900s (Naff 1987; Suleiman 1994, 39–43). Decades later, when immigrants from across the Arab world, not just from the Levant, began to arrive in large numbers, another designation emerged to replace "Syrians." "Arab Americans" became the latest minoritarian construct to subsume, without erasing, the ways in which Arab immigrants and their descendants identified themselves.

As for race, it did not have, and could not have had, any legal meaning in the ancient and thoroughly hybridized cultures of the Middle East. Nor did Syrians fit in the racial categories used to classify immigrants, in a country where, for well-known historical reasons, "without a clear racial identity a North American is in danger of having no identity" (Winant 3). The earliest immigration code in the U.S., that of 1790, allowed for the naturalization of "free white persons," and as Philip Gleason demonstrates, race and ethnicity have remained central to American identity from that time to the era of Affirmative Action. Not surprisingly, therefore, Arabs in the U.S. have experienced "a history of inconsistent racialization" (Majaj 2000, 321). Whether or not "Syrians" were white, and thus eligible for citizenship, at times depended on whether or not they were considered covered by Asian exclusion statutes from the 1870s to the 1920s (Samhan 1999, 210). Classified as Caucasians, "their popular perception as nonwhite was so pervasive that courts were willing to privilege common knowledge over scientific evidence when the two were at odds," as can be seen in "a series of cases involving Arab applicants between 1909 and 1915 and again in the 1940s, in which courts declared Arab applicants to be variously white and nonwhite" (Majaj 2000, 322). Judicial discrimination of this kind, coupled with various forms of racism experienced by the immigrants, including lynching and arson incidents in the South, often galvanized the Syrian community to action. Those incidents also spurred controversy over the community's racial, cultural, and national identity, and raised questions about whether Syrians had a future in America (Suleiman 1987, 42–46). Also debated was the question of whether being Arabic speakers constituted a cultural or a racial identity, and whether race was a matter of blood or of culture. Thus, for example, Hitti devoted the opening pages of his landmark *Syrians in America* (1924) to the question of "racial relationships," stressing that Syrians are neither Turks, nor Arabs, nor Assyrians, but "a mixed Semitic race" (Hitti 19–21). Hitti opted for blood, contrary to the historically and widely accepted notion that Arab identity is a matter of language and culture rather than race or ethnicity. Such ambiguities bedeviled the Syrians' attempt to articulate their group identity within what was to them the alien discourse of race.

Yet, as Philip Gleason shows, the concept of race was itself ambiguous in U.S. thinking about biology, ethnicity, culture, immigration, and American identity. The period of the 1860s to the 1930s witnessed the emergence of four ideologies of citizenship that attempted to define the nation's changing character, and which Arab Americans had to negotiate: Anglo-Saxonism, Anglo-Saxon conformity, the Melting Pot, and cultural pluralism. According to Gleason, during the period 1860–1924, "ethnicity assumed greater salience as an element in the national identity than it has had at any other time before or since" (Gleason 105). Accelerated immigration over the course of the nineteenth century, the Civil War, Reconstruction, and World War I all contributed to the prominence of ethnicity. As Protestant Anglo-Saxons gradually ceased to be the overwhelming majority of the U.S. population, mid-century anti-Catholicism evolved into Anglo-Saxonism, which regarded the ideals upon which the republic was founded to be either the political legacy of the original English immigrants or the product of the native genius of their "racial stock." Consequently, in Anglo-Saxonism only Anglo-Saxons were seen as fit for citizenship. According to a second, more liberal but closely related ideology, which came to be known as "Anglo-Saxon conformity," other immigrant groups were expected to conform to Anglo-Saxon customs and attitudes as a condition for "Americanization." Here, the ideals of the republic were not so much a matter of genetics as socialization and training in citizenship, something that various types of "Americanization" programs for immigrants sought to achieve. Eventually, however, Americanization came to be regarded as another form of racism, especially when the Ku Klux Klan adopted it. In both ideologies, "immigrants . . . were not regarded as having anything valuable of their own to contribute to the national culture or identity" (106–7) and only certain kinds of groups were fit for citizenship. The Asian Exclusion Act of 1924 translated that into official policy, which would not be reversed until the Immigration and Nationality Act of 1965, one year after the Civil Rights Act.

The other ideologies were the "Melting Pot" and "cultural pluralism." The idea of individuals from "different nations . . . melted into a new race of men" was first expressed by Michel-Guillaume Jean de Crèvecoeur in 1782 (quoted in Gleason 64), but it was popularized in Israel Zangwill's 1908 play, *The Melting-Pot*. Here, differences eventually blend into one homogeneous culture, while those elements that do not fit into the mix are burned off. Thus, unlike Anglo-Saxonism and Anglo-Saxon conformity, the ideology of the Melting Pot accommodates racial and cultural diversity and even allows for the transformation of the dominant Anglo-Saxon culture, but the goal was the elimination of difference, or as Gleason puts it, the stress remained on the *unum* rather than on the *pluribus* in the national motto (106). That emphasis was reversed in "cultural pluralism," the fourth ideology to emerge during that period and the one favored by Arab Americans.

First advocated by Horace Kallen in 1915, cultural pluralism was based on the view that, because of immigration, the U.S. is not so much one nation as a "federation of nationalities" within one political state, and that the goal should be to work toward harmony, not unison (Gleason 96–97). According to Kallen, Americanization and the imposition of conformity were antidemocratic. Instead, he called for "a possible great and truly democratic commonwealth" in the form of a

> federal republic . . . a democracy of nationalities, cooperating voluntarily and autonomously through common institutions. . . . The common language of the commonwealth . . . would be English, but each nationality would have for its emotional and involuntary life its own peculiar dialect or speech, its own individual and inevitable esthetic and intellectual forms. The political and economic life of the commonwealth is a single unit and serves as the foundation and background for the realization of the distinctive individuality of each *natio* that composes it and of the pooling of these in a harmony above them all. Thus "American civilization" may come to mean the perfection of the cooperative harmonies of "European civilization"—the waste, the squalor and the distress of Europe being eliminated—a multiplicity in a unity, an orchestration of mankind. (Quoted in Gleason 97)

Gleason points out that Kallen's vision is predicated on "romantic racialism," which, unlike Anglo-Saxonism and Anglo-Saxon conformity, "valued diversity as such and did not attempt to rank human groups as superior or inferior according to any absolute scale of racial merit. But he also resembled the romantics in attributing the distinctive characteristics of peoples to inborn racial qualities" (99–100). Kallen's racialism is often overlooked because cultural pluralism became known as a liberal ideology and because Kallen reconceptualized it in nonracial terms after racialism fell into disrepute following World War II (113). Another limitation in Kallen's formulation, which posed a more patent obstacle to Arab immigrants, was its Eurocentrism. "American civilization," for him, was to be a refinement of "European civilization." Thus all three ideologies that held out some potential for the acceptance of non-Anglo-Saxons (Anglo-Saxon conformity, the Melting Pot, and cultural pluralism) demanded assimilation into narrowly conceived models of national identity.

Since they were concerned about the effects of racial prejudice on their American-born children and the pressure on them to become "Americanized," which would alienate them from their traditions, Syrian immigrants' attitudes to the three ideologies were ambivalent. Anglo-Saxon conformity had little appeal for them. The Melting Pot, which was dominant in the 1920s–30s, represented both an opportunity and a threat: it endorsed the Syrian immigrants' right to citizenship, but at the forbidding price of cultural assimilation. The Eurocentrism of cultural pluralism undermined their claim to citizenship, but the ideology's racialist content seemed to safeguard their cultural identity, insofar as such identity is understood as an inalienable racial heritage. This explains why Arab American advocates of cultural diversity at the time, such as Salloum Mokarzel, W. A. Mansour, Abraham Rihbany, and others, conflated race and culture. For example, in a book that advocates the independence of the Arab world from European domination after the collapse of the Ottoman Empire, Abraham Rihbany found in the principle of absolute difference, which is central to Orientalism and racialism, a defense against cultural extinction:

> [T]he Eastern mind and the Western mind diverge so widely that any attempt to force them into a unity is foredoomed to failure. Whatever may have happened in the remote past, when the human species was still plastic and very sensitive to formative influences, is of the past. . . . The races of men whom we know at present as nations and peoples are types which centuries of evolution have shaped and hardened, *and which no hasty human processes can create or annul.* (Rihbany 1922, 288—emphasis added)

Such "hasty human processes" (as opposed to natural and evolutionary ones) include educational institutions implemented in European colonies and the assimilation of immigrants in U.S. society. He goes on to elaborate:

> The voluntary gathering of racial elements together in one country, like America, and the voluntary submission to new influences, may in the process of time evolve a human composite called a people with general characteristics strong enough to vouchsafe for it a peaceful and harmonious

> existence. Yet even here the fusion of such elements is creating staggering problems; and the success attained is the result of the constant elimination of the "newcomer" and the exclusion of the racial idea from the mind of his offspring. In other words, the new influences are not changing the old stock [of the immigrants], but killing it, and replacing it by a new breed. (288–89)

The "elimination of the newcomer," or Melting-Pot assimilation, is cultural rather than racial in content, for the "staggering problems" Rihbany refers to include the erasure of "racial idea" from the *minds* of second-generation Syrians. It is not, for him, a question of blood, as it was in European and American racial theory. Rather, it is that U.S.-born Syrians are becoming too Americanized to identify with their immigrant parents' culture. What he calls "the racial idea" is considered a positive thing because it preserves the richness of native traditions and could, in principle, contribute to the realization of a pluralistic, or what we would call today a multicultural, society.

Many immigrants were troubled by the fact that their children were not literate in Arabic and that they found it difficult both to identify with their parents' culture and to integrate in American society. This concern was behind the launching, in 1926, of the first English-language magazine, *The Syrian World*, after more than three decades of Arabic-language newspapers in the United States.[10] The editor, Salloum Mokarzel, aimed at connecting U.S.-born Syrians with their Arab culture, which was often romanticized and understood as a "racial heritage," and at bridging the sectarian divisions (Maronite, Syrian Orthodox, Druze, and Sunni Muslim) which Syrian immigrants imported with them into the U.S. and which defined their various organizations, clubs, societies, and newspapers. In other words, it was through the medium of English that immigrants became, in a cultural sense, "Syrians," a minoritarian identity forged in a foreign language, articulated within the framework of cultural pluralism, and expressed in racialist terms. In the foreword to the inaugural issue, Mokarzel declared that one of the goals of the new publication was to give immigrants' children "a broader vision of their racial heritage . . . to the end that our Syrian-American generation will come to better understand the country of their parents and appreciate more fully their racial endowments which constitute a valuable contribution to the country of their birth" (Mokarzel 2). Aligning himself with cultural pluralists and responding to possible objections from the advocates of Anglo-Saxon conformity and the Melting Pot, both of which were predicated on the eradication of cultural differences as a condition for Americanization, Mokarzel states "emphatically that not only is it farthest from our intention to alienate Syrian-Americans from their American allegiance, but that one of our chief objects in helping Syrian-Americans discover themselves is to breed in them a consciousness of appreciation for their racial qualities and inheritances so that they may comport themselves with a befitting sense of honor as citizens of this great American nation" (3). This theme was elaborated by the editor and a number of regular and occasional contributors, and debated in letters to the editor, in almost every issue of the magazine until its demise in 1932. Mokarzel's deployment of the concept of race clearly marks Syrian identity as an American product; but more importantly, by anchoring the question of culture in biology, Mokarzel makes Syrian identity a non-negotiable fact, something that is not subject to eradication through assimilation. He essentializes Syrianness by way of arguing that it cannot be burned off in the Melting Pot. In this way, racialization was the price of cultural preservation. To protect their cultural identity, Syrians had to frame it in racial terms.

However, the concept of race was anything but unproblematic to other Arab American writers at the time. For example, writing in the same magazine a few weeks later, Habib I. Katibah was highly suspicious of race as a category because it inevitably leads to "discussion on the biological merits of one 'race' over another," and he was doubtful as to "whether there is such a thing as 'race.'" Nevertheless, he could not dismiss race altogether, given its scientific status at the time: "We leave these subjects for scientists to discuss" (Katibah 16). Instead of biology, his focus is on "practical" and "moral" considerations of Americanism as a process of acculturation, rather than assimilation. He criticized the notion of "Americanism as conformity to some sacred residium of raciality" that is "Anglo-Saxon, or at least Nordic," and he also rejected "the slogan, once very popular, of 'the melting pot'" (18). Favoring a non-racialist form of cultural pluralism, he defined "Americanism" as "a pedagogical term . . . hav[ing] as its immediate objective the conversion of untutored foreigners into good, responsible Americans" (17), and understood American identity "as a composite product of the ideals represented by the different nationalities that have found a dwelling-place and a refuge in this vast land" (18).

Yet Katibah was in the minority among Arab Americans. In the late 1920s, Anglo-Saxonism was the reigning ideology, having just triumphed with the passage of the 1924 immigration restrictions. That may explain why most Arab Americans felt compelled to use racial discourse in an attempt to preserve their group identity as a minority in a society that was hyperconscious of race and in which they often experienced racial prejudice and discrimination. Yet in accepting the basic premise of racial theory and trying to adapt it to their situation, they effectively resigned themselves to being placed on the racial hierarchy and simply attempted to claim a higher position on it. Citing the example of Irish and Italian immigrants, Lisa Suhair Majaj writes, "Immigrants whose tenuous racial status compromised their ability to assimilate into white America often sought to move up the racial scale . . . by distancing themselves from people of color. . . . Similarly, Arabic-speaking immigrants, recognizing that perceptions of 'whiteness' turned upon relative distance form the 'darker' end of the spectrum, anxiously sought to assert their difference from blacks" (Majaj 2000, 325).[11] Not only was the strategy problematic in itself, but it was also bound to fail in inducing the American-born generation of Syrians to "appreciate more fully their racial endowments," as Mokarzel had hoped. As Shakir points out, many U.S.-born Arab Americans opted for passing as white during the middle decades of the century (Shakir 1996, 6). Meanwhile, by the late 1930s, cultural pluralism was becoming more prevalent; it shed the vestiges of racialism after the war, and by the 1970s and 1980s it had become known as "multiculturalism" and emerged as the dominant model of American identity.

With few exceptions, then, Arab Americans were willing to redefine themselves in terms of the dominant discourse of race in the 1900s–1930s. If their efforts to do so were marked by hesitancy, confusion, contradiction, and ambivalence, it is because, first, race was not a category with significant legal implications in their countries of origin, and second, race was itself an ambiguous category in the U.S., with several distinct ideologies claiming to define it, and consequently shifting policies on immigration and naturalization that were applied haphazardly to racially ambiguous groups. Arab immigrants could not, obviously, challenge the racialist premises of the nation's immigration law; on the contrary, they by and large accepted them and attempted to negotiate their identity in terms of race.[12]

Their approach to Orientalism, which as we have seen was itself racialized, was similar, though more nuanced. Just as they accepted race as a category, they also accepted Orientalist culturalism, central to which was the dichotomy between East and West. With Orientalism, early Arab immigrant writers were on more familiar ground than with race because of their familiarity with Europe. As with race, Orientalism represented an opportunity and a threat to early Arab immigrant writers: it condemned them to an inferior position in the cultural hierarchy, but it also afforded them an entry into the American scene if they could draw on the familiar tropes of Orientalism and act as interpreters or cultural translators between "East" and "West." One argument of this book is that no Arab immigrant in the U.S. could avoid engaging with American Orientalism in some fashion, considering its entrenchment in American culture, its inextricable links to race as a fundamental component of American identity, and the crucial role that the U.S. has played in the Middle East since World War II. As we shall see in the following chapters, some writers have pandered to American and Eurocentric cultural supremacy, but most others have challenged it in multiple ways that reflect not only their particular concerns, but also the transformation of American Orientalism from the nineteenth to the twenty-first century.

Numerous nineteenth-century American missionaries, journalists, scholars, and literary figures, including William Cullen Bryant, Ralph Waldo Emerson, Washington Irving, Herman Melville, Edgar Allen Poe, Harriet Prescott Spofford, Susanna Rowson, and Mark Twain, wrote about the Orient. As Fuad Sha'ban, Malini Johar Schueller, and Scott Trafton have pointed out, nineteenth-century American Orientalism was intimately connected to the construction of the country's religious, racial, and gendered national identity and its dreams of empire. In *Islam and Arabs in Early American Thought: The Roots of Orientalism in America*, Sha'ban notes that "American Orientalism is . . . a national cultural dialogue which derives from European background, heritage and influence on the one hand, and, on the other, stems from particularly American factors and experience" (vii), including the Puritans' view of themselves as "the chosen people and America [as] the land of promise . . . the symbolic Kingdom of God." In the early nineteenth century,

> America went to war against the North African Muslem [*sic*] states; commercial and diplomatic relations were gradually established between America and the various dominions of the Ottoman Empire; there was a

> surge of missionary enthusiasm and operations carried out by Americans in these dominions, especially the Holy Land; the Oriental tour became a popular American activity. As a result of these events and other contributing factors, the symbolic Kingdom of God in America was replaced by a more physical aspiration to establish that Kingdom in the Holy Land. (viii)

That aspiration was fueled by "Manifest Destiny, Adventist, and Millennial tendencies, patriotic enthusiasm, missionary zeal" (ix), which, combined with "the extensive knowledge and materials about Islam and Muslems which were available to Americans of all walks of life . . . preconditioned the American attitude to the Orient and Orientals" (x). In addition to this religious interest in the Orient, there was also a secular, literary appeal manifested in "the widespread popularity of the *Arabian Nights* and its imitations. In fact, because of this kind of literature, the Orient often represented to Americans a world of dreams and romance." Thus, "when Americans traveled to the Orient they were in most cases seeking to fulfill the vision of Zion or the dream of Baghdad" (x).

While Sha'ban stresses the religious component of American Orientalism, Schueller focuses on its imperial, and Trafton on its racial, character. As Schueller demonstrates in *U.S. Orientalisms: Race, Nation, and Gender in Literature, 1790–1890*, secular and religious American ideas about the Orient were racial and gendered: "The Orient served the dual purpose of containing national schisms and constructing an imperial nationhood" (Schueller 3). Trafton's *Egypt Land: Race and Nineteenth-Century American Egyptomania* focuses on the greatest of those schisms, race, which was behind the enormous interest in Egyptology, a branch of Orientalism that became highly relevant to debates about phrenology, polygenesis, and slavery. But like the American biblical Orientalism analyzed by Sha'ban, the secular American Orientalisms that Trafton and Schueller examine were connected to a notion of

> United States . . . imperialism, particularly with respect to the Orient, [which] could be constructed much more benevolently [than European imperialism], as teleology. Since the 'discovery' of the Americas by Columbus was popularly transmitted as the outcome of a vision to reach the Orient, contemporary arguments about seizing Oriental trade or civilizing Orientals through missionary activity were accompanied by visionary statements about completing Columbus's original mission. (Schueller 9)

Because of the instability of the idea of the nation in nineteenth-century America due to "the internal colonization of Native Americans and African Americans . . . the idea of a U.S. empire . . . was used to both mystify national instabilities and bolster the idea of a strong, expanding nation" (9). U.S. Orientalism is, therefore, inseparable from American racial discourse: "because of this attempted mystification, U.S. literary Orientalism became the site of a triadic encounter in which the Africanist and Native American presences returned to haunt and question the cultural and political hegemony of the New World" (Schueller 9–10).

Toni Morrison has argued that "the imaginative and historical terrain upon which early American writers journeyed is in large measure shaped by the presence of the racial other" (Morrison 46), and that each of "the major themes and presuppositions of American literature . . . is made possible by, shaped by, activated by a complex awareness and employment of a constituted Africanism" (44). Schueller cogently notes that this thesis "needs to be expanded to include the presence of Native Americans as well as various non-Western others that figure so prominently in the intellectual imaginary," such as the Chinese (Schueller 211, n.28); one can certainly also add other cultures and peoples against whom the U.S. defined itself: Egypt (Trafton), the Near East (Sha'ban 1991), and, of course, Europe (especially late-coming southern and eastern Europeans, who were mainly Catholic, Jewish, and Eastern Orthodox). Arab immigrants, or "Syrians," did not begin to arrive in the United States in significant numbers until the late nineteenth century, but they were already defined in American consciousness in racial and Orientalist terms. Consequently, anti-Arab racism, in the various forms and intensities it has assumed since the beginning of Arab immigration to the post-9/11 period, has always been wedded to American Orientalism. This is discernible in xenophobic attitudes dating back to the nineteenth century as well as, more recently, in Islamophobia and what has been called "political racism," all of which served to differentiate Americans from supposedly inferior races. For example, Frederick Bushée, a social worker, described the Syrian inhabitants of Boston's South End in 1898 in these terms:

> The Syrians are nearly all peddlers, if they are anything. Some are persistent candidates for charity. . . . Next to the Chinese, who can never be in any real sense American, they are the most foreign of all foreigners. Whether on the street in their oriental costumes, or in their rooms gathered about the Turkish pipe, they are always apart from us. They are hospitable in their homes, but they are also deceitful; and out of all the nationalities they would be distinguished for nothing whatever excepting as curiosities. (Bushée 46–47)

Such xenophobia also marked serious academic studies of immigration. In *The Old World in the New* (1914), sociologist Edward Alsworth Ross argued that various immigrant races are making "the older immigrant stocks more sterile, even as the old Americans become sterile" (Ross 303), and that "a people that has no more respect for its ancestors and no more pride of race than this [i.e. boosting its population with immigrants] deserves the extinction that surely awaits it" (304). The main "stocks" blamed for this calamity are Germans, Slavs, Italians, Portuguese, southern Europeans, and other "lesser groups." He adds:

> That the Mediterranean peoples are morally below the races of northern Europe is as certain as any social fact. Even when they were dirty, ferocious barbarians, these blonds were truth-tellers. Be it pride or awkwardness or lack of imagination or fair-play sense, something has held them back from the nimble lying of southern races. . . . The Syrians . . . are extremely untrustworthy and unreliable. (293)

Less openly hostile but no less rooted in Orientalism is the widespread fascination with the Middle East that advertisers have exploited throughout the twentieth century. The recent exhibit of Oriental ephemera at UCLA, titled "Seducing America: Selling the Middle Eastern Mystique" (which is in the process of being digitized), demonstrates the extent to which Orientalism has permeated American consciousness. The exhibit included such items as

> comic books from the 1930s, pulp fiction book covers with titles such as 'Desert Madness' and 'Spicy Adventures,' video games such as 'The Prince of Persia,' vintage sheet music for songs including 'The Sheik of Araby' and 'Rebecca Came Back from Mecca,' photos of topless women on the covers of CDs, fierce warriors on the covers of DVDs, 'Turkish' tobacco products, Egyptomania films, and various sundry consumer items such as Palmolive beauty products, Ben Hur flour, Sheik condoms—and . . . Shriner fezzes. (Gabriel 18)

Naturally, the popular appeal of such images was not lost on Hollywood film producers who, as Jack Shaheen demonstrates, have "vilified" Arabs "since cameras started cranking" (Shaheen 2001, 6).

With the emergence of the U.S. as a superpower after World War II, American Orientalism entered a new phase. The emergence of oil as a major strategic interest, the onset of the Cold War, and the creation of the State of Israel and the strong support it found among influential American organizations, all politicized U.S. Orientalism in unprecedented ways. Among other things, these developments had the effect of steadily intensifying anti-Arab racism since the late 1940s. Openly racist depictions of Arabs and Muslims in the U.S. have grown increasingly more vicious since then. Jack Shaheen has documented Arab stereotypes in hundreds of television and Hollywood films (1984, 1997, 2001, 2008) and Tim Jon Semmerling has analyzed the portrayal of evil Arab characters in some of those films. Edmund Ghareeb, Karim H. Karim, Abbas Malek, Edward Said (1997), Linda Steet, Michael Suleiman (1975, 1988), Elias Sam'o, and Janice Terry have analyzed news coverage of Arabs in the media. Ronald Stockton discusses their representation in political cartoons; Lori Ann Salem in popular theater in the 1930s–40s; and Gregory Orfalea (1988) and Reeva Simon in fiction. Derogatory and racist representations of Arabs have also been widespread in K-12 school textbooks, as Sharon Abu-Laban, William Griswald, Samir Ahmad Jarrar, L. M. Kenny, Glenn Perry, and Ayad al-Qazzaz demonstrate. Jarrar, for example, notes that "the image of the Arab as presented in social studies textbooks is very cursory, and more negative than positive," as a result of

> a number of factors that include . . . omissions, stereotypes, over-generalization, and lack of balance in presenting the materials. The Arab is portrayed as primitive, backward, desert dwelling, nomadic, war loving, terroristic and full of hatred. The Arab world is most often depicted as an area of desert and oil, lacking modernization, united in its hatred of Israel. (Jarrar 387–88)

Several other scholars have analyzed anti-Arab racism, including Nabeel Abraham, Steven Salaita (2006), Aladdin Elaasar, Amaney Jamal, and Nadine Naber, among others, while Moustafa Bayoumi and Louise Cainkar have written about the impact of post-9/11 hostility on Arab Americans.

Because of this widespread and intense hostility, even in the age of multiculturalism, Arabs have been called "the last ethnic group in America safe to hate" (cited in Orfalea and Elmusa xiv), and ironically, in view of the early immigrants' insistence on their whiteness, "the new blacks" (quoted in Bayoumi 2). In an address to the Association of Editorial Cartoonists, Sam Keen elaborates: "You can hit an Arab free; they're free enemies, free villains—where you couldn't do it to a Jew or you can't do it to a black anymore" (quoted in Shaheen 2001, 6). Needless to say, racism directed at people of African descent, Native Americans, Latinos, Asians, and Jews still thrives. Indeed, Stockton argues that anti-Arab racism is "primarily derivative, rooted in a core of hostile archetypes that our culture applies to those with whom it clashes," and that "the roots of these archetypes lie in ancient conflicts or cultural teachings that go back centuries or even millennia" (Stockton 120). He demonstrates, for example, how centuries-old anti-Semitic "Jewish images were superimposed on Arabs" (136). For that reason, as Salaita puts it, anti-Arab racism "exists only because racism existed before the first Arab arrived in North America" (Salaita 2006, 123–24). Nowadays, however, hate speech and the stereotyping of nearly all minority groups are considered anathema by the acceptable standards of public discourse. Yet when it comes to Arabs and Muslims, hate speech appears to be the standard, and it issues not only from the entertainment industry, but also from the mouths of some politicians and religious leaders. [13]

Yvonne Yazbeck Haddad points out that "[f]or over a century, immigrants from the Arab world have prospered in the United States. They have 'made it' by working hard, carefully shedding their particular cultural distinction, and blending in. They have not, as yet, been welcomed as a group into the American mainstream" (2004, 45). Even "in the post-World War II period, when the United States was reinventing itself as a pluralistic society, immigrants from the Arab world found themselves publicly and deliberately excluded from the mainstream of American politics" (46) and, moreover, reviled in the media. The reason for that was a new form of racism that is politically motivated. Scholars who have analyzed the development of anti-Arab racism since the late 1940s agree that the new and especially potent ingredient in it has been the shaping of public opinion in support of Israel-centered U.S. policy in the Middle East. As the pro-Israel lobby shaped foreign policy, Zionist organizations in the U.S. have targeted anyone who has dared to criticize Israel, from Arab American organizations to outspoken anti-Zionist Jews (including, most recently, Norman Finkelstein), Middle East studies programs, professors, politicians (Findley; Samhan; Abourezk 167–91; Yvonne Haddad 2004, 20; Salaita 2006, 35–39, 102–4, 110–20), and even a former U.S. president (Bosman). This has prompted some scholars to draw distinctions between, on the one hand, nineteenth-century American Orientalism and the xenophobia and religious prejudice that plagued earlier waves of newcomers, and on the other hand, what Helen Hatab Samhan calls "political racism" and its close associate,

Islamophobia. Samhan goes so far as to argue that anti-Arab racism has its "roots not in the traditional motives of structurally excluding a group perceived as inferior, but in politics" (Samhan 1987, 14), and that

> the Arab-Israeli conflict has been . . . the common denominator in most cases of anti-Arab discrimination since the 1960s. Had the cause been classic racial or ethnic antipathy, Arab Americans could not have reached the levels of mobility in business, the professions, education, residential choice, and even intermarriage that they have. . . . It has not been so much Arab origin as Arab political activity in America that has engendered a new form of "political" racism that takes prejudice and exclusion out of the arena of personal relations and into the arena of public information and public policy. (16)

Therefore, Samhan argues that the exclusion of Arab Americans from politics "is not so much by ignorance or prejudice as by political design" (26), for the purpose of

> monopolizing the discussion of the contemporary Middle East in the United States. Especially in the realm of public information and public policy, it has been American Jewish campaigns to protect Israel—on either an organized or spontaneous basis—that have allowed anti-Arab prejudice to grow. For in many instances, protecting Israel has meant discrediting, delegitimizing, and silencing pro-Palestinian work in American schools, political bodies, and the mass media. These efforts have been far reaching enough for the civil liberties of some Arab Americans to be threatened; for acts of violence and harassment to be met with little outrage; and for the recurrence of exclusion of organized Arab American participation in the political process. (11–12)

Samhan cites examples of the harassment of non-Arab American academics and politicians who have been targeted in smear campaigns for criticizing Israeli policies, and even for accepting campaign donations from Arab American constituents, as evidence of the political, rather than ethnic or racial, nature of this form of discrimination.[14] She adds,

> At the core of such tactics is the fear of some American Jewish organizations that any national exposure to the substance of Middle East issues, including Israeli injustice and Palestinian rights, will weaken the existing Israel-centered U.S. policy toward the region. In each of the . . . [cited] cases of exclusion—whether in academia or in politics—the common denominator is that Arab or Arab American participation is controversial, not in and of itself, but because it is perceived as such by American Jewish institutions. Such exclusion is not based on fair or democratic debate of real issues but on tactics reminiscent of the McCarthy era. In each case, there is an effort to establish guilt by association . . . with terrorism, anti-Semitism, and even anti-Americanism. (25)

As Yvonne Haddad points out, such efforts all too often succeed in enlisting the aid of "government agencies including the CIA, INS, FBI, IRS, the Department of State and the United States Customs Service, to coordinate monitoring the Arab American community in an effort to ferret out terrorists and intimidate the community, weakening its effectiveness and scaring off its allies and sympathizers" (Yvonne Haddad 2004, 47).

While there is much truth in Samhan's thesis, her denial of the role of other kinds of racial, ethnic, or religious prejudice contradicts the considerable evidence marshaled by the scholars mentioned above, who document the persistent recycling of old Orientalist stereotypes in television, cinema, school textbooks, journalism, political speeches, and religious services. The resurgence of Islamophobia, in particular, proves that present-day anti-Arab racism draws on multiple sources, from medieval to contemporary. The perception of Islam as a false religion or cult that represents a dangerous competitor to Christianity goes back to the medieval period, when it provided the theological justification for the Crusades. Antiquated as it is, this idea survives in messianic and millennial thought and in the worldview of radical Evangelicals today. The collapse of the Soviet Union and the terrorist attacks of September 11, 2001 have led "a growing number of political and religious officials [who] had been casting around for a new enemy . . . to designate 'fundamentalist Islam' as the imminent threat, 'the other' that needed to be eliminated" (Yvonne Haddad 2004, 41). Some fundamentalist Christian ministers "engaged in demonizing Islam and its prophet with gusto reminiscent of the discourse that launched the Crusades" (Yvonne Haddad 41); they also advance an Israel-centered U.S. foreign policy, on the view that supporting Israel hastens the Second Coming and the conversion of the Jews.[15]

Thus while anti-Arab racism and Islamophobia have become a political weapon in the hands of some Israel supporters, the potency of that weapon derives from the recycling and intensifying of pre-existing racial, cultural, and religious hostilities. Those hostilities are deep-rooted, derived as they are from medieval European discourses that helped consolidate Christian Europe's identity vis-à-vis the Arab-Islamic world. Transferred to the New World, European ideas about the East developed in a new context and served to consolidate U.S. identity, not only in opposition to Arabs and Islam, but also differentially in relation to Europe. As the U.S. defined itself as an outpost, indeed the fulfillment, of European (or "Western") civilization, while at the same time disavowing Europe's political and social structures, it adopted European attitudes toward the Orient but reinterpreted them in accordance with its own discursive and ideological needs. When modern Orientalism emerged in Europe in the late eighteenth century, it redeployed those older notions about the Orient in the service of the emerging colonial empires. In the U.S., that Orientalism had a different character and function: mitigating the instability of the national character, shoring up the biblically derived self-image of the nation as the New Jerusalem, facilitating the internal colonization of Native Americans and Africans (acquiring in the process a racial dimension), and fueling a discourse on American imperialism as part of Manifest Destiny. With the demise of Europe's colonial empires and the emergence of the U.S. as a superpower, American Orientalism underwent a corresponding development suited to new imperialistic needs.

The confluence of several forces has enabled a powerful critique of that discourse. Immigration reforms, the ethnic revival and Civil Rights movements in the U.S., national liberation movements worldwide, including the Palestinian movement, and the high pitch of anti-Arab racism during and after the 1967 Arab-Israeli War and in the wake of 9/11 have galvanized Arab Americans and demonstrated the necessity of self-assertion and political activism (Orfalea 2006, 213–41). Corresponding developments in the academy such as the rise of feminism, multiculturalism, and postcolonial theory all provided a fertile ground for the resurgence of Arab American writing. Edward Said's role in these developments cannot be underestimated. It was no coincidence that the critique of Orientalism, in both its European and American branches, was launched by a Palestinian American. That critique inaugurated the field of postcolonial studies, which in turn changed the face of literary studies in the U.S. and Britain. At the same time, Said's courageous political work on behalf of the Palestinian cause helped give it prominence and legitimacy in the U.S. Needless to say, he became a lightning rod for anti-Arab vitriol, but he also set an example followed by scores of writers of all backgrounds. All of this provided the context for the current renaissance in Arab American literature at the hands of new immigrants and U.S.-born Arab Americans, who have produced an enormous amount of poetry, fiction, autobiographical writing, drama, social and political critique, and scholarship. Similarly, after its brief initiation at the hands of Edward Atiyah in the 1940s, Arab British literature reemerged in the 1980s, exhibiting a similar concern with Orientalism, but with an emphasis on British colonial history in the Arab world and the growing Muslim minority in Britain. In fact, contemporary Arab British writers like Ahdaf Soueif and Leila Aboulela have developed, at the end of the twentieth century and the beginning of the twenty-first, what I shall be calling a "translational literature," which was initiated early in the twentieth century by the first Arab American writer, Ameen Rihani. In that sense, the two traditions dovetail and Arab immigrant writing comes full-circle, a testament to the strength of the discursive and political forces against which Arab American and Arab British writers have had to define their projects.

Cultural Translation

Said described the stance of the Orientalist as that of a translator:

> The relationship between Orientalist and Orient was essentially hermeneutical: standing before a distant, barely intelligible civilization or cultural monument, the Orientalist scholar reduced the obscurity by translating, sympathetically portraying, inwardly grasping the hard-to-reach object. Yet the Orientalist remained outside the Orient, which, however much was made to appear intelligible, remained beyond the Occident. (Said 1978, 222)

By writing in English, Arab immigrant writers have found themselves placed in that position, often expected to interpret their culture for their readers. However, they do not stand outside the "Orient," like the European or American Orientalist, since they are of the "Orient" by virtue of their background; but they are also of the "Occident" by reason of immigration and acculturation. Therefore, their position represents a merger of the two classic stances of the native informant and the foreign expert. Many Arab immigrant writers have seen this position as a privileged one insofar as it affords them a unique insider's perspective not only on the Arab world, but also on their adoptive country. In fact, a few of those writers, especially those who write in Arabic and English, have positioned themselves not only as interpreters of "Orient" to "Occident," but also as interpreters of the "Occident" both to itself and to the "Orient"—that is to say, as two-way translators. All in all, Arab immigrant writers have adopted translational stances that range from native informants to Orientalists; from mediators who attempted to question only certain aspects of Orientalism while leaving its conceptual edifice unchallenged to critics of that discourse who (following Said) have striven to dismantle it and to undo its basic premises; from reluctant translators who struggle with the burden of collective representation to those who eagerly embrace the role; and from opportunists who exploit it to activists who turn it into a site of contestation and opposition. In all events, writing in English has been, for Arab immigrants, always a politically charged translational task, heavily invested in discourses of cultural identity, and gravid with ethical and epistemological considerations.

Over the past two decades, translation theory has grappled with the politics, ethics, and epistemology of cultural-linguistic transfer in ways that help illuminate the subject of immigrant Arab American and Arab British literature. As Lawrence Venuti argues in *The Scandals of Translation: Towards an Ethics of Difference* (1998), "the formation of cultural identities" is "by far the most consequential" and "the greatest potential source of scandal" of all the effects of translation, since translation "wields enormous power in constructing representations of foreign cultures" (Venuti 1998, 67). First of all, translation can

> fix stereotypes for foreign cultures, excluding values, debates, and conflicts that don't appear to serve domestic agendas. In creating stereotypes, translation may attach esteem or stigma to specific ethnic, racial, and national groupings, signifying respect for cultural difference or hatred based on ethnocentrism, racism, or patriotism. In the long run, translation figures in geopolitical relations by establishing the cultural grounds for diplomacy, reinforcing alliances, antagonisms, and hegemonies between nations. (67–68)

Carol Maier puts it even more emphatically: "translation . . . has repeatedly obliterated rather than communicated a 'source' culture" (Meier 23).[16] According to Anuradha Dingwaney, this process often "entail[s] varying degrees of violence, especially when the culture being translated is constituted as that of the 'other.'" In (post)colonial settings, the power differential has often determined the ways in which "alien cultural forms and concepts or indigenous practices are recuperated (translated) via a process of familiarization (assimilation to culturally familiar forms or concepts or practices) whereby they are denuded of their 'foreignness,' even, perhaps of their radical inaccessibility" (Dingwaney 4–5).[17]

Venuti has also demonstrated how translation participates in the construction of cultural identities not only through reproducing stereotypes of the source culture but also by reinforcing dominant discourses and self-images of the target culture:

> since translations are usually designed for specific cultural constituencies, they set going a process of identity formation that is double-edged. As translation constructs a domestic representation for a foreign text and culture, it simultaneously constructs a domestic subject, a position of intelligibility that is also an ideological position, informed by the codes and canons, interests and agendas of certain domestic interest groups. Circulating in the church, the state, and the school, a translation can be powerful in maintaining or revising the hierarchy of values in the translating language. A calculated choice of foreign text and translation strategy can change or consolidate literary canons, conceptual paradigms, research methodologies, clinical techniques, and commercial practices in the domestic culture. (Venuti 1998, 68)

Nor is it only the agency of the translator that shapes the translated work:

> Whether the effects of a translation prove to be conservative or transgressive depends fundamentally on the discursive strategies developed by the translator, but also on various factors in their reception, including the page design and cover art of the printed book, the advertising copy, the opinions of reviewers, and the uses made of the translation in cultural and social institutions, how it is read and taught. Such factors mediate the impact of any translation by assisting in the positioning of domestic subjects, equipping them with specific reading practices, affiliating them with specific cultural values and constituencies, reinforcing or crossing institutional limits. (68)

Translation, in other words, is both carried out and received within a domestic discursive field that sets the condition for it and also inevitably lifts the translated work from its original context and reconfigures its meaning. Over and beyond the impossibility of total "fidelity" at the linguistic level, the work acquires the added dimension of being not only *of* the culture from which it emerges (say, a novel from Egypt), but ultimately *about* that culture in its totality (a novel about Egypt, *tout court*, rather than a particular event, idea, historical period, or whatever else it may be for Egyptian readers). Less directly but no less importantly, it also becomes a novel about the receiving or target culture, since consciously or unconsciously, readers look for an image of themselves reflected in the mirror of a "foreign" novel. Moreover, such a novel also ultimately becomes about the relations between Egypt or Islam or Arabs or the "East" (however the work may be marketed to, and/or received by, the reader) on the one hand, and the U.S. or the "West" on the other hand (however that may be constructed by translator, publisher, reviewer, and reader). Such reconfiguration is inevitable in any literary translation, which is not only an aesthetic but also a cultural (or cross-cultural), discursive, and political activity.

Hence Venuti's emphasis, signaled in the subtitle of his book, on the need to work "towards an ethics of difference" in translation, which he distinguishes from "a translation ethics of sameness" (82). Drawing upon the work of Antoine Berman, Venuti argues that an ethics of difference preserves the foreignness of the translated work (its potential to challenge domestic discourse), while an ethic of sameness "domesticates" the text by making it conform to the dominant discourse in the target, or receiving, culture:

> Bad translation shapes toward the foreign culture a domestic attitude that is ethnocentric: "generally under the guise of transmissibility, [it] carries out a systematic negation of the strangeness of the foreign work" (Berman 1992, 5). Good translation aims to limit this ethnocentric negation: it stages "an opening, a dialogue, a cross-breeding, a decentering" and thereby forces the domestic language and culture to register the foreignness of the foreign text" (4). (Venuti 1998, 81)

Berman and Venuti have contested some conventional notions about the ideal translation, such as the requirement that a translation be "fluent" in a way that renders the translator invisible and gives the reader the impression that the work is an original rather than a translation. Drawing on poststructuralism, Venuti has also questioned the very notion of the "original," with its implications of coherence and self-identity, suggesting that the "original" is itself always a translation; he further insists that rather than eradicating the foreignness of the translated text, a "good translation is demystifying: it manifests in its own language the foreignness of the foreign text" (Venuti 1998, 11). This kind of translation does not leave us with a comfortable sense of self-identity, let alone superiority. As James Clifford puts it, "in the kind of translation that interests me most, you learn a lot about peoples, cultures, and histories different from your own, enough to begin to know what you're missing" (Clifford 39).

The effect of estrangement in Berman's and Venuti's notion of ethical translation has been contested by some Arabists who share the concern for an ethics of difference. Berman (a French Germanist) and Venuti (a U.S. Italianist) work on cultural materials that are relatively easy enough to conflate: Romanticism in Germany and France, the Renaissance in Italy and England, respectively, and so estrangement in their case works to emphasize cultural specificity that is easy to overlook. When it comes to translating Arabic into English or another European language, however, the prism of Orientalism brings a whole new dimension to the picture. This is evidenced by the oft-cited fact that access to Arabic literature and culture in Britain and the U.S. has long been mediated by highly uneven translations. From the radically distinct nineteenth-century translations of *The Thousand and One Nights* by eminent Orientalists Edward William Lane and Richard Burton, to widely circulated translations of Nawal el Saadawi and Naguib Mahfouz today, the history of English translations of Arabic texts reveals the dynamics of power in the (post)colonial age. Roger Allen argues that "the general situation regarding the translation of Arabic literary works into English is probably the least satisfactory of all the European languages (my point of comparison is with French,

German, Italian, and Spanish), by which I imply a comment on the possibilities of publication, the amount and variety of Arabic literature available in the target language, and the receptivity among the readership for translated works" (Allen 2003, 1).[18] This situation prompted Edward Said to describe Arabic as an "embargoed literature" after one prominent New York publisher told him that Arabic was "a controversial language" (1990, 278). In this context, some scholars and translators of Arabic literature have taken issue with Venuti's valorization of estrangement as the guarantor of ethical translation. As Marilyn Booth puts it:

> my self-questioning, as I translate, centers on the issue of 'how foreignizing?' in terms of both extent and strategy. Arabic literature already faces so many obstacles to reader reception in this continent [North America] that I find myself asking whether foreignizing translations will productively challenge those power relations or whether this approach runs the risk of ironically contributing to current dominant notions among Americans by privileging difference in a way that serves an already rooted discourse of difference in the United States when it comes to producing 'Arabs,' 'Muslims,' 'Islam,' and the like. Too much of what we see in American print and visual media on the Middle East conveys a message of cultural untranslatability that isn't an invitation to work toward an understanding of and respect for difference, but rather an intimation of possibly unbridgeable otherness. (Booth 51)

Furthermore, as Tarek Shamma demonstrates in his reading of Richard Burton's translation of *The Thousand and One Nights*, foreignizing strategies "could be used to serve very different ideological agendas . . . [I]t could rationalize racial and cultural bias and blatant imperialist attitudes as well as oppose them"; by the same token, "the domesticating strategies that Venuti attacks may be equally unsusceptible to a priori formulations" (Shamma 65). Therefore, "if both domesticating and foreignizing strategies can have such varying effects, then the politics, as well as the ethics, of translation . . . must be seen as the outcome of a complexity of circumstances that comprise the intervention of the translator and the choices that he or she makes . . . , the larger context of reception, and the relation of the translated text to other texts in its cultural environment" (65–66).

While Arab immigrant writing in English is not translated from Arabic, its producers are nevertheless perceived, and many of them have also perceived themselves, as cultural translators all the same. Arab immigrant literature oscillates between the two strategies of domesticating and foreignizing, but it also demonstrates that the range of ideological and discursive effects described by Booth and Shamma can be produced through both strategies. Nowhere is this clearer than in the case of what I call "translational literature." By that I do not mean all immigrant writing, but, strictly speaking, those texts that straddle two languages, at once foregrounding, performing, and problematizing the act of translation. The prime examples of translational literature examined in this book are Ameen Rihani's *The Book of Khalid* (1911), Ahdaf Soueif's *The Map of Love* (1999), and Leila Aboulela's *The Translator* (1999), although translational novels can be found in other languages and literary traditions as well. Like other Arab immigrant narratives, those texts participate in the construction of cross-cultural identities, but because they thematize the processes of translation, those paradigmatic novels bring into sharp relief the conditions of immigrant Arab writing in general and draw a benchmark for the most contestatory kinds of cultural translation found in it. In other words, those texts offer the most radical form of cultural translation in Arab immigrant literature. While all bilingual and multilingual discourse dramatizes the interaction of languages, translational texts lay special emphasis on translation as a crucial component of cross-cultural contact. Translational literature exposes the problematics of translation as an interpretive process in its attempt to negotiate the complex critical, institutional, and commercial grids that govern the selection, translation, publication, and marketing of Arabic texts in Britain and the U.S. More crucially, translational texts are positioned to resist the power differentials that influence the work of the translator and reproduce stereotyped cultural identities. In performing acts of cultural translation in the "original" itself, translational literature at once problematizes the notion of the "original" and stages what Deleuze and Guattari describe as the deterritorialization of language.

For example, translational texts may "Arabize," "Africanize," or "Indianize" English, sometimes by transliterating words and expressions for which there is no English equivalent, then explaining them within the text or in a glossary or not at all.[19] Or alternatively, literal translation may be used to transfer the cultural-linguistic character of one language—its idiomatic expressions and its sensibility—into English, at the expense of fluency and immediate intelligibility.[20] In occasionally favoring what Douglas Robinson calls "radical literalism," translational texts point to the limits of translatability (Robinson xi). They transfer the rhetoricity of one language into another, reproducing not only sense, but also such cultural-linguistic phenomena as etymological derivation; conventional, idiomatic, and proverbial usage; and culturally embedded connotations of cognates and word associations. In "The Politics of Translation," a sustained reflection on the subject of literary and cultural translation that is grounded in her influential translations from Bengali and French, Gayatri Chakravorty Spivak argues that while the rhetoric of any language at times interrupts its logic, it is in the "jagged relationship between rhetoric and logic, condition and effect of knowing" that "a world is made for the agent, so that the agent can act in an ethical way, a political way; so that the agent can be alive, in a human way, in the world. Unless one can at least construct a model of this for the other language, there is no real translation" (181). Translational texts construct such models of language in the "original" itself. And yet those texts are not only concerned with translation techniques within a strictly linguistic register; they also present the act of translation as a central theme, metaphor, or structural principle.

In these ways, translation is not only the condition of the texts under consideration in this book, but also of much bilingual writing, and of translational literature in any language.[21] In the Francophone arena, Abdelkébir Khatibi has theorized bilingualism as the erotics of an "amour bilingue" (bilingual love), in response to the agonistic or antagonistic relationship between the languages of colonizer and colonized in many of the debates around the politics of language in (post)colonial settings.[22] Bilingual love begets a hybrid offspring, a language semantically infused by its Other, bearing the marks of linguistic and ideological contamination. Two telling examples of this phenomenon within an unsuspected politico-linguistic field are the novels of Israeli-Palestinians Emile Habibi and Anton Shammas. Habibi's novel, *The Pessoptimist*, is about the predicament of so-called 1948-Arabs, those Palestinians who were not exiled when Israel was created and became citizens of the new state. The novel is written in Arabic, but its language is infused with Hebrew in a way that reflects the anxieties, misunderstandings, mistranslations, and mixed allegiances of the Israeli-Palestinian minority.[23] Treating the same issues, Shammas's novel, *Arabesques*, is by contrast written in Hebrew, although he later translated it into Arabic, and translated Habibi's novel into Hebrew. Thoroughly trilingual, Shammas has also translated other writers into and from Arabic, English, and Hebrew. His deliberate choice of Hebrew over Arabic in *Arabesques* afforded him a certain artistic freedom (to write about family members in a language foreign to them), imposed on him a productive linguistic discipline (the cautious precision of a non-native speaker), and also allowed him discursively to divorce the Hebrew language from Zionist ideology, which conflates language, ethnicity, and nationhood, allowing him, as a non-Jewish Israeli citizen, to stake a claim to the language (Siddiq 163–4). For Shammas, "writing in any language, even that of the colonizer, is a form of love" (163-my translation)—although he differentiates his own situation as a multilingual writer enjoying the freedom to choose his medium from the predicament of those Maghrebian writers on whom French was imposed by a colonial system that proscribed Arabic literacy.[24] Writing in Hebrew or French allows writers like Shammas and Khatibi to appropriate the colonizers' language for themselves and to dissociate it from the ideologies of Zionism and "la mission civilisatrice."

A rigorously self-conscious conception of ethical agency governs the passage from bilingual love to love in translation—a crucial passage that defines the condition of translation from one language to another and of translational literature. Reverence for the "original" correlates that ethical imperative with the ecclesiastical sense of "translation," for to "translate" a saint's remains requires elaborate rituals the purpose of which is to sanctify the act and to ward off the evil consequences of sacrilege.[25] In the same vein, as Robinson shows, the translation of sacred texts was for millennia considered taboo, to be undertaken only by high priests on special occasions, such as initiation into divine mysteries. Such initiation radically transforms the initiate, who must be willing to surrender himself or herself to the divine power unleashed through translation. Robinson identifies a paradigmatic case in Lucius Apuleius's *The Golden Ass*, which involves multiple metamorphoses of the protagonist, culminating with his initiation into the cult of Isis (Robinson 3–45). Delineating a notion of literary translation that, in its respect for the original and emphasis on the transformative potential of translation, functions as a secular equivalent to Robinson's, Spivak invokes Luce Irigaray's discussion of the place of love in ethics to describe literary translation as "the most intimate act of reading." Spivak goes on to argue that the translator must "surrender to the text" in order to "solicit the text to show the limits of its language" (Spivak, "Politics" 183). Through that surrender, the translator "earns permission to transgress from the trace of the other" (180). Echoing Khatibi's metaphor of *amour bilingue*, Spivak argues that "the task of the translator is to facilitate this love between the original and its shadow, a love that permits fraying, holds the agency of the translator and the demands of her imagined or actual audience at bay. The politics of translation from a non-European woman's text too often suppresses this possibility because the translator cannot engage with, or cares insufficiently for, the rhetoricity of the original" (181). In extreme cases, this kind of translation forges or fabricates a text that reproduces the dominant ideology of the target culture—for instance, Orientalist representations of Muslim women (Amireh, Kahf). Forgery and fabrication represent the endgame of domestication and the secular counterpart to sacrilege. In Spivak's secular metaphor, translation becomes a species of forgery when deviation from the letter of the original, which is the condition of translation, is not authorized by an ethics of "fraying," i.e. "a disrupting, yet 'loving' rhetoricity that enters into the text's self-staging rather than searches for synonym, syntax, and local color" (Apter 102). In the religious register, translation becomes sacrilege when it is performed without ritual sanction or when intentional desecration occurs (as, for example, when, in Ahdaf Soueif's *The Map of Love*, British colonists desecrate—or translate—the remains of the Mahdi, who is revered by the Sudanese insurgents as a saint).

Spivak's theory rests on an ethics of difference that takes seriously the agency of the translator in the reform of cultural identities by subverting the will-to-power of colonial and other hegemonic ideologies. Translational literature is a product of cultural translation that performs that ethical imperative and undercuts the myth of autonomous cultural and civilizational identities.[26] By the same token, if the ethics of difference in translation depends not so much on the translational strategies used (foreignizing vs. domesticating) but on love of the Other, an ethics of sameness that informs hegemonic translation could likewise mobilize the same range of strategies. In contrast to translational literature, there are Arab immigrant narratives that embody an ethics of sameness, going so far sometimes as to "fabricate" the realities they purport to describe, so as to conform to, and to draw authority from, Orientalism. The following chapters examine several texts that in various ways derive their authority from Orientalism, but it is worth noting here the paradigmatic case of Norma Khouri's *Honor Lost* (2003). First published in Australia as *Forbidden Love* (2002), the memoir generated tremendous publicity and much praise for its author (not to mention sales of hundreds of thousands of copies) for recounting the "honor killing" of her best friend Dalia in Jordan. Subsequently, however, investigating journalists discovered that the sensational events never took place and that Dalia and other characters, places, and events mentioned in the book were fictitious. Steven Salaita, who devotes a chapter of his book *Arab American Literary Fictions, Cultures, and Politics* (2007) to the forgery and the ensuing scandal that led Australian and U.S. publishers to withdraw the book, writes,

> *Honor Lost* is virtually unreadable. It is poorly written with hysterical narration and clichéd description. It is worse methodologically, relying

> not only on spurious information and falsified data, but also on every imaginable American stereotype of Arab men and women. In a sense, the most interesting question *Honor Lost* raises is . . . how anybody read the book and actually believed it. I will have to argue that the book's believability . . . can be attributed in part to its appeasement of a long-standing cultural mythos in the United States and its ability to retroactively justify decades of aggressive foreign policy in the Arab world. *Honor Lost*, in other words, could be believed because its readers had already accepted its contents as true before it had even been written; had they not, it would have been impossible to write. (Salaita 2007, 88)

Khouri's example illustrates the shaping power of, and ideological investments in, a cultural discourse that constructs a collective "Western" identity according to an ethics of sameness vis-à-vis a barbaric Other. In this extreme case, an unscrupulous opportunist knew how to exploit both her national background and Orientalist stereotypes in posing as an authoritative cultural translator.

Khouri's initial success vastly contrasts with the general neglect of Arabic and Anglophone Arab writers, suggesting that many readers in English-speaking countries are only prepared to accept texts that confirm what they already "know." Consequently, certain kinds of narratives—in this case, of Arab women's oppression—are eagerly received not only out of concern for the plight of the victims (which in many cases is indeed grave), but also because they confirm stereotypes that function to justify U.S. foreign policy toward Arab countries. By contrast, narratives that cross discursive or ideological lines are censored altogether, if they cannot be remolded and beaten into shape by editors. In private conversation, many Arab American writers are all too eager to tell horror stories about press editors and marketing departments, but many of them are reluctant to write or speak publicly about their experiences for fear of antagonizing their publishers.[27] One glaring example of censorship on the part of an unusually candid editor is recounted in Gregory Orfalea's memoir, *Angeleno Days: An Arab American Writer on Family, Place, and Politics* (2009):

> My second novel, *Mirage*, was set in 1936 Palestine and featured a marriage between an Arab and Jew in old Haifa. It was being taken around New York [publishers] by a fine agent named Elaine Markson. So taken was she with the manuscript she told me, "This is going to be a great book. This is going to be an event." I told her, "Elaine, forget the event. Just get it published." Well, one day I received a phone call from Little, Brown's Frederica Friedman, a legendary editor who had done the bestselling historical novel on Japan, *Shogun*. She said to me, "Mr. Orfalea, you write very well. You are on an intriguing mission." I said, "Ma'am, I'm not on a mission. I just follow my instincts and obsessions." She said, "I want you to know I like your book very much, but I am not going to publish it." "Why?" I asked. "Because of who you are," she said. For a second I wanted to ask her, "Who am I?" But I just sat on the phone, speechless, until she filled the silence. "Greg," she said, "If you were Jewish, this

> wouldn't be a problem. People would believe the book. But because you are who you are, nobody will believe it."
>
> I have thought about this portentous conversation for a long time. Intermarriages in old Palestine between Jews and Arabs were not common, but they did happen, as they do occasionally today in Israel. I've met several people who were products of such marriages and interviewed a daughter of one extensively. Naturally, their views on the Palestine-Israel conflict are complicated and I think fascinating. Freddy Friedman was basically saying she agreed with my presentation of this complex reality and attitude, but because I was of Arab background, I couldn't get it right. I was, by dint of who I was, perceived as unable to be fair. I was, de facto, an unreliable narrator. (Orfalea 2009, 221–22)

The stark irony here lies in the contrast between the remarkable success of Khoury's fraudulent memoir and the censorship of Orfalea's still-unpublished novel. The one was judged as true, even though it was falsely presented as a memoir, the other was deemed unbelievable, even though it only claimed to be fiction. The one confirmed the reigning discourse on Arabs, the other contradicted it.

As cultural translators and members of an embattled minority, Arab immigrant writers pick their stances toward Orientalism along the discursive spectrum broadly defined by Berman and Venuti: domesticating (understood as conforming to, and thereby confirming, the dominant representations of Self and Other, or "East" and "West") and foreignizing (challenging readers' expectations, undermining stereotypes and idealized self-images, and proposing what Venuti calls reformed models of cultural identity). Those two approaches, as I understand them here, are not only a matter of procedure, translation strategy, or narrative form and technique, but more importantly of the underlying assumptions and ideological project of each writer. Nor are domesticating and foreignizing simple and straightforward alternatives. As the following chapters demonstrate, very few writers indeed can be classified with such either/or clarity—extreme cases, such as that of Norma Khouri, being rare. Instead, in most cases, identity construction involves complex negotiations among sometimes contradictory personal, social, cultural, religious, political, and ideological propositions that often defy straightforward taxonomies. After all, with mixed feelings toward both the home and the adopted country, immigrants are often conflicted creatures.

1

The Rise of Arab American Literature

We are not of the East or the West;
No boundaries exist in our breast:
We are free.
—AMEEN RIHANI

Cultural Translation and the *Nahda*

Ameen Rihani (1876–1940) is the author of the first Arab American poetry collection, *Myrtle and Myrrh* (1905), the first Arab American play, *Wajdah* (1909), and the first Arab American novel, *The Book of Khalid* (1911). Subsequently he published another poetry collection, *A Chant of Mystics* (1921), a treatise on *The Descent of Bolshevism* (1920), and *The Path of Vision: Essays of East and West* (1921). His first English-language publication, however, was a translation of selected poems by the great tenth-century Arab poet Abu al-'Ala' al-Ma'arri (1903), with another volume to follow in 1918. This is the first English translation of Arabic poetry by an Arab translator. Rihani was also the first Arab literary critic in English, with an important study on *The Lore of the Arabian Nights* (written in 1928–30 and unpublished until 2002) and three books on the Arabian Peninsula and the founder of the Saudi dynasty (1928, 1930, 1931). In Arabic, Rihani published poetry, literary criticism, essays, history, books on his travels throughout the Arab world, and studies of nearly all of its heads of state. In fact, he was already a celebrated writer in Arabic before he published anything in English. His *Nabdha fi al-thawrah al-firinsiyyah* (Treatise on the French Revolution) appeared in 1902, and numerous articles, speeches, short stories, and poems established his literary reputation in the Arab world by the turn of the century. He was the first to write prose poetry in Arabic and he spearheaded an important literary movement known as *Mahjar* (immigrant) poetry, which introduced European Romantic themes in Arabic literature. His collected Arabic works fill twelve volumes (1980–86).[1]

What unites this prolific output in Arabic and English is an overarching project of cultural translation that ambitiously aimed to reinterpret the "East" and the "West" to each other and bring about a civilizational synthesis, coupled with Rihani's tireless pursuit of Arab independence—first from the Ottoman Empire then from European colonialism—and of political unity. Although Rihani shared those twin objectives with many of his contemporaries, his approach was shaped by his location in the United States. The first objective dates back to the beginnings of the Arab *Nahda* (or renaissance) in the 1830s. In the wake of the French occupation of Egypt (1798–1801), it became all too clear to Egypt's ruler Muhammad Ali (1769–1849) that Europe's strength was the result of modern scientific knowledge, and it was in the interests of acquiring that knowledge that he began sending educational missions to France in the 1820s. In 1831, an Egyptian Islamic scholar called Rifa'a al-Tahtawi returned from one such mission in Paris to establish a school for translation that would disseminate modern European science and ideas. The core of *Nahda* reformism was selective appropriation: adopting modern European ideas, sciences, and institutions that would strengthen Arab societies while rejecting aspects of Europe that did not harmonize with Arab Islamic mores and values. Christian Levantine intellectuals who played an important role in the movement from the 1860s onward, and to whom Rihani was heir, contributed to the rise of secular Arab nationalism as an anti-Ottoman ideology.[2] But this impulse was not sectarian per se, for it was shared by many Muslim intellectuals and political leaders from the early part of the nineteenth century, contributing to the Arab Revolt of 1916, led by the Sharif Husayn of Mecca and coordinated with the British invasion of Palestine in the final phase of World War I. In the McMahon–Husayn correspondence of 1915–16 leading up to the Revolt, the British encouraged Arab aspirations to independence, only secretly to conclude the Sykes–Picot agreement with the French in 1916 that effectively divided the Arab world into spheres of influence, and then to issue the Balfour Declaration in 1917 promising the establishment of a Jewish state in Palestine.[3] None of this could have been seen by Arab nationalists as anything but a betrayal by the British, something that deepened the mistrust felt by many toward Europe and further complicated the task of social and political reform predicated on cultural translation and synthesis. Inspired by Woodrow Wilson's Fourteen Points, some Arabs hoped that the U.S. would play a more positive role in the Middle East than the European powers, whose colonial ambitions there had become obvious, and some even called for a U.S. mandate in the region (Khalidi 32–33).

The Syrian intellectuals who came to the United States in the late nineteenth century and established a number of Arabic-language newspapers in the 1890s were products of the *Nahda*. They wrote in Arabic and many were outspoken in their criticism of the Ottomans and of social conditions back home, especially religious superstition and the power of the clergy. Although many of those early immigrants imported with them local sectarian biases, espoused by the various newspapers at the time, gradually and under pressure from the larger society in which they became a racialized minority (Majaj 2000), those biases began to be fused into a "Syrian" identity in the U.S. and a nationalist politics with respect to events back home. For example, when Ameen Rihani emigrated to the U.S. in 1888 at the age of twelve, he was accompanied by his uncle 'Abduh Rihani and his teacher Naoum Mokarzel, who in 1898 founded a newspaper, *Al-Hoda* (Guidance), "to serve the cause of a Christian, Maronite-dominated Lebanese nation under French tutelage, independent of the Ottoman Empire." Mokarzel's impulse was to oppose the publishers of another paper, *Kawkab Amrika* (The Star of America), begun in 1892, which "did not espouse a religious bias" and "remained loyal to the Ottoman Empire, perhaps because of the [founder's] family's Damascene (rather than Lebanese) origin and Eastern Orthodox Christian faith, but more likely because this educated, elite family was among the advocates of the incipient Syrian nationalist philosophy," which "stressed Syrian unity through political and social reforms, respectful coexistence between the numerous rival religious sects, and Syrian patriotism—a patriotism aimed more at the concept of a Syrian people than a Syrian nation—and by implication, loyalty to the Ottoman Empire" (Naff 1987, 7). By contrast, *Mir'at al-Gharb* (Mirror of the West) was established in 1899 as the voice of the Syrian Orthodox and anti-Ottoman Arabism, while the Druze and Muslim immigrants founded *Al-Bayan* (The Explanation) in 1911 (8). In his early speeches and essays published in those papers, often against the grain of their sectarian biases, Rihani himself would be so critical of the Maronite Church he had been raised in that he was excommunicated in 1903, an event dramatized in *The Book of Khalid*. Similarly, Kahlil Gibran (1883–1931), also of Maronite background, wrote a number of short stories in Arabic dramatizing the corruption and tyranny of the clergy; those stories were directly influenced by Rihani (Naimy 21–22, 25–26). Rihani also advocated Arab unity and independence from the Ottomans, and later from European colonialism, a goal he hoped would be achieved with the aid of the United States. He believed that because of the ideals expressed in its Declaration of Independence and its historical experience as a former colony, the U.S. would be a natural ally in the Arab struggle for national liberation, which he hoped would come to fruition with the creation of the United Arab States, on the U.S. model, after the demise of the Ottoman empire. The task, therefore, was to explain both this historical affinity between the United States and the Arab world and the advantages of their forging an alliance. The aim of his freelance diplomacy in the 1920s and 30s was to cement the relations between Abdul-Aziz Al Saud, founder of the Saudi dynasty, on whom Rihani set his hopes for unifying Arabs, and the U.S. government. Rihani's Arabic travel books sought to bring the Arab world closer together, while his English travel books of the same period (self-translations from the Arabic originals) were intended to familiarize readers with Abdul-Aziz and his kingdom.[4]

Rihani's literary, intellectual, and political project is captured in the title of the published proceedings of a symposium held a few months after 9/11 to celebrate his life's work, *Ameen Rihani: Bridging East and West*.[5] Heir to two literary and cultural traditions, Rihani not only contributed to both but also tried to fuse them together. Writing in two languages throughout his life, such "bridging" involved constant translation, a process that immediately collided with the discourse of Orientalism. Rihani, Gibran, and Abraham Rihbany knew that addressing American readers required more than just the ability to write in a foreign language. They had to situate themselves in relation to a powerful discourse through which their readers had already formed their ideas about that distant culture. The shift from Arabic to English meant that Anglophone Arab American literature was to be constrained by that antecedent discourse, in relation to which the nascent literary tradition must constantly define itself. Obviously, when writing in Arabic, Rihani and Gibran not only had a different agenda, but also enjoyed greater discursive latitude in that, first, they did not have to explain Arab culture to Arab readers; second, they were not expected by their readers to be Oriental spokesmen; and third, they did not have to abide by discursive strictures imposed on their cultures by a conquering knowledge system, with its stereotypes, typologies, culturalist and racialist frames of reference, privileged texts and modes, and so forth—even when they could not free themselves entirely from its powerful imprint. They wrote within an Arabic cultural discourse and could ignore or dismiss simplistic or offensive Orientalist descriptions, or they could boldly and directly challenge their imperialistic underpinnings. When writing in English, however, they had to couch their message in ways that guaranteed or at least increased the likelihood of its acceptance—of *their* acceptance as writers—by American readers. As Evelyn Shakir points out, "the first generation of Arab-American writers (as might be expected of immigrants in an age of rampant xenophobia) dressed carefully for their encounter with the American public, putting on the guise of prophet, preacher, or man of letters. They could not hide their foreignness, but they could make it respectable" (Shakir 1996, 6). Some of those roles (such as Gibran's posture as a mystic or Oriental sage) are, of course, among the stereotypes circulating within Orientalism's regime of truth, while others (Rihani as a man of letters and Abraham Rihbany as a Protestant minister) were carefully calculated to challenge aspects of it, in an effort not only to "make foreignness respectable," but also to redefine the relationship between "East" and "West." The implied message was, "Here we are, we can produce literature that draws upon the most distinguished Western writers, and we can minister to American Protestant congregations, but we, too, are Orientals."

Moreover, early Arab American writers in English tried to appropriate that stance of Orientalist and, in fact, their implicit claim was that they were better equipped to interpret the Orient than European Orientalists. Immigrating to the U.S. in childhood like Gibran and Rihani (both at age twelve), or in youth like Rihbany (age twenty-two) out of economic necessity, they were intermittently educated in Arabic, French, or American schools in Lebanon and the U.S., and their self-education was eclectic. Like Edward Said, they came to Arabic studies belatedly.[6] It was inevitable for them, therefore, to subordinate their experience to the systematic, authoritative, and widely dispersed Orientalist knowledge. They nevertheless felt the kind of tension between that knowledge and their own lived experience which was to spur Said's critical project, but they did not have the benefit of a privileged family background that afforded him a first-rate education, or the conceptual tools with which to interrogate Orientalism as he would do seven decades later, or the historical advantage he enjoyed (or suffered) of witnessing the decolonization and Civil Rights movements, the catastrophic events in Palestine, and the rising tide of anti-Arab racism in the U.S. over the course of the twentieth century, all of which in different ways motivated and inspired the oppositional thrust of his work. In the early twentieth century, by contrast, it was still possible for Gibran to see British and French colonialism in Egypt, Syria, and Lebanon as a civilizing force (*Nusus* 60–65). It was also possible for Rihani to see the United States as a potential ally in the Arab struggle for independence. Rihbany went even farther; by an eerily familiar and thoroughly disturbing logic to us today, in books like *Militant America and Jesus Christ* (1917), he provided a religious argument for United States intervention in World War I, and in *America Save the Near East* (1918) he advocated U.S. stewardship over the region: "I do not say that America is the best 'colonizer,' nor that Syria's real need is to be 'colonized' by being tied to the chariot of a strong and *conquering* nation. The cry is rather for a big-hearted, disinterested helper, whose motives shall be above suspicion, and whose reward, the joy of helpfulness" (52; original emphasis).

Arab American writers' attempts to replace the Orientalist as interpreter or translator of the Orient was a way of claiming cultural space and voice, countering the negativity associated with the Orient, and mediating between it and the West for the sake of greater cross-cultural understanding. Said's book and the polemics it initiated, together with the areas of inquiry it opened up, such as postcolonial studies, represents a watershed in that contest over voice, representation, and discursive power in which early Arab Americans engaged. Said's critique of Orientalism and of the concept of the Orient puts into question the antithetical construct of the Occident or the West, but early Arab American writers did not go so far. They accepted the Orientalist distinction between the contrasting essences of East and West, the former seen as passive, mystical, spiritual, traditional, backward, and the latter correspondingly as aggressive, rational, materialistic, modern, progressive. What they wanted to contest was the hierarchy of values attached to the poles of this binary. They were angry at, and rebellious against, the oppressive rule of the Ottoman Empire and highly critical of social and political conditions in Syria and the rest of the Arab world. They correspondingly admired the social, political, and technological advances of western European countries and the United States. But they were also very conscious and proud of a great civilization's past history and rich literary heritage, to which they contributed through their Arabic prose and poetry, written in the United States.[7] They could not, therefore, accept the idea of the East's inferiority. Moreover, the prevailing attitude toward Europe within what Hourani calls the "liberal" school of Arabic thought from the 1830s onwards emphasized critically selective borrowing from Europe: only those ideas and sciences deemed compatible with Arab culture and necessary for the reform of its social institutions were to be adopted, while decadent and materialistic aspects of Europe were in need of reform and to be rejected. Given the balance of power and the challenges of social reform in their countries, *Nahda* intellectuals never imagined themselves on a mission to reform Europe, but they discriminated sharply between what they considered to be the advantages and disadvantages of its civilization, and advocated borrowing selectively from it.

Because of their location in the U.S., Arab immigrant intellectuals at the turn of the twentieth century saw themselves as reformers of East *and* West. The discursive challenge facing them was to replace Orientalist valuations with a model of duality without hierarchy, whereby the contrasting essences were seen as existing in a sort of metaphysical equilibrium and reciprocity: East and West complement, need, and have something to teach each other. Rihbany puts it succinctly: "The world needs a characteristic Oriental civilization as it needs a characteristic Occidental civilization" (*Wise Men* 159). Reform of the East depends on inspiration and material assistance from the West, but "if it is to be of significant value to either the East or the West, a new Eastern civilization must be genuinely Eastern. It must not be a replica of Western civilization, which itself needs a hundred reforms" (299–300). A "better East" (289) would be more suitable to Western business interests (299), yet would remain free from the material and spiritual ravages of industrialization discernible in "New York, Chicago, and London" (300). By the same token, "the Oriental must never cease to teach his Occidental brother, nor ever allow himself to forget his own great spiritual maxims which have guided the course of his life for so many centuries" (301). At the end of the day, East would still be East, and West West.

Others like Rihani (and less explicitly Gibran) envisioned a Hegelian dynamic that would eventually blend East and West into a higher synthesis of civilizations, and saw themselves in the role of two-way reformers and facilitators of that process. Like Rihbany, they accepted the Orientalist distinction between East and West but rejected its historical immutability in favor of a conception of East and West as values and attitudes of mind that are not geographically determined and can, therefore, circulate among cultures over long historical periods. This more plastic form of Orientalism can explain the erstwhile historical ascendancy of Phoenician and Arab civilizations. Thus, pride in their civilization's illustrious cultural heritage that has much to offer their new country is the content of Gibran's address, "To Young Americans of Syrian Origin," which appeared in the inaugural issue of *The Syrian World*, the first English language literary and cultural magazine in North America, launched specifically for the benefit of second-generation Arab Americans whose native language was English. Pride in Syrian heritage (coded as the "Syrian Race," for the reasons explained in the Introduction) is also the theme of a series of articles by the Reverend W. A. Mansur, published in *The Syrian World* throughout its six-year life (1926–32). Rihani clearly articulated this reconstructed Orientalism in the June 1927 issue of the same magazine. In an address originally delivered at the American University of Beirut two months earlier and titled "Where East and West Meet," Rihani declares that his title "implies a partial denial of the dictum of Rudyard Kipling, megaphoned to the world in a line of verse, 'East is East and West is West, and never the twain shall meet.'" Rihani goes on:

> I admit, at the start, that, from a surface point of view, the evidence is in favor of Mr. Kipling. The East prays, the West dances; the East dreams, the West thinks; the East broods, the West plays. What is a mark of respect in the East, is considered an offense in the West: the Oriental, when he enters your house, slips off his shoes at the door; the Occidental finds a hat-rack for his hat. . . . [T]he one is suave and insidious, the other is blunt and often crude. The Oriental is imaginative and metaphoric, the

> Occidental is literal and "matter-of-fact." Kipling's dictum is in this, at least, wholly to the point.

Rihani here validates Orientalist typology: East and West are homogenous, self-evident, autonomous, and antithetical to one another. However, those traits do not fall along the colonialist hierarchy of values that defines the East as primitive, childish, superstitious, and the West as advanced, mature, rational. Some of Rihani's pairs of opposites are value-neutral (praying/dancing, dreaming/thinking, imaginative/literal, metaphoric/matter-of-fact), others are moral equivalents (suave/blunt, insidious/crude), and one actually reverses Orientalist valuations (brooding/playing). In other words, while endorsing duality, he is undermining the hierarchy. Moreover, those traits are not irrevocably wedded to symbolic geography, but are variable and historical:

> Like all generalities, however, these traits are not without exception. They are characteristic, but not exclusive. Take, for instance, the fawning and florid Oriental, extravagant with the metaphor and the puff, he is not a type exclusive. He is a species produced by despotism and its pompous court. The aristocracy kowtows to the emperor; the lower classes kowtow to the aristocracy and to each other. . . .
>
> When absolute monarchies were the rule in Europe, the Europeans, on the whole, were quite Oriental in the art of fawning and adulation; while the extravagant manner, as much in evidence in the nation as around the throne, was revealed, not only in speech, but also in the dress of the period. Consider the ruffles and feathers of mylords at court; the flounces and trains of mylady in waiting; consider the dedications penned by needy scribes to their rich patrons. . . . As for the people, they follow, according to the Arabic proverb, their sovereign. (8–9)

A critical historical perspective relativizes Orientalist valuations, which become anything but timeless. If Europeans were at one time Orientals, and Arabs Occidentals, those identities become variable, dynamic, and interchangeable. What matters ultimately is

> the highest ideal of the prophets and the poets—the ideal of the soul—which includes the ethical and the practical aspects of life, and which is neither Oriental nor exclusively Occidental. It is supremely human. Before it every mark of birth disappears; and customs and traditions are held in abeyance, and the differences in nationality and language cease to be a hindrance to understanding. The soul seeking expression, the soul reaching out for the truth, is one everywhere. Confucius might be American in his ideal, even as he is Chinese, and Emerson might be Chinese, even if he is American. Cotama [*sic*] Buddha made manifest in London might be mistaken for Carlyle and Carlyle revisiting the glimpses of the moon in Japan might be mistaken for Cotama. Jelal-ud-Din Rumi, were he born in Assisi would have been a St. Francis; and St. Francis, were he born in Shiraz

> would have been a Jelal-ud-Din. . . . And genius everywhere is one. In the Orient and in the Occident the deep thinkers are kin, the poets are cousins, the pioneers of the spirit are the messengers of peace and goodwill to the world. Their works are the open highways between nations, and they themselves are the ever living guardians and guides. (9–10)

This transcendentalist metaphysics of the spirit, prophecy, and poetry trivializes Orientalist hierarchies, but also overlooks the material conditions of cultural and ideological production.[8] If "East and West meet" in a celestial sphere inhabited by Buddha, Rumi, St. Francis, Carlyle, and Emerson, they can remain safely and discretely separated in the material world. (The very worldly and avowedly agnostic Confucius seems oddly out of place in this company!) In its conciliatory, non-confrontational stance, it offers itself as an alternative to the dominant discourses of difference, but without exposing their internal inconsistencies or their affiliations with power. In fact, it offers an illusory sense of freedom that sublimates the dialectics of history. The same idea is expressed in Rihani's poem, "A Chant of Mystics," published in 1921 in a collection bearing the same title:

> Nor Crescent nor Cross we adore;
> Nor Budha [*sic*] nor Christ we implore;
> Nor Muslem [*sic*] nor Jew we abhor:
> We are free.
> We are not of Iran or of Ind,
> We are not of Arabia or of Sind:
> We are free.
> We are not of the East or the West;
> No boundaries exist in our breast:
> We are free. (84)

This passage is frequently quoted to illustrate the nobility of Rihani's endeavors to reconstruct a human community free from religious, ethnic, and cultural, chauvinism. Yet the fact that the entire collection contains not a hint of the historical and political conditions that were radically transforming the map of the Middle East in 1921, and in which Rihani himself was fully embroiled as a speaker, writer, nationalist, activist, and delegate to postwar conferences, points to the unbridgeable chasm between this rarefied metaphysics and material reality. Rihani's negotiation of Orientalism vacillates between this Sufi ideal that transcends dualism and the material, worldly transactions that confront it—that is, between metaphysical unity and cultural translation.

Translation and Orientalist Knowledge

It is highly significant that Rihani's first English-language book was not only an effort at cultural translation, but was itself a literary translation that directly challenged Orientalist scholarship. In his preface to *The Quatrains of Abu'l-Ala* (1903), which was expanded and republished in *The Luzumiyat of Abu'l-Ala* (1918), Rihani describes the classical Arab poet (974–1058) as "the Lucretius of Al-Islam, the Diogenes of Arabia and the Voltaire of the East" (1903, vi). Abu al-'Ala' al-Ma'arri was a skeptic and a rationalist whose example represented, first of all, an implicit challenge to the idea of an exclusively spiritual East. Yet this skeptical rationalism is tempered by a mystical, nonsectarian, anticlerical religiosity that centers around a nonpartisan God whose love embraces all humanity regardless of creed.

> Another prophet will, they say, soon rise;
> But will he profit by his tricks, likewise?
> My prophet is my reason, aye, myself—
> From me to me there is no room for lies. (*Quatrains* 57)
>
> These superstitions, Sacred Books and Creeds,
> These cults and Myths and other noxious Weeds—
> So many Lies are crowned, in every age,
> While Truth beneath the tyrant's heel still bleeds. (59)
>
> Muhammad or Messiah! Hear thou me,
> The truth entire nor here nor there can be;
> How can our God who made the sun and moon
> Give all his light to one Sect, I can not see. (*Luzumiyat* 35)

Rihani found in those beliefs a way to overcome religious and political schisms, including the polarity between a dreamy, stagnant, albeit spiritually rich East and a rationalist, progressive, yet drearily materialistic West. He believed that al-Ma'arri combined the best qualities of both and held out the hope of a future synthesis of civilizations. At the same time, al-Ma'arri demonstrates to the West that the germ of Enlightenment could be found in the East (and eight centuries before Europe, for that matter), the implication being that Orientalists either did not fully understand the East or deliberately misrepresented it. Secondly, through al-Ma'arri, Rihani questioned Europe's fascination with Omar Khayyam—Persian author of *ruba'iyyat* (Arabic and Persian for quatrains), famous in Europe in Edward Fitzgerald's translation—a fascination that represents at once partial and partisan knowledge. Thus, Rihani's argument that Khayyam was an imitator of, and a lesser thinker than, al-Ma'arri directly challenged the authority of Orientalists by exposing the inadequacy of their representation. Khayyam

> was an imitator or a disciple of [al-Ma'arri]. The birth of the first and the death of the second . . . occurred about the middle of the eleventh century. . . . [T]he skepticism and pessimism of Omar are, to a great extent, imported from Märrah. In his religious opinions the Arabian philosopher is far more outspoken than the Persian poet. I do not say that Omar was a plagiarist, but I say this: Just as Voltaire, for instance, acquired most of his liberal and skeptical views from Hobbes, Locke and Bayle, so did Omar acquire his from Abu'l-Ala. (xviii–xix)

Moreover, Khayyam appealed to English readers because of his rebellion against Islam, which made him easy to enlist in the discourse on the backwardness and fanaticism of that religion. Al-Maʿarri, by contrast, attacks all creeds, as well as tribalism and chauvinism of all stripes, and can, therefore, only be subversive to Orientalist culturalism.

Yet al-Maʿarri also exposes a fundamental ambivalence in Rihani's Orientalism: on the one hand, al-Maʿarri undermines the binary model that structures Orientalism. If the Orient had its own Hobbes, Locke, Bayle, and Voltaire, then the entire distinction between the rationalist scientific West and the superstitious and fanatical East collapses. On the other hand, al-Maʿarri demonstrates Oriental influence on the Occident, something that Rihani finds extremely significant because it reinforces the idea of Europe's indebtedness to the wisdom of the East in general, and to Arab civilization in particular, thereby undermining the supposed superiority of the West. Rihani's wavering between the impulse to deconstruct Orientalism and the temptation to play the game of cultural one-upmanship—his wanting to have it both ways—points to his own intellectual investment in the opposition East/West, which seemed unassailable in his age, but which also afforded him a platform from which to launch his revisionary discourse. For the dichotomy East/West was not only culturally and intellectually reductive, it was also enabling for Rihani insofar as he could reinterpret or "expand" it to the point where it no longer sustained cultural and political hegemony, but in a nonconfrontational, conciliatory manner suited to his reformist project of civilizational synthesis. His hesitancy is no doubt also due to his sense of being a minority writer, an outsider to the American literary scene, or, as he puts it in the introduction to the first collection of his own English verse, *Myrtle and Myrrh,* published two years later, "a stranger at thy [the reader's] gate" (1905, 5) who "relies on the hospitality and cordiality due a guest" (6).

Rihani is careful, in the preface to the 1903 translation of al-Maʿarri, not to challenge Orientalist knowledge explicitly:

> The English-reading public, here and abroad, has already formed its opinion of Khayyam, and let it not, therefore, be supposed that in making this claim I aim to shake or undermine its great faith. Nor am I so presumptuous as to think that one could succeed in such a hazardous undertaking. My desire is to confirm and not to convulse, to expand and not to contract the Oriental influence on Occidental minds. (xix).

However, by the time he sits down to expand the 1903 preface into the version that appears in the 1918 volume of translation, that hesitancy has all but disappeared. The above statement about not wishing to challenge Orientalist knowledge is reproduced, but he goes on to do just that anyway. Elaborating on the neglect and distortion that al-Maʿarri suffered at the hands of Arab scholars who tried to turn him into a great Sufi whose heretical ideas that were forced upon him by the strictures of Arabic prosody, Rihani registers his surprise "to find a European scholar like Professor [D.S.] Margoliouth giving countenance to such views, even repeating, to support his own argument, such drivel" (1918, 18). Sensing that the absurdity of such views may not necessarily be self-evident to his readers (given that inane pronouncements on the Arab mind, the Arabic language, Islam's responsibility for the backwardness of Arabs, and so on, are not rare in either Orientalist scholarship or popular culture), Rihani turns to al-Maʿarri's prose works to show how his ideas of religion as a superstition prevail there too. Rihani goes on to offer this powerful indictment of European scholarship that anticipates the sweeping nature of Edward Said's critique of Orientalism's ideological investments:

> The East still remains the battle-ground of the creeds. And the Europeans, though they shook off their fetters of moral and spiritual slavery, would keep us in ours to facilitate the conquests of European commerce. And the terrible Dragon, which is fed by the foreign missionary and the native priest, by the theologians and the ulema, and which still preys upon the heart and mind of the Orient nations, is as active to-day as it was ten centuries ago. Let those consider this, who think [German Orientalist Alfred Freiherr] Von Kremer exaggerated when he said, "Abu'l-Ala is a poet many centuries ahead of his time." (20–21)

The neglect suffered by al-Maʿarri results from a conspiracy between Orientalists (with Von Kramer and Reynold A. Nicholson as exceptions that Rihani makes sure to mention) and conservative Arab scholars—two groups whose ideological imperatives require a monolithic and static conception of the Islamic tradition. As a rationalist and free thinker, al-Maʿarri did not fit with that conception: from an Orientalist perspective, an Oriental rationalist is an oxymoron; for conformist Arab scholars, al-Maʿarri was a heretical thinker whose difficult writings demanded the sort of misreading that blunted their incisive edge or co-opted them altogether. For Rihani, al-Maʿarri disturbs both regimes of truth and, therefore, serves as a model for the kind of progressive intellectual that Rihani himself aspired to be. Al-Maʿarri also becomes a particularly appropriate subject not only for interrogating Eastern and Western self-images and particularly Western views of the East, but for renewing East–West dialogue as well, since he embodied the kind of synthesis between spiritual wisdom and skeptical rationalism that Rihani took for a civilizational ideal, one which he himself promoted and aspired to embody in his own work.

Within a few years of publishing his first translation of al-Maʿarri, Rihani attempted to extend this project of cultural translation through all three major genres, writing a poetry collection, a play, and a novel by 1911. Mikhail Bakhtin's favorite genre was better suited to carry the burden of the type of cross-cultural discourse that Rihani wanted to create, for it gave him greater latitude than either poetry or drama to juxtapose different ideological worldviews. The poems gathered in *Myrtle and Myrrh* are on the same themes as his Arabic verse and written in anachronistic idiom and conventional forms, and together with his second collection, *The Chant of Mystics and Other Poems* (1918), came across as exotic, quaint, and mediocre. They were "either ignored . . . altogether or damned . . . with faint praise" (Bushrui and Munro 16).[9] As for his play *Wajdah*, it "seeks to convey to Western readers a topic that is neither familiar nor usual to them. . . . Perhaps it is the first time that an Arab-American portrays to the West a defiant Arab woman who questions everything and defies all norms" (Publisher's Foreword 9–10). Such a theme, however, must have seemed totally foreign. The play, being heavily influenced by Shakespearean tragedy, and anachronistic in its language, style, and form, was never published or performed during Rihani's lifetime, despite his efforts to revise it. Rihani's poetry and drama may have exhibited more literary ambition than talent, but they nevertheless stand as a testimony to his effort to "expand" American consciousness of the Orient.

Translational Poetics

Much more complex and rewarding is *The Book of Khalid*. Rihani goes one step further in that novel than in his translations, *Myrtle and Myrrh*, *Wajdah*, or *The Chant of Mystics*, in that he attempts to fuse Arabic and European literature thematically, linguistically, formally, and structurally. This inaugural text of Arab American fiction and of the Anglophone Arabic novel remains relatively unknown, no doubt in part because of its baffling admixture of philosophy and mysticism, its paradoxical tone at once solemn and ironical, its confusingly overwrought web of literary allusions, its alternation between utopianism and cynicism, and its enigmatic protagonist who seems at once to embody and to satirize Rihani's own ideas. Like other immigrant narratives, it is a story of coming to America; but like numerous fictional and autobiographical travel accounts of Arab intellectuals, from Rifa'a al-Tahtawi's *Takhlis al-ibriz fi talkhis bariz*, the text that inaugurated *Nahda* in the mid-1830s, to the novels of Tayeb Salih and Ahdaf Soueif in the late twentieth century, it is also a story of returning home, of migration rather than immigration. And while immigrant narratives tend, for obvious reasons, to be written in English, migration narratives are, with few recent exceptions, written in Arabic. In one sense, therefore, *The Book of Khalid* situates itself outside of two traditions: in the one, it is the wrong kind of story, in the other, it is written in the wrong language. Furthermore, its English is not only archaic, but also at times nearly unintelligible to readers unfamiliar with Arabic and its cultural frame of reference. In addition to the verbal humor and ironic tone characteristic of the Arabic *maqama* genre, Rihani's English is infused with Arabic words, expressions, proverbs, and even rhetorical strategies characteristic of nineteenth-century Arabic literature, such as parallelisms and rhymed prose.[10] It is a language radically deterritorialized, in Deleuze and Guattari's terms, availing itself liberally of the resources of another language with different cultural, rhetorical, and literary norms. Those strategies signal the emergence, in Arab immigrant writing, of what I call here "translational literature"—texts that dramatize the process of translation and foreground the limits of translatability.

Whereas such strategies in the novels of later writers like Ahdaf Soueif and Leila Aboulela participate in the Saidian project of undermining Orientalist claims to authoritative knowledge, of "translating" the Orient and making it accessible, in the work of Rihani, who accepted some of the basic tenets of Orientalism but pursued the ideal of a Hegelian synthesis of East and West, translational strategies are part of the effort to forge a new language that would serve as the vehicle of a new genre, the Arabized English novel, or the Arabic novel written in English. This genre would represent a literary synthesis of East and West that heralds the cultural and political synthesis that he envisioned. *The Book of Khalid* embodies this quest in its style, its language, its intertextual references, and its themes. Unfortunately, this also meant that the ideal readers for this novel do not yet exist on any wide scale; only those bi-cultural hybrids like Rihani himself would be able to decipher the endless cross-linguistic word play, in-jokes, untranslated Arabic vocabulary, and literal translations of Arabic phrases that are sometimes accompanied by their idiomatic equivalents but mostly stand alone, and to follow the large number of meandering allusions across fourteen centuries of Arabic literature and four hundred years of European texts (after all, it is only modern Europe that interested *Nahda* intellectuals). As Geoffrey Nash observes, Rihani's language in many of his English language works

> is framed in a discourse clearly borrowed from the western Romantics, and at others in an idiom that reads like a literal translation from Arabic. What can be said of most of these writings is that in foregrounding the Arab and oriental constituency, they make little accommodation for a western readership in the sense of diluting or acculturating oriental idioms to suit occidental pre-dispositions and expectations. (1998, 18)

This has the effect of estranging or deterritorializing the English language by confronting its native speakers with linguistic difference within a deliberately hybridized discourse, challenging their assumptions and expectations. Readers are called upon to engage in a difficult task, the end result of which is a new cultural awareness—which is the effect of translational literature.

Nevertheless, the novel is formally, and quite explicitly, patterned after European models, principally Cervantes's *Don Quixote*, Voltaire's *Candide*, and Carlyle's *Sartor Resartus*. The central characters in those works, like Rihani's titular character, are idealistic, naïve, and/or out of synch with their times, and are treated with a great measure of irony by their respective narrators. All three texts involve travel, cross-cultural exchange, or translation: the fictional "real author" of *Don Quixote* is a North African who wrote the story in Arabic; after wandering throughout Europe and South America, Candide and his companions settle near Constantinople and are taught what in the discourse of the novel is the ultimate wisdom by a Muslim Turk; and Carlyle's narrator edits a German manuscript that has the potential to infuse British pragmatism with German idealism. Cervantes's and Voltaire's texts depict a cultural exchange between Arab or Muslim ("Eastern") sources and European ones; Carlyle fits in this company because of his highly appreciative assessment of the prophet Muhammad in *Heroes, Hero Worship and the Heroic in History*, which made a great impression on Rihani, and because *Sartor Resartus* constructs the kind of cross-cultural discourse that Rihani himself sought to achieve.[11] In all three texts, satire of social conditions is clothed (in Carlyle's metaphor) in the caricature of an idealistic protagonist who pursues an elusive utopia. In two of those novels, that pursuit leads to a series of travel adventures of the episodic, picaresque kind. The picaresque closely resembles the Arabic *maqama* genre; indeed, some critics speculate that the picaresque originated in the *maqama* by way of Muslim Spain (Allen 1998, 270). In those formal and thematic ways, Cervantes, Voltaire, and Carlyle serve as antecedent examples that authorize Rihani's cross-cultural discourse.

The protagonist is young, naïve, idealistic, and something of a Romantic rebel against social conventions and institutions in Lebanon. "Just as Candide, caught kissing the baron's daughter (rumored to be his cousin), is set upon by the baron and literally kicked out of the 'terrestrial paradise' of Westphalia, so—in a cock-eyed echo of that scene—Khalid, in love with *his* cousin, is beaten from the door by *her* father, whereupon he sets out on a journey not away from, but in search of, 'the Paradise of the World,'" America (Shakir 1996, 6). He leaves with a close friend called Shakib, the counterpart to Carlyle's Hofrath Heuschrecke in *Sartor Resartus* or Cervantes's Sancho Panza. However, Shakib is the educated one among the two, and the inverse relationship between formal education and intuitive wisdom in the characterization of Khalid and Shakib indexes Rihani's indebtedness to Rousseau and the Romantics. Khalid's education is like that of many prophets mentioned in the Bible and Qur'an: shepherding animals, wandering in the open, and meditating, or as Shakib puts it, "he loafs . . . after the manner of the great thinkers and mystics: like Al-Fared and Jelal'ud-Din Rumy, like Socrates and St. Francis of Assisi" (Rihani 1911, 11). By contrast, Shakib, whose biography of Khalid is full of "ecstasies about his master's genius," (19) recounts:

> When we left our native land . . . my literary bent was not shared in the least by Khalid. I had gone through the higher studies which, in our hedge-schools and clerical institutions, do not reach a very remarkable height. Enough of French to understand the authors tabooed by our Jesuit professors,—the Voltaires, the Rousseaus, the Diderots; enough of Arabic to enable one to parse and analyse the verse of Al-Mutanabbi; enough of Church History to show us, not how the Church wielded the sword of persecution, but how she was persecuted herself by the pagans and barbarians of the earth. . . . Now, of this high phase of education, Khalid was thoroughly immune. But his intuitive sagacity was often remarkable, and his humour, sweet and pathetic. Once when I was reading aloud some of the Homeric effusions of Al-Mutanabbi, he said to me, as he was playing his lute, "and in the heart of this," pointing to the lute, "and in the heart of me, there be more poetry than in that book with which you would kill me." (27)

This is only one instance of what Evelyn Shakir describes as "name-dropping" on the part of Rihani—"Dickens, Tennyson, Balzac, Shakespeare, Dante, Paine, Arnold, Montaigne, Epictetus, Swinburne, Diderot, Pascal, Ibsen, Homer, Marx, Spencer, and Rousseau," among others—apparently intended to establish Rihani's credentials: "here is an 'Oriental' who can run with Western writers, who can match their erudition, their tone, their wordplay, the particular flavor of their philosophical flights" (Shakir 1996, 6). Yet equally implicit in this kind of mimicry is the claim that Western writers are not enough, for Rihani also references a host of

Arab writers, poets, and scholars who would be known only to cultured Arab readers and to Arabists: al-Zamakhshari, al-Mutanabbi, Rabi'a al-'Adawiyyah, Ibn al-Farid, al-Makrizi, al-Auza'i, and others, so that even highly educated American readers who may be familiar with European writers would still feel inadequate vis-à-vis the author's bicultural frame of reference.

The passage also registers Rihani's attitude toward the Jesuits, who persecute Khalid in the novel (among other things, on the charge that he translated Carlyle's essay "On Jesuitism" into Arabic), and toward classical Arabic poetry, of which Abu al-Tayyib al-Mutanabbi (d. 965) is a chief representative. A decade earlier Rihani pioneered prose poetry in Arabic and introduced Romantic themes and language, so al-Mutanabbi here represents what he believes ought to be jettisoned in the Arabic tradition. Significantly in this context, "al-Mutanabbi" is not a real name, but a nickname by which the poet became known and which means "one who [falsely] claims to be a prophet" (he boasted that he could imitate the style of the Qur'an, which is believed to be the literal words of God and, therefore, inimitable as a matter of doctrine). Rihani's attack on al-Mutanabbi is an attack on the established canon of classical Arabic poetry, in which the wisdom of al-Ma'arri is marginalized and a "false prophet" is lionized. Instead, the novel offers the latter-day Romantic, visionary, and iconoclastic leadership of Khalid, which holds the potential for cultural, religious, and political reform—and here we can see the influence on Rihani not only of Romanticism, but also of Carlyle's ideas on heroism, particularly "the hero as prophet," exemplified by Muhammad. *The Book of Khalid* thus begins with an introduction titled "Al-Fatihah" (the opening), which is the title of the first chapter of the Qur'an, clearly drawing a parallel between Khalid and Muhammad as prophets and nation builders. But Khalid is also a Christ figure whose "voyage to America is a Via Dolorosa of the emigrant; and the Port of Beirut, the verminous hostelries of Marseilles, the island of Ellis in New York are the three stations thereof. And if your hopes are not crucified at the third and last station, you pass into the Paradise of your dreams" (Rihani 1911, 29). As the structure of the plot suggests, however, his experience in America proves to be harrowing and Khalid returns home to retreat to the forest, like the Buddha, or like Thoreau at Walden, for a period of meditation and introspection, before he emerges to preach social, political, and religious reform. The novel is divided into three parts, each corresponding to a stage of Khalid's life: "In the Exchange" depicts his early life and journey to the U.S., "In the Temple" his involvement in the U.S. political machine and subsequent retreat into nature back in Lebanon, and "In Kulmakan" (Everywhere) his emergence to spread his message, his escape from his persecutors to Egypt (a haven for Syrian intellectuals fleeing Ottoman persecution in the nineteenth century), and his disappearance there. The ending evokes the idea of the Messiah, the Mahdi, or the twelfth imam in Shiite doctrine, who returns after a period of absence to save the world.

But the novel's hagiographic structure and all the explicit and implicit attributions of prophecy to the protagonist are parodied in the text. The intoxicated customers of a Cairo hashish den sarcastically describe Khalid as a "prophet" and a "Muhdi" [*sic*] between loud peals of laughter (8), and his most devoted (and only) disciple is the ludicrous Shakib. Kahlid's naïve idealism and outlandish behavior do not escape the narrator's satire, either. In a perceptive reading of Carlyle's use of irony and satire in *Sartor Resartus* that applies to Rihani's novel, Wolfgang Iser argues that "as far as the [fictional] Editor [in *Sartor*] is concerned, poking fun at German transcendentalism implicitly asserts a British attitude which allows transcendentalism to be channeled into empiricism" (Iser 252). That attitude privileges experiential knowledge over transcendental abstraction, but asserting the value of experience through humor allows the Editor to temper empiricism with transcendentalism, and vice versa, in the act of editing the chaotic manuscript of the German philosopher (253). The philosophy that emerges from the Editor's labors, therefore, represents a higher synthesis reached through cultural cross-fertilization, and the novel thus becomes "a paradigm of translatability rather than an actual translation" (254).

A similar strategy is at work in *The Book of Khalid*. The narrator presents himself as an editor who discovers an Arabic manuscript written by Khalid in the Egypt's Khedival Library. Intrigued by the manuscript, he searches for the author and is led to Shakib, who has written in French a gargantuan biography of Khalid. The narrator-editor presents the novel as an historical account and not a work of fiction, based on two original manuscripts: the Arabic *Kitab Khalid*, Khalid's spiritual autobiography, short on facts and rich in abstractions and meditations, and the French *Histoire intime*, Khalid's biography written by Shakib, a chronological account of Khalid's life abounding in exaggeration, rhetorical flourishes, and tedious, pointless digressions. The English text, then, is presumably a soberly edited account that draws upon, or synthesizes, the best qualities of its Arabic and French sources. If Khalid's Arabic account is too mystical and abstract, true to the prophetic character of its author, and Shakib's French manuscript is too mired in romance and poetic excess characteristic of both medieval Arabic historiography and the European chivalric romance, *The Book of Khalid* is a narrative that embodies an evolved and discerning consciousness that is able to discriminate, select, and synthesize. Both original manuscripts, which are the counterpart to Cide Hamete Benengeli's Arabic manuscript in *Don Quixote* and Diogenes Teufelsdröckh's *Die Kleider ihr Werden und Wirken* in *Sartor Resartus*, represent Oriental and Occidental excess, supposedly displaying the quintessential characteristics of the mystical East and the decadent West—or at least as mimicked by Shakib, a French-educated Oriental.

The first paragraph of the novel expresses this vision of synthesis somewhat differently:

> In the Khedival Library of Cairo, among the Papyri of the Scribe of Amen-Ra and the beautifully illuminated copies of the Korân, the modern Arabic Manuscript which forms the subject of this Book, was found. The present Editor was attracted to it by the dedication and the rough drawings on the cover; which, indeed, are as curious, if not as mystical, as ancient Egyptian symbols. One of these is supposed to represent a New York Skyscraper in the shape of a Pyramid, and the other is a dancing

> group under which is written: "The Stockbrokers and the Dervishes." And around these symbols, in Arabic circlewise, these words:— "*And this is my Book, the Book of Khalid, which I dedicate to my Brother Man, my Mother Nature, and my Maker God.*" (v, original emphasis)

The location of the manuscript is highly significant, for it evokes the entire cultural history of Egypt: from Pharonic times, represented by the papyri of the supreme god Amen-Ra, to the illuminated Qur'ans of medieval Islamic Egypt, all housed in a library built in modern Egypt. If those markers designate the narrative past and present, the "modern Arabic Manuscript" in question looks to the future in which the civilization of Egypt, captured in the iconic image of the pyramid, fuses with modern American civilization, epitomized by a New York skyscraper. Those two symbolically charged structures are synthesized into the image of a skyscraper in the shape of a pyramid. The other image on the cover of the manuscript drives the idea home. The materialism of the West and the spirituality of the East combine in a dancing circle of stockbrokers and dervishes that evokes Sufi gatherings for *dhikr*, or trance-inducing rituals intended to bring mystics closer to God. The dedication fuses all distinctions between East and West, materialism and spirituality, past, present and future, into transcendental, universal, masculinist values that would presumably sustain an evolved form of civilization.

In New York, Shakib and Khalid live in a damp cellar and practice peddling, selling trinkets that they claim to be relics from the Holy Land, a common occupation for impoverished Lebanese immigrants at that time. Although he abhors formal education, Khalid voraciously reads second-hand books (representing second-hand knowledge not based on personal experience, introspection, or meditation), each of which he burns immediately after reading. This burning of books recalls the burning of Don Quixote's library, which was blamed for causing his insane delusions; in Rihani's case, burned books stand for the weight of tradition that threatens to ossify the mind. Khalid writes, "does not a systematic education mean . . . that a young man must go through life dragging behind him his heavy chains of set ideas and stock systems, political, social, or religious?" (70). Therefore, his search for the Truth involves internalizing—or consuming—the content of books while discarding their dogma, the inverse of the iconic scene of medieval censorship, the burning of subversive books to suppress their content. In a gesture of ambivalence toward the past, Khalid here burns the books after absorbing their content, as though to assert the primacy of his own experience and to preempt the hegemonic potential of tradition that turns into the dogma of "social and political guides, moral and religious dragomans," as he puts it (vii)—false knowledge like the contents of his peddling box. "We are pestered and plagued with guides and dragomans of every rank and shade . . . a Tolstoy here, an Ibsen there, a Spencer above, a Nietzsche below. And there thou art left in perpetual confusion and despair" (vii), but "the time will come, I tell thee, when every one will be his own guide and dragoman. The time will come when it will not be necessary to write books for others, or to legislate for others, or to make religions for others" (viii). In the meantime, apparently, he himself must write a book: "And so, the Book of Khalid was written. It is the only one I wrote in this world, having made . . . a brief sojourn in its civilised parts, and I hope to write other books in other worlds" (vii).

Rihani's satirical framing of his themes—a principal strategy in Carlyle's *Sartor Resartus*—is once again evident here in the simultaneous evocation and dismissal of European writers who influenced his craft, and equally in Khalid's contradictory stance of condemning and burning books, yet writing one of his own, and discrediting translators while posing as one himself. Rihani's depiction of Khalid as both a prophet and a laughably Quixotic madman is of the same order, as is the treatment of the central trope of translation, which Khalid brings up in equating writers with "dragomans." According to Iser, Carlyle's novel is more of a paradigm of translation than the actual translation it claims to be. Likewise, Rihani's novel claims to be a double translation from original sources in two languages, yet translation is dismissed as inherently deceptive. Such paradoxes make sense only in light of mystical thought, which sees truth as an inner quality (*batin*), hidden by outward forms (*dhahir*)—garments, in Carlyle's sartorial metaphor, a metaphor used repeatedly by Rihani in this novel and in his other writings. It is only by intuition that a seeker can reach the hidden truth, which cannot be expressed in formulas and dogmas, taught, or translated. Hence the burning of books and discrediting of translators apply also to Khalid and his autobiography; indeed, the fictional *Kitab Khalid* lay abandoned in the Egyptian Library until discovered by the editor, and even then it saw the light of day only as a *pre*-text for the editor's own book, *The Book of Khalid*—an outer garment on top of another outer garment, a veil upon a veil. In that sense, for Rihani, cultural translation is a chimera because it is a worldly transaction, a trafficking in forms not essences—especially when "genius everywhere is one" and "poets are cousins" (Rihani 1927, 10). Poets, prophets, and gurus can only ultimately try to give their disciples an intuition of "Truth," but they cannot communicate it because it is inexpressible; those who come after them turn it into dogmas and books fit for the furnace. Rihani's entire philosophy swings on this dialectic of the mystical and the political, the worldly and the otherworldly.

Eventually, Khalid burns his peddling box and abandons his trade based on deception. Living on Shakib's income, Khalid is drawn to the lecture circuits of atheists, with whom he becomes disillusioned. He works in a lawyer's office (in the service of Morality, as he tells himself), but is "fired" (in the narrator's ironic pun [1911, 82]) for dilly-dallying, absenteeism, and suggesting to his employer that he burn the Register's Office. Khalid then frequents the cultic milieu of New York and enters into liaisons with bohemian women ("huris," as he calls them [83]) who are drawn to his exotic background.[12] Disenchanted with that brand of spirituality, he is then introduced to the corrupt world of Tammany Hall (this time in the service of Democracy), only to be literally kicked out and then imprisoned on trumped up charges when he accuses a powerful politician of hypocrisy and deception. Shakib contrives to free Khalid and together they return to Lebanon. Khalid's rude introduction to the workings of American politics is recounted in the first chapter of the second part of the novel, "In the Temple"—the temple of Mammon, and then after his release from prison (in which he rereads Rousseau's *Emile* and Carlyle's *Hero-Worship*), the temple of nature. His experience with American politics convinces him that "Americans are . . . true and honest votaries of Mammon, their great God, their one and only God" (112). Nevertheless, he declares that

> my faith in man . . . is as strong as my faith in God. And strong, too, perhaps, is my faith in the future world-ruling destiny of America. . . . In this New World, the higher Superman shall rise . . . but he shall not be an American in the Democratic sense. He shall be nor of the Old World nor of the New; he shall be, my Brothers, of both. In him shall be incarnated the Asiatic spirit of Poesy and Prophecy, and the European spirit of Art, and the American spirit of Invention. Ay, the nation that leads the world to-day in material progress shall lead it, too, in the future, in the higher things of the mind and soul. And when you reach that height, O beloved America, you will be far from the majority-rule, and Iblis [Satan], and Juhannam [Hell]. And you will then conquer those "enormous mud Megatheriums" of which Carlyle makes loud mention. (113–14)

How such Hegelian-Nietzschean evolution may come about, Khalid does not explain, nor does the editor, who actually satirizes this prophecy in the chapter that immediately follows, entitled "Subtranscendental," in which he compares Khalid's jail-time pontification to "Hamlet's player, or even like Hamlet himself—always soliloquising, tearing a passion to rags" (115).

Back in Lebanon, Khalid retreats to the woods after more skirmishes with the Jesuits that lead to his excommunication and imprisonment, and now he takes on the Muslim establishment. In "the Kaaba of solitude," a chapter in which nature is described as a "glorious Mosque" (190) and which evokes Emerson, Baudelaire ("*La nature est un temple . . .*"), Wordsworth, and Thoreau, Khalid conceives of himself as a prophet and refers to "MY Holy Book" (191). The message he preaches when he emerges from the woods is the core of Rihani's philosophy: "I am equally devoted both to the material and the spiritual. . . . For the dervish who whirls himself into a foaming ecstasy of devotion and the strenuous American who works himself up to a sweating ecstasy of gain, are the two poles of the same absurdity, the two ends of one evil" (237–38). The editor further explains "the gist of Khalid's gospel" (240) this way, "To graft the strenuosity of Europe and America upon the ease of the Orient, the materialism of the West upon the spirituality of the East,—this to us seems to be the principal aim of Khalid. But often in his wanderings and divigations of thought does he give us fresh proof of the truism that no two opposing elements meet and fuse without both losing their original identity" (239). This truism clashes with the principle of absolute opposition that structures Orientalist discourse, which posits both the undesirability and the impossibility of precisely such fusion. This is where Rihani's project falters in its attempt to graft the Hegelian dialectic onto Daoist complementarity, and then to superimpose both onto Orientalist Manicheism:

> The Orient and the Occident, the male and female of the spirit, the two great streams in which the body and soul of man are refreshed,

> invigorated, purified—of both I sing, in both I glory, to both I consecrate my life, for both I shall work and suffer and die. My Brothers, the most highly developed being is neither European nor Oriental; but rather he who partakes of the finer qualities of both the European genius and the Asiatic prophet. (245–46)

In a classic Orientalist gesture, the Orient is reduced to mysticism (feminine) and the Occident to science (masculine); despite this culturalist and masculinist hierarchization, both also represent the harmonious yin-yang of humanity; and yet again, despite the eternal nature of those principles, they are somehow capable of evolving into a higher synthesis. The tension noted above between Rihani's resistance to and investment in Orientalism is hidden within that formulation.

This dubious philosophy yields the political vision of an Arab empire, to be built by "a Saladin of the Idea, who will wage a crusade not against Christianity or Mohammedanism, but against those Tartaric usurpers who are now toadying to both . . . the Turks" (302–3), an empire built on "American arms and an up-to-date Korân [*sic*]." The reformed Islam he champions is that of Muhammad ibn 'Abd al-Wahab, "the Luther of Arabia" (303) and founder of Wahabism, the puritanical movement whose leaders eventually collaborated with 'Abd al-Aziz Al-Saud in founding the Kingdom of Saudi Arabia. Historical hindsight permits us now to appreciate the ironies that allowed a cosmopolitan and progressive thinker like Rihani to set such high hopes on, and to lobby on behalf of, a conservative regime that forged an alliance of convenience with a fundamentalist movement, not to mention his having totally miscalculated the role the United States would play in the region.

When Khalid airs his views in the grand mosque of Damascus, he predictably incurs the wrath of the Ottoman authorities and the conservative Muslims, who attack and nearly kill him. He emerges from that mêlée "like Don Quixote after the Battle of the Mill" (327) and escapes to Egypt, where he eventually disappears after creating quite a legend for himself. The comparison to Don Quixote's hilarious adventure rescues the utopian vision that Rihani puts into the mouth of his character from ridicule; as with Carlyle's satirical treatment of Teufelsdröch that, in Iser's reading, preempts the reader's ridicule of German Transcendentalism, allowing it to infuse British empiricism, Rihani's framing of his protagonist makes the message palatable to American readers: here is an Oriental madman or prophet with fantastic dreams, but those dreams are indelibly marked by his American voyage, and they do, in a way, hold a mirror up to America. The image reflected in that mirror is not always a flattering one, not an immigrant's success story confirming the American Dream. Nonetheless, it is an image contoured by American ideals and gravid with America's potential as a world leader, even as America's faults and shortcomings are diagnosed, and the remedy to them is prescribed.

Because of these discursive deviations from the norms of immigrant narratives, Geoffrey Nash contends that "Rihani's biculturality is not of the kind that can be considered ethnic American . . . Rihani's writings do not fully register the 'cultural doubleness'" or the "'divided allegiance'" found in "those writers who chose to address themselves to the ethnic situation in America" (1998, 24). This judgment is unconvincing because it posits divided allegiance and identity crisis as a condition for authentic ethnic American writing, making no allowance for Rihani's more self-confident stance, which provides an alternative paradigm that is often overlooked in ethnic studies. Rihani accentuates or exaggerates the "Orientalness" of Khalid to the point of caricature, but it is a caricature that informs the consciousness of Americans and, consequently, that of Arab Americans. This is more than a discursive performance, for even as he wrestled with Orientalism, Rihani accepted its basic premises, including the essentialist concepts of "Orient" and "Occident," which continue to frame the discussions of Rihani's interpreters even today.[13] The novel raises some interesting questions: How does a writer like Rihani, who is self-consciously Oriental because he is so defined in the dominant discourse of his time, imagine an Oriental character in an American setting? How does *he* (for this is, after all, a deeply and unself-consciously masculinist stance, totally in line with the gendered assumptions of Orientalism) conceive of cultural translation and of the possibility of a cross-cultural discourse? How does he assess his native tradition and its relationship to the traditions of Europe and the United States?

However flawed, Rihani's project was a valiant effort that indexes the historical, ideological, and discursive conditions of the Arab world, Europe, and the United States during that period. His questioning of Orientalism and his efforts at cultural translation that aimed at two-way reform did not resonate in a culture that did not sense itself to be in crisis, at least not the kind of crisis Rihani diagnosed. As Iser points out, "as long as there is an overriding conviction that a culture rests on a firm foundation, the necessity for a cross-cultural discourse does not arise. For such a self-understanding of culture, a cross-cultural discourse can only mean a foreign intrusion" (Iser 261–62). A cross-cultural discourse was an urgent necessity for nineteenth-century Arab leaders and intellectuals who looked to Europe, and to their early twentieth-century counterparts who turned to the U.S., in search of models for cultural and political survival. That sense was not reciprocated, since neither Europe nor the U.S. felt the need to learn anything from the Arabs or any "non-Western" peoples; indeed, Orientalism was, as Said argued, an expression of mastery over weaker peoples, and not a manifestation of cultural sympathy or desire for dialogue. Orientals who wrote against the grain of Orientalism, as Rihani did when he challenged its modes of representation, were bound to be ignored, their works regarded as "cultural oddit[ies]" (Nash 1998, 25), while those who conformed to those modes, as Gibran did, could become immensely successful.

2

The Gibran Phenomenon

. . . a chameleon-like ease of adaptiveness

—JOSEPH GOLLOMB

Marketing Orientalism

Like Rihani, Kahlil Gibran (1883–1931) wrote in Arabic first, then turned to English. Both were part of a literary group known as the *Mahjar* (or immigrant) poets who achieved fame on the Arabic literary scene from their location in New York. Their Arabic poetry and prose engaged directly with the social and political conditions back home, without any reference to their immigrant status in the U.S. The other members of the *Mahjar* group wrote only or mainly in Arabic; they include Mikhail Nu'aimah (Naimy), Ilya Abu Madi, Nassib 'Aridah, Nudra Haddad, and Rashid Ayyub. The Arabic poetry of that group represents, in its own way, a minor literature that revolutionized modern Arabic poetry. They pioneered a movement that rebelled against the time-honored conventions of Arabic poetry, conventions which had recently been infused with new vigor by Mahmud Sami al-Barudi, Ahmad Shawqi, Hafiz Ibrahim, and others who, in the late nineteenth and early twentieth century, found inspiration in classical Arabic poetry. By contrast, the *Mahjar* poets were captivated by the poetic and political ideals of the European Romantics and American Transcendentalists and wanted a freer and more flexible poetic medium to express their rebellion against existing social and political norms. The immigrants also tended to lack formal education, the rigorous training in the classical Arabic language, literature, and prosody required of Arab poets, and systematic knowledge of the European literary tradition. They were also influenced by Orientalism, especially insofar as they accepted the East/West dichotomy. Their rejection of the classical Arabic heritage was, therefore, due not only to their lack of formal Arabic education, but also to the Orientalist denigration of Arabic language and literature in general.[1] It was not surprising, therefore, that in Arabic they introduced prose poetry, in addition to simpler form and diction, and that the influence of Rousseau, Blake, Wordsworth, Keats, Shelley, Emerson, Whitman, and Nietzsche (the writers to whom they were most drawn) on their work tended to be disproportionate, not to mention anachronistic in view of Euro-American literary history. Nonetheless, the *Mahjar* group's revolutionary role in the history of modern Arabic poetry fits with Deleuze and Guattari's description of the effect of minor literature on a major language. M.M. Badawi summarizes their achievement in this way:

> By introducing a new conception of poetry, by adding a spiritual dimension to it, so to speak, by turning away from rhetoric and declamation, by concentrating on the more subjective experience of man in relation to nature and ultimate questions, by introducing biblical themes and images into their poetry, by their preference for short meters and stanzaic forms, the *Mahjar* poets, especially of the United States, exercised a liberating influence upon modern Arabic poetry. Indeed their extremist views were often rejected, the revolt of some of them against Arabic versification which resulted in the once fashionable prose poetry of Rihani and Jibran [or Gibran], proved to all intents and purposes to be a dead end, at least until recently; their language was sometimes severely criticized for not being sufficiently correct or even grammatical, and the tendency of many of them to turn their back on the Arab cultural past was often violently attacked. Nonetheless, it would be difficult to exaggerate the significance of the role they played in the development of modern Arabic poetry, and of the subtle influence they exercised in shaping modern Arab sensibility. Without their seminal minds the course of modern Arabic poetry would in many ways have been different.[2] (203)

It is likely that Badawi wrote this with Gibran in mind, for after a falling out of sorts with Rihani after 1910, Gibran emerged as the leader of that group and president of *Al-Rabitah al-qalamiyyah* (the Pen League), founded in 1920. His writings also drew much of the criticism to which Badawi refers.

In the U.S. today, Gibran is the best-known Arab American writer. National monuments are dedicated to him in Boston and Washington, D.C. His best-known work, *The Prophet* (1923), remains Alfred Knopf's best-selling title ever, having sold over eight million copies and been translated into more than fifty languages. *The Prophet* was adapted as a religious drama and repeatedly performed at New York's church of St. Mark's-in-the-Bouwerie, where services entirely drawn from Gibran's poetry were also held. The pastor of that church described another of Gibran's books, *Jesus the Son of Man*, as "The Gospel according to Gibran" (Young 33), "thus making of Gibran the fifth Evangelist" (Shahid 2000, 324). Gibran's other English-language books, and translations of his Arabic ones, remain in print today, unlike the English-language works of his immigrant Lebanese contemporaries, which have long been forgotten. Gibran's phenomenal popularity is in large part based on his aura as spiritual guru or Oriental wise man, bolstered by his self-styled prophetic posture, his use of biblical idiom, his universalist, didactic, and often aphoristic writings, and his intriguing blend of the Romantic visionary, Nietzschean idealist, Eastern mystic, and Christian evangelist.

Gibran was not the first Arab American to publish in either Arabic or English. As we have seen in the preceding chapter, Rihani was already a celebrated author in Arabic before Gibran's first literary work, *Dam'a wa ibtisamah*, appeared in 1914, and by the time Gibran published his first English-language book, *The Madman* (1918), Rihani had already published a poetry collection, a novel, and two translations of classical Arabic poetry. Likewise, Abraham Rihbany had published the first Arab American autobiography, *A Far Journey* (1914), which was followed by other well-received books on Christianity, Syrian history, politics, and U.S.–Syrian relations. Yet Rihani and Rihbany are today known only to academic specialists, while Gibran's tremendous success and lasting fame have led many Arab American writers to find in him an exemplary and inspirational predecessor, and some even to regard him as the progenitor of Arab American literature. This lionization of Gibran is perhaps understandable for members of a U.S. minority that suffers from entrenched anti-Arab racism, and whose literary tradition struggles for recognition in the face of a market-driven culture industry. Reclaiming one of America's most beloved and commercially successful writers as the founding father of Arab American literature is one way of gaining favor with the mainstream. As Khalil Hawi writes, "the Lebanese immigrants . . . further[ed] the fame and the greatness of their prophet in the eyes of the Americans who looked down on them, considering them as members of the yellow race whose sole purpose in life was the accumulation of money. Gibran's spiritual writings in English furnished them with proof that they came from a better race and had higher aims in life" (Hawi 73).

Yet Gibran has never been taken seriously by scholars and critics, some of whom regard him as a "charlatan" (Shakir 1996, 4), or as a writer whose work is no more than "fast food" poetry (Orfalea and Elmusa xvi), a "welcome escape route" (Hawi 281) for those "ill adjusted to life" (280), or for "late romantics and seekers after the exotic" (283). Shakir's assessment is even more damning:

> Gibran . . . actually embrac[ed] and exploit[ed] his status as an Oriental. A native of the Lebanese hills who once claimed to have been born in Bombay, Gibran played to the hilt a role made up in equal parts of Far-Eastern swami and latter-day prophet from the Holy Land. In a sense, he plied the same trade—only at a more sophisticated level—as Syrian peddlers whose stock in trade was holy trinkets from Jerusalem. (Shakir 1988, 43)

Even in the Arabic literary field, in which Gibran made an impact on poetic form and style in the early twentieth century, his works are generally dismissed as juvenile literature that stirs up the enthusiasm of adolescents and the "annoyance" of adults (Kilito 3). There is a great deal of truth to these assessments, which do not chime with Gibran's astonishing popular success in the U.S. and internationally. Irfan Shahid has argued that such success is reason enough for Gibran's works to become part of the literary canon (2000, 322–23). While commercial success is no indication of intellectual or aesthetic value, the Gibran phenomenon is significant insofar as it reveals the conditions of possibility of Arab American literature, especially in view of the absence of that literature as a whole from even the multicultural canon of American literature. The real interest of Gibran for the study of Arab American literature does not so much lie in his works themselves, which do not reward rigorous analysis, but in the phenomenon—its rise, continuing success, and enduring significance for Arab American literature. That phenomenon is rooted in the contradictions of the Arab presence in a country where the popular imagination, at the turn of the twentieth century and now, remains steeped in Orientalism. Arab American writing must at once negotiate, utilize, and contest that discourse to carve a space for itself on the U.S. cultural landscape.

The compelling question, therefore, is not why Gibran has been left out of the canon of American literature, but what made him so popular in a country where his culture is denigrated and the books of those who share his background are neglected. To answer that question, we would need to consider the options available to a minority writer. Deleuze and Guattari's theory of minor literature sheds light on Gibran's work, which, in turn, helps us discern the theory's limitation. Of the three characteristics of minor literature identified by Deleuze and Guattari, "the deterritorialization of language" is clearly evident in Gibran's works in Arabic (as described by Badawi above) and English (aphoristic style, biblical diction, prophetic tone, and so on). However, while abundantly clear in his Arabic works, the second and third characteristics, "the connection of the individual to a political immediacy, and the collective assemblage of enunciation" (Deleuze and Guattari 18), are not apparent in his English works. Those works seem to be totally apolitical, at least when compared to his Arabic works, which earned him the reputation of a social rebel and revolutionary. By contrast, his English works stress—in fact, preach—the freedom of the individual from all familial and social constraints. As we shall see, some Arab American writers criticized this aspect of his work because it threatens to weaken a community in dire need of solidarity. I will argue here that the suppression of politics and the disavowal of collectivity in Gibran's Anglophone works were, paradoxically, part of a failed attempt to articulate a new humanism that would transcend the social and political pressures on Arab Americans in the early decades of the twentieth century.

If Gibran's case seems to complicate Deleuze and Guattari's theory of minor literature, it is because they do not account for other options available to a minority writer that were not available to Kafka. Gibran's relationship to Arabic and English was different from Kafka's relationship to German. Kafka wrote in German while living in Prague, whereas Gibran wrote in Arabic and English while living in New York. As Deleuze and Guattari put it, "the impossibility of writing other than in German is for the Prague Jews the feeling of an irreducible distance from their primitive Czech territoriality" (16). Gibran, by contrast, wrote first in Arabic, and even though he wrote outside of its conventional genres and styles, he helped revolutionize them, thereby occupying an important place within that tradition. He wrote in Arabic as a minor writer: a Christian with little formal education who lived in New York. He was able to deterritorialize literary Arabic in the way Deleuze and Guattari describe when they emphasize that "minor" includes "the revolutionary conditions for every literature within the heart of what is called great (or established) literature" (18). (This, incidentally, applies not only to Gibran, but also to the other *Mahjar* poets who contributed to Arabic poetry while living in the U.S. and South America during the first two decades of the twentieth century.)

He was also a minor writer in English. Like Rihani, Gibran's turn to English placed him outside of any tradition. In fact, since he and a handful of others were the first Arabs to write in English, they were quite consciously initiating a properly minor tradition of their own. The fact that Gibran and Rihani first established their fame as Arabic writers makes their turn to English a deliberate act and begs the question of the strategic choice of language and the discursive shift it entailed. In that respect, therefore, Gibran's choices were somewhat more radical than Kafka's, the model for Deleuze and Guattari's theory of minor literature. Gibran's bilingualism complicates Deleuze and Guattari's theory in what are, from their vantage point, some unexpected ways—unexpected because while they call attention to bilingualism and multilingualism (23), they do not examine the case of bilingual writers—and by that I mean writers who *wrote* in two languages.

What, then, is the significance of Gibran's turn to English? The answer is twofold. First, to write in English at all means confronting the discourse of Orientalism in the trenches. No writer of Arab heritage, whether immigrant or U.S.-born, could write in blissful obliviousness of that discourse; even denying one's ancestry and trying to pass involves a decision about how to deal with Orientalism. There is no escaping the legacy of Orientalism for an Anglophone Arab immigrant writer: the personal is the political and the individual meshes with the collective. Since the minority's status is ever determined with reference to the identitarian discourse of the majority, the minority writer may accept the premises of the reigning discourse and mobilize its representations, thereby reinforcing them, or s/he may question some or all of those premises and write against the grain. Accepting the discourse may lead to self-Orientalizing, self-hate, denying one's roots and trying to pass, silence, or any combination thereof. As for the critical stance, even though it crystallized only with the publication of Edward Said's *Orientalism* (1978), it is discernible in the work of earlier Arab American writers like Rihani, and to a lesser extent Rihbany, neither of whom could entirely liberate himself from Orientalist presuppositions. Between the two endpoints of acquiescence to and rejection of the discourse, most cases involve various types of negotiation. In the case of Gibran, such negotiation was closer to acquiescence than to critical disputation.

Second, the bilingual writer who explains one culture to another is necessarily a cultural translator. In the case of a writer of two languages, cultural translation is a two-way activity, since s/he explains each culture to the other. Moreover, since one does not write the same way in two languages, a two-way cultural translator draws upon a different discourse whenever s/he turns from one language to the other. This was precisely Gibran's claim, that he could be a critic of "East" and "West." Hawi reports that "the prevalent belief among his [Gibran's] Arab friends is that: 'He declared his revolt against the West by means of the spirit of the East, just as before he had declared his revolt against the backwardness of the East, drawing his inspiration from what is pure in the spirit of the Western renaissance'" (Hawi 111). That is, in Arabic he wrote as a Westerner (a Romantic, to be exact), and in English he wrote as an Easterner (a mystic, sage, prophet). His Arabic works are noted for their progressive (if at times naïve) social criticism, although he all but stopped contributing to Arabic literature in the 1920s. Meanwhile, in English, the vehicle of his creative work from 1918 until his death in 1931, his tone, themes, and stance evidence his disengagement from politics. His two-way cultural translation consisted of addressing the materialistic West on a spiritual level by means of parables and aphorisms that made a virtue of vagueness and abstraction, and the mystical East on a more material level that commented on social conventions, religious institutions, and politics. This reformist project had limitations that were all too clear and crippling, for this sort of translation is based on the Orientalist typology that posits a monolithic East characterized by mysticism, backwardness, and stagnation, against an equally monolithic West dialectically marked by materialism, modernity, and progressiveness. Orientalism, of course, assigns negative and positive values, respectively, to those constructs. Like Rihani and Rihbany, Gibran's contribution to the critique of Orientalism was not in questioning the validity of those constructs so much as challenging the assignment of values. Both "East" and "West," for him, are in need of reform, and such reform is possible by tempering the essential characteristics of each with the contrasting tendencies of the other. But whereas Rihani tried to unmoor and to historicize the characteristic traits of "East" and "West," Gibran left them intact and actually reinscribed them.

Gibran's approach to cultural translation is revealingly illustrated on the cover of his English-language books. The unmistakable Arabic ring of his name, both in its phonetic properties and in the use of the distinctively Arab pattern of three names, the first and third of which are identical (the grandson named after the grandfather, with the father's name in the middle), are erased when Gibran Khalil Gibran becomes Kahlil Gibran. The tertiary pattern is disrupted and the foreign sound of "Khalil," which reflects the correct Arabic pronunciation, is domesticated to Kahlil. According to his biographer-nephews, Jean and Kahlil Gibran, this alteration occurred when the twelve-year-old Gibran entered Quincy School in Boston two months after his arrival in the U.S.:

> Due either to the impersonal registration procedures or to clerical impatience with a too-foreign name, his name was misspelled and shortened to Kahlil Gibran. And so, except for a few attempts to continue calling himself Gibran Khalil Gibran, the Americanization of the little boy began with his ultimate acceptance of the abbreviated name which was obviously more compatible to the American bureaucratic ear and eye. (29)

This episode foreshadows the manner of Gibran's self-presentation to the American public later on: he embraces the persona projected onto him in the U.S., not only by accepting the Americanization of his name, but with it also American ideas about the Orient, particularly the role of Oriental sage or prophet that he came to impersonate. He conforms to it, whereby he also confirms it for his readers, and, in fact, he seems to have believed in it, or willed himself to believe it. Gibran was not a two-faced opportunist who manipulated stereotypes to his advantage, but he was not above self-exoticization in his attempts to win the heart of a woman (146–47), or lying about his family and class background in order to embellish his image to his readers (Gibran and Gibran 9–38; Hawi 67–70).

Gibran carefully constructed his own legend in light of the expectations and tastes of his mentors and benefactors at first, and later of his publishers, readers, and followers. The first of those patrons to recognize and nurture Gibran's talent as a fourteen-year-old boy was Fred Holland Day, Boston's leading publisher of avant-garde literature, a trendsetter, Keats enthusiast, photographer, and flamboyant dandy. As Jean and Kahlil Gibran point out, in the late nineteenth century, "like all the bright young men around him, Day was searching for relevant movements and causes at 'the sick little end of the century,'" as he used to call it, "something . . . that would lead them into the approaching century with a glimmer of hope. . . . After exploring Jacobism, spiritualism, and decadence, and after dressing young poets' words in fine new packages, he would explore one more art form—pictorial photography" (Gibran and Gibran 50). He would dress up young street urchins from the slums of South End in ethnic garments and photograph them. Day posed young Kahlil "in mysterious Arab burnooses, just as he dressed Armenians in turbans, blacks in Ethiopian regalia, Chinese with flutes, Japanese in kimonos. . . . [T]hrough Day's lens ghetto waifs became 'Armenian Princes,' 'Ethiopian Chiefs,' and 'Young Sheiks.'" Offensively exoticizing and stereotyping (albeit well-intentioned) as this may be, "Day's titles infused the children with an unexpected sense of privilege and dignity." After the first two miserable years that the sensitive boy experienced as a new immigrant living in appalling conditions in Boston's South End ghetto, "Kahlil . . . fortified his self-image and sought to overcome the reality of a poverty-stricken childhood with a vision of nobility and lineage. With Day's lofty labeling, he was no longer a slum child who lived in a dark alley; the silvery image of himself which he saw on Day's platinum-coated plates showed far more. Within a year, he was striving to live up to the grand illusions which Day had caught" (54–55).

Day was also Gibran's first publisher, using several of the promising boy's drawings to illustrate books published by Copeland and Day. His influence on Gibran must have been worrisome to his family, for they decided to send the fifteen-year-old back to Lebanon to finish his secondary education there and to learn Arabic, which at that time he could speak but neither read nor write. By the time Gibran sailed for Lebanon, he had managed to sell an entire portfolio of his drawings, "striking Oriental designs for book covers," to an editor at Scribner's. The writer who reported the incident in the April 2, 1898 issue of *The Critic* goes on to say that the drawings "remind one, not unnaturally, of the designs of oriental stuffs. Only one was Americanized, and that was the least successful. Now I wonder why more Syrians, Turks, and other Orientals with whom New York abounds have not tried their hands at this sort of work before" (quoted in Gibran and Gibran 65). Perhaps unwittingly, this writer pointed the way to success for "Oriental" writers and artists in the United States: they can thrive so long as they cater to the perceived public taste for the exotic, but not when they engage "Americanized" topics. As so many Arab American writers and artists have continued to discover in their experience with editors and publishers, self-Orientalizing is the key to success in the publishing industry. Immigrant and ethnic minority writers are limited in their choice of topics by the perceived demands of consumers, a reading public that is believed by the gatekeepers (accurately or not) to be uninterested in what minority and foreign writers have to say about American society—except within certain narrow parameters and narrative patterns. The maxim expressed by the reporter and grasped by Gibran was this: America will reward those writers and artists who confirm its image of itself and of their national, cultural, or racial background. Those who challenge those images are likely to experience various degrees of editorial censorship and/or benign neglect by reviewers.

With that in mind, and given that Gibran himself actively collaborated in exploiting his exotic potential, we can understand the way he was marketed in the U.S. The blurb on the dust jacket of *The Prophet* describes him as a "poet, philosopher, and artist [who] was born in Lebanon, a land that has produced many prophets," while the biographical note printed in the back of some of his other English-language books (*The Earth Gods* and *The Garden of the Prophet*), reads as follows:

> Kahlil Gibran, poet, philosopher, and artist, was born in 1883 into an affluent and musical Lebanese family. He was a college student in Syria at the age of fifteen, studied art in Paris at the Ecole des Beaux Arts, and had visited America twice before he came to New York to stay in 1912 and adopted English as his literary language.

The facts of his impoverished life and minimal formal education both in Lebanon and in Boston, where his destitute mother and her four children settled upon their arrival in the U.S. in 1895, contradict the account he gave of his background, not only to his publisher and readers, but also to his adoring disciple, Barbara Young, whose quasi-hagiographic book, *This Man from Lebanon*, amplified the legend. Other blurbs also cite a fabricated report of Auguste Rodin comparing Gibran's work to that of William Blake. All of this fits into a well-documented pattern of lies Gibran repeatedly told about his family background and education (Gibran and Gibran 325–6, Hawi 97–99).

The legend and the lies took their cue from the reception of Gibran's English-language works in the United States. As his namesake biographers point out, "by the time *The Madman* was reviewed, Gibran had been introduced to Americans as a mysterious hero and a ready-made genius—the Middle Eastern counterpart to Tagore" (326). The frequent comparisons to Rabindranath Tagore are not surprising, given the Orientalist construction of a monolithic mystical East; Tagore's reputation as a great mystical poet; the fashion for Tagore during the 1910s in Britain, where his *Gitanjali* was published with an introduction by William Butler Yeats, and in the United States, which Tagore toured after winning the Nobel Prize in literature in 1913; and more generally the influence of Hinduism on Emerson and other American Unitarians since the nineteenth century, all "created a favorable spiritual atmosphere for the reception of his [Gibran's] message" (Hawi 113).[3] As Mahasweta Sengupta demonstrates, Tagore was a great manipulator of his public image through his own English adaptations of his Bengali poetry, translations that were calculated "to conform to the 'image' of the East as it was known to the English-speaking world of the West" (Sengupta 160). Tagore's Orientalist translation of his poetry was responsible for his success in Europe and the U.S. and widely believed to have won him the first Nobel Prize awarded to a non-white writer. As such, to be compared to Tagore, even to be described, as a reviewer for *Call* put it, as "a far greater poet than Tagore" (quoted in Gibran and Gibran 326), was a tremendous boost for a writer who had just published his first English-language book, but also indicative of the dynamics of literary reception of "Oriental" writers at the time.[4]

There can be little doubt that such a reception played an important role in shaping the next phase of Gibran's career. Until 1918, he had written only in Arabic; after that date, he gradually came to publish almost exclusively in English. It was in that language that he developed the profile of an Eastern prophet that furnished the title of his best-known book in English. Yet Gibran was a different kind of Oriental sage from Tagore, a more familiar and cosmopolitan prophet who blended Eastern and Western wisdom, and fused biblical, Sufi, Hindu, Romantic, and Nietzschean influences. One interviewer perceptively put it this way:

> Tagore . . . is a figure from some canvas Sir Frederick Leighton might have painted of a religious mystic. Gibran is Broadway or Copley Square or The Strand or the Avenue de L'Opera—a correctly dressed cosmopolitan of the Western world.
>
> His dark brows and moustache and somewhat curly hair above a good forehead; the clear brown eyes, thoughtful but never abstracted in expression; the sensibly tailored clothes, smart but not conspicuous—there seemed to me a chameleon-like ease of adaptiveness about him. In his studio in West Tenth Street he looked a sensible denizen of Greenwich Village—for such there be. But had I seen him at a congress of economists, or in a Viennese café, or in his native Syria, I feel sure he would look equally in the picture in each instance.
>
> It is not a case of lack of individuality with him but on the contrary, an unusual common sense and sympathy which transcend differences and enable him to understand so well each environment in which he finds himself that *he neither feels nor looks the stranger*. . . . Notwithstanding his citizenship in the world as a whole, Mr. Gibran feels himself a Syrian. To him there is no contradiction here. He is working to bring about a world in which there is a great fellowship of mutual understanding and sympathy. (Gollomb 1, 10, emphasis added)

The exotic features are tempered by genteel, cosmopolitan dress and mannerisms—appealing but also cause for suspicion (only mildly expressed here), since the authentic Oriental is expertly disguised with chameleon-like ease. The full range of affects evoked by Otherness—from fascination and attraction (and mutatis mutandis) to fear and revulsion—is discernible just beneath the surface of this language of praise. The passage also points to a great paradox that defines Gibran's career after 1918, namely the incompatibility of the idea of building bridges of understanding, which Gibran professed and his reviewers celebrated, with the image of the chameleon that changes its colors to blend into its environment so that it does not "look the stranger." The chameleon does not try to connect two environments together, but quite the opposite: it changes its colors in order to blend into each environment; it adapts itself without attempting to change its surroundings. By contrast, critical cultural translation aims precisely at changing the environment in which it is conducted, through exposing it to new and potentially transformative ideas imported from elsewhere. The difference between transgressive cultural translation and chameleon-like adaptation is that while the former has the potential to interrogate and unsettle discursive and ideological presuppositions, the latter adheres to, and in effect confirms and legitimates, the reigning discourse. The one is transformative and oppositional, the other is complicit. Gollomb astutely identified the mode of Gibran's self-presentation as that of the chameleon, finding it somewhat suspicious. Characteristically, however, Gollomb misjudges the effectiveness of Gibran's efforts to facilitate "mutual understanding and sympathy" within a hegemonic framework. The popular success of Gibran's English-language works rests on this fundamental and widespread error in judgment.

From Rebel to Recluse

The chameleon's disguise is successful in precisely *appearing* as though it is not out of place—in effect, the goal is to disappear altogether and to become indistinguishable from its environment. As for *feeling* the stranger, that is a different matter, for Gibran's sense of isolation was enormous, as all of his biographers emphasize time and again. For instance, Robin Waterfield, who foregrounds the psychology of the immigrant and his desire for success and recognition, argues that Gibran's life in the United States

> evolved organically out of the persona he chose to adopt—that of wounded Romantic, shading into that of poet and prophet—but even an organic development of a persona remains two-dimensional. Whether Gibran was talking to friends or to a public audience, the impression he projected was the same. As an insecure young immigrant he soon learnt that this role could win him ready acceptance, and even adulation; such positive feedback entrenched the role-playing until it became second nature. But once in a while, his first nature prodded him into awareness. (Waterfield 4–5)

Hence his famous declaration to Mikhail Naimy, in a moment of clarity in 1921, that he was "a false alarm" (Naimy 171)—in other words, "that he really had no right to play the role of awakener himself" (Waterfield 3). Interestingly, that realization does not seem to have altered the course of his career. The timing of that well-known episode is significant. In 1921, Gibran had already tasted the success of his first two English-language books, *The Madman: His Parables and Poems* (1918) and *The Forerunner: His Parables and Poems* (1920), and he had for some years been working on *The Prophet* (1923). At the same time, he had already written his last significant Arabic works, the philosophical poem "Al-Mawakib" (1919, "The Procession," trans. in *A Treasury* 359–76) and his mystical play, *Irama dhat al-'imad* (1921, "Iram, City of Lofty Pillars," trans. in *A Treasury* 124–51). That is to say, the realization that he was "a false alarm" came at the moment when Gibran was changing course, exchanging Arabic for English. He no longer wrote major creative works in Arabic, despite the fame he had achieved in the Arab world.[5] Instead, he would focus on embracing more fully the role of Oriental prophet and hermit, both in his subsequent books, written in English as collections of parables and aphorisms, as well as in his private life, increasingly spent in the isolation of his Greenwich Village studio, where he wrote, drew, and literally drank himself to death. As Waterfield puts it,

> he found a home in the West as an exotic Easterner, and became famous in the East for vilifying Eastern customs from a vantage point gained as a result of reading Western romantics. He adopted a persona at an early age and identified with it so thoroughly that it became virtually impossible to find the man beneath the myth. Moreover, since the role he chose to play was that of poet-prophet, it proved hard to live up to. To my mind, then, Gibran was crucified on these dichotomies ['East and West' and 'Man and Myth']. We have seen occasional signs that he was, underneath it all, a deeply unhappy and unsatisfied man. (Waterfield 292).

It bears repeating that this is not a matter of hypocrisy or cynical manipulation of stereotypes, as one may be tempted to conclude, but of the gradual embrace of a role defined by Orientalist typology as his thought evolved. Gibran's shift to the prophetic mode is evident in his last two Arabic works, which "assert the oneness of spirit and body" (Hawi 217) and demonstrate the influence of William Blake. At the same time, the social rebelliousness of earlier Arabic works informs *Al-mawakib*, which expresses his rejection of society with its dualisms, in favor of the oneness of existence he claims to find in the jungle.[6] As Hawi points out, there is a

> unity of attitude which runs through both his Arabic and his English writings. He was not a mystic in the West and a rebel in the East at the same time, but developed from a youthful rebel into a mystic, expressing his later beliefs in both languages. *The Madman*, his first book in English (1918) was a violent declaration of revolt, while the thematic 'play' *Iram dhat al-'imad* was a discourse on mysticism, written in Arabic. (Hawi 111)

Nevertheless, this development soon manifested itself in a radical shift in language, readership, and therefore discourse—i.e., a bifurcation of purpose in his English and Arabic works after 1921. He no longer developed mystical themes in the short essays and addresses he wrote in Arabic, which demonstrated an increasingly mature understanding of Arab social and political conditions. By contrast, his creative activity in English intensified along the lines drawn in *The Madman* and *The Forerunner*. The clearest and most striking example of that bifurcation is that in 1923, the year *The Prophet* was published, he wrote a penetrating critique of Arab cultural dependency vis-à-vis Europe for *Al-Hilal* magazine, which ran a survey of Arab intellectuals' views on the relationship between the Arab *Nahda* and "Western" civilization (*Nusus* 235–44). In that piece, Gibran argued that under the conditions of European colonial hegemony over the entire Arab world, Arab renaissance was no more than slavish mimicry of Western thought and tastes, a superficial veneer of modernity (235–36), and that a true renaissance embodied in economic cooperation among Arab countries and their political unity and independence—the goal of many Arab nationalists of that period—would never be permitted under Western economic and military dominance, which pursued the policy of divide and conquer (239). This position reflects Gibran's disillusionment with European colonialism after Britain and France revealed their colonial designs in the Levant and reneged on their promises of Arab independence in exchange for fighting the Ottomans during World War I. This is also a radical change in his views, considering that during the war, he (like many Lebanese Christians) had imagined French colonialism to be not only benevolent but "the architect of our new house. France will help us become a living nation" (*Nusus* 228).[7]

Why did Gibran, after 1921, express his mystical views only in English and his political views almost exclusively in Arabic? (Recall that Rihani wrote on both themes in Arabic and English throughout his life.) At least one answer to that question lies in the degree of Gibran's uncritical acceptance of Orientalist typology, which provided him with a role he was eager to play. A book such as *The Prophet* would have made little sense to Arab readers. In the Arabic poetic tradition, the socially engaged poet often assumed the voice of the worldly sage who formulated wise, pithy, and didactic statements in memorable poetic idiom. Though this role overlaps somewhat with the European Romantic conception of the poet, there is a fundamental difference. In the Arabic tradition the poet could be a sage and a moralist (among other roles), but never a prophet. Al-Mutanabbi is a case in point: a supremely talented poet, his enormous pride once drove him to declare himself a prophet; ever since he became far better known by a derisive epithet, "*al-mutanabbi*" (i.e., "one who [falsely] claims to be a prophet") than by his real name. In Muslim cultures, there is a taboo on the claim to prophecy, which is understood strictly as a divine mandate given to biblical prophets and to Muhammad, who is believed in Islam to be the last true prophet for all time. Anyone who claims to be a prophet after Muhammad is ipso facto a false prophet. For that reason, Gibran's prophetic stance could not be expressed in works addressed to Arab audiences. A title such as *The Prophet* would have been offensive to Arab readers, and even though the book was later translated into Arabic, it remains, together with his other books translated from English, far less known than his earlier, Arabic works. At the very least, the idea of an Oriental sage would have been associated, for his Arab readers, with the Far East, something altogether remote and exotic; an Arab playing that role would have been laughable.

In that sense, Gibran's prophetic stance was in many ways a deliberate and phenomenally successful feat of self-Orientalizing on the part of an immigrant seeking acceptance, although it was also a logical (if not inevitable) development within his self-styled Romantic trajectory: from youthful rebel with "adolescent vision" (Hawi 280) to Oriental sage, and consequently from writing in Arabic to writing in English. For Blake and Shelley, the poet, the visionary, and the prophet were more or less synonymous, and, in following in their footsteps, "Gibran initiated nothing in the realm of thought, nor did he revive long-forgotten ideas" (Hawi 278). But to assume that role within the framework of Orientalism condemned his work, in Hawi's blunt assessment, to a lack in "social and cultural responsibility" and to being "retrogressive and immature," something that furnished the proof of Gibran's "primitivism and naivety" (280). As cultural translation, Gibran's introduction of European Romanticism into Arabic poetry was a significant contribution to that tradition, but his English works imported nothing of value from Arabic into American literature; instead, their anachronistic Romanticism merely recycled tired ideas about the East. The dynamics of literary reception of his work in each language reflected that: on the one hand, qualified critical acclaim for the technical innovations of his Arabic works, if not for their naïve sentimentalism; and on the other hand, tremendous popular appeal and justifiable critical neglect of his English works. Equally important, Gibran's career trajectory also led from poverty to financial security, and from obscurity to fame in his adoptive country.

The price, however, was his increasing isolation as he came to believe in his own act and strove to live by his impossible precept. Indeed, the reclusive suffering of his later years had already been foreshadowed in some of his earlier works and was part and parcel of his conception of the poet-prophet. The protagonists of his Arabic and English prose and poetry are variations on the social rebel who becomes an outcast after securing a following of disciples—a Christ figure minus the resurrection and godhead. For example, in an emblematic early story, "Khalil al-Kafir" (trans. as "Khalil the Heretic," in *A Treasury* 243–98), from *Al-Arwah al-mutamarrida* ("Spirits Rebellious"), Gibran's namesake protagonist rebels against the tyranny and corruption of the clergy, who call him a heretic; yet he succeeds in unmasking their hypocrisy in a lengthy public oration that galvanizes the villagers, who offer to make him their chief. He refuses that distinction and continues to live among them as one of them. This idealistic vision of the rebel emancipating his people and realizing a social utopia gradually gives way, in *Al-Mawakib* (1919, The Procession), Gibran's last significant Arabic work, to that of the detached moralist who, finding society irredeemable, glorifies an idealized jungle in which dichotomies dissolve into oneness of being. In his first English work, *The Madman* (1918), the social rebel becomes a total outcast, a prophetic madman who seems to speak in a void. In *The Prophet* (1923), he is the hermit al-Mustapha, who has lived in exile for twelve years and is about to depart his adoptive land for the country of his birth, before he is prevailed upon to deliver a final discourse. In *The Garden of the Prophet* (1933), which Gibran left unfinished when he died, al-Mustapha comes back to his birthplace only to find that he no longer belongs there; he decides, once again, to leave his disciples behind and to undergo another self-imposed exile.

These modulations on the theme of the prophet as a remote, lonesome reformer, isolated from, sometime rejected by, and sometimes rejecting his people, bespeak Gibran's own growing sense of alienation in both worlds. For a minority writer, this solitary posture represents a repudiation of the political and collective nature of writing—the second and third characteristics of minor literature—and amount to the marginalization of the poet, not just in mainstream society, but also within the minority group. This had none of the Romantic appeal to many of Gibran's contemporary and later Arab American writers that it had for Gibran himself. It is an aspect of his legacy that some Arab American writers have vehemently rejected. Thus while some have continued to celebrate Gibran's popularity and to embrace the universalism of his message, others have disputed that message and found that it leads to social irrelevance and contributes to weakening the ties that connect Arab Americans to each other and to their homeland. Those two contrasting attitudes to Gibran reflect his contradictory legacy within the Arab American literary tradition.

One example of the first tendency is the title of a pioneering anthology, *Post-Gibran: Anthology of New Arab American Writing* (1999), edited by Munir Akash and Khaled Mattawa, in which the Lebanese writer is given pride of place as the founder of the Arab American literary tradition. Intentional or not, the ambiguity of the title ("post-" in many cases denotes both temporal succession and critical opposition) points to a deep ambivalence toward Gibran that has haunted Arab American literature and demands scrutiny in any critical reading of the tradition. The following passage from the introduction to the anthology brims with adulation and urges contemporary Arab American writers to imitate Gibran:

> Kahlil Gibran found his way to the American heart, not because he was a great poet, but because he strove to manifest positive aspects found in our traditional writing. The traditions he mined from are not always concerned with the liturgical, cultic, and esoteric elements of the Gilgamishian spirit, but are nevertheless created according to its norms and principles, according to the concept of *man* as a bridge between heaven and earth, the *anthropos*, the Promethean, or, in the Qur'anic sense, the viceregent of God. (Mattawa and Akash xii)

This statement is problematic on several counts—from the metaphysics of a so-called "Gilgamishian spirit" to the assumption of a trans-historical continuity between ancient Mesopotamia and twentieth-century Arab culture, to the conflation of the Promethean defiance of the gods with the Islamic (and Abrahamic) subordination of man to the creator. Moreover, that statement succumbs to the Gibranian logic it attempts to describe—a logic derived from Blake, Shelley, and Whitman, according to which all opposites collapse into a oneness of being that Eugene Paul Nassar has aptly described as "the pseudo-wisdom posture of exultant dualism" (Nassar, *Essays* 84).[8] But before turning to that critique, it is important to dwell for a moment on what Mattawa and Akash appreciate in Gibran's spiritualism: the mélange of Hindu, Christian, Islamic, and Nietzschean ideas represents an attempt, however unsatisfactory, to articulate an alternative kind of humanism that answers to the materialism of European secular humanism and its fullest realization in America, by tempering it with "Eastern" spirituality. The idea of "Eastern" spirituality, it should be recalled, emerges out of Orientalist typology and denotes an undifferentiated, trans-historical monolith, the polar opposite of secular "Western" rationalism. In other words, this is a humanism steeped in Orientalism. But it is a humanism that asserts the equal value of Orient and Occident and the possibility of a reciprocal relationship between them. This implicit claim of equality and reciprocity is, in the final analysis, the only political content of Gibran's English works. Rihani and Rihbany held a similar view, but whereas they expressed it directly and forcefully, Gibran tried to embody that ideal Orient in his English writings and in his own life.

As such, the latent political project of Gibran's English works parallels that of the Négritude movement, which was to be launched a decade later in Paris by writers of African descent as an affirmation of Africanness in the face of white racism. Both projects were flawed insofar as they accepted the dualistic logic of racist discourse, which constructs European identity and its extension in North America in opposition to Africa and the Orient. If the hegemonic discourses of Orientalism and Africanism devalue Africa and the Orient in favor of Europe, Négritude and Gibran's (and his Syrian contemporaries') version of Orientalism simply reverse the values attached to Europe and its others, but without questioning the binary construct itself, so that now African primitivism and Oriental mysticism acquire positive content, while Western modernity and materialism are negatively valued. Jean-Paul Sartre criticized Négritude as an "anti-racist racism" (Sartre xl), a characterization eminently adaptable to Gibran's posture, which can accordingly be described as an anti-Orientalist Orientalism. By the same token, Frantz Fanon's defense of Négritude not as a philosophically valid creed but as an expression of the psychological needs of the oppressed at a particular stage in the development of their racial consciousness (Fanon 132–35) also applies to this early twentieth-century Arab American version of Orientalism. The persistence of this kind of thinking in the late twentieth century is evident in the inflationary language of "Gilgameshian spirit," which is followed, one paragraph later, by Akash and Mattawa's description of Arab American writers as "members of a demonized minority"—a testimony to the fact that, while anti-black racism has been banished from the registers of acceptable public discourse (and with it the need for Black racialism), anti-Arab racism continues to thrive. The continued celebration of Gibran, therefore, bespeaks a psychological need in Arab Americans similar to that identified by Fanon with respect to Négritude.

Paradoxically, however, the very assertion of Arab American identity and of a literary tradition that builds upon Gibran's success contradicts Gibran's message. In a crucial discourse on "Self-Knowledge" almost halfway through *The Prophet*, Almustafa says:

> Say not, "I have found the truth," but rather, "I have found a truth."
>
> Say not, "I have found the path of the soul." Say rather, "I have met the soul walking upon my path."

For the soul walks upon all paths.
The soul walks not upon a line, neither does it grow like a reed.
The soul unfolds itself, like a lotus of countless petals. (55)

Derived from mysticism and (as suggested by the image of the lotus) Buddhism, the idea of truth as multiple and personal rather than unitary or universal represents an alternative ethos to the rigidly hierarchical worldview propagated by Orientalism, racialism, and other ideologies of difference. This creed preaches tolerance and acceptance of difference, not only in spiritual matters, but in worldly ones as well. If Orientalism indelibly marked Gibran's career, his search for universal truths that transcend cultural and religious boundaries represents a countercurrent that, however implicitly, challenged the discourse's hierarchical logic. Nevertheless, that universality, which accounts for Gibran's tremendous success, remained at such high level of abstraction that it became effectively unmoored, in its otherworldly spiritualism, from any concrete historical circumstances in which it might have been intended to intervene.[9] The biblical style, the apostolic tone, the poet-prophet's addiçtion to solitude "among the summits where eagles build their nests" (*The Prophet* 90), and above all by the nebulous abstraction of his "teachings," not to mention the absence of any reference to Arabs or their culture in his English language works, all combine to divorce Gibran's work from the struggles over representation that have always preoccupied Arab American writers.

It was this disavowal of collectivity that some of those writers rejected. Gibran's prophetic posture was unsustainable for U.S.-born Arab Americans, who wanted to dissociate themselves from the Orient and to assert their Americanness. As Evelyn Shakir puts it, U.S.-born Arab Americans "who came of age in the 1930s, 1940s, and 1950s—costumed themselves as 'regular Americans' and hoped to pass, which may be why they produced so little literature" (Shakir 1996, 6). Others have been vocal in their resistance to Gibran's influence. From within the Arab American literary tradition, the most extensive critique of Gibran to date has come from the literary criticism and poetry of Eugene Paul Nassar (b. 1935). In his poetic rebuttal, "Disputation with Gibran" (one of two cantos that make up his poetic memoir, *Wind of the Land*), Nassar charges: "O my brother Kahlil, your style enchants but your substance cheats" (Nassar 1979, 125). For Nassar, Gibran's is a metaphysics of evasion: "Why this exultation in the contraries of life, Gibran, in Good and Evil as one, Life and Death as One, the Darkness as blessed as Light? Is it not simply an avoidance of the fact of death, evil, and darkness? " (132). Elsewhere, in a critical study of "cultural discontinuity" in Gibran's work, Nassar argues that "the continuity of tone that runs throughout the works of Gibran is that of lonely alienation, of a yearning for connections. Beneath all his prophetic masks . . . is the Gibran of unsureness, of profound melancholy, of tragic vision. Gibran is at home neither in the old culture nor in the new, an unresolved dualism vitiates much of the work when, as so often occurs, it pretends to resolution" (1983, 87–88). In a cogent discussion of such "dualism pretending to unity" (95) in the work of Blake, Whitman, and Gibran, Nassar argues that "all three poets labor under the burden of their transcendent self-projections of unitary truth, and are wholly convincing only when wholly absorbed in dramatizations of their dualistic experiences" (100). In "Disputation with Gibran," Nassar puts it differently:

> Can you not see that you will not satisfy man, Kahlil Gibran, with your cold abstractions of Love and Life beyond the personal love and life, with your Great Soul or Great Self, or Vast Man or Master Spirit? We have had it all before (postcards to Blake and Whitman). Man will have his Heaven with private rooms and his personal immortality with his shoes on. (1979, 107)

Emphasizing the perspective of Lebanese villagers, Nassar satirizes both Gibran's hermetic individualism and his rarefied abstractions:

> *Your children are not your children.* O my Gibran, have you ever made a greater miscalculation? No village rebel ever made a greater. *You may strive to be like them, but seek not to make them like you.* O my God, worse and worse! Watch out for Shafee'a, Kahlil, she will eat you alive! And Abdullah will expose your weaknesses to laughter.[10] (112, original emphasis)
>
> Almustafa the prophet should have married Almitra the seeress. Their gloom might have been dissipated by a child in the arms.
>
> Would he have left Orphalese if a sweet daughter-in-law had given him a granddaughter for the eyes of his old age? (138)

Another Arab American poet, Sharif Elmusa (b. 1947), strikes a similar note in his poem, "Dream on the Same Mattress":

> Do not eat from the same dish,
> said Gibran;
> but the prophet never married.
> Drink from the same cup,
> I say,
> and dream on the same mattress.[11] (Elmusa 233)

Nassar finds Gibran's enormous reputation within Arab America to be troublesome:

> And a young man has been reading to me
> the poetry of Kahlil Gibran
> And wise he is in many things, O my
> children, and schooled in sound,
> But his is not the needful poetry, O my
> cousins,
> For he is too lonely and would make a
> blessing of loneliness. (Nassar 1979, 147)

Elmusa and Nassar find particularly worrisome Gibran's distaste for family bonds, which are not only of supreme importance in Arab culture, but especially so for Arab Americans, for whom ancestral traditions represent a haven of security within a larger society that views them with suspicion. Nassar's address to "my children" and "my cousins" stresses the importance of family ties, which Gibran's writings repudiate; to heed his admonition to "seek not to make [your children] like you" amounts to severing their cultural ties to the Old Country, effectively to melt indistinguishably in the pot of Euro-America. The alternatives Nassar proposes in his poem are "the tales of our grandmother/and the wisdom from her lips," the love and security found within the family fold, and attachment to the values of the Old Country:

> America has indeed been lavish in the
> casting of flowers,
> Of flowers that do not grow in the old
> country villages,
> Generous, open, accessible in the highest
> of glories.
> But what of the flowers, the country
> flowers of the village,
> Simplicity, serenity, and joy, the
> sense of belonging? (146)

A descendant of Lebanese immigrants, Nassar is nostalgic for the land and culture of his ancestors, which he tends to idealize. Gibran's rejection of the family is a revolt against patriarchal tyranny, parental coercion, forced marriages, and so on, which he observed in his Lebanese homeland and began to attack in his earliest Arabic works. His rejection of religious authority and its abuse by corrupt and hypocritical clergymen also belong to the same order. It was this work that made Gibran famous as a progressive revolutionary in the Arabic literary field. We can see that his position toward those social structures persisted in his English works, albeit in more abstract, universalist terms. By contrast, the position Nassar describes as "thoughtful conservatism" celebrates the same patriarchal values that Gibran rejects, but for reasons that have to do with Nassar's status as a minority writer born in a society prejudiced against or ignorant of his heritage:

> Beneath the bravado of the prophetic robes, Gibran really had no adequate replacement for the richness of the cultural heritage, both peasant and intellectual, of the Christian East, that the bread and wine in the hill village in Lebanon is perhaps a better bet for a life than the winds of solitude at the top of a mystic mountain, or the studio apartment at West Tenth Street in Manhattan. (Nassar 1983, 100)

The strong family ties that Gibran found stifling are for Nassar nurturing, and the old customs that the former considered outworn are for the latter a reassuring link to his Lebanese heritage. The two poets represent contrasting tendencies that turn conventional wisdom upside-down, as the U.S.-born and raised poet rejects the American-style individualism adopted by the Lebanese immigrant: "out of / our sometime loneliness, O brothers, / Comes the memories of a past that was not / lonely" (Nassar 1979, 146). For Nassar, immigration and biculturalism are no passport to superior wisdom, and Gibran's case is an exemplary "drama of a talented émigré at home neither in the old country nor in the new" (1983, 101).

Put differently, the chameleon is a failed cultural translator. Gibran understood himself, presented himself, and was regarded by many as an intermediary between two worlds—indeed, as the prophet of a spiritual utopia. In fact, the Gibran phenomenon signals the triumph of Orientalism at the moment when cultural hegemony appears to have been surpassed. Indeed, it is the *appearance* of its elimination that evidences the staying power of hegemonic discourse, which functions all the more effectively for seeming no longer to exist. This kind of cultural translation does not carve a new space through dialogue and critique; on the contrary, it operates within the orbit of the dominant discourse. Gibran tried to negate Orientalist negation through Orientalist transcendence, a move that ensured the failure of his project on the personal, social, and intellectual levels, although it brought him tremendous popular and commercial success. That he has been so rewarded is both ironic and indicative of the forces that still shape public views of Arabs today.

3

The Emergence of Autobiography

"I like the Syrian people very much."

—GEORGE HADDAD

Whenever I open my Bible it reads like a letter from home.

—ABRAHAM RIHBANY

Minority Autobiography

The question of autobiography as a genre with an ambivalent relationship to historical fact and narrative convention has preoccupied U.S. and French theorists since the early 1960s, when autobiography began to command the attention of literary scholars.[1] There are at least two reasons for the canonization, in postmodern culture, of autobiography, which had previously been regarded as inferior to enshrined literary genres (Morgan 3–4). One reason is the

> generally perceived autobiographical turn in the literature of the [1970s and 1980s], both in Europe and the United States . . . particularly . . . among those contemporary novelists who appear to be playful practitioners of fictional games or who—from the perspective of their ethnic or marginal backgrounds—seem to be in search of their ethnic identity within a dominant white culture. (Hornung and Ruhe 9)

Another related reason is that feminist and minority criticism questioned the traditional literary canon and brought to the attention of scholars women's and minority writing, especially previously unknown or uncanonical texts, many of which were autobiographical, such as women's letters, fiction, and diaries, and African American slave narratives. Thus, at a time when theorists like Roland Barthes and Michel Foucault pronounced the "death of the Author"—as part of the poststructuralist critique of the transcendental subject of the Enlightenment—avant-garde novelists and those marginalized by gender, race, and/or ethnicity showed their vital signs through autobiographical writing (Morgan 11–12, Hornung and Ruhe 9).

Arab immigrant autobiography has played a major part in articulating Arab American identity. As we have seen in the two preceding chapters, the Anglophone writings of the two pioneers of Arab American literature, Ameen Rihani and Kahlil Gibran, represent a continuation and an outgrowth of their Arabic literary careers, albeit refracted through the prism of Orientalism. By contrast, the relationship between Arab American and Arabic autobiography is rather tenuous. In the Arabic literary tradition, autobiography has existed since the ninth century and been a scholarly concern throughout the ages.[2] And just as the publication of fiction and poetry written in Arabic in the United States preceded the emergence of Anglophone Arab American literature, so did the appearance of Arabic-language autobiography in the U.S. predate the first Anglophone Arab American autobiography. Interestingly, however, those first Arabic autobiographies were written neither by Arabs nor by immigrants, but by educated Muslim slaves captured in West Africa in the eighteenth and early nineteenth century, and, like other slave narratives, they were written at the urging of abolitionists.[3]

Arab American autobiography proper begins with Abraham Mitrie Rihbany's *A Far Journey* (1914), followed by George Haddad's *Mt. Lebanon to Vermont* (1916), and Rihbany's second autobiographical narrative, *The Hidden Treasure of Rasmola* (1920). These texts have more in common with immigrant autobiographies by members of other ethnic groups than with the tradition of Arabic autobiography. This chapter lays out a theoretical framework for interpreting Arab American autobiography's relationship to Orientalism and cultural translation, then considers the autobiographies of Rihbany and Haddad. Rather than engaging in debates over the definition, demarcation, and "policing of the borders" of autobiography as a genre, or even attempting to define a poetics of Arab immigrant autobiography, the more urgent question concerns the kinds of cultural, historical, and discursive intervention that such autobiography makes in the United States.[4] That is, I read Arab American autobiographies not so much as variations on a tradition or canon of autobiography, or as test cases for particular theories and definitions of a genre, but as distinct negotiations of Arab American identity.

Based on contemporary notions of reality as socially constructed in language, theorists of autobiography hold, contrary to conventional wisdom, that "autobiography is not and cannot be a way of simply signifying or referring to a 'life as lived' . . . there is no such thing as a 'life as lived' to be referred to. On this view, life is created or constructed by the act of autobiography" (Brunner 38).[5] Further, the dialogical, interpersonal dimension to all kinds of narrative erases conventional distinctions between fiction and autobiography, on the one hand, and on the other, between autobiography and other kinds of nonfiction writing, including historiography, philosophy, literary and cultural criticism, and so on. If novels are always to some degree autobiographical ("Madame Bovary, c'est moi!"), autobiography is inevitably novelistic, always making use, whether consciously or not, of familiar conventions and techniques of storytelling (Eakin 295, Gergen 90). In fact, Henry Miller went so far as to hold that all "writing is autobiography," and likewise Paul Valéry believed "that there is no theory that is not in fact a carefully concealed part of the theorist's own life story" (Klinkowitz 118). This is not, of course, to suggest a return to crude notions that fiction is to be interpreted in terms of the author's life, or vice versa, that all autobiography is nothing but fiction (the hybrid genre of autobiographical fiction can be located precisely along that artificial boundary), but rather that the autobiographer, like the novelist and the theorist, constructs a particular kind of discourse. Autobiographical discourse could be said to consist "in combining witness, interpretation, and stance to create an account that has both verisimilitude and negotiability" (Brunner 46). Brunner defines "stance" as the "autobiographer's posture toward the world, toward self, toward fate and the possible, and also toward interpretation itself" (45); in other words, it is the autobiographer's ideological worldview. As for "negotiability," it is "whatever makes it possible for an autobiography to enter into 'the conversation of selves'" (47); that is to say, the forms of its engagement with sanctioned narratives, cultural codes, discursive norms, ideological imperatives, and textual procedures that prevail among its readers and which produce for them the truth-effects of the autobiography. Therefore, discussion of autobiography would more profitably focus on its ideological project and the kind of discourse it constructs than on "truthfulness" in any absolute sense.

From this perspective, I propose a reading of the autobiographies under consideration in this book as negotiations of Arab American identity. Like the social identity of women and of minority groups such as Native Americans, African Americans, Asian Americans, and Hispanics, that of Arab Americans is constructed dialectically in relation to the male-dominated majority culture. Molly Hite argues that for marginalized groups, "self-writing tends to be participation in the multiple discourses that establish and reestablish this 'self.' It is by definition a revisionary activity, inasmuch as it reinscribes a prescribed subjectivity in another register, intervening in the social construction of identity" (Hite xv). Thus the negotiation of identity in minoritarian autobiographical discourse tends to perform a double operation: contesting the identity assigned by the dominant majority discourse while at the same time utilizing its sanctioned narrative procedures to enter into its regime of truth. In other words, it is not enough for the marginalized autobiographers to undermine socially constructed identity; they must be able to engage the dominant discourse dialogically in order for their intervention to negotiate a viable identity. As Leigh Gilmore points out, "[w]hether and when autobiography emerges as an authoritative discourse of reality and identity, and any particular text appears to tell the truth, have less to do with that text's presumed accuracy about what really happened than with its apprehended fit into culturally prevalent discourses of truth and identity" (ix). Jerome Brunner enumerates some such discourses, which he calls "conventional autobiographical genres" that

> reflect idealized cultural patterns. Many are familiar: the selfless seeker after the public interest, the sacrificing family man, the *Bildungsroman* with its assurance of learning from experience, the ironic and detached observer of the absurdities of the contemporary human condition (in any age), the guardian mother shielding the young, the seeker after

> spontaneous self-expression, the forgiving victim of society's outrages, the apologia of the misunderstood public man, and so on. (Brunner 40)

It is important to emphasize here that those "idealized cultural patterns" represent both choices for the author and a set of readers' expectations; they are often factored into the complex grid of editorial pressures, publishing decisions, marketing strategies, and reviewers' judgments.

While it is impossible to measure with any accuracy how all of this influences, shapes, or censors (including self-censorship) the published autobiography, I would venture to say that most American readers expect an Arab immigrant's autobiography to follow two general trajectories: the self-reliant (male) achiever of the American Dream, and the Arab Muslim woman who escapes from the oppressive patriarchy of her culture to freedom and independence in the U.S. (As we shall see in later chapters, fiction by women is also often expected to conform to this master narrative.) From this perspective, it is possible to advance the thesis that Arab American autobiography is often constrained by two unspoken requirements: first, that it construct a selfhood that is intelligible in light of American paradigms of subjectivity, and second, that it address Orientalist ideas about Arabs and Muslims. The first condition requires Arab American autobiography to construct narratives of self-emergence that conform to the doctrine of individualism (usually with some variation on the theme of pursuing personal freedom, independence, and the American Dream), while the second requires such narratives to foreground issues such as cultural differences, religion, and Middle East politics. Arab American autobiography's "apprehended fit into culturally prevalent discourses of truth and identity" (Gilmore ix) depends on meeting those ideological requirements—that is to say, on effectively *translating* personal experience into familiar patterns of autobiographical narration.

To elaborate on the first requirement, all of the immigrant autobiographies considered in this book are success stories; they call attention, by default, to the fact that it is only immigrant success stories that tend to be written. Unsuccessful migrants whom the American Dream eludes and who return to their country of origin, would probably write in their native language, if they were inclined to write autobiographies at all (and who likes to tell the story of their failure?). Those who remain in the U.S. would simply have no story that would be deemed worthy of publication, either by themselves or by publishers. Stories that deviate from the norms of immigrant autobiography are, therefore, largely irretrievable, except in non-autobiographical registers such as news stories, court records, sociological and historical studies, oral history, and so forth. That is, "immigrant autobiography" is, by definition, a genre with strict sociological and ideological, if not formal, boundaries. To write in that genre already means that the autobiographer enjoys certain privileges (education, economic means, leisure time) and subscribes (or at least pays lip service) to particular ideological imperatives—for example, the doctrines of individualism, America as the land of freedom and opportunity, the American Dream. The second requirement implies that Orientalist assumptions, stereotypes, and narratives shape the reception of texts by and about Arabs and Muslims. Not surprisingly, Arab American autobiographers have by turns confirmed and challenged those dominant ideas. As with the work of Rihani and Gibran, the early immigrant autobiographers considered in this and the next chapter by and large confirmed both Orientalist ideas about their homeland and American self-images. Only subtly and indirectly did they ever challenge the dominant discourses. It was not until the last quarter of the twentieth century that many (though by no means all) Arab American autobiographers would do so forcefully and explicitly, along with novelists, poets, and cultural critics.

Untutored Counter-Orientalism

George Haddad (1866–?) attended an American missionary school in his Lebanese village of Barook before turning to trade at the age of sixteen. He emigrated to the U.S. ten years later, worked as a peddler of oriental goods and became a successful merchant. The title page of his autobiography, *Mt. Lebanon to Vermont* (1916), announces that it was "taken down by his daughter Emily Marie Haddad with the assistance of Berenice Rachel Tuttle." The book is a minimalist chronicle of life events that displays few intellectual interests. Whether such a text qualifies, strictly speaking, as an autobiography, and the degree to which the agency of its ghostwriters shaped the narrative, are interesting questions that lie beyond the scope of this discussion. What interests me here is Haddad's narrative negotiation of Arab American identity, especially the ways in which his book sets off the elaborate textual machinery of Rihbany's more learned texts, discussed in the next two sections of this chapter.

Precisely because Haddad's education was limited, his text stands as a rare example of an Arab American autobiography that is relatively free of Orientalist procedures, although it is manifestly written against the grain of dominant representations of the Orient. For that reason, it may be well to disregard strict chronology and start with Haddad's text. *Mt. Lebanon to Vermont* chronicles Haddad's life before and after immigration, without any of the usual accounts of struggle—whether social, economic, or psychological. Indeed, the most striking feature of *Mt. Lebanon to Vermont* is the conspicuous absence of any introspection and of any hint of negative experience, whether in Lebanon, the U.S., or the many countries he visits along the way and in subsequent business trips. Even the Atlantic Ocean and the Mediterranean are always calm and serene during Haddad's numerous travels. There is nothing but praise for Syria, America, and everything and everyone there and in between. So minimal is the narration, so sanitized, and so seemingly intent on projecting a positive image of Syria to America, and of America to itself (he reports praising America to Syrians and Turks during his visits home), and of all of Haddad's narrated experiences that one must wonder what intense negativity the book must have been intended to counter. It is true that the personality that comes across the narration (and in the frontispiece photo of Haddad and two of his children) seems to be that of a jolly, good-natured, successful, and contented man, yet this narrative of highly contrived reticence begs the question of to what it was meant to respond. For one thing, the book is full of praise for America; the first chapter contains little else: the Sphinx in Giza reminds him of George Washington (George Haddad 49), American missionaries in Syria are "very intelligent, well-loved, and a great help to Syrians" (67), the Statue of Liberty means everything to him (68), American stoves are better than British and French-made stoves (83), and on and on.

At the same time, his account of the Old Country is also all positive, so that if praise for America is intended to flatter his readers, praise for Syria and Syrians recommends them to Americans and even ventures to correct some negative perceptions. For instance, early in the book Haddad seems to endorse the notion that the Orient is plagued with inter-faith prejudices and populated, among other things, by bloodthirsty Arabs: "From Haifa to Jaffa . . . [t]he way was said to be very dangerous on account of treacherous Arabs, but I did not fear them as I had friends with me." The phrase "treacherous Arabs," which in Arabic would be understood to refer to nomadic Bedouins who sometimes raid villagers or rob travelers, in English evokes an Orientalist stock image of hostile Muslims threatening Christians. Some Christian Lebanese immigrants, including Rihbany and Salom Rizk, reproduce that stereotype in their writings in order to stress the confessional bond between themselves and their American readers, over and against a religious Other. In Haddad, however, the following sentence breaks the implicit promise of a lurid adventure of the kind encountered in sensational travelogues and Orientalist romances: "About fifteen miles outside the city we were stopped by five of them on horseback but all they did was ask me for tobacco" (33–34). The most dramatic moment in the entire book delivers an anti-climax that ever so subtly deflates the stereotype. Haddad goes on to stress the good neighborly relations among Christians and Druses in his native village of Barook and the fact that religious difference does not lead to antagonism. There are several examples of this: "Besides being the patron saint of England and of the Christians of Syria, St. George is a much beloved hero of the Moslems and Arabs" (95); St. John's shrine is housed within the grand mosque of Damascus and Christians are allowed to pray there (110–11); Haddad presented a silver candlestick to the mosque (73); "Emperor William" (Wilhelm II of Germany) placed golden wreaths on the tomb of Saladin (113). What emerges from between the lines is this: Syrians are normal, happy, friendly, peaceful people who get along with each other despite religious differences; they like America and make good immigrant citizens. This last point is not left for the reader to discern, but is emphatically put in the mouth of a high-profile American. Haddad makes a point of documenting his meeting with Admiral George Dewey, who says to him: "I like the Syrian people very much, I know many of them; they make good citizens and are very good workers" (100). This strong recommendation sums up the thesis of this unusual book.

Haddad's is the only autobiography by a pack peddler, a popular occupation among the poorer Syrian immigrants. His profession must have brought him into contact with many Americans and exposed him to typical attitudes of the time. Even though neither Haddad nor Rihbany mention encountering racial prejudice against Syrians, it is most likely those attitudes and misconceptions, rather than Orientalist literature in any formal sense, that Haddad's narrative undertakes to correct, artlessly albeit shrewdly. His autobiography also inaugurates one of the lasting conventions of Arab American literature, namely the celebration of Arabic food. While part I of the book tells Haddad's life story in a hundred and twenty-eight pages, part II of the book is a forty-three page collection of Syrian recipes used by his wife. A century later, Arab American fiction, poetry, and autobiography continue to celebrate Arabic food, the one aspect of Arab culture, it seems, that has escaped negative stereotyping and is, therefore, inordinately emphasized, even fetishized, not only as an unproblematic link to Arab culture, but also as a positive contribution to America.[6] Moreover, the appendix includes a reprint of an article by L. Hussakof, previously published in the *Bulletin of the American Museum of Natural History* (vol. XXXV, art. VX, pp. 135–37) and titled "A New Pycnodont Fish, Coelodus Syriacus, from the Cretaceous of Syria," based on a fossil collected by Haddad near Beirut (Haddad 173–76). Apparently, the unusual appendix was intended as another example of Syrians' contributions to America. Charmingly naïve it may be, but this confident assertion that Arab immigrants had something to offer America is unique among autobiographers during the first and second phases of Arab American literature. By contrast, in Rihbany, Rizk, Ihab Hassan, and others, the overwhelming emphasis is on the gifts that America had to offer those lucky enough to leave their destitute homelands, which seem to have nothing of value to give in return. However modest and untutored, *Mt. Lebanon to Vermont* proposes that Syria and America share the same values and aspirations and can enjoy mutually beneficial cultural and commercial exchange.

East Is East: Rihbany's Biblical Orientalism

A very different approach is found in the works of Abraham Mitrie Rihbany (1869–1944). Like Rihani and Gibran, Rihbany accepted many of the basic tenets of Orientalism but wrestled with the brand of inferiority with which it stamped his culture. As narrative engagements with Oriental discourse, Rihbany's two autobiographical texts, *A Far Journey* (1914) and *The Hidden Treasure of Rasmola* (1920), are more complex than Haddad's, but Rihbany also authored several books, most of them on East–West relations: *The Syrian Christ* (1916), *Militant America and Jesus Christ* (1917), *America Save the Near East* (1918), *Wise Men from the East and from the West* (1922), *The Christ Story for Boys and Girls* (1923), *Seven Days with God* (1926), and *The Five Interpretations of Jesus* (1940). I will focus on the two autobiographies in this section and on the other books in the next one.

Rihbany came from a humble rural and Maronite background in Lebanon, where he apprenticed as a stonemason, enrolled in an American missionary school, and converted to Protestantism as a teenager. He emigrated to the U.S. in 1891, at the age of twenty-two, and eventually became a minister in various Midwestern churches before settling in Boston. He knew the Arabic language reasonably well (he was the literary editor of *Kawkab Amrika*, the first Arabic-language newspaper in the U.S.), but it is doubtful that he was well read in its literature; his theological studies in the U.S. were far more important to his intellectual formation than his Arabic education. He was the first prolific Arab American author to write exclusively in English, but he was not in any way affiliated with the *Mahjar* group. Literature was not his primary vocation, although *A Far Journey* was the first Arab American autobiography ever to be published, and *The Hidden Treasure of Rasmola*, billed as "a true story and personal experience of mine" (Rihbany 1920, vii), reads like an adventure romance. Like Rihani and Gibran, he elaborated his own version of Orientalism, presented himself as an authority on "Eastern" and "Western" civilization, and posed as a cultural translator. Like Rihani, in particular, Rihbany wrote and lectured extensively on the political situation in the Middle East during the 1910s and 1920s, and advocated an active U.S. role there.

Rihbany's first publications were autobiographical essays in *The Atlantic Monthly* magazine. The positive response he received encouraged him to write *A Far Journey*, and the series of books that followed expanded on the theme of East–West relations central to the autobiography. In other words, Rihbany's career as an author grew directly out of his telling of his life story. Rihbany's success, and the warmth with which audiences and readers greeted that story, was due to the fact that his narrative confirmed Americans' cherished cultural norms and national self-image. We shall see in the next chapter that a similar reception allowed Salom Rizk to make a career of telling his life story to thousands of live audiences.

Rihbany's two autobiographical works draw heavily upon the Bible and *The Arabian Nights*, respectively, evoking what Fuad Sha'ban calls "the vision of Zion" and "the dream of Baghdad," the two main ingredients of nineteenth-century American Orientalism (Sha'ban 1991, x). The contradictions between those two registers necessitated that Rihbany write two autobiographical works, not one, as we shall see below. As the first Arab American autobiography, *A Far Journey* had no precedents except other immigrant and minority autobiographies, with which it shares two primary gestures:

> This narrative's excuse for being is, I believe, to be found, first, in that it is the story, not of an individual, but of a type. There are many other children of other lands who have come to the New World as learners of the modes of life and thought of a superior people; who have succeeded in discovering America on its ideal side, and who know and love this country as that Commonwealth of free, enlightened, and beneficent citizens. Second, this story justifies its existence by being a testimony to the unparalleled opportunities of America. (Rihbany 1914, viii)

The autobiographer asserts (against the obvious) that this is not the story of an individual, but of a "type" (out of many conceivable types); in a gesture that confirms the second characteristic of minor literature in Deleuze and Guattari's theory, the autobiographer here merges with members of his community, for whom by such a gesture he claims the right to speak. This gesture, obviously, monopolizes representation: he does not name the other "types"—less successful ones, or ones that did not discover the "ideal" America of which he speaks. Such types are suppressed in his discourse, for they would undermine the project of the autobiography as he defines it.

This authoritative voice also ingratiates itself with its readers through unreserved praise, flattery, and confirmation of their idealized self-image: free, democratic America, the land of opportunity inhabited by "a superior people." The narrative that follows is a success story, from Oriental rags and backwardness to American civilization and riches. This is "America on its *ideal* side"; in the rest of the book, he refrains from describing what he would consider to be its "real" side. It is not until later books, published in 1922 and 1926, that he points to some of America's social problems. For now and in the four books that follow, he seems eager to be accepted as a writer and to promote his vision of the role of the U.S. in the Middle East. Apparently, he believed that challenging his readers directly would impede his attainment of those goals; instead, he assumes the posture of the obsequiously grateful immigrant.

Rihbany's autobiographical discourse and his intellectual project as a cultural translator are located at the intersection of biblical and Orientalist discourses, both of which validate his message and his tactful balancing of implicit critique with explicit endorsement of the adopted country's discursive norms. As Evelyne Shakir argues, however, in comparing Rihbany's to Gibran's biblical discourse,

> While crammed with biblical allusions, [Rihbany's] was a calmer, more Protestant discourse, neither prophetic, nor hortatory. It was instead the unthreatening and familiar voice of the good-humored teacher/minister explicating a text on a Sunday morning (which is exactly who Rihbany was and what he did). In interpreting East to West, Rihbany relied on a religious mythology more deeply rooted in the Western psyche than was a titillating Orientalism. The Bible was the best answer to the *Arabian Nights*. (Shakir 1988, 43).

As we shall see below, Rihbany did, in fact, resort to the exoticism of the *Arabian Nights* in *The Hidden Treasure of Rasmola*, so that contrary to what Shakir implies, he was not trying to undermine "titillating Orientalism." Still, "Rihbany demystifies his Eastern society by drawing it in within the realm of familiar Bible stories, turning its landscape into a Sunday School pastoral. And he consecrates it. The message is clear that a special privilege or mystique attaches to those born in the Holy Land, however impoverished its current circumstances" (44). This consecration and the mystique of the Holy Land give Rihbany a unique authority as a Christian minister that he elaborates upon in his next book, *The Syrian Christ*, published two years after *A Far Journey*.

This posture also gives him authority over the representation of the Orient. As an insider, he knows best what his people and their circumstances are like—that is, he knows the community better than those outsiders who claim to know it: European and American scholars, tourists, politicians, journalists, and missionaries. In effect, Rihbany valorizes the position of the native informant over that of the foreign expert; indeed, the native informant here displaces the Orientalist, but without undermining Orientalism. And, as native informant, his perspective suffers from the classic limitation noted by ethnographers: he projects the provincial norms of his own village, clan, religious sect, and social class onto the entire culture that he claims to represent authoritatively. His limited, and at times prejudicial, knowledge is normalized through the figure of synecdoche: the village of el-Shweir, located in the Christian hills of Mount Lebanon with textbook precision

(Rihbany 1914, 29), stands in effect for all of Syria, and sometimes for the entire "East"; his family and acquaintances represent all Orientals; and the sectarian prejudices of his Christian background provide the only perspective. (This notwithstanding the fact that, by his own account, of this "Orient" he knew only the villages of el-Shweir and Betater, and his "visit to the great city of Beyrout [*sic*] was an epoch-maker" [79].) The provincial, prejudicial knowledge of the native informant is thus projected as universally true of the homogenized world over which he claims authority—an authority belied ironically by the fact that even at the small scale of his village, inter-clan conflict and prejudice are mentioned in the very first paragraph of the book (3).

The biblical framework of the autobiography rests on a cornerstone of Orientalist discourse: the idea of an eternal, unchanging Orient that lies outside the sphere of history. In Rihbany's first two books, this idea manifests itself in biblical style and allusions used to describe contemporary life in Lebanon. Thus, at his birth, visitors "brought their presents with them as did the 'Wise Men' of old on their historic visit to Bethlehem. They sang and were exceeding glad, because unto them a child was born, a son was given" (4). The roof of his father's house "was the Biblical earth-covered flat roof, such as the one on which Peter went up to pray in ancient Joppa" (8). Characteristic of some styles of peasant houses in the mountainous regions of Lebanon and susceptible to leaking on rainy days, Rihbany describes this problem as one that has plagued (all of?) "Syrian" households for millennia: "The writer of the book of Proverbs did not at all exaggerate the ugliness of the situation when he said, 'Continual dropping in a very rainy day and a contentious woman are alike' " (8–9). Village women "carry the water from the fountain, as did the woman from Samaria whom Jesus met at Jacob's well" (11). "The Orient in general has never troubled itself about sanitation . . . in my early years the country was just as Isaiah and Paul left it" (34). In this way, the Orient is "demystified," as Shakir puts it—made familiar by being frozen in mythical time.

The religious discourse of the book encompasses the narrative of his "Americanization," which follows the pattern of the spiritual journeys of saints, prophets, and believers. The trajectory of the book follows the classic pattern of spiritual (auto)biography and saints' lives, moving from false belief to accepting the true faith, followed by doubt, then a moment of epiphany that reconfirms the faith, banishes doubt, and clarifies the straight path. His conversion to Protestantism in the American missionary school in Lebanon represents his acceptance of true religion. The secular equivalent to that conversion is his naturalization as a U.S. citizen, which is described as a spiritual experience: "My heart never thrilled with a holier emotion than when I assented to the oath of allegiance" (218). His devotion to America is very much a religious devotion that follows upon his conversion to Protestantism, and his claim to American identity is an act of faith. This is followed by hardship and doubt—the test of faith. He decides to leave "cosmopolitan . . . New York" (246), where he spent his first eighteen months associating only with other Syrians, for the Midwest so as to know the "real" America (246). He tries to earn a living as a "lecturer on Oriental customs" (255), but the English language becomes one of the many obstacles he faces, along with lack of education, poverty, ignorance of American customs, and social rejection. This phase is described as "my Wilderness-of-Sinai discipline since I left New York" (268). At the height of penury, he "longed for the first time for the 'flesh pots of Egypt' and wished that I had never left Syria. . . . Sobs and tears poured forth simultaneously with, 'Why did I ever leave Syria?' 'Why did I not stay in New York?' 'Is this what America has for me?'" (262–62). Those doubts were dispelled later on in Mount Vernon, Ohio (echoes of Moses at Mount Sinai?), where

> I learned my first lesson in patriotism. Soon after my arrival in that town I strayed into the public square where stands a fine soldiers' monument. It seems to me that my attention had never been strongly challenged by a similar object in this country before . . . [A]s soon as my eyes beheld that significant memorial, I forgot for the moment my weariness and poverty and yielded myself to the mighty challenge of the thought that I was in a country where men died willingly and intelligently for their flag and all it symbolized, and that what the flag did symbolize were ideals worth dying for. (266–67)

This moment of epiphany or enlightenment is a prelude to (and condition for) the improved circumstances that come shortly afterwards: he is permitted for the first time to speak to a Pennsylvania congregation, whose sympathetic attitude seems to have persuaded him to enter the ministry. This decision is reinforced later on in the same year (1893), when his speech on "Turkey and America Contrasted" was repeatedly interrupted by "loud and prolonged applause, regardless of the fact that the service was essentially religious, the time Sunday, and the place a Presbyterian Church" (284–85). Three years later, he became "the regular minister of an American congregation. . . . America, the mother of modern wonders, began to reveal itself to me and in me. I soon became possessed by the consciousness that . . . I had the privilege of being *born again* in a land which more than any other on our planet establishes the truth of the New Testament promise, 'Ask, and it shall be given you; seek, and ye shall find; knock, and it shall be opened unto you'" (275–76, emphasis added). In this way, the secular and fairly common coming-to-America story is consecrated as a spiritual autobiography that bolsters his status not only as a successful immigrant (representative of "a type,"), but also as man of God in a tradition that goes back to St. Augustine.

Rihbany's strategy clearly has the effect of couching his narrative within what Leigh Gilmore calls "culturally prevalent discourses of truth and identity" (Gilmore ix), in this case biblical discourse and that of America as "the new Zion," the fulfillment of human destiny. He simultaneously inscribes himself within what Brunner calls "idealized cultural patterns" (Brunner 40), in this case the immigrant who comes to the U.S., rises from poverty to achieve the American Dream, and confirms his adopted country's self-image as the land of freedom and opportunity. He goes even further than most other immigrants by confirming the superiority of the dominant American religion not only to Islam, about which he has little good to say, but also to Eastern Christianity, into which he was born. At the same time, he does not dare criticize the society in which he wanted to be accepted. Instead, he frequently flatters it and confirms its idealized self-image. This image bears little resemblance to that found in his contemporary W. E. B. Du Bois's *The Souls of Black Folk* (1903), for instance, with its well-known declaration that "the problem of the Twentieth Century is the problem of the color-line" (Du Bois 1). Upon reading about the Civil War, Rihbany glosses over the entire issue of slavery and says that his "soul was fired with admiration for the devotion, heroism, and endurance of the American volunteer soldier, of both the North and the South," and that the experience allowed him "to see clearly what this country, which we newcomers found ready for us with all its unparalleled privileges, cost in blood and treasure to preserve its unity and guard its institutions" (Rihbany 1914, 290). In eliding the core issue of slavery, the direct cause of the Civil War, Rihbany endorses the racial hierarchy and covers over those contradictions in the American system that complicate the idealized image of America as the land of freedom and democracy. Predictably, Rihbany's failure to make the link between the institutional racism that disenfranchised African Americans and the racialization of Arab Americans, which already in his own day was beginning to threaten the immigration and naturalization of Arabs, did nothing to combat the rising tide of xenophobia that culminated in the 1924 immigration laws. The failure to initiate such a critique also disempowered U.S.-born Arab Americans of the next generation, many of whom would internalize anti-Arab racism and try to distance themselves from their immigrant parents' culture.

Rihbany's almost instantaneous success as a speaker in the 1890s, despite his broken English; the launching of his career as a minister; and the authority with which he went on write several books on the Orient, are all due to the remarkable success of this strategy of telling his story squarely within the dominant discourse on American identity, including American Orientalism and racialism. He is stauncher in his adherence to venerable Orientalist mantras like the absolute distinction between East and West than Rihani, who wrestled with them from his earliest works and throughout his career. In comparison, Rihbany is far less critical, and his intellectual project in his first six books consists of elaborating on and further inscribing them. Thus, East is East and West is West, and the twain can never meet except along the developmental logic that posits Orientals as children and Occidentals as adults, or the gendered logic that describes the ones as feminine and the others masculine, or the opposition between a mystical East and a rational West:

> the impassable gulf between my Syrian life and my American life is only seeming, and not real. I am conscious of no loss of continuity. Just as manhood *fulfills* rather than *destroys* childhood, so does America's large, tumultuous life tend to realize the possibilities with which the ancient, mystic, dreamy Orient endowed me. So to Syria, my loving, untutored mother, as to America, my virile, resourceful teacher, I offer my profound and lasting gratitude. (ix)

The only link between those everlasting and contrasting essences is Rihbani himself. His narrative is that of an evolved, reconstructed Oriental, and that is precisely what authorizes his voice and justifies his stance as interpreter of East and West. That is, his autobiographical discourse and his intellectual stance in subsequent books are equally invested in the construct of the Orient (hence his self-Orientalizing) and in the myth of America and "the West." The fascinating thing about Rihbany's texts is the way in which he tries, through logical acrobatics, to rehabilitate the Orient while holding on tenaciously to the typology of Orientalism, with its dichotomies and its hierarchy of values. This is the crucial paradox animating his work, and when he tries to move beyond it in his last book, as we shall see, his project exhausts itself.

In *The Hidden Treasure of Rasmola*, Rihbany continues this self-Orientalizing albeit in a different mode, that of Oriental romance, which operates within the framework of *The Arabian Nights*. First published in abbreviated form in the *Atlantic Monthly* in 1914, the year *A Far Journey* was published, *The Hidden Treasure of Rasmola* (1920) is presented as a supplement to *A Far Journey* that would have constituted too great a digression had it been included in the book. *The Hidden Treasure* reads much like an adventure story, complete with, as the title promises, treasures hidden in secret caves (reminiscent of "Ali Baba and the Forty Thieves"), magical potions, mysterious magicians, and—in an Orientalist twist on the original stories that foreshadows Disney's *Aladdin*—hostile, threatening "Mohammedans." It is the story of a youthful Rihbany who, still working as a stonemason, discovers an underground chamber while excavating the foundation of a new house. The discovery hints at a hidden treasure guarded by an evil spirit, hence the need to enlist the services of a magician and a local thug who eventually makes off with the booty. The entertainment and humor of the story depend on its skillful patterning after the classic formula of the quest narrative, but in a lighter key than in epic and medieval romance, for the element of the supernatural, which in those genres solemnly connects the human world with the metaphysical realm, is reduced here to the laughable ravings of primitive, irrational Orientals, hopelessly mired in ancient superstitions and irredeemably childish, naïve, and impractical in their pursuit of grand illusions. Not surprisingly, therefore, this is an unfulfilled quest narrative, a farcical variation on the heroic genre. Read in the context of *A Far Journey* and its ideological project, *The Hidden Treasure* could not possibly have ended with the attainment of wealth in Lebanon. Success, whether material or spiritual, could only come when he is able to "relate myself to the higher life of America" (1914, 253), in view of which material wealth in Lebanon would be hollow.

In that sense, *The Hidden Treasure* complements the project of *A Far Journey*, but in a different key. One book draws heavily upon biblical style, imagery, and themes, while the other relies on the *Arabian Nights* as a frame of reference. Syrians of today are indistinguishable from their biblical forebears, or, we now learn, from characters in the *Arabian Nights*. This discrepancy in mode is symptomatic of a deeper contradiction in Orientalist discourse and it necessitated that Rihbany's autobiography be split into two books, the one a solemn spiritual and cultural "journey," the other a light and entertaining romance. The decision to separate the two stories, therefore, represents astute literary judgment on Rihbany's part, but the question remains why he felt the need to write his life story in two different and discrepant modes. The purpose he gives for the Rasmola story is this: "The character of this adventure made it possible for me to introduce my readers to such regions of Oriental psychology and life as I had no occasion to traverse in my former books [*A Far Journey, The Syrian Christ, Militant American and Jesus Christ, America Save the Near East*], and which in reality constitute the essential value of the present publication," and also "as the fullest known commentary on the parable of the 'treasure hid in the field' (Matt. 13:44), and I ardently hope that our life-quest may be the wealth recommended in that parable, and not mere silver and gold" (1920, vii–viii). The Oriental romance is allegorized and inserted within a biblical framework, as a way of reconciling or bridging the two registers of American Orientalism. "The regions of Oriental psychology and life" that he reveals in *The Hidden Treasure*—superstition, magic, intrigue, thievery—are less dignified than those other spiritual regions connected with the Bible, its prophets, and the Holy Land. The Oriental now emerges as a walking contradiction, one that is inherent in Oriental stereotypes: at once spiritual and superstitious, dignified and base, sincere yet a liar, irrational but crafty, and so on.

To his readers, this validates the belief that the Orient is entirely knowable within the framework of the Bible and the *Arabian Nights*, the two registers of nineteenth-century American Orientalism. In fact, Rihbany seems to imply that the Orient and its inhabitants *cannot* be fully known outside of that dual framework. Although he apprehended the irreconcilability of those two registers in a literary sense, he failed or refused to draw out its epistemological implications. Instead, pseudo-scientific generalities about the "Oriental mind" and "Oriental psychology" are recycled and reaffirmed by an Oriental who claims inside knowledge: "The scenes here portrayed are not only real phases of the life of the common people of Syria, among whom I was born and brought up, but were in one way or another connected with our activities in the secret and dread enterprise" (viii). In a show of humility that serves to bolster his authority, the native informant implicates himself in that representation—although, of course, readers are meant to understand he has since been weaned from infantile Orientalness by his conversion to Protestantism and by America, his "virile tutor."

Yet in a move that seems to undermine his assertions about the representability of the Orient, Rihbany gives us a rare glimpse of the creative process under such conditions of discourse when he adds that the events of this narrative "have been reproduced in this work with only such dramatization as every writer knows is necessary to raise such a piece of literature, as far as possible, from the sphere of mere photography" (viii). That an ostensibly autobiographical account needs to be "dramatized," that it constitutes "a piece of literature" that ought to be "raised" above the level of "mere photography" are all rare admissions of artifice on the part of any autobiographer, given autobiography's claim to truthful and objective narration of real events. Autobiography's truth claim can only be undermined by its association with such strategies as romanticization, exaggeration, and dramatization, for while contemporary theories of autobiography find those and other literary and discursive strategies to be inevitable and consider truth and objectivity no more than discursive effects, autobiography works by maintaining the illusion of true-to-life objectivity. Thus, while serving up a highly romanticized narrative, bolstered by the authority of Orientalism and by his own experience, Rihbany seems simultaneously to undermine the narrative's truth claim by framing it as "dramatization" and as "literature," which inevitably anchors the work in the fanciful world of the *Arabian Nights* rather than in historical reality. This point may, of course, be lost on readers who are under the impression that the *Arabian Nights* depicts the Arabs of today, a belief propagated by Richard Burton in the "Terminal Essay" (1883) he appended to his translation of the medieval Arabic work.[7] Yet Rihbany's implicit differentiation between the truth-claims of autobiography and the conventions of Oriental romance, and his tacit acknowledgement of the disjuncture that Said would later on describe between lived experience and Orientalist description, indicate Rihbany's ambivalence about both. On the one hand, he is committed to Orientalism as a frame of reference, one to which he could envision no alternative (and indeed had no vested interest in such an alternative, be it sectarian, professional, or ideological, considering how skillfully he manipulated the discourse to serve his purposes). On the other hand, he sensed the discrepancy between stereotype and experiential knowledge and could not reconcile himself to the inferiority of his "race"—of himself—despite his unquestioning acceptance of racialism as a doctrine and his obsequious flattery of "Anglo-Saxon" superiority.

The Oriental Occidentalist

This contradiction is more pronounced in Rihbany's theological and political books than in his two autobiographies. In those books, the exaggerated show of humility masks an assertion of (personal, if not cultural) superiority: he not only knows the "Orient" better than Orientalists, he also knows the "Occident" better than it knows itself, by virtue of his intermediary position. He does that while acknowledging the authority of Orientalism; in fact, he assumes the stance of the Orientalist vis-à-vis the "Orient," before turning a proto-Occidentalist gaze toward the U.S.

In *The Syrian Christ* (1916), Rihbany tries to explain how negative stereotypes of Orientals—that they lie, exaggerate, and mistreat women—are misconceptions resulting from the ways in which the Oriental's rhetorical excess tends to be misinterpreted, in the same way that biblical events and attitudes sometimes do not harmonize with American social norms (107–39, 313–39). This he tries to do without critiquing the process of stereotyping itself; he is unhappy only with some negative stereotypes but has no problem perpetuating others. Indeed, his approach to interpreting the Orient relies heavily on stereotyping. Thus, the Oriental's "heart is in the right place. He is quick-witted, kind, generous, pious, obedient to parents, and a lover of his home. So far as all these fundamentals are concerned, I find no great difference between the Easterners and the Westerners." But difference there is, and it lies in the level of development: "compared to his Western cousin, the son of the Near East has only a slight acquaintance with the *art* of living. The working-out of details with the view of creating harmony has always seemed to him vanity and vexation of spirit. His intense desire for simple, spontaneous, easy living has always refused to be encumbered by exacting standards. In this respect he is a boy in man's clothing" (319).

Yet that state of primitive innocence enjoys a spiritual advantage. The premise of *The Syrian Christ* is that Jesus and the writers of the Bible are Rihbany's fellow Syrians. Since Syria and Syrians do not change, and since he is a Syrian himself, he has greater insight into the life and teachings of Jesus, as well as the temperament and rhetorical style of the Bible, than Westerners do. The book interprets scenes from the Bible in light of the author's knowledge of his homeland, which supersedes Western knowledge of both:

> From the fact that I was born not far from where the Master was born, and brought up under almost the identical conditions under which he lived, I have an "inside view" of the Bible which, by the nature of things, a Westerner cannot have. And I know the conditions of life in Syria of to-day are essentially as they were in the time of Christ, not from the study of the mutilated tablets of the archaeologist and the antiquarian, precious as such discoveries are, but from the simple fact that, as a sojourner in this Western world, whenever I open my Bible it reads like a letter from home. (5)

The audacious feat accomplished here almost amounts to subverting "Western" knowledge of Christianity, even while cementing and basing his argument on one of the central tenets of Orientalism. Yet it is not only the idea of the eternal Orient that in Rihbany's hands becomes a double-edged sword; Orientalist racialism and culturalism are likewise turned against the "West" by an Oriental Occidentalist who speaks of the "Western mind" with the authority of a veteran Protestant minister in American churches:

> [W]hat I have learned from intimate associations with the Western mind, during almost a score of years in the American pulpit, is that, with the exception of the few specialists, it is extremely difficult, if not impossible, for a people to understand fully a literature which has not sprung from that people's own racial life. As a repository of divine revelation the Bible knows no geographical limits. Its spiritual truths are from God to man. But as literature the Bible is an imported article in the Western world, especially in the home of the Anglo-Saxon race. The language of the Scriptures, the mentality and the habits of life which form the setting of their spiritual precepts, and the mystic atmosphere of those precepts themselves, have come forth from the soul of a people far removed from the races of the West in almost all the modes of its earthly life. (7)

The polite nod to the "few specialists" is closely followed by a near dismissal of all of Western knowledge of one of the pillars of its own cultural identity, the Bible and Christianity. The West, it turns out, does not quite know itself as well as the

Oriental Occidentalist knows it. The Syrian immigrant's attitude toward the society and "race" he describes parallel exactly the Orientalist's attitude toward the Orient. In both cases, the Other is homogenous (with a single "mind"), diametrically different, and entirely knowable to the foreign expert in ways that it cannot know itself.

The difference is in the relative strength of the expert and the society described (an Oriental describing the Occident rather than an Occidental describing the Orient), as well as the motivation, function, and intended audience of that description. If, as Said demonstrated, Orientalism was and continues to be imperialism's tool, a high-handed and condescending discourse on peoples it regards as inferior, Rihbany's discourse is addressed to the United States, which he reveres as the pinnacle of civilization, and the one Western power he deems capable of answering the plea in the title of one of his subsequent books, *America Save the Near East* (1918)—a plea for U.S. intervention to save Syria from European imperialism and to establish a federal government there under U.S. protection after World War I. (His 1917 book, *Militant America and Jesus Christ*, advanced a religious argument for U.S. military intervention in the war.) Contrary to the prevailing views of Arab leaders and intellectuals, including Ameen Rihani, Rihbany took the view of British and French officials who considered the Arabs unprepared for political independence at that time (1918, 142–43), which is not surprising in view of his Orientalist belief in a childish East. What he wanted for the region was U. S. rather than British or French tutelage. In effect, Rihbany maintains at once an Orientalist attitude toward the Orient (Orientals can neither speak for nor govern themselves; they need both American protection and Americanized Orientals to speak for them), and the idea of the wisdom and spiritual maturity of the East as the fountainhead of Christianity, which affords him his unique expertise on the Bible and special insight into the workings of "the Western mind." The first gesture is one of flattery and ingratiation in pursuit of a political aim, the second bolsters his claim to authoritative knowledge.

What undergirds Rihbany's incredibly bold, albeit contradictory, argument is the racialist, culturalist logic of Orientalism itself, which he closely follows all the way to its inevitable conclusion. In *Wise Men from the East and from the West* (1922), he undertakes to describe the Eastern and Western "minds" by way of commenting on European colonialism in the Arab world and the post-World War I settlement, which he tried to influence as a representative of Syrian Americans at the Paris peace conference. This is Rihbany's most political book, half of which is devoted to outlining the diametrical differences between East and West, while the other half details the history of European colonialism in the Arab world until 1922. "East is East and West is West" is the title of part I, which begins thus: "There is an Oriental mind, and there is an Occidental mind. They are two distinctive types of mind. The twain may meet, but they never can be so joined together that they cannot be put asunder. The difference between them is like the difference between the metals; it is constitutional" (1922, 17). He further opines, "The essential differences which appear between the races of men must have been in the beginning in the mind of the Creator. They could not have been 'accidental variations from type'" (18). The Oriental and the Occidental emerge as perennial "passive and aggressive types" (35–45), respectively. Their character traits, sociopolitical behavior, and religious attitudes are polar opposites. Not surprisingly, and in view of the supposed Oriental indolence, aversion to machinery, and passivity, Rihbany cannot account for the flourishing of Arab Islamic civilization and its military conquests in the early centuries of Islam, or those of the Ottoman Turks later on. He simply ignores all of that in this astonishing passage:

> For many centuries the East has been invaded by the West and intermittently placed under its domination. In successive waves the 'superior culture' of the West has flowed over the more ancient and passive East. The Greeks, the Romans, the Crusaders, and the more recent imperialistic colonizers of Gauls and Saxons have, all of them, sought to awaken the East from its deep slumber and lead it to the fresher springs of their own respective civilizations, but to little purpose. The horse has been led to the water, but could not be made to drink (23, repeated on 173).

By what evidence the Crusaders can be said to have had a superior civilization to that of Islam at that time is not entirely clear, neither is the reason why Rihbany omits such decisive events as the Arab conquest of Spain, the eventual defeat of the Crusaders, and the Ottoman expansion into Europe, all the way to the gates of Vienna. They simply do not fit with the discursive norms he obeys, whether out of historical ignorance, which is unlikely, or ideological imperatives. Rihbany also reveals his endorsement of the medieval Europeans' justification for launching the Crusades (the animal imagery he uses in that passage is revealing) and echoes the attitude of some Maronites who claim descent from Frankish Crusaders or from the Phoenicians so as to distance themselves ethnically from Arabs and Islam.

Given the logic of that passage, British and French colonialism become a historical necessity: the British "found themselves (in the case of India and Egypt) compelled to assume the responsibility of rulers, much against their own original intentions" (166). In 1882, they

> *had* to act in order to save the situation. . . . The British entered Egypt, and the 'turbulent' state of the country compelled them to stay in it for so many years in order to save it from anarchy. It would seem that the English never went forth seeking an empire, but that the empire which they now control in some unaccountable way fell into their hands. The French could tell a somewhat similar story with regard to their colonial possessions. (166–67)

The hesitant and barely noticeable irony here becomes more apparent when he goes on to describe the colonizers' competition among themselves for control of the East. What transpires then is that even though the European powers' motives may not be pure, colonization itself is inevitable, even justifiable, because it is in the nature of the dynamic, aggressive, virile West to invade the passive, static, feminine East. The "only question," for Rihbany, is

> How shall the renewal of the life of that Old World be effected? Shall the West swallow up the East and obliterate its distinctive characteristics? Even if that were possible, it would be an irreparable loss to the world. The world needs a characteristic Oriental civilization as it needs a characteristic Occidental civilization. That colorful, poetical Oriental type of life must not be utterly destroyed. Yet the West cannot fundamentally change the soul of the East without causing such destruction. On this the imperialistic colonizers seem to be bent. (159)

Rihbany's criticism of European colonialism is tempered with rapturous praise for "the Anglo-Saxon race," especially "the American Anglo-Saxon" (10–11). He is careful, in other words, not to criticize "the West," per se, but to play the well-rehearsed tune of American exceptionalism, which places U.S. intervention above the "European intrigues" he invoked earlier (1918, 142–47). However, by late 1922, when the book was published, it had become clear that the U.S. was not going to "save the Near East" by obtaining a mandate there, as Rihbany had wished, yet he still hoped that the U.S. would exercise a stabilizing influence in it (1922, 263–64).

Rihbany's stance is far more conformist than Ameen Rihani's, but in his defense, it must be noted that Rihbany understood that the best he could do with his own and his culture's foreignness in America was to try to "make it respectable" (Shakir 1996, 6). Yet he could not do that in the early twentieth century while explicitly challenging dominant discourses (American Orientalism, culturalism, racialism, Manifest Destiny), even if he did not accept them (he probably did) and had the tools to do so (which he did not, given his background, education, and intellectual orientation). Even if he did, an oppositional stance would have ill-suited his purpose of being accepted by the conservative mainstream to which he sought to belong, and whose politics he largely shared. What he does, therefore, is retool those discourses to his advantage. Racial theory, which assumes a hierarchy of the human races, can be modified to defend the right to racial difference. Orientalism, which posits eternal and opposing characteristics of East and West, can be mobilized against what he saw as colonial efforts to westernize the East and obliterate its cultures. An appeal to Manifest Destiny can induce America to check European imperialism and to implement political and social reform. The utopian vision he proposes is, therefore, one of selfless "help" (298) from the strong to the weak, the two becoming "cooperative friends" (299). However, "if it is to be of significant value to either the East or the West, a new Eastern civilization must be genuinely Eastern. It must not be a replica of Western civilization, which itself needs a hundred reforms" (299–300). It is not a question of a Hegelian synthesis of East and West, as Rihani advocated, but rather of creating a "better East" (298) that would be more suitable to Western business interests (299), yet would remain free from the material and spiritual ravages of industrialization discernible in "New York, Chicago, and London" (300). A "reconstructed" Oriental would be able to "teach his Occidental brother . . . [the] great spiritual maxims which have guided the course of his life for so many centuries" (301). At the end of the day, East would still be East, and West West.

Within this scheme, the question of cultural translation is raised in terms reminiscent of the *Nahda* discourse in the nineteenth-century Levant:

> The agencies of contact between those two worlds must be friendly intercourse and amorous spiritual interpenetration, and not the creeping tentacles of the invader. Whatever the East may have to borrow of Western thought must be translated in transmission in order that it may do its beneficent work. Like poetry, when translated from one language into another, the thought of the West must be translated to the East according to the spirit and not the letter. The East should be allowed to borrow from the West on the East's own terms. Its own thinkers and wise men must be its mediums of transmission and agencies of transformation. They must not receive Western thought as they would merchandise, but absorb, so far as may be desirable, the spirit of the West and reëxpress it to the East in its own forms of thought. Only in this way can the East distil wisdom from Western civilization and assimilate it into character. If it is to be of significant value to either the East or the West, a new Eastern civilization must be genuinely Eastern. It must not be a replica of Western civilization, which itself needs a hundred reforms. (299–300)

Cultural translation here is a transformative process of selective and adaptive borrowing rather than slavish mimicry. This ideal translation can be an agent of positive transformation and a buffer against its potential function as a vehicle for cultural imperialism. Like the ideal form of cultural exchange Rihbany proposes, his notion of translation seems utopian under the historical conditions he has just outlined in the book. Like his use of racial theory and Orientalist discourse, it is another form of defense against imperialism and cultural extinction. Unlike the leaders of the *Nahda*, however, whose stance toward Europe was much more confident and critically selective (in part because of their intellectual formation and partly also because they conceived their reform project before the spread of European dominance), Rihbany advances this view from a position of acquiescence to imperialism.

Rihbany performs a similar kind of translation in his own books. He wrote in English for American readers and had been a Protestant preacher and lecturer on Syria before becoming a writer. His success in both vocations led him, by way of publishing well-received autobiographical essays in *The Atlantic Monthly* magazine, to publish *A Far Journey*. Encouraged by its success, he continued to write books that, like his lectures and his autobiography, explained—or translated—the East to America according to the precept he explains in the passage cited above: by rendering it in terms intelligible to Americans, "according to the spirit and not the letter." He may be said to have done so according to both the spirit and the letter, not of the "East," as such, which is after all an Orientalist construct, but of the "West," the East's discursive and ideological counterpart. An example of this is his habit, throughout his books, of referring to Muslims as "Mohammedans" and to Islam as "Mohammedanism." Whereas Christianity takes its name from that of Christ, Islam (which literally means "surrender [to God]") differentiates itself from Christianity both by denying the divinity of Christ and Muhammad, who are revered as human prophets, and by negating the Christian doctrine of the Trinity and asserting the oneness of God. To Muslims, "Mohammedan" and "Mohammedanism" are offensive terms used by Europeans, out of ignorance or malice, to imply worship of Muhammad. Christian Arabs never use those terms, as Rihbany without a doubt understood, so his word choice (which is a translational choice) constitutes a validation of Euro-American prejudice or ignorance, and a missed opportunity to improve cultural understanding. His translation, therefore, effectively recreated a "Western" text on the "East" that confirmed his readers' fundamental ideas of themselves and their civilization's Other. But he tried to nuance some of those ideas and to increase their positive content. If the outlines of the Orient could not be redrawn, he could perhaps manipulate light and shade, modify color and perspective, but all the while maintaining the religious prejudices of his own background in Lebanon, which coincided with the religious prejudices of his American readers. The limitations of this approach—historical and ideological limitations which nonetheless allowed him to reap some personal advantages—restrict the scope of Rihbany's project and reduce his books and the form of translation they practice to being an instance of what Said described as the modern Orient participating in its own Orientalizing (*Orientalism* 325).

In his last book on the subject of "East" and "West," *Seven Days with God* (1926), Rihbany attempted to complicate some of those representations, especially the evolutionary scale he had used in *A Far Journey* and *The Syrian Christ*, depicting Orientals as children and Occidentals as adults. He also further questioned, as the title of one chapter indicates, "Misconceptions of Eastern Life." *Seven Days with God*, in fact, asserts the equality of East and West, but stops short of explicitly contradicting his previous book:

> In my other publications I did not refrain from pointing out what seems to me to be the defects of Western civilization; nor do I feel like shirking such a duty in the present volume. But I deem it also my legitimate duty to confess and proclaim the fact that, as one whose youth was cast in an Oriental mould, I find human life in the West to rest on the same everlasting arms which sustain the inner life of man everywhere in the world. (6)

With this commonality also goes mutual misunderstandings: "Easterners in general have acquired an incorrect understanding of the word 'materialism,' and Westerners in general an incorrect notion of the word 'mysticism'" (6–7). Clearing those misunderstandings up prepares the way for future synthesis between East and West, which are in equal need of each other, after all:

> Just as the East to-day is adopting the discoveries of the West in the field of science, so did the West adopt the discoveries of the East in the field of religion. Its task, therefore, has been to restate and interpret those ancient systems of religion so as to make them fit its own mentality and serve its own peculiar needs. The struggle in this field never was more strenuous than it is to-day. The Old and the New are face to face in the field of

> honor. The one is armed with the venerable idea of fixity and certainty, the other with that of movement and inquiry. To which is the battle? To neither, it is neither the Old because of its age, nor to the New because of its youth. *The selective processes of experience and constructive criticism will bring together whatever is true, good, and beautiful in both systems, and thus make of the twain one new order which shall possess both the stability of age and the progressiveness of youth. The future belongs to that form of thought which possesses spiritual health and belongs to it only so long as it has that quality.* (19–20, emphasis added)

The synthesis envisioned here represents a departure from Rihbany's view, expressed in *Wise Men from the East and from the West*, published four years earlier, that the East will always be East, the West West, and from the position he took in his earlier books that positive influence flows in one direction only, from superior to inferior cultures. Whatever may have occasioned that shift in Rihbany's position is not entirely clear, but his contradictory project seems to have exhausted itself. In the eighteen years between the publication of this book and his death in 1944, Rihany wrote only one more book, *The Five Interpretations of Jesus* (1940), which focused on contemporary debates in biblical scholarship, with no reference to politics or East–West relations. It may also be that by 1926, he felt his position as an American and as a respected writer and public figure to be secure enough for him to question the dominant discourse, whereas earlier he felt compelled to abide by it, and even went the extra mile to justify it. It may also have something to do with *Seven Days with God* being the most theological and least worldly of his books until that point, and the synthesis proposed in it being a version of the messianic restoration of prelapsarian wholeness.[8] Humanity's "seven days with God," as the title prophesies, would be the fullness of historical time, a triumph over evil and schism, including the dichotomy between East and West. Not so much a negation of Kipling's dictum as an addendum to it: never the twain shall meet—in this world.

4

The Retreat of Cultural Translation

> In my early show days, "Arab" and "acrobat" were synonymous.
>
> —GEORGE HAMID
>
> The more miserable I made my story, the more they enjoyed it.
>
> —SALOM RIZK

"Arabian" Acts

The middle decades of the twentieth century saw Arab American writers retreat from the project of cultural translation that harnessed the efforts of their predecessors. That project was formulated by immigrants who conceived of themselves as two-way interpreters and reformers, and was predicated on bilingualism and cultural symbiosis. The 1924 immigration law halted the arrival of newcomers who might have continued that effort. Growing up during the internationally isolationist and domestically assimilationist decades following World War I, the writers who came to the U.S. as children before the 1924 laws, or who were not otherwise affected by them, all but repudiated their heritage. By the time they wrote their books in the 1940s, the Depression, the rise of Fascism in Europe, and World War II had further solidified the prevalent attitudes toward immigrants and things foreign. The autobiographies of Salom Rizk, *Syrian Yankee* (1943), and George Hamid, *Circus* (1950), are immigrant success stories, yet, unlike the earlier autobiographies of Abraham Rihbany and George Haddad, Rizk's and Hamid's texts evidence a turning away from the pioneers' declared goal of facilitating a better understanding between cultures.

George A. Hamid (1896–?) arrived from Lebanon as a child in 1906 to work as an acrobat. His autobiography was written down "as told to his son George A. Hamid, Jr." (Hamid 3). A legendary tumbler, Hamid takes pride in that in his "early show days, 'Arab' and 'acrobat' were synonymous" (9). The circus acts in which he participated bore names like "Sons of the Desert" (90) and "Streets of Cairo" (157) and featured Arabian costumes, sword fights, bellydancers, and tom-toms (159). Shortly after he came to the U.S. at the age of eleven to work in his uncle's troupe, which had been touring with Buffalo Bill's circus, the latter put him in "Arab" (read Bedouin) regalia and taught him how to ride a horse for the show. Eventually, Hamid formed his own "Arabian" troupe. Reading his autobiography, one sees how his and his companions' very survival sometimes depended on securing one of those acts, and how starvation was for them a constant threat. Hamid proved to be a resourceful manager and astute businessman, rising to become a circus owner and organizer of state fairs. His is a rags-to-riches story, and his account of it is, characteristically, fast-paced and action-packed. There is hardly any introspection or reflection on social or political matters, and the Orientalist burlesque that sustained his career is not seen as problematic from his narrative perspective.

Nor was cultural identity, although his self-identification is inconsistent: he is an Arab in the statement quoted in the epigraph to this chapter and found in the first paragraph of his book, but when his future mother-in-law objects to his courtship of her daughter on account of her being "Jersey City aristocracy" and his being "just an Arab," he begs to differ: "I am Lebanese." This elicits the response that "Arab, Syrian, Lebanese—they're all the same to her" (149). That is the only instance of prejudice that he recounts, and it does not deter his plans for marriage. Elsewhere, he is able to use religious difference to his advantage. When two Moroccan acrobats in his troupe refused to eat the pork served by the cooks, he explained the taboo to the circus owner and secured for his troupe fancier meals of lamb, beef, and veal, so that the other performers' "eyes popped when they spotted our meal that night—and every day and night thereafter" (174). Hamid and his two cousins, also acrobats in the troupe, were Christian, a fact that he did not care to reveal. When suitable, his Arab background was cunningly conflated with Islam.

Like George Haddad more than three decades earlier, Hamid illustrates the fact that the relatively untutored autobiographer is less likely to follow the discursive protocols of Orientalism than better-educated writers. Haddad's and Hamid's autobiographies were ghostwritten by their children, and their professions did not require any serious engagement with the Euro-American tradition of Orientalist writing, even though both professions were based on profiting from Americans' perceptions of Arabs: one was a merchant trading in "Oriental" goods, the other an "Arabian" showman. Yet both endeavored to paint a more positive image of their culture than they encountered in the U.S. Though they did not tackle the question of representation directly in any sustained or theoretical manner, and only rarely did they mention their encounters with prejudice, it is not difficult to discern the sorts of pressures they sought to resist in their artless, matter-of-fact chronicles of their lives. Their individual success stories give intimations of their desire to project a positive image of their people, although they were circumscribed by representational norms of which they were not always or fully aware.

More American Than Americans

Salom Rizk (1909–73) was quite different in that respect, for he projected an image of himself as, first and foremost, a super-patriotic American and denigrated the Old Country in declaring his devotion to a new one. Rizk was born in the village of Ain Arab to a Lebanese father and an American mother who died in childbirth while his father, brothers, and uncles were in the U.S. He was raised by his grandmother, "Kbashy the Magnificent," as he calls her in the title of the first chapter of his autobiography, *Syrian Yankee* (1943), but she hid his eligibility for U.S. citizenship from him in order to prevent him from leaving her, as her children had done. He describes her as a Shahrazad figure who tells stories to educate and tame fearsome and unspeakably cruel Muslim males, who, like Shahrayar, are thirsty for the blood of their helpless wives at the least suspicion of infidelity (Rizk 3–13). Rizk proves to be as skillful a storyteller as his grandmother, and this familiar *Arabian Nights* script empowers his grandmother but also reinforces some of the most prevalent stereotypes. The powerful Kbashy contradicts the stereotype of the downtrodden Arab woman but reinforces others that emerge from the same discursive register. Moreover, even though she cares for him and teaches him through storytelling, she stands in the way of his success, hiding his right to U.S. citizenship from him and delaying his immigration for years. If Kbashy stands for tradition (Shahrazad as the repository of cultural wisdom), this is a tradition that opposes everything that the U.S. comes to represent for Rizk: freedom, opportunity, progress, and modernity.

Upon Kbashy's death, Rizk goes into the care of his other grandmother, Gontoosy, after a period of homelessness. Another powerful figure, she travels far over dangerous territory to secure grain for the village on the eve of World War I and upon her return is "hailed as a Joseph bringing salvation to a starving village" (45). Encouraged by her success, ten village men attempt to do the same and are never seen again (ten is probably a proverbial number here, so that she would have been described formulaically as a woman worth ten men). She is no wise storytelling Shahrazad, but a heroic Joseph. With Gontoosy, the frame of reference shifts to the Bible. As Rihbany did earlier, Rizk reproduces the Orient within the twin frameworks of American Orientalism. Potentially subversive examples of strong women are tamed—Orientalized—in observance of discursive strictures.[1]

A schoolteacher who knew his father in the U.S. informs Rizk of his mother's nationality, further explaining that the U.S. is "not like Syria. It is really a country like heaven" (70). By the end of the interview, the child is in ecstasy:

> the land of hope . . . the land of peace . . . the land of contentment . . . the land of liberty . . . the land of brotherhood . . . the land of plenty . . . where God has poured out wealth . . . where the dreams of men come true . . . where everything is bigger and grander and more beautiful than it has ever been anywhere else in the world . . . where wheat grows waist high, shoulder high, sky high, and as thick as the hair on your head . . . (71–72)

This goes on for another half-page, then: "Now it grew too big, too miraculous, too heavenly. It sounded like the fairylands my grandmother used to tell about" (72). It takes several years, however, to prove his identity to U.S. consulate officials in Beirut, before he finally arrives in Iowa to join his relatives. Still speaking no English, he works in a slaughterhouse, where he quickly encounters hostility from other workers, who call him "a foreigner," much to his consternation, since he thinks of himself as an American. Recalling his woeful disappointment and feelings of rejection, he writes, "I forget how many stages of descent are in Dante's *Inferno*, but there aren't as many as there are in a packing plant. . . . I actually wondered if this was America, the America I had dreamed so much about, the land I was ready to give my soul to come to" (139). At the bottom of despair, he wonders, "Why did I have to be born in Syria, anyway, and fall heir to all this contempt, ridicule, and abuse?" (159). Eventually, the provocations anger him enough to retaliate and to quit the job (144–45), but the driving force in his life from that point on is to prove his worthiness as an American.

Working as a cobbler, learning English, and attending school, his strategy is to tell his life story, in which he contrasts Syria and America and preaches the virtues of the latter. Unlike Rihani, Gibran, Rihbany, and Haddad, Rizk is not interested in improving American understanding of Syria. Rather, his concern is with improving America's understanding of itself. Like those earlier writers, Rizk presents himself as an immigrant with superior knowledge; however, that knowledge does not derive from the "East's" reserves of wisdom, as Rihani, Gibran, and Rihbany claimed, but rather from its poverty and backwardness, which give Rizk a greater appreciation of America than Americans have. The Orient serves not so much as a mirror but as a foil; it has little to teach America except by negative example. Its shortcomings amplify America's greatness, which is not well enough appreciated by its native-born citizens. He shares Rihbany's reverence for America and his strategy of flattery, but, unlike him, Rizk attaches no biblical mystique to Syria, even though he describes it at times in the same terms: "In the backward parts of Syria life is as primitive as in Biblical times" (16–17). This "primitiveness" is simply "backward," without any of the spiritual appeal found in Rihbany or Gibran. With nothing to recommend it to America in Rizk's account, the Old Country's reputation reaches its lowest level in the accounts of immigrant writers: in Rihani's novel, it is a place to return to after the shortcomings of America are revealed; in Gibran and Rihbany, it is the land of prophets and spiritual wisdom, however fallen on hard times; in Haddad and Hamid, it is a cherished homeland, repeatedly visited with pleasure; in Rizk, however, it is a godforsaken place the only merit of which is that it sets off the greatness of America. If for the Arab American writers who came before him first-hand knowledge of two cultures authorized their perspective and their role as cultural translators, with Rizk that knowledge validates his claim to a greater appreciation of America than Americans have; and while earlier Arab Americans worked to close the gap between cultures, Rizk widens it.

Like Rihbany two decades earlier, Rizk's success as a speaker and autobiographer is due to his ability to frame his life story within dominant American discourses. He is, first of all, the destitute immigrant for whom America represents salvation. Secondly, although he experiences great difficulties at first, his success confirms his faith in America as the land of opportunity. Third, he argues for the superiority of the U.S. not only to the Old Country, but also to Europe, something that underwrites American exceptionalism. Rihbany used this recipe for success earlier, but Rizk adds two more ingredients to it: he freely endorses the denigration of Arabs and Islam, and he loudly proclaims his sympathy with Zionism. I will illustrate those five points in the remainder of this chapter.

The first two points are evidenced in his account of his first lecture, delivered at the Rotary Club in Ames, Iowa, in the late 1920s:

> I forgot my prepared speech and told my story just the way I had told it to the kids at school [where his teacher had asked him to tell his story to his classmates]: How I was born in Syria and my mother died, leaving me to be cared for by my grandmother. How the death of my grandmother left me a miserable and ragged orphan in war-torn Syria. How I managed to survive by eating raw birds' eggs and roots in the hills. How I learned I was an American citizen. How it took five long, painful years to prove it. How at last I came to America, and how I felt when I saw this vast, rich land with its great farms and teeming cities. How I almost lost America in a packing plant, and how I found it again in a public school. How I appreciated the privileges and opportunities of this great and miraculous land, the friendliness and helpfulness of its people, especially those who had helped me so much in Ames. (Rizk 193–94)

Later on he would admit that "the more miserable I made my story, the more they enjoyed it" (303). But from early on, he understood why the exaggeration of his sufferings so enthralled his audience:

> When I got through, I sat down and everybody else stood up. They applauded until Mr. Davis motioned me to stand up, too. I knew they were not applauding me. They were applauding America, the land where something like this could happen to anybody, a land where a man was free, with the help of his fellows, to work out his destiny. I knew that I was living proof to them of what America was and what America could be. They were proud of a nation because of me. But I could not feel proud. It was a very great and a very humbling experience. (194)

He immediately found out that telling his story in that way not only guaranteed his acceptance, but also that he would be richly rewarded for it:

> When the meeting broke up, everybody came to shake hands with me. People invited me to their homes. They wanted me to meet their children. They asked me to speak to their clubs. They offered to lend me money to fulfill my ambitions. All this sudden flood of warmth and hospitality, all this friendliness and generosity awakened in me a feeling I had been trying to capture from the first day I landed in America—the feeling that I belonged here, that I was accepted. (194)

This vivid picture of the powerful effect of his rhetorical performance explains how he could go on telling the same story over and over again, first at the invitation of schools and social clubs, then as a professional speaker on the lecture circuit, before securing the sponsorship of the *Reader's Digest*—a better career than washing dishes and repairing shoes, which is what he had been doing before he began lecturing. As with Gibran and Rihbany, Rizk used his background as an avenue to respectability and success, although, unlike them, he did so by diminishing it. Rizk was perceptive enough to realize that his success had less to do with his personal struggle than with the ideological significance of his narrative to his audience, and he used his talent as a storyteller and orator to amplify that effect. He was able to key his narrative to a collective psychic need in the thousands of audiences he addressed—the need to confirm a national myth that was so severely tested during the Great Depression and challenged by the rise of Fascism in Europe as to require for its shoring up the fervent testimony of a humble, plain-talking immigrant.

The Depression, in particular, tested Rizk's faith in America by destroying his shoe-repair business. "If even in rich, abundant America men were fated to poverty, then the earth was hopeless" (228). This suspicion is echoed by "the campus cynic," an unnamed interlocutor who seems to be more of a type than an individual, and who stands for those whom Rizk describes at one point as "chronic grumblers" (304):

> I feel sorry for you foreigners. . . . You are so naïve, so foolishly optimistic. You work so hard in this little shop. You actually think that by hard work and study you will get somewhere. You still believe that old line that America is the land of freedom and opportunity and all that stuff. Well, it used to be, but not any more. . . . Now we are all slaves in the hands of sixty-two millionaire families, and there's no way to escape them. (229)

Interestingly, Rizk does not refute that argument; on the contrary, he says, "sometimes I was almost in a mood to agree with him" because "the depression became a black and ugly thing" (229). But if economic opportunity seems no longer to be what distinguishes America, he praises the freedom of speech that allows a cartoonist to ridicule a U.S. president (238–39).

The third reason for Rizk's success is his ability to use his account of a trip back to Lebanon via Europe "in the spring of 1933, the year that Hitler became Chancellor of Germany" (240), as an occasion to belabor American exceptionalism by contrasting Fascist Europe with democratic America. Rizk's strategy is to cite criticism of America at some length before refuting it in a passionate defense. In doing so, he confronts his audience with weaknesses in their country, but without antagonizing them. He uses the words of others as a warning against social ills, while attributing to himself the defense of American ideals. For instance, in France, he reports a lengthy discussion with a group of people representing "a score of nationalities" (243) and who confront him with stereotypes of America as a country of rapacious bankers and gun-toting gangsters, where people care only about money. An Englishman adds that "Americans regard the whole world as their banquet table" (246) and that they are

> very smug. . . . You believe yourselves to be immune from the diseases which afflict us. But don't forget that someday America will wake up to find herself in the same mess as Europe. You know, Macaulay once said

> that the chief difference between the United States and Europe is that your country is always about sixty years behind us—and that goes for the evil in us as well as the good. (249)

Rizk allows such criticism to stand without refutation, but he speaks at length about America's freedom and democracy. By the end of the meeting, he leaves the international set in awe of his country: "My friends listened like little children, their eyes filled with wonder. You could see that everyone of them was wishing in his inmost heart that he might go to my country and live there forever" (250). His passage through Italy and Germany provides an opportunity for scathing accounts of Nazi horrors and fulsome praise for Jewish immigrants to Palestine. In Lebanon, he so dazzles the inhabitants of his native village with accounts of America that they are pathetically driven to despair: "'Please take me with you,' they cried. 'Put me in your pocket. . . . Put me in your suitcase. . . . Let me be your servant. . . . Buy me a ticket.' And when I assured them that all that was impossible, they begged and pleaded with me to use my power, my influence, and the influence of my friends to get them into America" (273). Back in the U.S., he says,

> every hill and valley, every field and tree and stone, every chimney, steeple, and spire, every smokestack and every water tower shone with an inward light. . . . Even the begrimed and sooted cities, with their ghostlike factories, closed by calamitous depression, glowed with the promise of better days. Bad as things were here, I knew they were infinitely better than in Europe or, for that matter, anywhere else in the world. (275–76)

Rizk's journey gives his message added urgency in the context of the war:

> In Europe I had heard men tell how vicious demagogues exploited desperate people to lift themselves to power. I had heard and seen how dictators had organized hatred and intolerance into ruthless machines of violence and destruction. . . . There was soil in America for the same sort of deadliness to take root: racial prejudice, poverty, unemployment, discontent, despair of democracy. Even before going to Europe I had sometimes felt uneasy at reactions I encountered. Mussolini's brags about Fascismo solving poverty had found welcome lodging in certain American ears. Hitler's maltreatment of Jews appealed to some of my friends as good common sense. There were those, especially disillusioned young people, who applauded Stalin's arbitrary arrests, killings and starvation. . . . (277)

In addition to justifying his claim to American identity, praise for America in the 1930s and 40s becomes a political rallying cry in a time of crisis, a warning against external threats compounded by domestic problems: "we have hate in America, too—snobbish, superior people who think they are better than the poor or than the foreigners. But that isn't America. America is kindness and helpfulness and friendliness and tolerance, and it is getting more that way every day. You see, America isn't all born yet. It is still growing, still happening over there. America is a dream" (271–72). In a sense, this is what Rihbany called "America on its ideal side" (Rihbany 1914, viii), but whose "real" side he rarely ever dared to name, let alone decry in the 1910s and 20s. During the Depression, however, Rizk could catalogue America's less than ideal conditions, sometimes in his own words but mostly by quoting others. He was also able to turn such criticisms into patriotic exhortations, one of which was later famously echoed by President John F. Kennedy: "I wanted to tell them [his audiences] that if we did as much for America as America has done for us, we need never worry about the outcome, no matter how long and hard the road" (275). Telling his story became a patriotic service to his country. A friend who later became his promoter said to him: "Sam, you've got a message that every American ought to hear. . . . [T]hat's the best story I've ever heard, and the most enlightened Americanism to boot" (281). This friend also offered the ultimate validation of Rizk's Americanness by arguing that he was, in effect, a better American than his U.S.-born compatriots:

> Sam, there ought to be some way for you to get your story before more people. It's just the sort of thing a lot of us smug Americans need today. The trouble with most of us is that we were born with our citizenship, which is just about the easiest, cheapest, and worst way to get it. We're inclined to take our opportunities and liberties for granted. We seldom or never stop to think what life would be like without them. But your case is different. You had to earn your citizenship. You were born where all these privileges were denied you. And you know the difference. You have felt the difference in your flesh and bones. You've got to tell the rest of us what it feels like. You can wake us up. (280–81)

Rizk further amplified this image into that of the super-patriotic immigrant performing selfless and heroic service to his adopted country:

> Often nothing but the harrowing drift of events and the infectious enthusiasm of my audiences kept me going, for I was still barely meeting expenses. . . . On and on I went, shuttling back and forth across the country, sometimes driving a thousand miles at a stretch, fighting wind and ice and snow and rain and sleet, car trouble and the common cold to meet the next date, and always I felt more than amply rewarded by the appreciation of the people. (302–3)

When *Reader's Digest* offered to sponsor him, it was "the richest, most inspiring opportunity America had afforded me . . . to become a life servant of the country where I had found life so good" (307). While there is no reason to doubt his patriotism, there is no question that Rizk skillfully shaped his narrative in light of his audience's responses and sensibility. He knew exactly how to restore the self-image of a country still reeling from the Depression and now in the grip of war, and how to present himself as a grateful, super-patriotic immigrant who is more American than Americans.

Rizk also amplified the negative representations of Arabs and Islam, which stand in stark contrast to his resounding endorsement of Zionism—two more keys to his spectacular appeal. Throughout the 1920 and 30s, Palestine witnessed rising tensions, strikes, and violence as a result of British mandate policies and increased Jewish immigration from Europe. Writing his book in the early 1940s, Rizk's account of his 1933 trip to Europe and Lebanon presented the situation from the single vantage point of Zionism, confirming the propagandistic myth of "a land without a people for a people without a land." He speaks glowingly of heroic Jewish immigrants "resettling" Palestine, as though the land had been empty; they are farming the desert, as if there had been no Palestinian agriculture; and the Palestinians are described as "hostile" and "constantly agitated" (261). Rizk witnessed the shocking condition of Jewish refugees escaping Nazi persecution and sympathized with their plight. Moreover, he had been warned against going to Germany because his nose "looks too Jewish" (251). But there is no acknowledgment whatsoever in his account of the Arab point of view, which both Rihani and Rihbany had endeavored to explain to the American public during the 1910s and 20s (Rihani 1967; Rihbany 1918, 101–24 and 1922, 265–87). Instead, the Zionist line is uncritically repeated, which is amazing for an Arab who had grown up in the region and who must have known what the Zionist project meant for Palestinians. Their dispossession in 1948 was still several years away when Rizk wrote his book, but the gravity of the situation, the British policies, the intentions and behavior of the settlers, and the worries of the Palestinians demonstrated to those with any familiarity with the region that the situation was far more complex than the simplistic narrative of Jewish "return" to "a land without a people." Yet that was the prevailing narrative in the U.S., and Rizk was not one who liked to challenge his audience with complexity, much less to voice controversial views.

In the same vein, two pages after his eulogy of the Zionist movement, Rizk describes his arrival in Lebanon, which he disdainfully depicts as a backward desert country inhabited by primitive people:

> My first impression of Beirut was that it had shrunk terribly. The buildings which had once seemed so tall, the shops, stores, and public buildings which had looked so large and prosperous, the Grand Hotel Victoria which had been so magnificent, all now had become small and modest, almost poor and shabby by contrast with America. This impression struck me even more forcibly in Ain Arab [his village]. As I approached the village, in a Model T taxi, it looked like a lifeless skeleton bleaching in the desert. (264)

What is the purpose of reporting this highly unflattering first impression, except to emphasize the "contrast with America"? Interestingly, he never gives us his second impression—how he felt about his homeland a day or a week later, after the reverse culture shock had worn off, or what he thought of that experience years later when writing the book. The shock of the returnee is always strongest upon first encounter, but the perspective gained afterwards is usually more nuanced. It seems, however, that if he had any, he chose to withhold it.

Next, he endorses anti-Muslim prejudice by describing Islam as essentially un-American. Along the winding dirt road to his village, he is impatient with the slow speed at which the car is travelling, sharing the road with "donkeys, goats, or camels from the road. But worst of all, my driver was Moslem. At one point, he stopped the car . . . , performed his ablutions, . . . and then, spreading his prayer rug, knelt toward Mecca" (264). As he waited, Rizk

> amused myself trying to picture a Moslem America. I saw fast trains coming to a stop out in the country, after which the engineer leaped from his cab and spread his rug on the right of way, followed by all the Mohammedan passengers. I imagined taxi drivers on Fifth Avenue suddenly halting their cars and hitting the pavement, and street-car conductors, bus drivers, street cleaners, bootblacks, doctors, merchants, and public officials. I saw golfers kneeling on greens and fairways, and policemen interrupting the pursuit of a criminal to keep the faith. I saw workers in an automobile assembly line let a car go through without a carburetor or minus a fender in order to keep their tryst with Mecca. . . . Presently the Moslem finished his prayers, picked up his rug and climbed into the car. His face was filled with indescribable serenity and peace. I wouldn't have robbed him of that bliss for anything. (265)

In this caricature, Islam is reduced to a ridiculous ritual that is incompatible with modernity. It would bring the busy traffic of a modern city to a halt, impede the social order, obstruct justice, and disrupt economic activity—in short, undo civic society. Implied here is the Orientalist claim that Islam is responsible for the backwardness of Muslim societies. Yet, the serenity and peace on the face of the faithful indicate that they are content with their backwardness and would not exchange it for anything, nor should anyone try to save them from it. By depicting Islam and Muslims as un-American, Rizk stresses his religious difference from them, implying that to be Christian (like him) is to be American.

Two things in the Old Country escape this harsh treatment. First, the kindness of the people overwhelms him during his stay in Ain Arab. His grandmother greets him with "the glorious phrases of gratitude and hospitality which always make me glad I was born a Syrian. This was the real thing. Maybe I was normal after all. But it was the people and not the place that made me feel that way" (266). The people may be ignorant, backward, and destitute, the victims of French oppression (268–70), but they are kind, warm, and hospitable. This seems to come as something of a surprise for him, making him reconsider not just his opinion of them, but of himself. That opinion had been at a very low point when, shortly after his arrival in the U.S. a few years earlier, he was met with so much hostility in the slaughterhouse that he regretted his birth in Syria (159). Rizk seems to have internalized some of that racism, and he propagated it in his zeal to prove his worthiness of U.S. citizenship. Finding himself back in the middle of his people, their warmth forces him to reconsider, and it is with relief that he is able to celebrate them and to reclaim some of his pride. But he is careful to note that he maintains his disdain for the country.

The second is his depiction of Syrian immigrants. First of all, the title of the book deliberately conjoins two descriptors that, at a time of isolationism, xenophobia, and official anti-immigrant policy, must have seemed not only unusual, but improbable. (The typeface on the spine of the book dramatizes this effect: "*Syrian* YANKEE," the adjective italicized for emphasis, the noun cast in assertive capital letters.) A "Yankee" may be a New Englander, a Northerner, or more generally an American, but rarely if ever does the word conjure up the figure of the immigrant. The word implies being a native-born U.S. citizen because it designates cultural characteristics that distinguish white Americans from Europeans, especially Britons. Unlike its later equivalent, "Arab American," which springs from the register of multiculturalism with its ideology of a pluralistic, racially and ethnically diverse polity, both "Syrian" and "Yankee" are heavily steeped in the racialism of the late nineteenth and early twentieth century. Rizk's neologism "Syrian Yankee" was, therefore, in itself a bold assertion that a Syrian can be an American, the paradox being, of course, that it is only possible when he repudiates Syria.

The theme of Syrian eligibility for "Yankeeness" is emphasized in the final chapter of the book, entitled "Two Syrian Americans." In it, Rizk contrasts two immigrants. The first, who goes unidentified, is a cynical politician who only cares about enriching himself and feels no gratitude to the country that gave him the opportunity to succeed. The second, Dr. Michael Shadid, is a grateful immigrant who "pioneered the first co-operative hospital in the United States at Elk City, Oklahoma" (315). This is the same Michael Shadid who in 1927 wrote to *The Syrian World* complaining of racial prejudice, ostracism, and discrimination, and urging fellow Syrians to return home because he felt that they would never be treated fairly in the U.S. That letter spurred a debate that raged on the pages of that magazine for several months (see Halaby). Rizk makes no mention of that controversy, but he quotes what Shadid told him "recently" (315):

> When I was peddling jewelry from door to door those first years in America . . . I saw a lot of America. And the more I saw of it the more I loved it. But some things disturbed me. Here and there were injustice, oppression, and discrimination. I knew they didn't belong here. They were un-American. They didn't fit into the picture I had of this country. But there they were. Farmers paying outrageous interest rates and losing their farms, workers being overworked and underpaid, thousands of children denied their full educational opportunity, and hundreds of families not getting proper medical care. Of course, things were improving right along. I met people who were busy making this country, already the best in the world, even better. I decided I ought to do my share. I owed a debt to America for the opportunities she had given me, and I felt I ought to repay it in some concrete way. This hospital is part of my payment. Let's say it's the down payment. (316–17)

In closing the book with those two examples, reduced as they are to a simple contrast and shorn of the personal history of the two men, Rizk shows himself to be a writer and speaker more concerned with his ideological message than with the facts he marshals to support it. Shadid had a famously and very publicly complicated relationship to the U.S., culminating in his decision to move back to Lebanon with his family in 1928; he retuned to the U.S. only when his American-born children insisted. In closing the book with a highly abbreviated account of Shadid (and an even sketchier account of the unnamed politician), Rizk makes several points. First of all, by giving the example of another Syrian immigrant like himself who shares the same passion for serving his country, Rizk answers the skeptics in his audience by showing them that he is not unique (the personal is the collective, according to Deleuze and Guattari). Second, contra the xenophobes and racists, Rizk makes a compelling case that immigrants enrich the life of the country (although their contribution has nothing to do with their cultural background, only with their gratitude to America). Third, the two contrasting examples show that not all Syrians are alike, and that one cannot generalize about an entire group. Fourth, what matters in the end, he argues, is not ethnic or racial origin, but dedication and service to the nation: "There are a lot of people like Dr. Shadid in this country. Some trace their ancestors through Plymouth Rock and some through Ellis Island. But regardless of origin, they are working quietly, obscurely, and unstintingly to give democracy the victory in one area of life or another" (317).

There is no doubt that those are valid arguments and that Rizk did, indeed, perform a valuable service to the nation at a difficult period in its history, while at the same time attempting to rehabilitate the reputation of immigrants during a time of widespread and officially sanctioned ethnic and racial prejudice. The trouble with his approach, however, is that the type of patriotism he advocated so fiercely (in part out of his avowed desire to prove his worthiness to be an American) was monolithic, exceptionalist, and chauvinistic. It is not possible to preach so insistently that one's country is the greatest in the world without at the same time promoting national arrogance, disdain for other cultures, and even xenophobia and racism. Moreover, this attitude necessarily requires the stereotyping of others, as Rizk's Orientalist depiction of Arabs and Islam shows. The impression he gives is that his Arab origin seems to be an advantage only insofar as it enables a greater appreciation of America, but not as a point of pride in itself. With Rizk, the East/West dichotomy that structured the early writers' discourses has weakened with Europe succumbing to Fascism, but the new paradigm unabashedly establishes a new hierarchy with the U.S. occupying such a high position at the top that all other cultures blur into irrelevance. They have nothing of value to offer the U.S., except by negative example. That being the case, there is no longer any need for cultural translation.[2]

5

Exilic Memoirs

"Son, do not sell your piece of land. Come home and walk over the earth, sit on its rocks and plant some of your tears there. Your tears will grow into tall trees and will bear tear fruits and on the branches your name will be recorded for eternity. Even when you are no longer in this world, your land will remember you."

—AZIZ SHIHAB

People in struggle don't operate in a vacuum when they go about creating their self-definitions.

—FAWAZ TURKI

I occasionally experience myself as a cluster of flowing currents. I prefer this to the idea of a solid self, the identity to which so many attach so much significance.

—EDWARD SAID

The Task of Representation

Nowhere is the truth of Deleuze and Guattari's observation on the conjunction of the private and the collective, the personal and the political, more evident than in the memoirs of Palestinians exiled in 1948. It is also no coincidence that the first Arab American writers to challenge Orientalist discourse directly and unapologetically were Palestinian exiles. For Palestinian Americans, the logic that defined Europe's relations with its colonies, and which continues to define U.S. public opinion at home and foreign policy in the Middle East, reached a catastrophic conclusion with their collective expulsion from Palestine and the creation of the State of Israel. While for many European Jews it was the answer to anti-Semitism, Zionism combined elements of biblical nostalgia, Orientalist discourse, and colonialist attitudes into a narrative of the Jews' "return" to Palestine, a country described in a popular Zionist slogan as "a land without a people for a people without a land." Taking no notice of the Palestinians, Theodor Herzl argued in

Zionism's founding text, *The Jewish State*, that Jewish European settlers would form a state that would be "a portion of the ramparts of Europe against Asia, an outpost of civilization as opposed to barbarism" (96). Whereas Palestinian society was ancient, complex, multi-confessional, and highly structured, Zionist advocates imagined only nomads roaming the desert, hardly an obstacle to the creation of a modern, European-style state by civilized settlers. When this myth collided with the reality that Jewish immigrants found on the ground in Palestine, a two-pronged strategy was devised: the eviction of the Palestinians from the land and, following 1948, the insistence that the refugees were not Palestinians per se—i.e., not a society with a distinct culture that can have any claim to national self-determination—but Arabs, indistinct from the inhabitants of surrounding Arab countries, which should, therefore, absorb them. "Who are the Palestinians?," Golda Meir notoriously asked. "They do not exist" (quoted in Turki 1974, 44).

In the decades after 1948, therefore, the question of representation was for Palestinians one of survival. If Orientalism denied the humanity of Arabs through stereotype, Zionism as a particular mutation of Orientalism negated the very existence of Palestinians. For Palestinian exiles publishing in the U.S., the chief sponsor of Israel and where Zionism has acquired a monopoly on public opinion and the foreign policy establishment, writing and speaking has been a far more urgent—and sometimes perilous—task of cultural translation than it ever was for Arab Americans who wrote and spoke against settler colonialism in Palestine before the 1940s, such as Ameen Rihani and Abraham Rihbani. After 1948, the year known in Arabic as that of the *Nakba* (catastrophe or disaster), the task for Palestinian American writers was to construct a counter narrative that would not only prove that they exist, but also expose the racism and the terrorist tactics used to cleanse Palestine ethnically so as to fulfill the fantasy of a land without a people. This Palestinian perspective was familiar not only in Arab countries, but also around the world, shared by Third World revolutionaries and their supporters, from Mahatma Gandhi to Che Guevara and Jean-Paul Sartre, and adopted by the United Nations General Assembly in its Resolution 3379, which equated Zionism with racism. Yet the challenge for Palestinian American writers lay in presenting the Palestinian case effectively to a U.S. public whose views on the conflict have been shaped almost entirely by the Zionist narrative, and whose government has been the chief sponsor of the Jewish state, and further to do so at a time when anti-Arab racism reached unprecedented proportions as a direct result of the Arab–Israeli conflict, especially after the Six Day War of 1967. In such an environment, the Herculean task was to demonstrate how the "independence" of one people was another's "disaster."

This radical act of translation was already in the making even before Edward Said's critique of Orientalism. The first and best-known Palestinian activist writing in English before Said was Fawaz Turki, author of no less than three memoirs: *The Disinherited: Journal of a Palestinian Exile* (1972), *Soul in Exile: Lives of a Palestinian Revolutionary* (1988), and *Exile's Return: The Making of a Palestinian American* (1994)—in addition to two poetry collections, *Poems from Exile* (1975) and *Tel Zaatar Was the Hill of Thyme* (1978). Of course, Said contributed more than any other scholar to the emergence of a collective Palestinian narrative, and his *Out of Place: A Memoir*

(1999) provided the personal dimension. Other Palestinian American memoirs include Jamil Toubbeh's *Day of the Long Night: A Palestinian Refugee Remembers the Nakba* (1998) and Aziz Shihab's *Does the Land Remember Me? A Memoir of Palestine* (2007). Those writers belong to a generation that suffered the *Nakba* in their childhood and early youth (Shihab was born in 1927, Toubbeh in 1930, Said in 1935, and Turki in 1940), and their narratives recount their traumatic memories of 1948 and how it affected them and their families. Those autobiographies, and others by Palestinian exiles living in other countries and writing in numerous languages, play a role similar to that of slave narratives, prison memoirs, and testimonies of survivors of genocide and war crimes, in that they concretize a historical trauma that may seem abstract to those unfamiliar with it, anchoring collective tragedy in individual experiences, and adding the human dimension often missing from historical accounts and ideological claims and counter-claims. In taking direct aim at the Zionist negation of their rights, the memoirs of 1948 Palestinian exiles challenge the authority of the dominant discourse in the U.S. They also revolve around the problems of identity, home, and belonging—persistent themes in ethnic American autobiography in general, but with significant variations that sometimes run counter to the usual patterns in which immigrants, including non-Palestinian Arabs, have staked their claim to American identity. In what follows, I will briefly describe the treatment of those themes in Shihab and Said, before concentrating in the rest of this chapter on the highly complicated case of Turki and his three autobiographical narratives.[1]

Identity, Home, and Belonging

The concept of home in Palestinian American autobiography is tied to the loss of the homeland. With few exceptions, and contrary to the norms of other immigrant and Arab American autobiography, the titles of many Palestinian American memoirs evoke exile, loss, and memory quite explicitly, thereby stressing a profound attachment to Palestine and the centrality of the concept of *al-'Awda* (return or repatriation to Palestine, the end of exile). The word "exile" is in each of Turki's book titles; Said is "out of place"; Shihab evokes the anthropomorphic attribution of memory to the land in Palestinian folklore when he wonders whether his land still remembers him after decades of exile; and Toubbeh stresses his status as "refugee," a condition narrated in its historical and human dimensions by all of those memoirists. Consequently, their coming-to-America stories revolve around loss and deracination, rather than fulfillment of destiny, attainment of a goal, or reaching a final destination, as in many titles by Lebanese American and Egyptian American autobiographers who left their countries of origin voluntarily: *A Far Journey*, *Mt. Lebanon to Vermont*, *Syrian Yankee*, *Out of Egypt*, *A Border Passage: From Cairo to America*, and so on.

Consequently, Palestinian American autobiographies rarely display the sentimental effusions about coming to America that are typical of Rihbany, George Haddad, Rizk, Ihab Hassan, and immigrant autobiographers of other ethnicities. On the contrary, coming to America is often a mixed blessing, fraught as it is with the pain of dispossession and complicated by frustration and anger over the U.S.

support for Israel. On the one hand, for example, Shihab declares that "coming to the United States was the greatest gift from God," that he "feels sad for the people who were not equally blessed" (Shihab xxi), and that he is "lucky . . . compared to them [relatives in Jordan, the West Bank, and Arab countries]. I was a refugee also, but in a country where I had more freedom and more opportunities. . . . Palestinians who took refuge in other Arab countries were, and are still, treated like dirt" (23). On the other hand, his

> dilemma was to live quietly and obediently in a country that helped make me a refugee and that I chose to make my home, pretending it is the greatest home for justice in the world. Or I could go back to Palestine and live miserably under Israeli occupation and possibly die fighting injustice. I chose the lesser of two evils. But I was boiling inside to find out that convincing even one American of the truth of what had happened to my people and my homeland was quickly and continuously negated by press coverage portraying my victimized brothers as terrorists. At the same time, the U.S. press described the killers of my brothers and sisters as heroic people fighting for "security" with American weapons paid for by tax dollars to which I contributed. (2)

At the end of the narrative, he confides, "when the U.S. Immigration official said, 'Welcome home,' I did not feel that the United States was my home" (148). Such contradictions bespeak the conflicted feelings of those forced out of their homeland, as opposed to those who left it voluntarily and for whom the adopted country represents a far less problematic place.

Thus the concept of home in Palestinian American autobiography is provisional, fraught with anger and guilt, bitterness and nostalgia, hope and frustration, neither stable nor taken for granted. Not surprisingly, the journey "home" is often contradictorily twofold, containing some variation on the Palestinian concept of *al-'Awadh*, and at the same time the idea of the United States as the new home. The return to Palestine is an aspiration and a political project to be realized in the future, while the return to the United States is a pragmatic, existential necessity. The journey back to Palestine is sometimes narrated as an episode in the memoire, as in Toubbeh and Said, and sometimes it furnishes the framework for the whole memoir, as in the case of Shihab's book and Turki's *Exile's Return*. In fact, one of the most recurring scenes in Palestinian writing after 1967 is that of the dispossessed coming back to knock on the doors of their houses, now inhabited by Jewish immigrants.[2] "No more," a man from Brooklyn says to Shihab, "God gave it to us. It is ours now," before slamming the door in his face (54). Turki, whose beard and long hair cause him to be mistaken for an Israeli, is made to feel like an intruder in the old house by its Eastern European inhabitant who initially agreed to let him look around, not knowing that he is Palestinian (Turki 1994, 4). As for Said, he decides against knocking on the door once he finds himself in front of the house (Said 1999, xii).[3] Those journeys do not represent the end of the Palestinian diaspora, since the returnees are not allowed to stay, but become instead occasions to contemplate the loss of home.

Shihab's narrative centers on the problem of home, which is embedded in the question of whether or not to sell his plot of land in the West Bank village of Sinjil, near Ramallah. Originally from Jerusalem, his family became refugees in 1948 and settled in that village. He immigrated to the U.S. in 1950 and became a journalist at the *Dallas Morning News*—a career that allowed him to see firsthand how Zionism manipulates public opinion through the media (Shihab 24–25, 148–49). The occasion of Shihab's trip to Palestine in the mid-1990s was his mother's imminent death at the age of 106. The mother's longevity, especially given her exhortations for him to return to build a house on his land, comes to symbolize the endurance of Palestinian identity and the measure of his own attachment to his roots:

> [M]y mother was begging for me to return to Sinjil village . . . and begin construction of a red stone house so she could be proud of me before she died. . . . Palestinians had wearied of seeing Jews build prefab settlement houses on their occupied land seemingly overnight. Arabs felt an urgency to build their own houses before Israelis claimed whatever land they had left. My mother once said that I could become a president of the United States and would still be nothing in the eyes of the villagers until I built a house. . . . For several years I had been entertaining the idea of selling my small piece of property in Palestine. (Shihab 3)

For his mother, his relatives, and the villagers, selling his land would literally be selling them out: "Don't sell your holy piece of land, my son, it is your link to your past and to your people who have been stepped upon with the heavy boots of the people you live among these days, the Amrikanis" (5). Another villager is more blunt: "'First, let me warn you . . . that you should never even think of selling to foreigners'—meaning Israelis. 'Second, I advise you not to sell it to anyone from outside this village. And third, you would be a fool to sell it. You should return to your homeland, build yourself a stone house on the land, and live right here among your own people'" (95). Eventually, Shihab makes up his mind to do that "someday" (99). With the plot of land bearing such a heavy burden of symbolism—an entire society's fight for survival—it becomes far more than a piece of private property; the predicament of the individual is insoluble in isolation from that of the collective. And since the fate of the Palestinian people remains in limbo, the resolution of the individual's dilemma of home and belonging is likewise indefinitely postponed.

As we can see from Shihab's predicament, the question of identity for people who have suffered a collective calamity is rarely conceived in individualistic terms, but rather in a dialectical tension between individual and community. Private property, private feelings, and private life are inextricably woven into the fabric of collective history. Needless to say, such indissoluble ties exist in all human contexts, but in an extreme situation like that of Palestinians living in exile or under occupation, it is impossible to obscure such ties. The implication of this for Palestinian American autobiography in relation to other kinds of coming-to-America narratives can be understood in the contrast between, on the one hand, Ihab Hassan's claim that he "is in the American grain, a tradition of men and women who crossed an ocean to reinvent themselves" (Ihab Hassan 1986, 251), implying free and unfettered reshaping of the self in a new context; and on the other hand, the sense of historical determinism in Fawaz Turki's insistence that "people in struggle don't operate in a vacuum when they go about creating their self-definitions" (Turki 1988, 102).

Flowing Currents

Most Palestinian autobiographies illustrate that point. Toubbeh's slim volume contains no more than a bare outline of his own life, while the rest is devoted to the *Nakba* and the growing Zionist influence in the U.S., where he has resided since 1951. Turki's memoirs, which will be discussed in detail below, also devote far more space to Palestinian history than to the author's personal life. Said's memoir is the exception that proves the rule. *Out of Place* is devoted almost entirely to his private life, even though the resonance of history is always there in the background. Throughout his enormous *œuvre*, Said's personal experience is closely intertwined with his intellectual work as a literary and cultural theorist and with his political activism. The importance of *Orientalism* cannot be overstated here; it revolutionized the study not only of the Middle East, but also of colonialism and imperialism worldwide. While belaboring the importance of what is arguably the single most influential academic volume of the last quarter of the twentieth century is hardly necessary here, it is worth noting not only the crucial role that Palestinian dispossession played in the conception of the book, but also the way Said anchored his project in his lived experience in the Arab world and the U.S.:

> My own experiences . . . are in part what made me write this book. The life of an Arab Palestinian in the West, particularly in America, is disheartening. There exists here an almost unanimous consensus that politically he does not exist, and when it is allowed that he does, it is either as a nuisance or as an Oriental. The web of racism, cultural stereotypes, political imperialism, dehumanizing ideology holding in the Arab or the Muslim is very strong indeed, and it is this web which every Palestinian has come to feel as his uniquely punishing destiny. (Said 1978, 27)

So if *Out of Place* appears to be unique among Palestinian autobiographies in how much collective history it leaves *out*, that is because Said's work as a whole was inspired by that history, in which the personal and the political are ever present and inseparable.[4] Precisely because Said's prolific and intensely committed scholarly and political writing carries so much of the weight of collective representation, the genre of the memoir returns, in his case, to being a record of personal experiences, the story of individual self-becoming, which is nonetheless embedded in collective, political history.

In fact, so completely did Said himself come to embody the Palestinian struggle that his memoir came under attack even before it was published.[5] Said was the most prominent Palestinian American, so the mixed reception of his memoir reveals the ideological investments in narratives of identity. *Out of Place* is a lyrical and poignant account of the early life of a prominent intellectual and a searing narrative of the tragedy of Palestinian dispossession. Here, the autobiographical project not only constructs the subjectivity of the individual author (a success story of individual self-emergence), but also the collective experience of a people, and in so doing it undermines the truth claims of a dominant ideology (Zionism), which insists that Palestinian collective subjectivity does not exist. In Said's case, we can observe two simultaneous discursive operations: his entry into what Jerome Brunner calls a "conversation of selves" (Brunner 47) in the U.S. conforms to a prevalent notion of subjectivity, while at the same time anchoring the individual in the collective Palestinian experience. The two operations in a sense justify Said's lifework as a committed scholar and political activist, work that begins with his entry into professional and public life in the mid 1960s—the point at which the memoir ends—so that the memoir provides a personal context and prehistory to his lifework. In fact, it is possible to read his *Reflections on Exile* (2000), a collection of essays written between 1967 and 1998, as an intellectual autobiography, written on the margins of his major books, which picks up a life story from the point at which *Out of Place* (1999) leaves off, the titles of both books clearly modulating the theme of individual and collective displacement.

Said conceived of the idea of writing an autobiography in response to being diagnosed with leukemia and his realization "that I had at least entered, if not *the* final phase of my life, then the period—like Adam and Eve leaving the garden—from which there would be no return to my old life" (Said 1999, 216). He adds, "As one of the main responses to my illness I found in this book a new kind of challenge . . . a project about as far from my professional and political life as it was possible for me to go" (217). Furthermore, the rhythm and pace of writing the memoir were fundamentally different: "whereas with other sorts of work that I did—essays, lectures, teaching, journalism—I was going across the illness, punctuating it almost forcibly with deadlines and cycles of beginning-middle-and-end, with this memoir I was borne along by the episodes of treatment, hospital stays, physical pain and mental anguish, letting those dictate how and when I could write, for how long and where" (216). Said's response to the intensely private and immensely isolating confrontation with his mortality is two-fold: soldiering ahead with public responsibilities that impose their own temporal constraints on his faltering health, and seeking relief from both illness and public life in the private world of childhood memories that he reconstructs as a way, to use his favorite Gramscian metaphor, to "compile . . . an inventory" of his life (Said 1978, 25). The contrasting rhythms of the two responses reveal a conflict, exacerbated by the existential weight of his predicament, between the demands of public and private life, whereas before his illness he was able to devote so much of his energy to public life that he "unconsciously turned [his] back" on "holidays and relaxation, all that passes for middle-and upper-class 'leisure,'" and even sleep (1999, 217).

Out of Place is a story of self-emergence that is deeply marked by this tension between the public and private: "The underlying motifs for me have been the emergence of a second self buried for a long time beneath a surface of often expertly acquired and wielded social characteristics belonging to the self my parents tried to construct, the 'Edward' I speak of intermittently, and how an extraordinarily increasing number of departures have unsettled my life from its earliest beginnings" (217). The first of those motifs involves the individualistic urge to escape from the persona and role defined for him by his parents: the ideal "Edward" they envisioned vs. the "delinquent son" (18) he appeared to be. Hence "the extreme and rigid regime of discipline and extracurricular education that my father [created] and in which I became imprisoned from the age of nine," and which threatened to stifle the real or hidden self struggling to free itself. This is a classic story of Oedipal conflict and individualistic struggle against pre-established social order. The second motif concerns the "departures" or "displacements from countries, cities, abodes, languages, environments that have kept me in motion all those years" (217), and which give the memoir its title. Those displacements occur for all sorts of reasons—class (Anglophile Palestinian upper bourgeoisie), family history (the Jerusalemite family's primary residence was in Cairo), language (he spoke Egyptian, not Palestinian, Arabic but his formal education was in English), education (in British and American schools in Cairo and Jerusalem, then in the U.S.), religion (an Anglican minority within Orthodox and Coptic Christian minorities in predominantly Muslim countries), citizenship (born a U.S. citizen in Jerusalem, raised mainly in Cairo and spending summers in Lebanon), history (dispossession in 1948, with his father losing his business in Palestine and the extended family dispersing all over the world), and finally personal (what he considered to be his banishment from Cairo to Mount Hermon School in Massachusetts at age fifteen).

Those private and collective forms of displacement are impossible to disentangle. As a result, even though the dispossession of the Palestinians in 1948 affected Said the least among all of the exiled autobiographers under consideration here—his family's flourishing business in Cairo allowed his parents to shelter the children ("cocoon" them, as he puts it [294]) from the catastrophe that struck an entire society—the heroic example of his aunt Nabiha, who devoted her life to helping Palestinian refugees in Cairo (119–22), and his sense of historical responsibility (perhaps also the guilt of privilege) prompted him to devote his life to the struggle for the rights of Palestinians less fortunate them himself. By the same token, the loss of Palestine had the unique psychic effect on him of producing "a secret but ineradicable fear of not returning," a fear that compelled him to pack too much luggage when traveling and also paradoxically to "fabricate occasions for departure, thus giving rise to the fear voluntarily. The two seem absolutely necessary to my rhythm of life" (217).

Because the *Nakba* seems to have been only one in a series of dislocations in his childhood, it was 1967 that for him

> embodied *the* dislocation that subsumed all other losses, the disappeared worlds of my youth and upbringing, the unpolitical years of my education, the assumption of disengaged teaching and scholarship at Columbia, and so on. I was no longer the same person after 1967; the shock of that war

> drove me back to where it had all started, the struggle over Palestine. I subsequently entered the newly transformed Middle East landscape as a part of the Palestinian movement that emerged in Amman and then in Beirut in the late sixties through the seventies. This was an experience that drew on the agitated, largely hidden side of my prior life—the anti-authoritarianism, the need to break through an imposed and enforced silence, above all the need to draw back to a sort of original state of what was irreconcilable, thereby shattering and dispelling an unjust Establishment order. (293)

1967 was, of course, a turning point for the Palestinian national movement as a whole because Palestinians realized that they could no longer rely on the Arab states to defend them, that they had to take matters into their own hands. Said's response to the war was part and parcel of a broad mobilization of Palestinian energies, even as his antiauthoritarianism had roots in his private struggle to free himself from the strict discipline imposed on him by his father. The struggle for Palestinian national self-determination became the political correlative of the struggle of his inner self against the "Edward" defined by his parents.

Thus political values like antiauthoritarianism, speaking the truth to power, and the insistence on "irreconcilability" or nonconformity to the "established order" all originate in private life and childhood experience. They shape his sense of home as something dialectically defined by rupture, and his notion of freedom as a state of being irremediably "out of place":

> My search for freedom, for the self beneath or obscured by "Edward," could only have begun because of that rupture [coming to the U.S. at age 15], so I have come to think of it as fortunate, despite the loneliness and unhappiness I experienced for so long. Now it does not seem important or even desirable to be "right" and in place (right at home, for instance). Better to wander out of place, not to own a house, and not ever to feel too much at home anywhere, especially in a city like New York, where I shall be until I die. (294)

His coming to America was enabling, but not for the usual reasons found in other immigrants' autobiographies. What is central for Said is the experience of *leaving* home, rather than *coming to* the U.S. Said here echoes a favorite passage by Hugo of St. Victor that Erich Auerbach cites in *Mimesis*, which states that "the person who finds his homeland sweet is still a tender beginner; he to whom every soil is as his native one is already strong; but he is perfect to whom the entire world is as a foreign land" (quoted in *Culture and Imperialism* 335). For Said, as for Auerbach, being nowhere at home, the condition of the exile, is not just a wrenching experience, but a necessary one for "transcend[ing] the restraints of imperial or national or provincial limits . . . to the negative freedom of real knowledge" (335–36). Yet paradoxically, Said identifies New York as the locus of both home ("where I shall be until I die") and homelessness itself ("not ever to feel too much at home anywhere, especially in a city like New York")—the ultimate state of homelessness is to be at-home-in-homelessness, the site of "the negative freedom of real knowledge." It is a negative freedom because it is predicated on the destruction of unitary identities that inevitably generate ethnocentric hierarchies:

> No one today is purely *one* thing. Labels like Indian, or woman, or Muslim, or American are not more than starting-points, which if followed into actual experience for a moment are quickly left behind. Imperialism consolidated the mixture of cultures and identities on a global scale. But its worst and most paradoxical gift was to allow people to believe that they were only, mainly, exclusively, white or Black, or Western, or Oriental. (1993, 336)

Only, mainly, exclusively one thing or the other—such reductionism is the stuff of stereotype, self-stereotyping as well as the stereotyping of others. Instead of those unitary and essentialist conceptions of identity that posit "a solid self," Said suggests a more fluid notion of subjectivity as "a cluster of flowing currents." He explains:

> These currents . . . require no reconciling, no harmonizing. They are "off" and may be out of place, but at least they are always in motion, in time, in place, in the form of all kinds of strange combinations moving about, not necessarily forward, sometimes against each other, contrapuntally yet without one central theme. A form of freedom, I'd like to think, even if I am far from being totally convinced that it is. That skepticism too is one of the themes I particularly want to hold on to. With so many dissonances in my life I have learned actually to prefer being not quite right and out of place. (1999, 295)

As they flow in nonsynchronous, occasionally contradictory and unharmonious motion, each along its own course, those currents represent a mix of influences and inclinations—historical, societal, familial, personal—none of which can be considered the defining characteristic of identity. It is a form of freedom that is limited by contradiction, confusion, and skepticism—that habit of mind which can be at once liberating and paralyzing. Appreciating the rewards and the frustrations of this condition takes the kind of intellectual courage born out of the pain of dislocation and the anxieties of permanent exile.

Dialectics of Exile

If Said's articulation of the relationship between exile and identity in the image of the "cluster of flowing currents" stresses its liberating potential, Fawaz Turki's memoirs dramatize its tragic contradictions. In many ways, Turki's life as a Palestinian exile, his work as an activist and writer, and his memoirs could not be more different from Said's. The latter's family was affluent; they resided mainly in Cairo, where his father ran a successful business and where the family was at the actual time of the 1948 disaster. He received the best education available at the most prestigious schools and universities in Egypt, Palestine, and the United States. He was born a U.S. citizen because his father had been naturalized after serving in the U.S. military during World War I, so, unlike Turki, Said did not suffer the indignities of statelessness. Said's family deliberately sheltered him and his siblings from the tragedy in Palestine, never discussing it at home, and he led a nonpolitical life until 1967, by which time his distinguished academic career at Columbia University was underway. By contrast, Turki is the child of a poor grocer from Haifa. An eight-year-old at the time of the *Nakba*, he underwent the harrowing experience of fleeing on foot with thousands of other refugees, witnessing along the way unimaginable suffering (the sight of a woman screaming with the pain of labor by the side of the road during the exodus from Haifa would haunt him for decades). He grew up in Burj al-Barajnah refugee camp and on the streets of Beirut, in the thick of Palestinian misery, and was dependent on scholarships for his formal education. He became politically active as a teenager during the 1950s. This was followed by stints as a farmhand in the Australian Outback, a hippie in South Asia during the 1960s, then a bohemian writer in Paris, Boston, and Washington D.C., where he has lived since the mid-1970s.

Because of that tempestuous life, not to mention his fiery temperament, the existential predicament of homelessness and exile is painfully and dramatically captured in Turki's three memoirs. They chronicle his wrestling with his sense of identity and his role in the Palestinian movement. Written in Paris and first published in New York and London in 1972, his acclaimed memoir, *The Disinherited: Journal of a Palestinian Exile*, powerfully attacked the myths surrounding Israel and the Palestinians. He came to the U.S. in 1973 and published *Soul in Exile: Lives of a Palestinian Revolutionary*, his second memoir, fifteen years later, in 1988. Despite the differences in time and location, those two books are more or less continuous with one another, the one retelling, amplifying, and updating the other. In both, he assumed the stance of a Palestinian revolutionary who is totally dedicated to the cause, and framed his discourse in Fanonian, Third-Worldist terms. However, in his third memoir, *Exile's Return: The Making of a Palestinian American* (1994), Turki takes on the PLO, Palestinian society, and Arab culture in general in an all-out attack that falls back on Orientalist discourse. In the first two memoirs, very little of his own personal narrative is told, and no more than passing references are made to the apolitical years he spent in Australia and South Asia. It is not until the third memoir, with its alternating chapters describing his personal and public lives, that some balance between the demands of the personal and the collective is struck. This mercurial shift is fascinating enough in itself, but it is also accompanied by a radical shift of perspective that powerfully dramatizes the trials of Palestinian exile and the crushing historical burden it lays upon the individual.

Turki's stance in his first two books anchors the predicament of the minority writer in the posture of classical Arab poets: "our poets have appropriated the role of speaking the language of the people, of drawing on the universality of their struggle rather than on the particularity of a personal malaise" (Turki 1974, 46). He also asserts that "people in struggle don't operate in a vacuum when they go about creating their self-definitions" (1988, 102). Accordingly, Turki's preoccupation with his people and "the universality of their struggle" takes precedence over his own "personal malaise," and he defines himself first and foremost as a Palestinian exile and revolutionary. This is signaled immediately in the title of his first book, *The Disinherited: Journal of a Palestinian Exile*, which refers at once to himself and to the Palestinian people as a whole, while the indefinite article in the subtitle designates both a particular individual (the author) and any individual, the Palestinian Everyman. In the final chapter, he writes,

> In a way, all that I have written on the preceding pages is really a journal. My own and the journal of thousands of Palestinians like myself who grew up in the Middle East over the last two decades. I have written it to satisfy myself and those who want to know that our struggle has not been merely for a place in the sun and a standard of living, but a struggle for dignity and national identity. (1974, 149)

A form of autobiographical writing, the journal is a private chronicle of events, recorded with personal reflections as the events unfold in time. The record grows as new events unfold and the writer's understanding of them develops. The journal is, therefore, a narrative under construction, subject to renarration, reassessment, and reinterpretation, in an ongoing effort to give shape to a past that constantly swallows the present. If autobiography and memoir recount a finite period in the past (even as the author's life unfolds), a journal is open-ended, and in a sense unending; its events will acquire final meaning from an unattainable point in the future—that is, unattainable from within the journal itself. The speaking subject of a journal has not, and cannot, transcend the open-ended temporality that he or she inhabits so as to write a finite narrative like that of a novelist, autobiographer, or memoirist who works with a temporally bracketed narrative. The journal ends not when the story ends, but when the writer stops writing, sometimes abruptly, *in medias res*, perhaps even in mid-sentence, at any rate still looking ahead into the future. In Turki's "journal," therefore, the storyline flows beyond the back cover and spills into the next book, another installment of the journal that retells, amplifies, updates, and reinterprets the story told in the previous book(s), and on and on until the writer lays down the pen for the last time. This is the distinctive feature of Turki's books, which attempt to tell not the story of an individual life (e.g. Said's life up to the 1960s, or Shihab's trip to Palestine/Israel over the course of a few weeks in the mid 1990s), but of an exiled nation's ongoing struggle for survival.[6] Therefore, in *The Disinherited*, the story begins several decades before Turki's birth, in 1896, when Theodore Herzl published *The Jewish State*, the book that first articulated the Zionist project, while Turki's third memoir ends with the dream of a future Palestinian state that may not be realized in his own lifetime.

Despite significant differences among Turki's three memoirs, they share two features that underscore the temporal open-endedness of the journal, one stylistic and the other formal. First, he always recounts the events of his life in the present rather than the past tense, lending a sense of immediacy to his reactions, thoughts, and the meaning he derives from his experience, as though each book were a contemporary record of events as they unfold. Second, all three books end by projecting forward into the future: *The Disinherited* closes with a chapter on

"What Is to Be Done?"; the last few lines of *Soul in Exile* mitigate his despair at the world's indifference and his sense of the futility of his own writing by asserting his faith that "our children . . . will understand"; and *Exile's Return* ends with a "fantasy," a "dream" in which he sees himself returning in ten years' time to an independent Palestinian state presided over by the young leadership of the Intifada, a new generation that he hopes will succeed where his own has failed. This open-endedness of narratives that refuse closure and look resolutely into the future denotes a refusal to accept the status quo or to give up on Palestinian aspirations, despite a seemingly endless series of frustrations. At the same time, by recognizing that those aspirations may not be realized in his own lifetime, Turki refuses to settle for an individualistic sense of self that repudiates collective identity. Consequently, as we have seen in Shihab, the resolution to the question of home is indefinitely postponed.

So completely does Turki strive to embody Palestinian national consciousness that very little of his own personal history comes through in *The Disinherited* and *Soul in Exile*. Disconnected scenes from the family's exodus from Haifa, wretched existence in the refugee camp, childhood and adolescent delinquency, persecution and humiliation on the streets of Beirut, and early political activism are reported in both books to illustrate not the evolution of an individual consciousness or psychic life, but the condition of a nation in exile, especially that of a generation growing up in refugee camps. In striving to write the autobiography of a people, at a time when no Palestinian narrative existed in English, Turki allows only fragments of his own life story to creep in, separated by conspicuous gaps. For example, in the last sentence of the second chapter of *The Disinherited*, he tells us that in 1958 "he graduated from high school and was granted a scholarship to study in England, where I stayed for three and a half years" (1974, 74), but the next chapter begins with his return "to the Middle East more embittered, more disillusioned, more unhappy than when I left" (75). Not another word is written about that interval in England. Likewise, no more than passing references are made to his immigration to Australia in the early sixties and the three years he spent in Nepal from the late 1960s until he arrived in Paris in 1970 and began writing the book. His Australian experience is briefly described in his second book, *Soul in Exile* (1988), but without an account of his relationship with an Australian woman with whom he had a child or of his hippie phase. Those two episodes are finally recounted in *Exile's Return* (1994), even though he had already lived through them before writing *The Disinherited*. It took him two decades to able to give shape to a personal story that deviates from, although it remains intelligible only in the context of, the narrative of Palestinian dispossession. This collective narrative leaves little room for the story of the individual; the political subsumes the personal in the first two installments of the journal.

That being the case, *The Disinherited* opens with this emblematic statement, which defines Turki's project in this and subsequent works: "The major source for this book is *my* own recollections of what *we* have endured and *my* own conviction that *ours* is a just cause, a cause long forgotten by the Western world (self-righteous in its overly easy conscience) and long mutilated by the Arab world (self-satisfied in its mercenary games)" (7, emphasis added). The entire trajectory of the first two books is captured in the swift and constant movement from first-person singular to first-person plural pronouns, as though the singular voice exists only as a conduit to the plural, anchoring it in the concreteness and specificity of localized, lived experience. Such anchoring is necessary in the face of Zionism's attempt to negate the existence of Palestinians, and the U.S. and Western Europe's willingness to turn a blind eye to their plight. This "overly easy conscience" with regard to the Palestinians is the flipside of Euro-American guilt over the Holocaust, which Zionism has exploited to full effect. In the same sentence, Turki differentiates Palestinians from other Arabs by way of asserting Palestinian identity in the face of Zionists' negation of it.

Deeply Orientalist and inherently racist, the proposition that Arabs are all the same flies in the face of a fact that Turki is at great pains to emphasize, namely that Palestinians have suffered expulsion, indignity, and massacres at the hands of Zionists *and* Arab regimes. If Menachem Begin's Irgun, Yitzhak Shamir's Stern Gang, and the Haganah used systematic terror to cleanse Palestine ethnically of its non-Jewish inhabitants during the 1940s, Jordan's King Hussein, Syria's Hafez Assad, and Lebanon's Fascist Phalangists also massacred Palestinians in Black September (1970), Tel Zaatar (1976), and Sabra and Shatila (1982), respectively. (*The Disinherited* was written as the first of these tragedies unfolded, and *Soul in Exile* opens with the Palestine National Council convening shortly after the third of those massacres.) The Arab regimes, in other words, cynically exploited the plight of the Palestinians or treated them just as savagely as the Zionists. To make things even worse, those regimes failed to represent the justice of the Palestinian cause effectively to the world: "Despite the absurdity of the Zionist claim for a 'return' to Palestine and the injustice inherent in the act of taking from the Palestinians to give to the Jews for a crime committed by the Nazis, the real issues involved in the Palestinian problem and the hope for its solution got buried under the heavy weight of the first speech pledging the driving of the Jews into the sea" (1974, 128). Thus "the battle to remain myself, as a Palestinian belonging to a people with a distinctly Palestinian consciousness" (8) is waged against both the Zionists and reactionary Arab regimes that see the Palestinian resistance movement, which emerged after their defeat in 1967, as a populist threat to their illegitimate authority.

In *The Disinherited* and *Soul in Exile*, Turki describes in detail the emergence and tribulations of the Palestinian movement, which finally dispelled the myth that Palestinians did not exist. Branded as terroristic for a slew of sensational bombings and hijackings and the murder of Israeli athletes at the Munich Olympics (which occurred after the publication of *The Disinherited* and provided the occasion for an epilogue added to the 1974 reprint), Turki attempts to "offer some notes toward an understanding of what we are doing now and an insight into the way and the how of it" (8). He attempts to do so by interpreting the Palestinian predicament in terms of the struggles of the oppressed everywhere, especially the Abolitionist and Third World liberation movements, as well as the existentialism of Jean-Paul Sartre. Evoking Fanon, Turki writes, "The Palestinian revolutionist viewed his struggle as identical with the one waged by all the wretched of the earth for liberation and dignity" (Turki 1974, 116). He also advances an argument that echoes Frederick Douglass and Aimé Césaire: "the venomous consciousness of the occupiers turns inward in time as they subjugate their victims by the rule of the gun, thus destroying for themselves what there is of humanity in humans and restoring in them what there is of beast. For brutality has a way . . . of seeking vengeance on those who unleash it" (1988, 128).[7] He also interprets his situation in existentialist terms:

> Mine is an existential problem having to do with the yearning for my homeland, with being part of a culture, with winning the battle to remain myself, as a Palestinian belonging to a people with a distinctly Palestinian consciousness.
>
> If I was not a Palestinian when I left Haifa as a child, I am one now. Living in Beirut as a stateless person for most of my growing-up years, many of them in a refugee camp, I did not feel I was living among my "Arab brothers." I did not feel I was an Arab, a Lebanese, or as some wretchedly pious writers claimed, a "southern Syrian." I was a Palestinian. And that meant I was an outsider, an alien, a refugee, a burden. To be that, for us, for my generation of Palestinians, meant to look inward, to draw closer, to be part of a minority that had its own way of doing and seeing and feeling and reacting. To be that, for us, meant the addition of a subtler nuance to the cultural makeup of our Palestinianness. (1974, 9)

In this existential condition, the "outsider" is not an alienated individual but an alienated generation from an alienated nation. True to Sartre's legacy, this condition entails political commitment to a just cause, which Turki describes in Fanonian terms. He draws inspiration from the Algerian war (129, 141), a bloody but ultimately successful struggle against settler colonialism that was still a fresh memory when he wrote *The Disinherited* and, indeed, more than a decade later: *Soul in Exile* opens with the Palestinian delegations arriving to attend the sixteenth session of the Palestine National Congress in Algiers, where they are received as heroes in the airport VIP lounge. But not only Algeria: "If the black people of South Africa, Zimbabwe, Angola, and Mozambique would not accept apartheid, racism, and colonialism, why should the Arabs?" (1974, 182) Fanon's argument, in *The Wretched of the Earth*, that national consciousness does not predate colonialism but is forged during the violent struggle for liberation, reverberates in Turki's emphasis on his generation's acquisition of a unique sense of Palestinian identity, distinct from that of the earlier generation by the "subtler nuance" gained from growing up in exile. Palestinian armed resistance is apprehended within Fanon's theory of revolution as a violent Manichean struggle between colonizer and colonized: "Palestinian violence does not occur in a vacuum. It is best understood in the dichotomy that exists between the oppressor and the oppressed, the occupier and the occupied, the colonizer and the colonized, the master and the slave" (1974, 167). That violence forced the Zionists and their supporters to recognize the existence and the claims of the Palestinians:

> Only when we took to armed violence did the world stop calling us "the Arab refugees" and start calling us Palestinians. Responsible statements were heard from world leaders suggesting that for the first time since their diaspora, the Palestinian people's position was now being understood. President Nixon, a man not noted for his consideration of the oppressed peoples of the world, said in his State of the World message in February 1971 that no Middle East peace was possible "without redressing the legitimate aspirations of the Palestinian people." This was significant only inasmuch as it indicated the great shift toward understanding the Palestinian cause occurring in American policy, and in that it was the first statement of its kind by an American president. (136)

This shift also occurred among Israelis, as evidenced by Shlomo Avineri:

> Those like Golda Meir who continue to ask, 'Who are the Palestinians?' seem increasingly out of touch with reality; for it is Palestinian organizations that send their members to kill and maim Israelis, and it is against Palestinian organizations that Israeli patrols lie in nightly ambush in the Jordan Valley. Under such conditions anyone still questioning the existence of Arabs who call themselves Palestinians is talking ideology not facts. (quoted in Turki 1974, 138)

While Fanon's Manichean theory of violence, which developed in the context of colonial war, provides Turki with a paradigm for interpreting Palestinian violence to his readers, it also imposes a discursive limit. As a theory of absolute opposition between antagonistic principles, Manicheism is highly adaptable to the Orientalist dichotomy between Orient and Occident. In colonial discourse, that Orient/Occident opposition placed Europe at the top of the hierarchy of civilization. We have seen that Ameen Rihani and Abraham Rihbany attempted to annul that hierarchy without undoing the opposition by interpreting the culturalist dichotomy in terms of Hegelian synthesis or yin-yang complementarity. In Fanon's revolutionary theory, the dichotomy reappears as an opposition between the colonial power and the wretched of the earth, an opposition that reverses the hierarchy of values by giving the moral upper hand to the oppressed, while reinforcing the binary. This is a necessary move in the context of armed liberation struggle, but when used as a paradigm of cultural translation, the Manichean model theoretically forecloses any possibility of mutual comprehension. This slippage in Turki's discourse is evident in the 1974 epilogue:

> It becomes ever more difficult every day for a Third World person to communicate the essence of his experience to people in the West; not only because they remain so unyielding in their attitudes, their myths, and their blatant racism. Not only because he finds it increasingly urgent to return to his roots and scour the culture of the West off his back. Rather it is because a Third World person's linear development, his idiom and his metaphor, will forever remain alien to Western society. He is located in a

> spatial and temporal reality where his sensibilities respond to issues and feelings that to a Westerner are an abstraction. (174)

The number of totalizing judgments, essentialisms, and masculinist assumptions crammed in this short passage is impressive. People in the Third World are as homogenized as those of the West; their collective experience is unitary and their worldviews and reactions are identical, undifferentiated by culture, gender, class, religion, or local history. That being the case, it would seem pointless to write a book that, as he states in the first edition of 1972, seeks to "offer some notes toward an understanding of what we are doing now and an insight into the why and the how of it" (8). The historical moment to which the 1974 epilogue belongs does not validate the logic of that statement, but explains the frustration evident in it: written in the U.S., where Turki arrived in October 1973, it was a reaction against the bitter hostility toward Palestinians and Arabs in the U.S., which had been accentuated in the aftermath of the Munich Olympics and compounded even more by the 6th of October (Yom Kippur) War and the Arab oil embargo. A recent arrival and a sought-after public speaker, Turki describes that period in this way: "I give lectures to American audiences around the country and they ask me racist questions. . . . When I first arrive in this country I am a patient speaker who wants to disseminate information, debate, talk rationally. I keep my voice calm. I am so patient. I am so moderate. Three months later, I no longer want to expose myself to indignities or contain my anger" (181–82). "In the States, I come close to the most racist society that I had ever lived in, including the ones in Australia and France" (185). His defensive reaction is to declare that the reality of the Palestinians and Third World peoples as a whole is simply beyond the West's capacity to comprehend.

If the argument for total incomprehensibility in the 1974 epilogue is an extreme and defensive formulation, he nevertheless recognizes that the struggle for Palestinian rights remains, in one sense, a struggle over interpretation, a war of definitions and of narratives and counter-narratives, that can be won only through effective representation and cultural translation. Early in the book, he declares disdainfully,

> I am neither concerned nor qualified to indulge in the game of quote and counter-quote adopted by those whose business or ideology drives them to espouse the position of one or the other. I have discovered that with enough diligence, the historian can present a devastatingly convincing version of the Zionist/Israeli/Jewish (call it what you wish) claim in modern Palestine. Another historian, with equal diligence and partisan to our own claims and grievances, can come up with a perfectly valid and at the same time diametrically opposite view. (8)

This irreconcilability of discourses driven by antagonistic ideologies crystallizes in the question of how to describe those who undertake violent resistance: "terrorists," according to Zionist discourse, which dominates mainstream liberal and conservative U.S. media and the foreign policy establishment; "guerillas," in leftist and Third Worldist discourse; or in Palestinian and Arab discourse, "*mujahideen*" (those who conduct holy war) and "*fedayeen*" (those who sacrifice themselves for others), terms laden with religious (Muslim and Christian) associations not found in the secular discourse of Fanon and Third Worldism. Turki's explanation of those nuances in *Soul in Exile* (1988, 47) indicates that he still believes it to be possible for his American readers to understand a different cultural discourse. And indeed this second book, written many years after settling permanently in the U.S., is another attempt at explaining the Palestinian case. Yet at the end of the book, he describes his reaction to the Israeli invasion of Lebanon, the massacres of Sabra and Shatila, and the seeming indifference of the world in this way: "I withdraw to write . . . There is nothing else to do. I am forty-five and I find no emotional logic in my introspections, no relevance in my dogmatic certitudes. A new generation, bringing with it a new order of reality, an alternative order of meaning, is emerging to supplant ours" (1988, 202). It is for that generation of Palestinians (the generation of the Intifada on which Turki pins his hopes in his next book, *Exile's Return*) that Turki implies that he is writing: "People who die for the freedom of others are, like women who die in childbirth, difficult to explain except to those for whom they died. Our children have drunk all our suffering. . . . They will understand" (1988, 204). He is torn between, on the one hand, a sense of futility that persists after over a decade of writing for newspapers and speaking on television and in countless public lectures, and on the other hand the belief in the possibility of comprehension that drives him to write, speak, and reconstruct his narrative again and again.

The Making of a Palestinian American

Even though he had been living in the U.S. for fifteen years by the time his second memoir, *Soul in Exile: Lives of a Palestinian Revolutionary*, was published in 1988, Turki does not present himself in it as a Palestinian American. As the subtitle indicates, he remains a representative of a people, completely identified with a national struggle—except for the intriguingly plural noun in the subtitle. This plurality is belied, however, by the continuing suppression of any mark of individuality. The word "lives" merely hints that there may be something more to the author, other lives besides that of a revolutionary, which alone occupies the full space of the book. Turki had an unimaginably difficult childhood not only because of the *Nakba*, but also because of a tragedy that ended his sister's life and alienated him from his family forever. He was an Australian citizen when he came to the U.S. in 1973, and he became a U.S. citizen afterwards. He had an Australian wife and son, then a Jewish American wife, whom he met in Paris and followed to Boston, and with whom he had a daughter. He spent years in Australia and South Asia trying (by his own admission) to escape his Palestinianness. He was addicted to drugs and alcohol during the time he wrote *Soul on Exile*. The only sign of those "lives" is the mark of the plural in the subtitle. They remain outside the book, spilling out only in the third memoir, published in 1994, in which Turki implies that everything in his past was a preparation for his acquisition of a new, American identity: *Exile's Return: The Making of a Palestinian American*.

The radical nature of this shift in self-identification in the 1994 book cannot be appreciated without first noting his extremely negative assessment of the U.S. in the 1988 book. Keeping in mind that he came to the U.S. in 1973, such an assessment cannot entirely be explained by the culture shock of a new émigré. In *Soul in Exile*, Turki has no qualms about voicing his disdain for the U.S., its culture, and its people. Boarding a plane from Paris to New York at the outbreak of the October 1973 war, he wonders, "What the hell am I going to do there? What am I going to do in the United States? Do people there hold demonstrations every day the way they do here in Paris? . . . [G]o to political rallies every other evening, and live in a city that gives shape to the poetics of an outsider's life, and throws its shadow against every line he has written and every word he has uttered?" (1988, 116). He complains about American racism and dismisses many of the country's cherished self-attributes, such as the American Dream, political diversity, and super-power status. The American Dream is vacuous, symbolized by McDonald's (1988, 117), where, interestingly enough, he eats on the next page. He identifies with fellow Palestinians who have

> the cynicism of the rebellious outsider and the counterpolitics of the disinherited acquired by all Palestinians who have spent their late youth in the West. They see themselves as hip activists to whom the traditional concepts of the Arab nation and Arabism are a camp joke, and America and its dream are issues mockingly remote from their vision, their reality, and their aspirations. To these Palestinians living in the United States, Americans are naïve, uninformed, hick. (1988, 118)

Not only mainstream America; the American left, too, is a sham:

> Cambridge has all manner of . . . political groups. I have very little patience with them, especially with 'left-wing' groups calling themselves by high-sounding names who, when debating the Palestine question, sound like they are playing university politics. And liberal Jewish groups that called themselves 'non-Zionist,' whose members debated whether they were 'Jewish radicals' or 'radical Jews.'
>
> Is this the American left? Is this all there is to it? Having just arrived from Europe, where the revolutionary left is a movement with a genuine ideology and established party politics—drawing on a long intellectual tradition—I was shocked by my encounter with its American counterpart. (1988, 131)

Even many Palestinian Americans are subject to his disdain for displaying an attitude that, as we have seen in previous chapters, characterizes the stance of earlier Arab American autobiographers: they "assume a defensive posture, preoccupied with pleasing their audience. We are really, honestly, the injured party in the dispute and we are really, honestly, a nice, peaceful people once you get to know us. Then you'll realize the justice of our cause and your government will correct the wrong committed against us." After appearing on television, publishing articles in national newspapers, and giving public lectures, they would approach him

> with the complaint that I was a bit too harsh. Too blunt. Too radical. How are we going . . . to gain the sympathy of Americans with such intemperate language? How are we going to have the United States on our side if we . . . alienate Americans? . . . There were, however, some of us who could not, because of our political background and social experience, drop the implacable harshness of tone we had set for ourselves as revolutionaries and adopt in its place the rhetorical sophistry of people aiming to please. We could not become Uncle Ahmads. (1988, 136)

As for the American policy makers and strategists whom those "Uncle Ahmads" want to please, they are, in the words of one of his friends,

> fools. They are new at the game of big power. . . . They see history, and human struggle, mechanistically, as a forward motion of events dependent on the law of causality—A leads to B and B leads to C—with everything else constant. But one event in the life of a people in struggle—an invasion by a foreign army, a defeat in battle, the imposition of an unpopular regime, economic destitution, colonial occupation, civil war, name it—could, in the dialectic of things, unlock forces antithetical to the goals intended by a policy move, forces that may have otherwise remained dormant but now, once emergent, will overcome the policy and its initiators. (1988, 191)

Turki has nothing positive to say about the U.S. The condemnation is all encompassing, not only in the 1972 and 1974 editions of his first memoir, but also in 1988. Even taking into account the journal-like quality of his memoirs, this assessment of the U.S. is striking in that it is not nuanced at all over the course of the fifteen years between his arrival in the U.S. and the point at which the book ends in 1988.

Yet a mere six years later, in *Exile's Return*, he reversed his assessment not only of America, but also of Palestinian culture: instead of racist and "hick," the former is now open, democratic, and liberating, while the latter has turned from being revolutionary to decadent, from vibrant to moribund, from progressive to "neo-backward." His self-definition in the subtitles of the three books also changes from a "Palestinian exile" (1972) and "Palestinian revolutionary" (1986) to "Palestinian American" (1994). The "return" of the title is correspondingly puzzling: is it his visit to Palestine/Israel in 1990–91 for the first time in thirty years, or his anxiously awaited return to the U.S. at the end of that trip, or the definitive return to a future Palestinian state that he imagines on the last page of the book?

Exile's Return is framed by that visit. Alternating chapters narrate "the journey to the homeground," as he calls it in the first chapter, and the story of his life starting with the 1948 exodus. What is new in this third narration is what has been suppressed before: his own personal story of labor in the farmlands of the Australian outback, hippie years in South Asia and Europe, pilgrimage to Mecca, and alcohol and drug addiction that nearly killed him in the U.S. In *Soul in Exile*, Turki writes that immigrating to Australia, he wanted to "enjoy anonymity in a social reality that is the complete opposite of mine. I can be invisible" (1988, 74). No personal reasons are given for this desire; the reader is left to assume that the life of a refugee in Lebanon or Syria (where he visits an uncle and is disgusted by the repression of the Syrian police state), and the untold story of Turki's experience in England, are the reason. However, in *Exile's Return*, he reveals a family tragedy that lay at the core of his rebellion against Palestinian and Arab culture in general—the "honor killing" of his sister by his elder brother. This event furnishes the third and most personal of Turki's memoirs with a central metaphor, that of "the land behind the mountains," his sister's childhood imaginary wonderland, which for Turki comes to stand for the future that the Palestinian movement strives to realize.

Like his two previous books, *Exile's Return* is an account of the ongoing series of frustrations of that dream and of its continuing affirmation on the part of the Palestinians. However, while the previous books exposed both the racism of the Zionist project and the persecution of the Palestinians by Arab regimes, the third book takes on the repressive patriarchy of Palestinian culture, especially the lack of personal and sexual freedom, and the incompetence and corruption of the PLO, with which he was involved from the early 1970s to the late 1980s. In fact, he was on the payroll of the PLO at one point during the 1980s, and he admits avoiding any criticism of the organization during that time (1994, 220).

Equally dramatic is his newly found identity as a "Palestinian American," a development that results in some contradictions and inconsistencies in his account. For example, he writes in *Exile's Return*, "It was there [in the U.S.] that I discovered that I wanted to be—needed to be—Palestinian again. *America has a way of allowing people to experience the defining feature of their old culture, after they have given themselves to a new one*" (8–9, emphasis added). Earlier, in *Soul on Exile*, he said the same thing about Paris: "This city has returned me to my original, genuine core of Palestinian selfhood. I am again engaged in Palestinian politics, in revolutionary ideas, as I had been . . . in the streets of Beirut so many years before" (1988, 103). It is true that new places sometimes give one a new perspective on life and expand one's sense of identity, yet what he says in *Exile's Return* implies that only America is able to do that for him, for there is no recollection or acknowledgment of Paris having earlier done the same thing. The effect is to underwrite the uniqueness or exceptionalism of America. Is this simply a matter of a lapse in memory, or is it a deliberate revision of his account? In any event, the new identity brings about a shift in perspective, as he now writes from a position similar to that of other immigrants who have espoused the dominant discourse on American identity. Thus, America is a "new" culture that "allows" ("makes" is probably a more accurate word) immigrants see "their old culture" as "old." It is from the "new" perspective (apparently afforded by neither Australia nor France) that the culture of origin appears "old," not in the positive sense of possessing a long or rich tradition (as in Rihani, Gibran, and Rihbany), but as outworn, outdated, obsolete, backward (as in Rizk, or indeed in colonial discourse). Turki here endorses some of the main ideas in the discourse on America's Manifest Destiny, which Arab American autobiographers from Rihbany to Rizk to Ihab Hassan have confirmed by way of pledging allegiance. Nowhere does Turki explain this radical revision of his attitude toward the U.S.

Nevertheless, his new self-definition as a Palestinian American (rather than simply a Palestinian) has a remarkable consequence, also indicated in the italicized sentence above: the "old" culture now appears to have "a [i.e., one] defining feature" that supposedly was not at all obvious before. Predictably, this reduction to a singular characteristic deemed essential—this essentialization—cannot but throw an unfavorable light on its object. From here follows an all-out attack on Palestinian and Arab culture generally that reproduces crude Orientalist ideas and generates a simplistic analysis of what he considers to be the problem with contemporary Palestinian and Arab culture. This problem, or "defining feature," is what he calls "neobackwardness": "The legacy of Western penetration of the Arab world . . . [which] not only consolidated Arab backwardness but guaranteed its transformation (through the introduction of bastard modes of social experience) into a more subtle form of backwardness" (1994, 117). It is a circular argument that goes as follows: Arabs were backward before colonialism; Europe's civilizing mission failed because it introduced "bastard modes of social experience"; by the same token, "legitimate" ones could not be found because of Arabs' preexisting backward condition, given that backwardness is the authentic Arab mode of being; therefore, Arabs are inherently incapable of progress.

Needless to say, none of those propositions survives scrutiny. Exactly what constitutes "backwardness," and by whose yardstick is it measured? Is it a matter of economics, military strength, social institutions, political stability? How does backwardness become more backward? And what constitutes progress? The barely articulated premise here is the Hegelian notion of the march of history in the footsteps of Europe, of European history as the embodiment of Spirit. As such, any form of development not following the example of Europe is necessarily a deviation, deformation, or distortion. This is the rationale for Marx's equivocal support for British colonialism in India, which Edward Said interprets as Marx's inability to think of India outside of Orientalist discourse (Said 1978, 153–56). It is also the logic of Hisham Sharabi's thesis on "neopatriarchy" as a form of "distorted development" in the Arab world that resulted from an alliance between traditional patriarchy and colonialism as a capitalist venture (Sharabi 1988, 6). Sharabi's theory of "neopatriarchy," advanced in a book by that title and published just a few years before *Exile's Return*, evidently inspired Turki's notion of "neobackwardness," which however lacks the sophistication of Sharabi's careful and insightful, albeit Eurocentric, analysis.

Nowhere does Turki acknowledge his obvious debt to Sharabi. Instead, he goes on to offer this contemptuous and racist stereotype by way of illustrating what he means by "neobackwardness":

> We see it in the spectacle of an Arab who seemingly possesses all the attributes of modernity—who has a university degree, works in a high-tech office, speaks several languages, travels extensively, and appears normal to the naked eye—but once you scratch beneath that veneer, you find him infected with the germ of traditionalism. He is convinced that he has made the leap into modernity already; that his transformation is not

> shallow and superficial; that he is not a mere caricature, a Westernized Arab. . . . Neobackward Arabs, like alcoholics, will continue to deny their affliction as long as they can. (Turki 1994, 117)

This generic and unregenerate specimen, who "appears normal," is anything but. What is normal and by whose standards it is measured are apparently obvious enough for Turki that no clarification seems warranted. His implied readers are now those Americans who are predisposed to such views; he seems no longer to be writing for "our children" (1988, 204). The "normalcy" of a "neobackward" Arab is a mask that may fool the "naked eye," but not the expert with a knowing gaze (Turki, of course, and the Orientalists he now parrots and whose posture he adopts). What the scientific and objective eye of such experts sees is what the afflicted cannot admit: that he is a wog—a Westernized Oriental Gentleman—the contemptuous caricature that British colonial officials made of those natives who aspired to the condition of their betters through colonial mimicry. Like junkies in denial, those cheeky natives desperately need intervention—except that this colonialist attitude does not envision rehabilitation, even though it prescribes it. The point of such arguments is to justify perennial colonial tutelage. The natives are inherently degenerate; their efforts to improve themselves can only be "shallow and superficial"; colonial rule is necessary to keep them from doing harm to themselves and to others.

This attitude underlies the damning evidence that Turki presents, and which reveals his uncritical borrowing of racist ideas and acceptance of Eurocentric history. His sophomoric account of the *Nahda*, for instance, reduces that nineteenth-century movement to "a mimetic Westernized elite" who "borrowed ideas freely [from Europe], imported them voraciously, and applied them senselessly" (116). Equally simplistic is the notion that "the European leap from medieval backwardness to the modernity of the Renaissance had occurred in response to decisive social changes triggered by internal and spontaneous forces" (116). He does not suggest what those forces may have been, but he seems unaware of the decisive roles played in this "European leap" by Arab civilization's achievements in every sphere of knowledge, the Crusaders' encounter with a more advanced culture, and the fact that Europe's economic and industrial development would have been inconceivable without its worldwide imperial conquests, initially spurred by economic competition with the Muslim world, and yielding the rich spoils of unimaginable devastation. None of those forces are simply internal or spontaneous.

Other criticisms he marshals are no less surprising both for their contradictoriness and for the way they seem simply to repeat some of the most trite, arrogant, and ignorant anti-Arab and anti-Muslim propaganda. For instance, he states that Islam is an inferior religion because it is not centered on Christian love (125), although elsewhere he claims that he admires Islam as a religion and laments the way it is used to justify oppressive practices in Muslim countries (211, 256). Though he disdainfully boasts that he has never learned the Muslim daily prayer (28), he nevertheless describes it as "a mindless ritual [that] has turned Muslims into zombies" (144).

He expresses his admiration for the Qur'an, even though he has not read it. Without bothering to check his sources, he attributes to the Qur'an statements from the *hadith* (144). He rejects organized religion in principle, yet he goes on a pilgrimage to Mecca in a farcical attempt to stir religious feeling in himself, and to find something to believe in (203), as though going through the motions would be enough. The devotion of other pilgrims does not escape his sarcasm (203).

Turki reserves some of his most venomous attacks for the Arabic language. Arabic has, of course, been a favorite target for some Orientalists. Edward Said devotes many pages in *Orientalism* to Ernest Renan's dichotomy between Indo-European and Semitic languages and his claim that the latter constitute "a phenomenon of arrested development in comparison with the mature languages and cultures of the Indo-European group. . . . [T]he Semitic languages are inorganic, arrested, totally ossified, incapable of self-regeneration" (Said 1978, 145). By the time it filters down to twentieth century American Orientalism, that dichotomy degenerates into increasingly absurd and simple-minded assertions about the Arabic language specifically (310, 320). Turki uses this discourse selectively: he describes Modern Standard Arabic (MSA) in the same terms, but he admires classical Arabic and the Palestinian colloquial. It is clear from the sometimes wildly scratchy translations he volunteers of Arabic words, expressions, and verses of poetry, that he has mastered neither MSA nor classical Arabic. Not only that, but Turki did not even speak the vernacular for a whole decade at a stretch (Turki 1994, 186). Nevertheless, he feels confident to repeat judgments that betray his ignorance of how language works: "Formal Arabic [is] a language unsuited to logical thinking" (213); it is "a language whose constraints contributed to regimenting personal behavior and helped to systematize the rules and corruptions of the Arab establishment" (62)—the sort of judgments that Ameen Rihani described as "drivel" nearly eight decades earlier (Rihani 1918, 18).

Some British- and French-educated Arabs whose schools made them functionally illiterate in MSA and classical Arabic and taught them to despise their culture imbibed this Orientalist hostility to Arabic. But Turki has an additional axe to grind. MSA is the lingua franca of the Arab world and was, therefore, also the vehicle of pan-Arab nationalist discourse of the 1950s–60s. From his first book, Turki declared his enmity to pan-Arabism and its political representatives, principally Egypt's president Gamal Abdel-Nasser and Syria's Hafez Assad, and to official Arab culture generally, from education to the media, all of which used MSA (or what he calls "Formal Arabic"). He erroneously defines it as

> the exclusive lingo of the ruling elite, the Westernized intelligentsia, representatives of state power, the bureaucrats, the *mukhabarat* [state security] sadists, and the effete literati, Formal Arabic . . . is a kind of secondhand derivative of Classical Arabic, replete with pretensions and artifices imported from the West. . . . It was in Formal Arabic . . . that Nasser and the Voice of the Arabs Radio from Cairo spoke to the Arab masses . . . as did Saddam and the Voice of the Mother of All Battles Radio. (121–22)

Hence, his attack on MSA is part and parcel of his otherwise entirely justifiable attack on the Arab political establishment, except that it is nonsensical to blame language for the sins of some of its users—for it is not true that it is "the exclusive lingo" of the groups he names. MSA is also the language of a vibrant literary culture that is often politically dissident and critical of a whole spectrum of social norms far broader than the problems on which Turki focuses. Clearly, he has no familiarity whatsoever with modern Arabic literature, yet he proclaims that "much of what passes for Arabic 'literature' today should be remaindered as quickly as it is published" (124).

The problem with *Exile's Return* is not that Turki criticizes Palestinian and Arab societies. No society is free of weaknesses and, like any other society, there is much to criticize in the Arab world—patriarchy, authoritarianism, sexism, conservatism, corruption, nepotism, sectarianism, limited personal freedoms, homophobia, and so on. The trouble is that he seems incapable of doing so without resorting to the most bigoted and simple-minded inanities found in anti-Arab propaganda, as though his new self-identification as a "Palestinian American" required him to adopt racist views. Some of his criticisms are obviously justified and reformist in spirit, but they are mixed in with astonishingly sweeping generalizations—astonishing because he ought to know better and because they contradict his earlier books so glaringly. The net effect of this is to explain the catastrophic modern history of the Palestinians by their own weaknesses, a tendency that Said and others exposed in *Blaming the Victims: Spurious Scholarship and the Palestinian Question* (1987). It is one of the strategies used to negate Palestinian rights and to absolve Israel and its supporters of any responsibility for the egregious injustices upon which the Jewish state was founded, and which it continues to perpetrate.

When a Palestinian exile who once described himself as a revolutionary resorts to that discourse, it is obviously not out of indifference to Palestinian suffering or support for Zionism. To adapt Thomas Pynchon's brilliant formulation, Turki veers so far to the left that he ends up on the right (Pynchon 88–89). He understands Palestinian psychology well enough to argue that "the narrow inwardness that Palestinians retreated to . . . after 1948," when they felt betrayed by the Arabs and abandoned by the rest of the world, is a "defensive" posture:

> Palestinians are alone in the world. Which means you don't criticize your own people, your own cause, your own movement, when with outsiders. In the end, this was inevitably to mean: You do not criticize Palestinian society even when with your own kind. This was to translate into a kind of resolute provincialism that would make Palestinians turn a deaf ear to the attractions of another way of thought and social conduct. (Turki 1994, 22)

This insight acknowledges the immeasurable pressure placed on a society facing the threat of annihilation. Its very survival, against the odds, is due in large part to the resiliency it gained from such "defensiveness," which, of course, came at a price. No society emerges unscarred from a collective trauma of such magnitude. Without a doubt, Turki's intent is reformist: "I am a Palestinian, but also one who has come to believe that the spirit of Palestinian society will not become hot to the touch until Palestinians escape the prison of their moribund cultural norms" (1994, 31). However, in his blindingly violent zeal and his desperation at the frustration of Palestinian aspirations over several decades, what he seems to forget is that attacking the symptoms alone risks diverting attention from their causes.

Nevertheless, at times he questions both his ability to diagnose what ails Palestinian society and his right to prescribe the cure. His first visit to "the homeground" in over three decades leaves him, first, with the unmistakable impression that his experience and worldview differ significantly from that of other Palestinians living in Israel and the Occupied Territories; and second, the suspicion that his harsh judgment on those other Palestinians may be misguided and condescending. In Jerusalem, he realizes the following:

> I am a Palestinian exile by upbringing and an American leftist by choice. [There is no explanation given for this unexpected rehabilitation of the American left!] I am here to be one, if only for a moment, with the Palestinians who have never left Palestine. But I have to admit that to be a Palestinian, like them, is not like a glove that an exile can slip on at will. Nor can these people slip into my glove. . . . Palestinians in the homeground are shaped by the irremediable suffering in their daily lives. I can no more pretend to feel the way they do about that suffering than they can afford a welcome to my way of being Palestinian. (33)

He describes Ramallah as "A Heart of Darkness" due to the horrendous conditions of life under occupation, which he experiences for the first time, even though his American passport and foreign appearance protect him somewhat from the routine harassment meted to other Palestinians—curfews, road blockades, power cuts, and midnight raids by occupation forces that seem to have no other objective than to terrorize the population. This makes him wonder, "What conceit I bring with me to this place. Who am I, after all, to come here from my comfortable exile, to foist my fancy musings on the homeground?" (73)

Homeground, Home, and Homelessness

Turki reports a conversation with a friend who describes himself as "a Palestinian Jew" and "an anti-Zionist Israeli," and who accuses Turki of being "a self-hating Palestinian." Far from denying the charge, Turki concedes and tries to justify it: "Self-hatred . . . helps you relinquish those lunacies that cling to your history and soul and language and integrity. . . . Like otherness, self-hate is something visited upon you by others. It is the poison they give you because you've challenged their tradition. And if it doesn't kill you, you emerge from it transformed, since it can trigger fundamental energies of adjustment that will take you beyond your fixed meaning" (217). This is then yet another way in which, within the same book this time, Turki casts doubt on his earlier assertions. If in *Exile's Return* he undermines the narrative he so eloquently constructed in his two previous memoirs (or "journals"), here he undercuts the vociferous criticism of Palestinian society that he has advanced until this point in the third book. Implied in his conception of self-hate is that it is a phase that one goes through. This book is then another dramatic episode in an unfolding narrative, another flight from the stress of Palestinian history, not unlike his flight to Australia and South Asia in search of "invisibility" thirty years earlier. Like an installment of a journal, this episode does not proceed in a linear fashion from where the previous one ended, but casts a new light on what came before from an ever shifting vantage point. This temporal open-endedness of the narrative has the effect of postponing any closure, since closure is a luxury afforded from a yet unrealized future perspective. Indeed, this scathing book ends, surprisingly (not to mention illogically, given his argument that Palestinians are the most neobackward Arab society [189]), with a powerful affirmation of Palestinian aspirations. In the penultimate chapter, he meets two leaders of an underground Intifada cell in Haifa who impress him with their organization, democratic spirit, and dedication, and who represent for him the only glimmer of hope. He emerges from the meeting reassured: "*Now I am ready to go home*. I love this land. . . . But I am also weary of it" (266, emphasis added). On the final page of the book, he describes a "fantasy" and a "dream" in which he sees himself returning ten years later to live in an independent Palestinian state, presided over by one of the two Intifada leaders he met in Haifa. With the frustration of that dream (as of this writing a Palestinian state has not materialized), it remains to be seen if another installment of Turki's journal, another memoir, will be forthcoming.

Once again, "home" is ambivalent in the extreme. In that sentence, home is Washington, D.C., where he has lived since the mid-1970s, "longer than in any other part of the world" (273). He finds "the idea of the nation [to be] absurdly wrong . . . [and] nationalism to be obscene" (272). He believes that

> forty-five years of exile are homeland enough. Anywhere where one is free . . . is homeland enough. I need not live in Nablus or Jericho or Gaza. I could live anywhere I am with my people—those from any part of the world with whom I share a commonality of values and a certain way of life. Paris, Sydney, or New York will do—especially New York, because New Yorkers are like Palestinians in many ways. (273)

But the idea of the *'Awda* persists because it is "necessary to the lives of Palestinians in exile"; "like the square root of minus one, the *'Awda* was a big lie, an imaginary notion, a state of fancy . . . an imaginary value [that] is integral to the order of mathematics" (271). Indeed, the book ends with Turki "succumbing to the fantasy" and dreaming of his own return to live in a Palestinian state (274). The idea of home, then, remains emotionally, imaginatively, and psychically linked to Palestine, even though practically it is not tied to any specific locale, but to a notion of freedom of action, thought, and association. This extra-territorial notion of home remains rooted in Palestinianness (a Palestinianness predicated on exile from Palestine), and he feels it embodied not in Washington, D.C., but in New York, where he has never lived:

> New Yorkers are like Palestinians . . . born of tragedy. Their ancestors landed at Ellis Island after escaping a czar, . . . a tyrant, . . . a colonial oppressor, or were brought to the U.S. as slaves. Like Palestinians, New Yorkers are a little mad, a little lonely, a little disgruntled. They live with no regard for the concerns of the rest of the planet and stare with murder in their eyes if you dare suggest that there is any place better than where they come from. (273)

Arriving at this recognition may be Turki's claim to American identity. Hence his "read[iness] to go home" to the U.S. after meeting the Intifada activists. Nevertheless, the ultimate "exile's return" is the return to Palestine that he dreams about on the last page. This hesitation, ambivalence, even contradictions in the meaning of home—historical Palestine (and Haifa, in Turki's case), a future Palestinian state in the West Bank and Gaza, anywhere that one is free, or anywhere inhabited by people shaped and scarred by exile like the Palestinians—parallel the equally discontinuous ways in which Turki defines and redefines his identity: a refugee and a rebel against his society; an escapist and a revolutionary; a bohemian and an activist; a PLO functionary and a critic of the PLO; a stateless Palestinian, an Australian, a Palestinian American.

Exile's Return is a fundamentally flawed book, but it has at least one merit: it nuances and adds depth to the representation of the Palestinians by differentiating Turki's experience from that of those living inside Israel, those in the West Bank, and the myriad experiences of those, like himself, who scattered to the four corners of the earth. In his previous books, Turki narrated the history of the Palestinian people so eloquently at a time when such narrative was nonexistent; but this he did at the expense of homogenizing the Palestinian experience, of not giving a sense of the range of ways of being Palestinian. Of course, that may have been neither his intent nor the politically expedient thing to do in 1972, 1974, or even in 1988, whereas, by 1994, the Oslo Accords and the so-called historic handshake between Yasser Arafat and Yitzhak Rabin on the White House lawn in September 1993, to which Turki refers in first line of *Exile's Return* (v), signaled that the battle to prove the existence of the Palestinians and the legitimacy of their aspirations has been won, and that therefore he is free to criticize the PLO (which by then, incidentally, no longer paid his "meal ticket" [220]). The time seemed ripe also to turn his attention to building a new society, something that calls for unsparing assessment and self-critique. Yet it also becomes clear that the nearly complete self-negation of the first two memoirs was a reaction against his previous attempt, during the 1960s, to distance himself from the Palestinian cause:

> As a child, I had felt a certain apartness as a Palestinian. As an Australian, I had felt—despite my at-homeness there—a sense of conscious acquisition of the cultural idiom. As a citizen of the Woodstock Nation, I had always felt the stress of extraterritoriality that the nation's members claimed for themselves. In each of these worlds, my identity was provisional, a partial construct. Wanting to be Palestinian now [in 1971] must mean, I suppose, that all the facets of my identity could be defined at once

> by Palestine's 'national' struggle. What better place for a flower child, fleeing the ruined Eden of Woodstock, to seek a pivot for his identity?
>
> I was now . . . more Palestinian than any of the activists I came to know in Paris. (1994, 185)

Gone here is the kind of totalizing statement found in the 1974 epilogue to *The Disinherited*, in which he claimed that "Third World" people and "Western" people had homogeneous and oppositional views and experiences. At the same time, the third memoir asserts his Americanness and his individuality by representing his background in terms familiar to his U.S. readers—much like Abraham Rihbany, Salom Rizk, and Ihab Hassan had done before, except that unlike his conservative (Rihbany and Rizk) and liberal (Ihab Hassan) predecessors, Turki is a "flower child," a "citizen of Woodstock Nation," and an "American leftist." He also strives to be more American than Americans in his harsh condemnation of the Palestinians—just as he had had tried to become more Palestinian than Palestinians. Ever a man of extremes by temperament, he remains tragically torn between self-definitions, his sense of identity as provisional in the 1990s as it was in the 1960s, 1970s, and 1980s. There is nothing necessarily wrong with that, except that he experiences the provisional nature of his identity as a crisis and seems continuously desperate to reconcile all its "facets" and to find a central "pivot" to it.

Turki's insistence till the end on a unitary identity explains both his tragic sense of fragmentation and his charge that Arabs as a whole "suffer from multiple personality disorder" (115), since they identify themselves by "three names—Arab, Moslem, the national name [i.e. 'Lebanese, Palestinians, Jordanians, Kuwaitis, and so on']. They belonged to one. They belonged to none" (120). Nothing can be more different from Edward Said's argument that "No one today is purely *one* thing" (Said 1993, 336) or his sense of himself as a "a cluster of flowing currents" that "require no reconciling, no harmonizing," rather than as "a solid self, the identity to which so many attach so much significance" (1999, 295). As we have seen, Turki comes close to Said's notion of selfhood when stressing his affinity with people of all backgrounds who share common values, but elsewhere he clings to the old notion of a solid self. Neither a precise thinker nor a rigorous analyst, Turki nonetheless shares with Said the kind of skepticism that questions ideological imperatives, religious and political dogmas, and social pieties. Ironically, however, when he directs that skepticism to Palestinians and Arabs, Turki falls back on reductive ideas about language, culture, social mores, and religion; discursive strategies like generalizations, stereotyping, and spuriously totalizing judgments; and a condescending, disdainful, and arrogant tone—all of which are characteristic of the kind of racism that Said identifies in post-1948 American Orientalism. It is as though Turki could find no language to express his justifiable dissatisfaction with the state of Palestinian and Arab politics and society outside of that discredited register, and no way to assert his newfound Americanness except by validating the prevailing prejudices against his own people. To date, no literary embodiment of the ravages of Palestinian history is more bitterly ironic than Turki's trilogy of memoirs.

6

Academic Itineraries

> My story began in Egypt, continues in America. But how tell that story of disjunction, self-exile? In fragments, I think, in slips of memory, scraps of thought. In scenes and arguments of a life time, remembered like the scattered bones of Osiris.
>
> —IHAB HASSAN

> And I am now at the end point of the story I set out to tell here. For thereafter my life becomes part of other stories, American stories. It becomes part of the story of feminism in America, the story of women in America, the story of women of color in America, the story of Arabs in America, the story of Muslims in America, and part of the story of America itself and of American lives in a world of dissolving boundaries and vanishing borders.
>
> —LEILA AHMED

Out of History

While the memoirs of Palestinians exiled in 1948 broke the mold of both the immigrant autobiography described by Jerzy Durczak and the Arab immigrant writing analyzed in earlier chapters, the memoirs of Ihab Hassan, *Out of Egypt: Scenes and Arguments of an Autobiography* (1986), and Leila Ahmed, *A Border Passage: From Cairo to America—A Woman's Journey* (1999), were departures of their own in Arab American literature. The first of their kind by Egyptian immigrants, they were also the first by U.S. academics who happen to be of Muslim background. Unlike all the other immigrants discussed so far, Hassan and Ahmed did not leave their country out of economic or political necessity, being highly educated and from upper-class backgrounds when they emigrated to the U.S. Both belonged to Cairene families that had enjoyed considerable privilege then suffered (in the 1940s in Hassan's case, in the 1950s in Ahmed's) a reversal of fortune when they fell out of favor with the regime. Both received first-rate European education in Egypt, learning both English and French; their Arabic was so poor that their most traumatic school experiences in Cairo had to do with their mediocre achievement in Arabic (Ihab Hassan 1986, 61–2; Ahmed 1999, 147–8). Both harbor bitter recollections of the colonial era in Egypt. While in secondary school, Hassan dreamt of entering the military academy to become an officer in the army and drive the British out of Egypt (Ihab Hassan 1986, 66–7), a task later undertaken by a group of army officers led by Nasser. Ahmed meanwhile resented the racism and chauvinism of British colonial schoolteachers and curricula (Ahmed 1999, 143–6, 151–2, 154) and felt enormously betrayed by the British during the Suez Crisis of 1956 (166–70). Both declare in no uncertain terms their appreciation of the U.S. These similarities account for their choice of the U.S. as their adoptive country over England or other European countries where they could have settled. Both despised the corruption of King Farouq, and Nasser's authoritarian rule destroyed Ahmed's father and all but derailed her academic dreams (179–205). However, the similarities end here. Their engagements with Orientalism and approaches to cultural translation are as widely divergent as can be.

Ihab Habib Hassan "was born on October 17, 1925, in Cairo," but remarks that "though I carry papers that solemnly record this date and place, I have never felt these facts decisive in my life" (Ihab Hassan 1986, 2). He paints in very broad strokes the picture of a childhood spent moving from one place to another (his father was governor of several rural provinces), punctuated by visits with what he describes as unspeakably cruel, unscrupulous, and pathetically dysfunctional uncles and aunts. As a schoolboy, he "grew up with fierce fantasies of liberating Egypt" from British rule (24), and he despised Britain's pawns, "a decadent royal house and a landed oligarchy, inept, venal, and vain" (25). When his parents forced him to study engineering, he came to see it as his ticket out of Egypt. He worked very hard, hoping to win a government scholarship to the U.S. and secretly planning to stay there. In the U.S., he earned an MS from the University of Pennsylvania before abandoning engineering for literature, earning an MA and a Ph.D. in English, and launching a distinguished career as a literary critic who pioneered the study of postmodernism in the U.S.

Hassan does not draw a distinction between criticism and autobiography and believes that "there is no theory that is not in fact a carefully concealed part of the theorist's own life story" (Klinkowitz 118). Thus, in the postmodernist fashion which he helped to shape, Hassan's own critical (and "paracritical") works are interlaced with entries from his journals, as in *The Right Promethean Fire*, which opens with "A Personal Preface" where he describes the book as "a fragment of an autobiography, meditation on science and imagination" (Ihab Hassan 1980, xxi). His other scholarly books abound in autobiographical reflections on his temperament, personal life, and journey from Egypt to the U.S. Further, he has written about autobiography as a genre (especially in *The Postmodern Turn, Selves at Risk*, and *Rumors of Change*). By the same token, his autobiography is the product of a "'sabbatical to write a book about the humanities' that turned out to be more a book about myself" (1986, 5). In *Rumors of Change*, he asks rhetorically:

> Can a life ever be translated into words? . . . Can a life still in progress . . . ever grasp or understand itself? . . . Can we ever distinguish between fact

> and fiction in autobiography, any more than we can in our media? Is not memory sister to imagination, kin to nostalgia or self-deceit? . . . Is not autobiography, therefore, itself a quest rather than the record of a quest, a labor of self-creation no less than of self-cognizance or self-expression? . . . And does not this quest, this labor of self-creation, in turn affect the real, living, dying subject? (1995, 188–89).

Out of Egypt must then be read as an effort not so much to render Hassan's "life as lived," but as a "quest" and a "labor of self-creation" that complements and extends his work as a critic, and at the same time as a discursive reinvention of his identity. Since the boundaries of the book are so mutable, that autobiographical discourse spills out into theoretical interventions, and vice versa.

Hassan's autobiographical discourse constructs his identity as an American—not an Egyptian American or Arab American, but one whose chosen national and intellectual affiliations abrogate any ties to Egypt: "Roots, everyone speaks of roots. I have cared for none" (1986, 4). He presents himself instead as one who wholeheartedly embraces that most cherished of American doctrines, individualism, positing an ahistorical, transcendental selfhood: "I am in the American grain, a tradition of men and women who crossed an ocean to reinvent themselves" (1995, 251). Significantly, his scholarly work focuses primarily on American literature, and his philosophical orientation is, once more, characteristically American—Emersonian self-reliance and the pragmatism of William James. This is to some extent surprising, given that postmodernism, Hassan's primary interest, is most often inspired by French theory—deconstructive, speculative, anti-foundational. In other words, Hassan's "American" brand of postmodernism can be read autobiographically as an expression of his "reinvention" of his American identity.

This aim is discernible throughout *Out of Egypt*, which opens thus: "On a burning August afternoon in 1946, brisk wind and salt of the Mediterranean on my lips, I boarded the *Abraham Lincoln* at Port Said and sailed from Egypt, never to return." Surveying the scene (dominated by the building of the Compagnie de Suez and the statue of Ferdinand de Lesseps) from the deck of the "Liberty Ship," he "could only think: 'I did it! I did it! I'm bound for New York!'" (1986, 1). This opening scene—which inaugurates a nonlinear, discontinuous narrative incorporating mystical and philosophical speculations, reflections on *King Kong* and *Beauty and the Beast*, and self-reflexive meditations on autobiography that include an imagined interview between "Autobiographer" and "I.H." (91)—announces Hassan's relationship to Egypt. This Egypt belongs equally to Orientalist ("Eternal Egypt" [14]) and biblical (land of bondage) discourse. The rapturous disbelief of the twenty-one-year old at having earned a passage to freedom—from a despised family and a colonized, "prodigal, corrupt, cruel" Egypt (4)—to the Promised Land, and the pride taken by the autobiographer forty years later at having never returned, set the tone for the narrative and establish its trajectory. In retrospect, the gratuitous symbolism of what he at one point calls the "Great Escape" (87), by sea like the ancient Israelites, aboard a "Liberty Ship" named after the U.S. president who freed the slaves, turns almost into a sign of fate, suggesting a divinely ordained destiny. Hassan's opening move, the evocation of colonial stereotype and the biblical myth of the Exodus, clearly appeals to what Gilmore calls "a culturally prevalent discourse of truth and identity" (Gilmore ix) that establishes the autobiographer's claim to American identity.

Hassan describes himself as a "psychological exile" (Ihab Hassan 1986, 106) and reports that during the decades following his Exodus, he was beset by a recurring nightmare of being forced to return to Egypt (108–9). Coming from a wealthy, influential family, he did not, like the biblical Israelites and so many immigrants to America, flee from persecution or poverty: "What . . . had I really hoped to discover in America? It was . . . scope, an openness of time, a more viable history. I also looked for some private space wherein to change, grow; for I had not liked what I foresaw of my life in Eternal Egypt. And so I left—no, fled" (107). Numerous other statements reinforce an essentialist conception of Egypt, repeatedly described as "Eternal" not to evoke its long history, but to brand it as "something closer to a curse, a fate" (16), a land static, unchanging, irredeemable (14, 92–3). Once, in Athens, he had an "intuition of Egypt":

> a stifling moment of heat, dust, noise, young men in short sleeves drifting through shabby streets, old ornate buildings, their cornices, caryatides, peeling on hovels below—most of all, the sense of durance, merciless contraction in the gut. It was, finally, an intuition of prisons: hospitals, asylums, monasteries, dungeons, any occluded relation or caved-in self. (108)

On Egypt "the sun rose in the clear, dry dawn of history and now has set, perhaps never to rise again" (112); as for America to which he "deliriously" emigrated, it is "a land violently dreaming the world into a better place." Egypt is trapped and crumbling under the weight of the past, while America is making the future—"Out of Egypt, into middles, passages, falling into true time" (113). Those final words of the text more than fulfill the expectations carefully elicited in the opening scene. The romance of America is undiluted: the Promised Land, the Shining City on the Hill, the Land of Freedom and Opportunity, the polar opposite of Egypt. As Jerome Klinkowitz observes in his study of Hassan's literary criticism, Hassan "believ[es] with William Blake that America is indeed another portion of the infinite" that "reject[s] the history of the world" (Klinkowitz 120). This metaphysics of America lift it, like Egypt, out of history.

It would be warranted to dwell on the ironies involved in the fact that one who fled Egypt because he could not liberate it from the colonizers recycles Orientalist stereotypes, or that one of the prophets of postmodernism trumpets Manichean metaphysics. Like the autobiographies of Abraham Rihbany and Salom Rizk, Hassan's *Out of Egypt* depends on the East/West dichotomy that structures Orientalist discourse and constitutes a fundamental rejection of history. If his Egypt is "eternal" and unchanging, his America is Utopia (which etymologically means a "non-place"). How is it possible to maintain this romance after forty years of living in the U.S.? Partly, it is possible because his Egypt never changed, for he began to "ignore" it altogether shortly after leaving it (14), but partly also because the memoir itself is a highly self-conscious discursive performance in which his "labor of self-creation" strategically depends on the Egypt/America opposition. Interestingly, some critics have complained that, unlike so many other immigrants' autobiographies that tell of painful transition, difficult adjustment, and the challenge of racial, ethnic, or religious prejudice (Durczak 143), Hassan says very little about his transition *into America* (Beard 24, Falcoff 48–9). He is content to offer only a "brief celebratory assessment of an open and friendly America" (Durczak 143), implying an easeful Americanization (144, n. 19), and rejects cultural and historical roots in exchange for a transcendental conception of selfhood consistent with idealized patterns of immigrant autobiography in America: "the country's autobiographers have told usually optimistic stories, in which they praised the power of the individual, or the cult of hard work and success" (12).

It is not surprising, therefore, that Hassan feels no affinity with, and indeed becomes highly critical of, recent developments in the humanities that have foregrounded questions of colonialism, race, and ethnicity in critical and theoretical debates. Postcolonial studies is for Hassan the product of an alien "ideological world" whose inhabitants, he writes with subtle nuance, "speak to [him] in a mildly foreign accent" (Ihab Hassan 1995 244, emphasis added). Hassan regards himself as a true American whose "birth in Cairo [was] fortuitous, an accident, not a destiny" (243) and proclaims to be "in the American grain" (251). For him, postcolonial studies is no more than "self-absolution" of foreigners who "locate all virtues in the colonized, all vices in the colonizer" (249). As for ethnic and minority studies, which emerged after hard-won battles for Civil Rights in the 1960s, giving voice in the academy to the long-suppressed experiences of African Americans, Native Americans, women, and other marginalized groups, they are merely "tribal" and "ludicrous." He, therefore, rejects for himself the title of Arab American. "Arab-American is to me redundancy, pleonasm. Is not America a land of immigrants rather than exiles?" (250). Besides the obvious omission of Native Americans, who were colonized and decimated, Africans brought to the U.S. by force as abducted slaves, and Palestinians driven from their homeland, the statement ignores vast inequalities based on gender, ethnic, racial, and national origin, and which postcolonial, ethnic, gender, and cultural studies make central to their inquiry. The statement also endorses the normalization of white, middle-class, male perspectives, tastes, and judgments. It is an incontestable fact that the U.S. remains among the freest and the most hospitable countries to immigrants and exiles, but Hassan's insistence on a romantic, idealized notion of America ignores the fact that, as in all other countries, here too some have always been freer and more equal than others.

Into History

Leila Ahmed takes a radically different stance. Born in 1940 in Cairo, she was the child of an upper middle-class Egyptian father and an upper-class mother of Turkish ancestry. She attended British schools in Egypt, then Girton College, Cambridge, where she obtained a degree in English. When she returned to Egypt, her family's circumstances began to change dramatically. A prominent engineer, her father chaired the Nile Water Control Board and the Hydro-Electric Power Commission when he opposed, for ecological reasons, Nasser's project to build the High Dam. After he defied Nasser's orders to keep silent, the government viciously persecuted and harassed the family, including refusing for four years to issue their daughter a passport so that she could return to England to pursue her graduate work at Cambridge. Enormous effort and the intercession of family friends finally enabled her to leave, and eventually she earned her doctorate. After brief employment in England, she went to work in Abu Dhabi, where she was appointed to a commission charged with planning women's education. Her exposure to American feminist texts and the intellectual upheavals in the U.S. academy in the 1970s eventually drew her to the U.S., where she became for many years a professor of women's studies at the University of Massachusetts at Amherst, before joining Harvard Divinity School in 1999.

While Ihab Hassan's Egypt remains suspended in mythical time, Ahmed's Egypt (like that of Ahdaf Soueif) is firmly anchored in contemporary history, with nothing to confirm the preconceptions of readers for whom Egypt is little more than a place of ancient archaeological interest, biblical myth, and Oriental romance—a place summed up by a handful of images and clichés: King "Tut," sand dunes, camels, veiled women, and Hollywood mummy thrillers. *A Border Passage* belongs to the new direction in Arab immigrant writing, which undermines Orientalist assumptions and fosters new knowledge. While the defining moment in Hassan's relationship to Egypt is his "escape," as he puts it, what defines Ahmed's relationship to the country is a sense of nostalgia and irreparable loss. And while Hassan's autobiographical discourse serves to embalm his Egyptian past and to substantiate his claim to American identity, Ahmed's functions to disentangle and reconstruct her past in Egypt and England and to connect it more vitally to her American present. Thus while Hassan's narrative is fragmentary, elliptical, and whimsical, *A Border Passage* is unified, discursive, and expository. Hassan polarizes Egypt and America, whereas Ahmed connects them and undermines essentialist representations of them. Hassan also conforms to the classic American ideology of (masculinist) individualism, whereas Ahmed works with another conception of selfhood that emphasizes the influence of social, cultural, and historical variables on individual consciousness and agency.

Many of their differences are ideological, but they can also be attributed to gender and generation. Hassan was born in 1925 and published his most significant work between 1961 and 1980, in the waning years of New Criticism and its insistence on literature's insularity from politics and history; Ahmed was born in 1940 and began to publish in the early 1980s, in the wake of the Civil Rights movement in the U.S. and the revolution it incited in the academy, with the rise of feminism, women's and ethnic studies programs, and postcolonial studies. These changes occurred after Hassan had established his fame as a critic and have left him and some scholars of his generation cold and bemused: people like Said and Ahmed speak to him with "foreign accents."

As the autobiography of an academic scholar, *A Border Passage* is, like Said's and Hassan's narratives, both an extension of Ahmed's academic work and an exposition of its prehistory. A noted scholar of women's studies, Ahmed has made the question of women in Islam the focus of her academic career since her arrival in the U.S. Her major book, *Women and Gender in Islam: Historical Roots of a Modern Debate* (1992), surveys the history of gender discourses in the Middle East from ancient Mesopotamian and Mediterranean civilizations to those of Judaism and Christianity, the emergence of Islam, and on to the present. Ahmed also makes the question of gender in Islamic societies central to her autobiographical narrative, the subtitle of which announces that the book is "*A Woman's Journey*." This gesture immediately addresses the implicit requirement of immigrant Arab women's autobiography that it comment on the status of women in Muslim society. Contrary to some expectations, however, the book does not narrate the story of a woman's "great escape" (to use Hassan's phrase) from an oppressive Arab or Muslim society to freedom in the U.S. In fact, she seems deliberately to conjure up Orientalist themes such as the East/West opposition and Islam's oppression of women in order to refute the assumptions on which they are based. Negotiating those stereotypes is part and parcel of her claim to Arab American identity, a claim that remains, nonetheless, fraught with unresolved tension.

Connections and Disconnections

A Border Passage presents itself as a narrative of connectedness rather than polarity. It begins and ends in Cairo, sounding a note of nostalgia and yearning that comes to resonate for Ahmed with Jalaludin Rumi's Sufi conception of the human condition; she prefaces the narrative with an epigraph from his poetry: "To hear the song of the reed / Everything you have known / must be left behind" (Ahmed 1999, ix). She then notes that "in Sufi poetry this music of the reed is the quintessential music of loss" and that in Rumi's poetry,

> the song of the reed is the metaphor for our human condition . . . Cut from its bed and fashioned into a pipe, the reed forever laments the living earth that it once knew, crying out, whenever life is breathed into it, its ache and its yearning and loss. We too . . . says Rumi, remember a condition of completeness that we once knew but have forgotten that we ever knew. (5)

The autobiographical relevance of the metaphor of the reed is all too obvious—the immigrant cut off from her native land and culture, "the living earth [she] once knew," who writes about what she considers to be her exile in order to recover the condition of "completeness." That condition is recoverable only through connecting, or reconciling, the past and the present. In contrast to Hassan, whose resort to biblical and Orientalist discourses of opposition forecloses such connection, Ahmed's autobiography—her own song of the reed—seeks to dissolve dichotomous discursive and ideological constructs.

The theme of connectedness frames the autobiography. She opens the narrative of her life thus: "It was as if there were to life itself a quality of music in that time, the era of my childhood, and in that place, the remote edge of Cairo. There the city petered out into a scattering of villas leading into tranquil country fields. On the other side of our house was the profound, unsurpassable quiet of the desert" (Ahmed 1999, 3). In the Epilogue, Ahmed writes of a recent trip back to Egypt and a visit to Cairo's City of the Dead; contemplating the use of burial chambers, which dates back to Pharaonic times, she thinks of Rumi's funeral, when "Jews, Christians, Buddhists, and Hindus, as well as Muslims, walked in his procession, weeping." She then closes the autobiography with this anecdote: "Rumi's cat, who had meowed piteously through his last illness, refused to eat after his death and died a week later. Rumi's daughter buried her at his side. Symbol, she said, of Rumi's deep connection with all beings" (307). The theme of connection is embedded in Sufi thought (Rumi being one of its best known representatives) which seeks to uncover the oneness of being; in the gratuitously symbolic geography of her parents' house at the edge of the city, connecting the urban with the rural and the desert; in the physical congregation of the dead in burial chambers; in the communal grief of members of all faiths over Rumi's death; and finally in the emotive bond between Rumi and his cat, which joins him in the grave. Along the way, she finds this sense of connectedness in the Qur'an, in Mahatma Gandhi's philosophical outlook which combines British education with Hindu philosophy, in Hassan Fathi's architecture, in her father's ecological vision, and in the work of "Rachel Carson, Barbara McClintock, and other women pioneers of Western scientific thought . . . [whose] originality . . . sprang in part from their rootedness in a different cultural ethos—a women's ethos of connectedness—different from the ethos of competitiveness and individualism of the men of their culture" (35). This ethos of connectedness sharply distinguishes Ahmed's autobiographical discourse from Hassan's, which revolves around individualism. The deep sense of connectedness also guides Ahmed's autobiographical discourse as it undermines Orientalist conceptions of Egypt, the Arab world, and Islam that impede sympathetic understanding of them.

Ahmed's autobiographical discourse, then, constructs a personal identity that departs from individualist notions of the self's autonomy, in that selfhood is inconceivable outside of its cultural and historical context, both in Egypt and in the U.S. Yet in a shrewd move, her rejection of the dominant ideology of individualism is couched within the biblical myth of the Fall (repeated in the Qur'an), so that she in effect exchanges one "culturally prevalent discourse of truth and identity" for another (Gilmore ix). For instance, she begins with recollections of her happy, early childhood "in a world alive . . . with the music of being," a world confined within the walls of the family home's garden, where she communes with the trees, learns to identify the distinctive sound the wind makes ruffling the leaves of each kind, and watches the distinct shapes of their shadows falling on her bedroom wall at night. She then provocatively declares that

> it is not in those days and those moments that my story begins. Rather, it begins for me with the disruption of that world and the desolation that for a time overtook our lives. For it was then that I began to follow the path that would bring me—exactly here.

> And so it is with those years and their upheaval and with the politics that framed our lives that I must begin. (Ahmed 1999, 5)

The immediately noticeable thing here is that she refuses to locate the starting point for her story in what she describes as an Edenic childhood, a time unmarked, as it were, by any significant events, being instead a temporally undifferentiated period of primordial harmony and bliss. The function of this gesture is at once to dramatize the moment of "disruption"—the Fall—as the true beginning of her story. As in the story of Adam and Eve, expulsion from Paradise signals the beginning of human history on earth. Likewise, for Ahmed, the social upheavals and the national politics of the day forever disrupt "the music of being" and become impossible to disentangle from her life. The autobiographical project then becomes an effort not to distill an individual life out of history, but to reconstruct that life and the identity of the autobiographer more fully in the context of history.

This conception of selfhood necessitates locating the individual life within the intersecting grids of national, class, gender, and racial identity in Egypt, England, and the U.S.—intersections that are sometimes charged with unresolved traumas that evidence *dis*connection. In Egypt, for instance, national identity becomes problematic for her in 1952, when she is punished by a schoolteacher for failing, then refusing to try, to read from her Arabic textbook. Arabic had been a neglected subject in the colonial schools she attended, and although the family for the most part spoke Egyptian Arabic at home, she was not well educated in Modern Standard and classical Arabic. Her father was an upper middle-class professional who was enthralled by Europe and none too keen on having his children learn Arabic. The mother did not share the father's enthusiasm for British schools, but by virtue of her Turkish upper-class background, she was accustomed to leaving the day-to-day activities of raising children to a Croatian nanny who did not know Arabic. The revolution of 1952 inaugurated a new era of pan-Arab nationalism. The teacher was a Palestinian refugee dispossessed in 1948 and obviously with enormous stakes in the idea of Arab nationalism. The rebelliousness of the twelve-year-old against the newly required study of the Arabic language, followed by pain and shock at the corporal punishment she receives, not only represent a childhood trauma, but become central to Ahmed's intellectual development as she later investigates Egypt's millennial sense of identity, the history of European colonialism in the Arab world, the rise of Arab nationalism in the region and the pivotal role of the British in promoting it before and during World War I, Jewish settlement in Palestine, Egypt's complex involvement in the conflict over Palestine since the 1920s, and the emergence of the Muslim Brotherhood. This leads Ahmed to the belief, which she finds historical arguments to substantiate, that since Egypt has not always been Arab, it should not necessarily be considered Arab (10–11).[1] The autobiography investigates the enormously complex history of this and other issues, not in the manner of a historical survey, but tracing Ahmed's own developing understanding of them as she probes her own past:

> My relations with Miss Nabih [the Arabic language teacher] were only a symptom of the times: of the battering and reshaping of our identities that the politics of the day were subjecting us to. I would be marked by everything that was happening, not just by Miss Nabih. Only when, in the process of writing this book, I began to examine this memory and others, and the history in which they were entangled, would I come to that realization. (148)

The numerous lengthy sections of historical narration reflect Ahmed's own personal development as an individual and as a scholar. The result is a life story that gives a personal perspective on Egypt's history in the twentieth-century. Understanding or recounting the personal life is impossible without reconstructing that history, at the same time that the personal perspective illuminates the collective history with insights that often escape standard historiography—such as, for instance, the extent to which Nasser's brand of Arab nationalism destroyed intimate social and personal relationships among Muslims, Christians, and Jews (172–5). As we shall see, Ahmed's relationship to the Arabic language, Arab nationalism, and Arab identity remains vexed throughout the book.

In England, the question of identity immediately becomes even more entangled as she suffers "the mute, complicated confusions of my exilic Arab identity, my identity as an Arab in the West" (238). This "exile" is of special kind, since she was not an exile in the common sense of one banished from her country; if anything, she was *prevented* from leaving it by the government. It is rather the inverted exile of one forced into a particular category, "Arab," to which she feels she does not belong as an Egyptian. The reasons for this feeling of nonbelonging have to do with her abhorrence of Nasser and of Arab nationalism, and with her discovery later of Britain's role in encouraging Arab nationalism during World War I in order to weaken the Ottoman Empire, a role that rendered Arab nationalism and Arab identity for Ahmed (who problematically conflates the two) a colonial invention and an instrument of colonial rule (265–69). However, in England, and later in the U.S., Arab identity, as well as a host of other categorizations, are imposed upon her willy-nilly:

> 'One is not born but rather becomes a woman,' goes Simone de Beauvoir's famous dictum. I obviously was not born but became black when I went to England.[2] Similarly of course, I was not born but became a woman of color when I went to America. Whereas these are political identities that carry, for me, a positive charge, revealing and affirming connection and commonality, my identity as an Arab, no less a political construction, is an identity that, in contrast, I experience as deeply and perhaps irretrievably fraught with angst and confusion. (237–38)

When complicated by racism, Arab identity becomes a source of anxiety, for in Britian she could not "[e]motionally . . . fully side with the Arabs insofar as Nasser was their spokesman and universally adulated hero. But it was even less possible for me to side with the bigoted British racists and their stupid diatribes against Nasser and the Arabs" (239).

> In Egypt the sense of falseness and coercion would be there in a political sense, but at least in ordinary daily life I'd just be another Egyptian, whereas in the West it's impossible for me ever to escape, forget this false constructed Arabness. It's almost always somehow there, the notion that I am Arab, in any and every interaction. (255–56)

Like the words "African" or "Negro," "the word 'Arab' . . . comes, in European tongues, internally loaded in the negative" (266):

> 'Arabs' meant people with whom you made treaties that you did not have to honor, arabs being by definition people of a lesser humanity and there being no need to honor treaties with people of a lesser humanity. It meant people whose lands you can carve up and apportion as you wished, because they were of a lesser humanity. It meant people whose democracies you could obstruct at will, because you did not have to behave justly toward people of a lesser humanity. And what could mere arabs, anyway, know of democracy and democratic process? (267)

Furthermore, in Britain, "being Arab was profoundly implicated, of course, in what has proven to be one of the most painful and intractable political problems of our day, the Palestinian-Israeli conflict" (239), not just on a political or collective level, but on a mundane, personal level as well. A perfect stranger on a bus in Cambridge once asked her with a broad smile if she was Israeli, only to spit on her when he realized that she was Arab! There are, then, she concludes, "two notions of Arab that I am trapped in—both false, both heavily weighted and cargoed with another silent freight": the Euro-American notion steeped in negativity (and which she writes as "arab"), and the Nasserite notion, which subsumes all historical and geographical particularities into a monolithic identity. Both notions "imput[e] to me feelings and beliefs that aren't mine. They overlap in some ways, but they are not . . . identical" (256).

Those two false constructs aside, there is certainly a third possibility that Ahmed does not consider, and that is the notion of Arab identity as a function of a common language, culture, and history, and a sense of solidarity in the face of a common historical challenge, which the appalling behavior of the Cambridge stranger on the bus illustrates with crude eloquence. There is little doubt that Ahmed's class background, which availed her of a first-rate colonial education that deliberately proscribed any viable grounding in the Arabic language, literature, and heritage—the historical repository of Arab cultural identity—foreclosed the development of a secure sense of Arab identity that could resist colonial, nationalist, and racist constructs. This dimension of Ahmed's "exilic Arab identity" remains unresolved in her narrative, although it reveals itself in a highly resonant encounter with Hanan al-Shaykh, a renowned Lebanese novelist who writes in Arabic. At a lecture in Cambridge, al-Shaykh's

> paper, about how she became a writer, was full of evocations of . . . her youthful discoveries of the classics of contemporary Arabic literature, and of poetry read and heard and ideas exchanged under apple trees. It

> began, almost at once, to work its enchantment. As the minutes passed, the faces around me grew perceptibly happier, mellower, more relaxed. . . . I found myself thinking enviously that this was what I would like to be writing, something that would affirm my community in exile. Something that would remind its members of how lovely our lives, our countries, our ways are. How lovely our literature. What a fine thing, whatever it is people say of us, what a fine thing it is, in spite of them all, to be Arab; what a wonderful heritage we have. . . . What wouldn't I give, I sat there thinking, listening to her quote Arab poets, to have had that in my past, all that wealth of Arabic literature that nurtured her as a writer; what wouldn't I give now to have all those poets and writers to remember and write about and remind people of?

Soon, however, the antipathy Ahmed has felt toward literary Arabic since that traumatic childhood incident with the Arabic language teacher resurfaces, and, together with her lack of Arabic education, compels her to admit that she appreciated the lines al-Shaykh recited "only the way I might the poetry of a foreign tongue" (253). At a more intimate gathering with al-Shaykh afterwards, her skepticism about Arab identity returns, leaving her feeling

> like a Judas among these friends. . . . Was it even imaginable that . . . sitting there among them—two Lebanese, one Palestinian, one Iranian, three of the four of them having been made homeless one way or another by Israeli aggression or by some spin-off of that conflict—was it conceivable that I could say, "Well, actually I am looking into this whole question of the Arabness of Egyptian identity, I am trying to really look at it, deconstruct it . . ." It was completely unimaginable, impossible, inconceivable. (254)

At that moment, she feels the need to convey "to them solidarity and support." Yet at the same time, in the absence of a strong bond with the Arabic language and its heritage, the notions of Arabness propagated both by Nasser and by anti-Arab racism render the quest for identity extremely vexed for someone who "just do[es] not want to live any longer with a lie about who I am" (255).

Harems

Anti-Arab racism and Islamophobia justify themselves, in part, by perpetuating the perception of women's status in Arab and Muslim societies as oppressed and degraded. For centuries now, the harem has inspired an endless array of fantasies—literary, artistic, cinematic—about the Orient. Ahmed's story of growing up female in Egypt of the 1940s and 1950s picks up that thread, but characteristically, she pulls it in such a way as to unravel those representations. Two chapter titles in *A Border Passage* announce the theme: chapter 5 ("Harem"), which depicts the daily life of her female relatives in her Turkish grandfather's house, and chapter 8

("The Harem Perfected?"), which narrates her life as an undergraduate at Girton College, Cambridge. Here, Ahmed evokes a stereotype in order to undermine it by pointing to a structural similarity between Islamic and European institutions. In Cairo, her mother and aunts repaired daily to their mother's rooms in the family house after their husbands left for work in the morning. The daily routine transported them to a space that was exclusively for women, since life in their own households (with their Egyptian husbands) was not only desegregated, but quite Europeanized—Ahmed's parents, at least, engaged a European nanny for their children, educated them in European schools, and sent them to college in Europe. Yet when Ahmed arrived at Girton, which was still a women's college at the time, she found it to be

> a deeply familiar world to me. In some ways indeed Girton represented the harem perfected. Not the harem of Western male sexual fantasy or even the harem of Muslim men, fantasy or reality, but the harem as I had lived it, the harem of older women presiding over the young. Even the servers here . . . were women, and from these grounds . . . the absence of male authority was permanent.

These women's spaces, she finds, were nurturing, and she regrets their disappearance: "I have been privileged to live in two harem communities, a Turco-Egyptian one and a British one. And it has been my destiny, too, alas, to live through the ending of both" (183). (In post-1952 Egypt, "Land Reform" and other nationalization policies effectively transformed the lifestyles of the upper classes, and in England, Girton was desegregated in the late sixties.) She contends that, while they lasted, those spaces sustained what was in effect a women's ethos, a women's way of knowing, and even a women's Islam, all of which were distinct from men's (121–24).

Looking retrospectively from a point in time when militant fundamentalism has spread widely, she recalls that "Islam, as I got it from them [her grandmother, mother, and aunts], was gentle, generous, pacifist, inclusive, somewhat mystical." She further describes this Islam as a way of being in the world rather than "elaborate sets of injunctions or threats or decrees or dictates" (121). She sharply distinguishes it from "the official (male, of course) orthodox interpretations of religion," derived from ancient commentaries and still propagated, a thousand years later, by male clerics. What she describes, in effect—accurately or not—is, on the one hand, a dynamic, female, orally transmitted religious culture, and on the other hand, a static, rigid, militant, male, religious culture of literacy. Ahmed herself comes back, half-heartedly, to complicate this gendered dichotomy by saying that

> after a lifetime of meeting and talking with Muslims from all over the world, I find that this Islam is one of the common varieties—perhaps even *the* common or garden variety—of the religion. It is the Islam not only of women but of ordinary folk generally, as opposed to the Islam of sheikhs, ayatollahs, mullahs, and clerics. (125)

The latter is "the Islam of the arcane, mostly medieval written heritage in which sheikhs are trained, and it is 'men's' Islam . . . [a] minority of men" (125–26). The

Islam of women and "ordinary folk generally," she contends, is based on the "oral and aural" experience of the Qur'an:

> what remains when you listen to the Qur'an over a lifetime are its most recurring themes, ideas, words, and permeating spirit, reappearing now in this passage, now in that: mercy, justice, peace, compassion, humanity, fairness, kindness, truthfulness, charity, mercy, justice. And yet it is exactly these recurring themes and this permeating spirit that are for the most part left out of the medieval texts or smothered and buried under a welter of abstruse "learning." (126)

Arguing (the scholar here extrapolating on her autobiographical experience) that this "oral and aural Islam is intrinsic to Islam and to the Qur'an itself, and intrinsic even to the Arabic language" (127), predating literacy (written Arabic was not codified until the eighth century), Ahmed claims that "literacy has played a baneful part both in spreading a particular form of Islam and in working to erase oral and living forms of the religion" (128). Once again, Ahmed's old grudge against Modern Standard and classical Arabic drives her to blame literacy as such (Arabic literacy, not English or French, for example), rather than medieval scholasticism. It is doubtful if those "oral and living forms of the religion" are in any danger of disappearing, for they obviously thrived until they were transmitted to her in the mid-twentieth century. But the greater problem here lies in Ahmed's polarization of literacy and orality, and further in the conflation of this polarity with another, that of male/female, which in turn is superimposed on yet a third, fundamentalist/moderate Islam. Hardly does one encounter such slippage in the work of the Arab scholars, critics, philosophers, and theologians who have in recent decades been actively challenging patriarchy, traditional interpretations of Islam, and fundamentalism. Mahmoud Muhammad Taha, Hassan Hanafy, Nawal el Saadawi, Muhammad Sa'id al-'Ashmawi, and Nasr Abu Zayd, to name but a few, have never dismissed literacy, classical Arabic, or the *shari'a* out of hand. On the contrary, they have engaged traditional clerics and fundamentalists in critical debate. Thus the linguistic dimension of Arab identity that Ahmed wrestles with throughout the book, and which remains unresolved, also shapes her scholarly outlook, giving it a tint of the prejudice against the Arabic language that has persisted from Ernest Renan to Fawaz Turki.

This form of alienation may have played a role in Ahmed's decision to move to the U.S., but at any rate she gives two reasons for choosing the U.S. over England or elsewhere in Europe. One was the possibility of professional advancement for an Arab: "All three [of her siblings] had found that in Europe (England, Switzerland, and Germany had been their bases) they simply could not advance in their professions beyond a certain point. In America, they told me, things were different. Even though people had their prejudices, if you had the ability and the qualifications you could move forward in America" (291). The other was the rise of feminism:

> In America, social ferment and activism formed the backdrop to the new intellectual perspectives that were emerging. In England, or at least in

> Cambridge, there was no parallel ferment either on issues of race or of gender that I might have connected with. By the end of my graduate student days I had essentially acquiesced in and accepted my own proper invisibility from scholarship and the proper invisibility and object status of my kind. The passion and joy of thought and understanding would come back into my life only after I had gone to Abu Dhabi to work and begun to feel driven by my need to understand, as the Iranian Revolution crested, our history as Muslim women, and the possibilities that lay ahead; simultaneously I began to read the exhilarating feminist books coming out of America. Placing Muslim women at the heart of my work was in a way . . . a refusal of my invisibility. (237)

Once in the U.S., however, she was confronted by anti-Arab racism and Islamophobia within the feminist movement itself. In the early eighties, she remembers, she and other Muslim feminists were met with belligerent responses at women's studies conferences "for trying to examine and rethink our traditions rather than dismissing them out of hand," the assumption being that

> whereas they—white women, Christian women, Jewish women—could rethink their heritage and religions and traditions, we had to abandon ours because they were just intrinsically, essentially, and irredeemably misogynist and patriarchal in a way that theirs (apparently) were not. In contrast to their situation, our salvation entailed not arguing with and working to change our traditions but giving up our cultures, religions, and traditions and adopting theirs. (292)

But such prejudice was also directed at other non-White feminists, and Ahmed found herself in the company of other minority feminists—African Americans mainly—who challenged it (293). As she states toward the end of the book in the passage quoted in the epigraph to this chapter, her life in the U.S. is defined by her minority status—as a woman of color, an Arab, a Muslim, and a feminist, among other things—"a cluster of flowing currents," as Edward Said puts it in his memoir, which in their dissonance and contradictoriness respect neither borders nor boundaries.

Twenty years after moving to the U.S., Ahmed's professional success confirmed the truth of her siblings' counsel, which had reiterated the idea of America as the land of freedom and opportunity. But she understands her position in the U.S. as already predetermined, in relation to the majority culture, as a woman of color, an Arab, and a Muslim, regardless of how conflicted she may feel about some of those constructs. Rather than submitting to the ideological content of these representations, her autobiographical discourse turns those predetermined positions into sites of contestation, critique, redefinition, and reinvention of identity—that is, sites of transformative cultural translation. This critical engagement with the dominant discourses in the U.S. is matched by her efforts to "rethink," as she writes in the passage just quoted, the heritage of Islam, and to "argue with" and "work to change" her native traditions. Her critique of *shari'a* and her attack on what she considers the "lies" of nationalism are efforts—however laden with unresolved tensions—to reform conditions back in Egypt. These efforts bespeak a dialogic conception of Arab American identity that works backwards and forwards to establish productive and transformative connections between cultures "in a world of dissolving boundaries and vanishing borders" (296). It is a project that harkens back to Ameen Rihani's conception of cultural translation, while discarding the East/West dichotomy which paralyzed the efforts of early Arab American writers.

Becoming American, then, has involved two radically different negotiating strategies for these two Egyptian immigrants. Both strategies are embodied in autobiographical narratives that have what Brunner calls "verisimilitude" and "negotiability" (Brunner 45), allowing them to enter into a "conversation of selves" (47) with their American readers. However, they do so by drawing upon the resources of two different "culturally prevalent discourses of truth and identity" (Gilmore ix). Hassan marshals biblical and Orientalist stereotypes of Egypt in order to distance himself from his country of birth and to prove that he is an American at heart. As in Abraham Rihbany and Salom Rizk, this strategy appeals to essentialist notions of national and cultural identity based on the colonialist belief that "East is East, and West is West, and never the twain shall meet." By contrast, Ahmed's negotiation of identity draws upon multiculturalist discourses—feminist and postcolonialist, mainly—to interrogate essentialist conceptions of identity and to affirm her right to difference. In a sense, the two autobiographical discourses and their negotiating strategies embody what came to be known in the early 1990s as the "Culture Wars." Hassan and Ahmed have sided with different warring camps, and part of their claim to American identity rests on the fact that they have pledged allegiance on the same American battlefield.

7

Postcolonial Translation

'Hubb' is love, 'ishq' is love that entwines two people together, 'shaghaf' is love that nests in the chambers of the heart, 'hayam' is love that wanders the earth, 'teeh' is love in which you lose yourself, 'walah' is love that carries sorrow within it, 'sababah' is love that exudes from the pores, 'hawa' is love that shares its name with 'air' and with 'falling,' 'gharam' is love that is willing to pay the price.

—AHDAF SOUEIF

Beginnings of Arab British Literature

Literature that emerges from what Edward Said called the "Anglo-Arab encounter" may be traced back to works by travelers, rather than immigrants or descendants of immigrants in Britain. Said used that term in a review of Ahdaf Soueif's *In the Eye of the Sun*, and he complained of the dearth of English-language novels written by Arabs, mentioning Palestinian Jabra Ibrahim Jabra and Egyptian Waguih Ghali as predecessors to Soueif. However, the first work to fit Said's designation is probably *A Voice from Lebanon* (1847), the autobiography of Assaad Y. Kayat, chief interpreter to the British consul in Syria, who visited England three times and gave a number of lectures there. Surprised by his audiences' lack of knowledge about his background (he was mistaken for, among other things, "a prince, . . . a Chinese ambassador, a merchant, . . . a Jew, . . . a Turk, a missionary, a philosopher" [2]), he resolved to write his life story so as "to give information respecting details little known, and to interest the public feeling in favour of Syria" (4). As for Jabra, a well-known novelist in Arabic, literary critic, and translator of Shakespeare, he wrote only one novel in English, *Hunters in a Narrow Street* (1960), about a Palestinian refugee who settles in Baghdad in the early 1950s. Ghali's *Beer in the Snooker Club* (1964) focuses on an anglophile Egyptian aristocrat living at the expense of a wealthy aunt and an Egyptian Jewish lover who takes him on a trip to England, after which he settles back in Egypt. Ghali himself committed suicide while in exile in England, but his novel is mainly about the life of Cairo's cosmopolitan elite in the late 1950s and early 1960s (see Starr).

As I use it here, Arab British literature is the work of immigrants and their descendants, although the designation is not as standard as its North American counterpart. Indeed, Geoffrey Nash uses Said's term "Anglo-Arab encounter" as the title of his book on Arab British novelists and autobiographers such as Soueif, Jamal Mahjoub, Tony Hanania, Fadia Faqir, and Leila Aboulela, three of whom are immigrants and two half-British by birth. My preference for "Arab British" stems from my focus in this book on the work of immigrants as distinct from that of travelers, such as Kayat, Jabra, and Ghali, in whose case the "encounter" remains between cultures that are presumably separate and discrete. The case of travelers lends itself to that perception, although as I have been arguing throughout this book, identity constructs that posit autonomous entities such as "East" and "West"—entities that the notion of "encounter" leaves intact—are ideologically motivated, epistemologically untenable, and ethically suspect. By contrast, "Arab British" (like "Arab American") denotes an identity that is fused, hybrid, straddling and subversively mixing together constructs that can no longer be imagined as monolithic. Without pushing this argument about semantics too far, or even entering into debates about whether or not to hyphenate ethnic designations (arguments which can easily turn into hair-splitting exercises), the point is that the experience of immigrants is one of cultural admixture and interpenetration, not to mention the multiple and complex loyalties that the traveler or temporary resident does not always or necessarily share. The immigrant experience adds extra dimensions to the task of cultural translation that the "encounters" depicted in travel literature may lack.

This is clearly illustrated in the work of Soueif and Leila Aboulela, the focus of this chapter and the following one, respectively, as well as in that of Edward Atiyah (1903–64), a British-educated Lebanese who settled in England after a career in the British intelligence service in Sudan and who may be described as the first Arab British writer. The title of his autobiography, *An Arab Tells His Story: A Study in Loyalties* (1946), suggests that it shares Kayat's purpose of explaining his life to British readers, except that, unlike Kayat's Britain, Atiyah's was now an imperial power in control a of large swath of the Arab world. In the century separating the two writers, William Babington Macaulay's program of English education, first devised in British India, was exported to other parts of the empire. One of its beneficiaries, Atiyah was indeed "English in taste, in opinions, in morals, and in intellect" (Macaulay 1952, 729); as his subtitle suggests, the central conflict in his autobiography is between his belief in the inherent goodness of British colonialism in the Arab world (which underwrites the reconciliation of his two loyalties to the Arab world and to the British) and the racism he faced when he began to work for the British government in Sudan. Atiyah went on to write six novels, only two of which are on Arab themes. Geoffrey Nash describes those two novels in this way:

> A Sudanese setting is to be found in *Black Vanguard* [1952], a novel which develops out of the colonial context . . . and has as its main protagonist an Oxbridge-educated Sudanese, Mahmoud, who rejects the harem-world

> of his native womenfolk and marries a Scotswoman with whom he has greater cultural affinity. In its treatment of the colonial issue, the novel is the polar opposite of Tayeb Salih's *Season of Migration to the North*, as well as Jamal Mahjoub's *Wings of Dust*. Atiyah unashamedly advocates the westernization of Arab societies, and his novel of Lebanese social manners, *Lebanon Paradise* [1953], has the message that Arab Muslims must catch up with Arab Christians in order to recuperate the catastrophic effects of Zionism.[1] (Nash 2007, 47)

In Atiyah, then, we have a writer who embodied Macaulay's vision of the colonial intellectual. Yet Atiyah went further by writing as an Englishman in crime novels such as *The Thin Line* (1951) and *The Crime of Julian Masters* (1959), which are set in England and populated by English characters, and in *The Eagle Flies from England* (1960), a historical novel about Napoleon. Although his last work, *Donkey From the Mountains* (1961, published in the U.S. as *The Cruel Fire* [1962]), is set in Lebanon, it is a crime novel that does not thematize cultural relations. Like Rihani and Rihbany, Atiyah also wrote three books on Arab history and the political situation in the Middle East (1948, 1954, 1955), and his whole-hearted embrace of Englishness closely parallels Rihbany's quasi-religious belief in America. These writers did not only write as Arabs encountering Britain and the U.S., although they did so at the beginning of their writing careers; they wanted to write as Americans or Englishmen.

Soueif and the Politics of Reception

The generational and ideological gap separating Ihab Hassan and Leila Ahmed parallels that between Atiyah and Soueif, who represent the colonial and the postcolonial periods of Arab British literature, respectively. The best-known contemporary Arab British writer, Soueif was born in Cairo, Egypt, in 1950, to two British-educated professors at Cairo University (her mother, Fatma Mousa, was a prominent literary critic, translator, and professor of English). At the age of four, Soueif moved with her parents to England, "so that English was practically another first language" for her, and she learned to read first in English (Pakravan 275). Four years later, the family moved back to Egypt and Soueif went on to study English literature at Cairo University. In 1973, she traveled back to England for postgraduate work, eventually earning a Ph.D. from Lancaster University. Since then, she has divided her time between Cairo and London, where she frequently writes on literature and politics for *The Guardian*, *The Times Literary Supplement*, and *The London Review of Books*, among others. She also writes in Arabic for numerous newspapers and magazines and translates into and from Arabic and English.[2] Her fiction, however, is written in English: two short story collections, *Aisha* (1983) and *Sandpiper* (1996), and two novels to date, *In the Eye of the Sun* (1992) and *The Map of Love* (1999). Another collection, *I Think of You* (2007) contains a selection from *Aisha* and *Sandpiper*.

Exhibiting all three characteristics of minor literature identified by Deleuze and Guattari, Soueif's fiction focuses not so much on Arab British identity as on Arab

British relations in the (post)colonial period; it is more "postcolonial" than "ethnic" literature. Its concern with Orientalist representations of the Arab world can be seen to increase steadily from Soeuif's earliest short stories to her latest novel, as she becomes more aware of the politics of reception of Arab writers, especially women, in Britain, and of the politics of writing in English—i.e., of her predicament as a minority writer who continues to identify primarily as an Egyptian, even though she is a dual citizen of Britain and Egypt. This awareness creates a tension between the personal and the collective, or the individual writer's need for unfettered expression and the political exigencies of representation under Orientalism's regime of truth. That tension triggers the most sustained reflection on literary and cultural translation found in Arab immigrant writing since Ameen Rihani, for in contrast to many of those earlier immigrants who accepted the basic premise of Orientalism—the East/West dichotomy—and sought acceptance as writers by validating that discourse, Soueif (like Said and Ahmed) rebels against the role it assigns to her. In what follows, I chart the trajectory of her fiction as it reflects her growing realization of the implications of being a minority Arab woman writer in Britain, then turn to her novel, *The Map of Love*, a paradigmatic text for what I have been calling "translational literature."

When she first started to write fiction, Soueif conceived of herself as an Egyptian and an Arab—not an Egyptian British or Arab British—writer, one who happened to write in English while following in the footsteps of Yusuf Idris (1927–91) and Tayeb Salih (b. 1929), major novelists who analyzed sexual mores and gender politics in Egypt and Sudan during the 1960s. This is the theme of several of her works, including her first two short stories, "The Wedding of Zeina" and "Her Man" (from her 1983 collection *Aisha*), which depict Egyptian peasants. The title of the first story unmistakably echoes that of Salih's novella *The Wedding of Zein*, which is also about a peasant wedding, although unlike Salih's story where the groom achieves individuation and social status through marriage, Soueif's story is told from the troubling perspective of a traumatized young bride whose virginity is taken in a ritualized rape scene as part of the wedding ceremony.[3] The other story focuses on the Machiavellian intrigue by which one co-wife deceives her polygamous husband into divorcing his new bride. In an interview with Joseph Massad, Soueif said this about the two stories:

> "The Wedding of Zeina" and "Her Man" were the first things I ever wrote, and at that time, I wasn't really aware of "the politics of reception." I had sat down to write, and I had assumed that I was going to write in Arabic. But the words didn't come, the Arabic didn't happen for me, the words came in English. That was the area where I was struggling. I kept trying to write in Arabic, because I hadn't thought that I would write in English. Eventually, it was a choice between writing in English or not writing at all, so I wrote in English. So the whole problematic of what it meant to be writing in English had not occurred to me at all—these early stories might just as well have been written in Arabic. (Massad 86)

A thoroughly bilingual writer who specialized in English literature, Soueif also read modern Arabic fiction and grew up knowing some of its writers (she recalls that Latifa al-Zayyat [1923–96], a pioneer of women's fiction in Egypt, was a family friend whom she "adored" [Soueif 2000, 110]).[4] Thus even though she had conceived of herself as a writer within one literary tradition, modern Arabic fiction, by writing in English she found herself being *read* within another, namely Orientalist literature. She adds,

> These are the two stories that I feel most distant from now, but they got me a lot of attention in England and were very popular. I think that in itself tells us something . . . , that there is a certain amount of, I hesitate to use the term "exoticization," because again that wasn't something that I was doing consciously. If it's there at all, it's because genuinely for me these stories describe an exotic world. So in the sense of what I was doing, I was doing something genuine and real. I was turning into fiction stories or fragments of stories that I had heard. But reading them now, I can see that they do present Egypt or the East in terms that perhaps the West is comfortable with: as a world that is very traditional, very close to magic, ritualistic, a little brutal, and very sensual—our world as perceived by aficionados of the *Arabian Nights*. And that is possibly why they struck a chord immediately. Because that was the Eastern world that the West was comfortable with and wanted to read about. (86)

Here, the author's creative impulse was given free rein without any constraint being placed on it by considerations of audience, medium, or the politics of cross-cultural reception. The reception of those stories in England allowed Soueif to see that what for her was a "genuine" representation participated in what Edward Said described as self-Orientalizing, and that it was this aspect of her work that earned her praise in England. This was, of course, the same discovery made earlier in the U.S. by Gibran, Rihbany, Rizk, and Ihab Hassan, who had accepted the basic premises of Orientalism and understood the rewards reaped for confirming them.

Unlike those writers, and similar to Ameen Rihani, Soueif refused to capitalize on readers' expectations, and the object of her critique shifted from gender politics in Egypt to Orientalist discourse. Nevertheless, as her own unproblematized (and very frequent) use of categories like "the Eastern world" and "the West" demonstrates, the creative freedom she describes was not unconstrained by Orientalist discourse when she wrote the stories in the early 1980s, nor did she completely discard those categories at the time of the interview, in 1999, even though by then she had written *The Map of Love*, with its powerful critique of Orientalism. Her metafictional discourse deploys the East/West dichotomy even as her mature fiction undermines it. And she concedes Massad's point that the early short stories are problematic, "even were I to read them in Arabic, given the middle-class Cairene and urban Egyptian attitudes and exoticization of the village and poor urban folks" (86). In fact, "The Nativity," another story in the same collection, actually stages the quasi-Orientalist classism to which Massad refers. In that story, an upper-middle class woman is drawn to what to her is the strange, fascinating, and primitive world of an ancient working-class district of Cairo. A strong-arm man whom she has befriended, and who, from the perspective of his class-based masculinist ethos, interprets her interest in him as sexual, rapes her in the final scene.

Until that point, the protagonist's gallant attitude of benevolent and generous tourist echoes that of nineteenth-century European travelers in Egypt, such as Gustave Flaubert and Gérard de Nerval, for whom the sexual possession of the Oriental female encodes colonial desire—just as being raped by an Oriental male (as in "The Nativity" or in E. M. Forster's *A Passage to India*) tropes the fear of the gendered colonial Other. The important difference is that the protagonist's is a "class Orientalism," if I may call it that: the upper-middle class Egyptian with a European education comes to see the lower classes of her own society from an Orientalist perspective shaped equally by European travel writing and Egyptian class attitudes. That is, Orientalism here frames not only the relations between Egypt and Britain (described, tout court, as "East" and "West" and cast in the gendered terms of colonial discourse), but also class relations within Egyptian society.

Soueif's first collection of short stories also contains autobiographical narratives about a young Egyptian girl growing up in London, where she suffers from alienation, prejudice, and loneliness. Hardly celebratory of England in the way that nearly all Arab Americans praise the U.S., those stories predictably did not generate much interest among reviewers, even though they are no less expressive of the same creative impulse as Soueif's unself-consciously Orientalist ones, having all been written at a time when she did not give much thought to the politics of reception. Her subsequent works are indelibly marked by her acute awareness of that politics, and in her two novels to date she set out to contest readers' assumptions and expectations.

Her first novel, *In the Eye of the Sun* (1992), tells the story of Asya al-Ulama who (like Soueif herself and roughly her age) studies English literature at Cairo University. There Asya falls in love with a fellow student named Saif Madi, whom she marries after graduation. A brilliant, indulgent, seemingly open-minded, and in many ways "ideal" husband, Saif turns out to be old-fashioned at heart, repressed, and incapable of understanding or communicating with his wife, who cannot, as far as he is concerned, be anything more than a "princess" or a "pussycat." Following Asya's miscarriage, Saif refrains from lovemaking with her until, several years later, when she is writing a dull, laborious, and uninspiring doctoral thesis in the north of England, she begins an affair with Gerald Stone, a crude, nagging, and obsessive 1970s hippie. Burdened with the combined frustrations of her marriage, love affair, and dissertation, Asya eventually has to deal with the shocked rage of Saif, who, like Gerald, had apparently never imagined her as capable of independent thought. The plot places Soueif's preoccupation with sexual politics in Egypt in a postcolonial context, where it is complicated by Egyptian–British relations in a manner reminiscent of Tayeb Salih's *Season of Migration to the North* (1966). *In the Eye of the Sun* echoes Salih's novel in which the Arab African student's journey to England becomes an occasion to interrogate the gendered violence of colonial discourse and patriarchal violence back home.

The novel is a semi-autobiographical *Bildungsroman,* a genre that, like autobiography, emphasizes the inner life and development of the individual. Yet the novel also, much like the memoir and the historical novel, paints a vivid picture of an era, in this case Nasser's Egypt during the late 1960s, and chronicles in meticulous detail the unfolding, hour by hour, of the June War of 1967, a crucial event in the life of the protagonist and of Soueif herself. This war chronicle is framed within a historical narrative that stretches back to the Sykes–Picot Agreement of 1916, in which the British and the French divided the Arab world into spheres of influence in anticipation of the fall of the Ottoman empire, and forward to the Camp David Accords of 1979 between Egypt and Israel. This historical narrative provides a context for the plot, the events of which span the period 1967 to 1981. In fact, the historical narrative overwhelms Asya's story in the first half of the novel, so that from a structural point of view the novel may be said to be flawed in that no direct connections are made between the inner development of the protagonist and the collective history. Readers are apparently meant to understand that the historical overdetermines or at least frames the individual narrative, but without the exact nature of the relationship between the two narratives being developed. They intersect only at the very end in a decisive scene when Asya finally, 723 pages through the massive novel, declares her independence, so to speak, by gathering enough courage to break up with Gerald, accusing him of being a "sexual imperialist" who likes to feel superior to his Third World girlfriends (Soueif 1992, 723). From this point on, she is no longer dependent on him, or on her husband Saif, or even on her mother who comes to her rescue more than once, as Asya begins to take control of her life. The sentimental education of the protagonist is complete only when she is able to interpret her personal life in the context of both imperial history in the twentieth century and the millennial history of patriarchal hegemony. The final scene of the novel depicts Asya in the presence of a newly excavated statue of an ancient Egyptian woman who has symbolically lain face down in her sandy grave for thousands of years.

Reviewers criticized the novel for its length, which is partly due to the inclusion of material such as news reports on the 1967 War and numerous quotations from Asya's oppressively dry doctoral thesis—material not normally found in a *Bildungsroman*. This structural untidiness of the novel is a symptom of the tension between the individual voice and the need for collective representation. Soueif's project was to give free rein to both, that is to say, to represent fully the interiority of the protagonist but also to frame it within a version of collective history that is not readily available to her readers. Written in English, *In the Eye of the Sun* incorporates substantial background worthy of a historical novel, background that had a profound material and psychological effect on her generation and was perfectly known and understood by Egyptian readers. Had she been writing in Arabic, it would not have needed much elaboration, but since she was writing in English, she felt it necessary to weld together, albeit clumsily, two genres of narration into a hybrid form, a sort of historical *Bildungsroman*.

Yet another aspect of the politics of reception revealed itself as the novel began to be reviewed in the Egyptian press. *In the Eye of the Sun* was on the whole very warmly welcomed as an Egyptian novel written in English that painted a nuanced and sympathetic image of the country to the outside world. However, what shocked a few readers was the frank discussion of sexual taboos and the explicit depiction of an Arab Muslim woman's sexual encounters not only with her husband, but also in an adulterous relationship with an English lover. Doing so in the English language, rather than in Arabic, was especially problematic for some scandalized readers, one of whom protested that the novel had "defame[d] her sisters, defame[d] Arab women, and defame[d] Islam" (Pakravan 282). It is noteworthy that nobody had accused Tayeb Salih of defaming Arab men by depicting a sexual predator in *Season of Migration to the North* (1966), something that reveals not only the double standard involved in judging what male and female writers can do, but also the different implications of writing in Arabic and English. In the context of (post) colonial relations, notions of female honor take on added symbolism: its "protection," "violation," or "surrender" become a measure of national honor and allegiance. To represent such relations in English is to assume a corresponding, overdetermined stance vis-à-vis the former colonizer, so the charge of "defamation" implies a sort of discursive treason—that Soueif, in effect, sold her culture out in exchange for fame and fortune in Britain.

Many established critics in Egypt and elsewhere in the Arab world rushed to defend Soueif and to refute that myopic, sexist, and paranoid accusation, some even asserting that "although it was written in English, it was an Egyptian novel, and one of the most important novels to come out of the Arab world in the last twenty years" (281). Those reviews "struck a note of pride that a book written by an Egyptian, that contained such affection for the country and was clearly born of that culture, found an audience in the West. I also received a lot of letters, mostly from women but also from men, saying how much they sympathized with the book and how it speaks of our generation" (282). Soueif adds, "When I went home [to Cairo], I was received very, very warmly. There were demands for interviews, demands for readings. At one reading there were over a hundred people, most of whom had read the book—a book in English, 800 pages long, and very hard to come by in Cairo! I was heartened and encouraged and proud" (281).

Nevertheless, the episode is exemplary for what it reveals about the politics of writing in English for an Arab writer, especially a bilingual writer who maintains an active presence on the Arab cultural scene. In Soueif's case, English afforded a certain freedom to discuss private and especially sexual concerns that would have been more sensitive in Arabic, but also imposed restrictions on the choice of subject matter and its treatment, in view of the Orientalist biases to which she refuses to cater. By the same token, Arabic imposes certain restrictions yet affords satisfactions of its own that are not available in Britain—the freedom from the sense of being besieged by hostile representations of one's background and the sense of belonging that Soueif has never felt in England (283–86). In other words, the bilingual Arab writer, especially the female writer, must negotiate not one but two kinds of reader expectations, and different sets of culture-specific conditions of reception. Each context affords her certain freedoms and also imposes limits of its own. Within each context of reception, an Anglophone Arab writer is seen as a representative of the Arab world. He or she is, therefore, a minor writer in relation to two literary traditions and has no choice but to embrace fully the limitations of her or his minority status (the representational burden of knowing that everything personal or private is always political and collective), as well as the opportunities it affords to transform language and genre, to forge a new discourse, and to expand the cultural worldview of each society.

Thus while Soueif has collaborated on the Arabic translation of her short stories and her second novel, *The Map of Love*, she has not allowed *In the Eye of the Sun* to be translated. Her rationale for doing so amounts to a theory of cultural translation. She says:

> [B]ecause my native language is Arabic, I really do care about what it would sound like in Arabic. I would be really distressed if it sounded like a translation. That being said, I don't think that a literal translation would do. It would have to be a reworking, almost a rewriting of the book. In whatever language you write, you write against a backdrop of that language, of that culture, of the assumptions of the native speakers, of what has been done before in the literature of that language. Now take the odd problematic passages . . . from *In the Eye of the Sun*, and look at them against a Western background. Let's say that [they] might be a little bit shocking, but not very shocking. If for convenience, we give it a scale of shock value from 0 to 10, let's say that the book as I wrote it would shock its reader 2 out of 10. Now translate this book into Arabic and you have to look at it against a different background, because it is, in a way, an Arab or Egyptian novel. You would have to judge it on the background of what has been done in the literature and the social context of Arabic. And that 2 on a scale of 10 shock value would become 9 out of 10. Your readers would possibly not want to continue to read the book, and even if they did you [would] have changed the whole balance of the book so that the things that were shocking have become vastly more important because you just gave them more weight, you foregrounded them, you pushed them at the reader a lot more than you did in the original. What I would love to see would be a genuine translation . . . one that would preserve the shock value, so that you would still startle your reader into sitting up and paying attention, but to that 2 on a scale of 10, not 9 out of 10. You are not doing social anthropology; you are writing a work of fiction, a work of art. What matters is the effect you have on your reader. You must have the same effect on the Arab reader that you had on your Western reader. (282–83)

Soueif here recognizes that all translation, no matter how "faithful," necessarily involves a kaleidoscopic distortion of the original text that overemphasizes some aspects of it and de-emphasizes others, and that the greater the cultural difference, the greater the distortion. She also warns against the Eurocentric assumption that an Arabic or a Third World literary text is an unmediated reflection of social reality, not a work of art that imaginatively transforms that reality. For readers who make that assumption, the Third World writer is less an artist than a native informant. In this situation, literary translation needs to be undertaken with great care so as to prevent the work turning into "social anthropology." According to that logic, Soueif argues that in the case of a novel like *In the Eye of the Sun*, translation need not even be attempted in the first place.

But Soueif's theory leaves many unanswered questions: is what she calls a "genuine translation" possible? Can the work be recalibrated to maintain its score on the scale of shock value across different languages and cultures with widely divergent mores and sensibilities? Would such translation not in effect be an altogether different work from the original? Would it not be an original work in its own right rather than a translation? Does this requirement not place a *de facto* prohibition on all translation? And what, after all, are the stakes involved? Why should a translation not shock and disturb differently in its translational "afterlife," to use Walter Benjamin's metaphor—an afterlife which is, by definition, qualitatively different? Why should translation conform to its readers' expectations and confirm their assumptions, leaving them in the comfort of received ideas? This is, of course, the complaint made about careless or prejudiced English translations of Arabic works that domesticate or even distort them, turning them into reflections of Orientalist biases rather than edifyingly unfamiliar perspectives that challenge and enrich. Soueif's novels serve precisely this defamiliarizing function in English, both in their content and style: by offering political perspectives that challenge received ideas and by deterritorializing English by infusing it with Arabic. Obviously, if the style, themes, structure, and form of the "original" are all calculated to play such a transformational role within the Anglo-American cultural-linguistic context, no such aspects of Soueif's work would survive in Arabic translation. Linguistic deterritorialization would fizzle, and the critique of Orientalism would be moot. The shock value in Arabic would be much lower than in English.

But this is not what worries Soueif, who was happy with her mother's Arabic translation of *The Map of Love* (in fact, both of them collaborated on the translation), and eager for it to appear in Arabic (Massad 89–90). The interdiction is restricted to translating *In the Eye of the Sun*, which would produce a significantly higher shock value in Arabic than in English: nine out of ten, compared to two out of ten. For Soueif, this would be an unacceptable distortion that renders *In the Eye of the Sun* untranslatable into Arabic—not because the novel resists linguistic transfer in a similar way to poetry or the Arabic *maqama* (Kilito 2008, 16–18, 42), but because a cultural translation of *In the Eye of the Sun* would be impossible; it would be the wrong kind of intervention in the Egyptian literary field. Its implied challenge to sexual mores and gender politics in Egypt—while much less powerful compared to the writings of Ihsan 'Abd al-Quddus, Yusuf Idris, Nawal el Saadawi, Tayeb Salih, Ghada al-Samman, or, more recently, 'Ala' al-Aswany—would be tainted by guilt of association with imperialism. Written in English and published in London and New York, it recalls the perceived "treason" of a Salman Rushdie or the anti-Arab and anti-Muslim bias that more recently fueled the Danish cartoon controversy. Those defensive readers who accused Soueif of defamation saw no difference between an Egyptian author of a controversial English book and a hostile European writer. Interestingly, some of those who defended Soueif did so also based on the fact that the novel was written in English, so in both camps, the politics of language and location was paramount. And while Soueif's theory of "genuine" cultural translation implies that two-way cultural translation is impossible, her success has to a great extent been due to her location and her translational use of English:

> In the West, I think that part of why people liked my work is because they felt that it gives them an insight into another world, into the hearts and minds of people they would not have access to otherwise. Because the books are written in English—without the medium of translation—because the form is familiar to them, they find that they respond to it, and they are able to empathize. In the East, people have said that even though the writing is in English, that this is an authentic Arab voice, and authentic Arab *wigdan* [soul, passion, or sensibility], which is being expressed in English. It is as if they're their emissary to the world at large. So, I guess I'm lucky—to have the Arab *wigdan* and the English language. (Massad 89)

Minoritarian Dialectics

The reception of *In the Eye of the Sun* in Egypt was another watershed in Soueif's fictional project, just as the reception of her early short stories in England represented an earlier turning point. If two-way cultural translation is impossible, she has to pick her battles and focus on one side. Her next novel, *The Map of Love*, which was a finalist for the Booker Prize in 1999, is an extended meditation on the possibilities and limits of translation, but it is also much more focused on the critique of Orientalist discourse, British colonialism, and U.S. imperialism than on sexual and gender politics in Egypt. The novel goes beyond what Deleuze and Guattari call the "deterritorialization of language" (the first characteristic of a minor literature) in that it not only Arabizes English, but also makes literary and cultural translation a central thematic and formal concern. I will turn to this aspect of the novel in the next section, but first, I would like to dwell briefly on the problematic of the individual and the community, the personal and the political—the second and the third characteristics of a minor literature, according to Deleuze and Guattari—by way of concluding the discussion of the politics of reception.

In her first novel, Soueif's preoccupation with balancing the individual and the collective, the personal and the political, resulted in an uneasy welding of the historical novel and the *Bildungsroman*. In her second novel, she opted for the collective and the political, and hence for the historical novel, at the expense of the private voice.[5] *The Map of Love* has several narrators and central characters. The plot consists of two love stories that take place in the 1900s and 1990s and that mirror each other, just as the cultural and historical backgrounds that overdetermine them reveal similar patterns of imperial dominance: first the British military occupation of Egypt (1882–1956), and later U.S. foreign policy and its self-serving advocacy of "free"-market globalization. The principal characters represent branches and generations of a multinational family that extends from Egypt to England, France, and the U.S., undercutting the myth of autonomous national or cultural identities. In the early twentieth century, Lady Anna Winterbourne, the English widow of an embittered veteran of the 1898 British campaign to reconquer Sudan, is drawn to Egypt both by the desire to retrace the steps that destroyed her husband and by the mystery of the East represented in the Orientalist paintings of John Frederick Lewis. In Egypt, she falls in love with and marries Sharif Pasha al-Barudi, an Egyptian aristocrat and nationalist who is working to improve educational and economic conditions in his country and to liberate it from British rule. The multinational descendants of Anna and Sharif are Omar al-Ghamrawi, a prominent Palestinian American pianist and political activist who is a thinly veiled fictionalization of Edward Said, and Isabel Cabot, a young American journalist; they meet in 1997 and fall in love. Thus the plot links two cross-cultural love stories at the beginning and end of the century, each involving an Egyptian and a citizen of the world's most powerful empire at the time, so that the personal and the political are inextricably intertwined in them. Soueif paints a vast panorama involving scores of historical figures in a minutely researched and documented portrayal of Egypt's struggle for independence from Britain. Through this panorama, she portrays the ravages of colonial history and unmasks Orientalist stereotypes through the eyes of Anna Winterbourne, who is a sympathetic observer of Egypt and an avatar of Lady Mary Wortley Montagu. Anna loses her husband to the nationalist struggle for independence, just as decades later, on the eve of the new millennium, Isabel, who in turn is an avatar of Anna, comes close to losing Omar to the Palestinian struggle for self-determination—a reflection, no doubt, of the death threats that for many years plagued Omar's real-life model, Edward Said. In fact, in his largely negative review of the novel, Bruce King complained that the last pages of it read like a lecture by Said and that the characters are on the whole little more than two-dimensional portraits of idealized Arabs and British sympathizers with Arab causes, and stereotyped "British, Americans, and 'Zionists.' . . . *The Map of Love* seems like a Harlequin Romance for the anti-Western intelligentsia" (King 453).

There is a kernel of truth to this otherwise reductive dismissal of the book. In this polyphonic novel with multiple narrators, there is hardly any sense of inner complexity to the characters. There is much to be said about the structural symmetry of the plot, the meticulous historical research that enriches the vivid recreation of a little known decade of Egyptian history (the 1900s), and the intensely humane vision that prevails throughout the novel, but characters lack psychological depth, and the only interiority depicted in the novel is spatial, not psychological. The harem, for example, is revealed to Anna (as in Montagu and Leila Ahmed) to be contrasted to Orientalist fantasies about it, which figure in the enchanting paintings of John Frederick Lewis that Anna saw in the South Kensington Museum before her visit to Egypt. Psychological interiority, which was the hallmark of Soueif's first novel, is replaced in the second novel by spatial interiority, which serves to undermine Orientalist stereotypes.

So complete is this erasure of psychological interiority that the only character painted with any hint of inner complexity is Amal al-Ghamrawi, the principal narrator, who never allows her story of a broken marriage, estranged children, and a barely articulated sense of guilt vis-à-vis her privileged position in Egyptian society, to become part of the larger narrative that she pieces together out of letters, diaries, newspapers, memoirs, and oral family history—fragments of private voices that keep interrupting one another and erasing her own. Amal's narrative is repeatedly hinted at but constantly repressed. She avoids thinking about it as she lives vicariously through the characters whose lives she is reconstructing—indeed her preoccupation with their lives and the history that shaped them serves as a distraction from her own unhappy story. The collective subsumes the individual experience, reducing it to a fragment of political history.

But the irony of King's criticism of the novel as a "Harlequin romance" is that that is precisely what the publishing industry wants from a writer like Soueif. She reports:

> After *In the Eye of the Sun* was published, I met up with a friend who had become a literary agent, and she wanted to talk to me about possibly switching agents and going with her, and she said, "Why don't you write a best seller? Why don't you write a pot-boiler—big thing, sort of East-West, and romance, and so on? I can get you a huge advance for that. And bits of *In the Eye of the Sun* show that you can do sexy scenes. You can do this—just do it!" And I went away and thought about it. And I said no. . . . But it got me thinking along romantic lines, and what I became interested in was the idea of the romantic hero, the Byronic hero, as in Mr. Rochester and Heathcliff, and all the characters that we find in Mills and Boon novels—tall, dark, handsome, enigmatic, a stranger, proud, aloof, yet you just know that if you get close you'll find these depths of sensitivity and empathy and passion and tenderness, and so on. And this hero is very often kind of Eastern, but he isn't ever really Eastern. And I've read novels and stories where he's meant to be Egyptian and really isn't at all. He's completely fake . . . they have to make him Christian because they can't go into the whole Muslim bit, but yet he's called Ali or Mohammed because that's what Easterners are called—very odd, pastichey things like that. And I thought, what if I make a hero who's larger than life . . . a real, genuine Egyptian, of that time, with the concerns of that period, and so on. So that was behind the making of Sharif al-Barudi (Soueif 2000, 102).

The novel's indebtedness, however negatively, to the genre of romance may in part account for the flatness of the characters, their ideological clarity, and the melodramatic love story. However, one must not take lightly the pressure exerted by editors and publishers on writers like Soueif, who could not afford to ignore the politics of what Emily Apter has called "the marketing of Third-World difference" within a publishing industry "subject to stratified and specialized 'niche' marketing, with strategically targeted communities of readers ghettoized according to nation, class, education, race and gender"—the very categories that Soueif's fictional project seeks to disrupt (Apter 100).[6] In that sense, Soueif is working to evacuate the ideology of the Oriental romance, but to be effective she has to use its conventions, to write an "East–West" romance that undermines the Orientalist premises of the genre.

Thus whereas *In the Eye of the Sun*, a novel that privileged the individual experience but attempted to frame it historically, was criticized for its structural untidiness and its length, and praised for the psychological depth of its characters, the opposite happened with *The Map of Love*, a novel that privileged the collective and the political at the expense of individual history and private experience, and consequently was praised for its structural complexity and damned for the flatness of its characters, and by some for its politics, which may have cost it the Booker.[7] Yet had it been written in the manner suggested by the literary agent, the novel would have probably been spared Bruce King's ideologically motivated attack, even though as a specimen of a subliterary genre, a Mills and Boon romance, King would have probably not deigned to comment on it. This critical catch-22 demonstrates, first of all, that the second and third characteristics of minor literature, in Deleuze and Guattari's theory, involve not so much a simple equation between the personal and the political, the individual and the collective, but a dialectical tension that writers must constantly negotiate in view of editorial pressures, conditions of reception, politics of location, and the writer's ideological and aesthetic projects. The second implication is that under the regime of Orientalism, it is sometimes impossible for Arab immigrant writers, especially women, to negotiate that tension with any degree of nuance without inviting criticism not only on explicitly ideological grounds, but also on aesthetic grounds, which provides a more subtle way of dismissing or marginalizing the work. The task, and the ethical burden, of the cultural translator is to face those risks as she speaks the truth to power.

A Map of Translation

Notwithstanding, in *The Map of Love* Soueif achieved something that no other Arab immigrant writer had attempted since Ameen Rihani's *The Book of Khalid*, namely to write a novel that bridges Arabic and European literatures discursively, thematically, formally, and stylistically. Indeed, Soueif was much more successful at this than Rihani, whose novel passed quietly out of print after one edition, due in part to its making no concession to readers who do not know the Arabic language and its literature. By contrast, rather than being itself unreadable, Soueif's novel skillfully stages unreadability, multilingualism, and translation as themes, plot devices, stylistic features, and discursive strategies. The novel maps translational strategies: from literal to literary translations, from domesticating to foreignizing translations, and from epistemically violent translations that pursue the will to power to the extremes of forgery to loving translations that surrender to the experience of alterity. The novel pits those forms of translation against one another, juxtaposing the unidirectional intentionality of imperial ideology and the countervailing forces of transculturation.

Translation structures the plot and is one of the explicit themes in the novel. The story of Anna Winterbourne and Sharif al-Barudi is pieced together by Amal al-Ghamrawi out of diaries, letters, books, newspaper clippings, and oral family history in Arabic, English, and French. The plot depends on Amal's multidirectional translations, just as the dialogues in the novel take place in different languages. The novel also highlights the politics of multilingualism. The four main Egyptian characters are bilingual or trilingual, while Anna (who is bilingual to begin with) and Isabel begin to learn Arabic while in Egypt. English and French enjoy the prestige and appeal of the imperial powers whose languages they are, so it is not surprising that Egyptians learn them. By contrast, interest in learning Arabic, the language with lesser political power though with an immense cultural heritage stretching back to the sixth century, generally serves in Soueif's fiction to identify travelers to Egypt who have a genuine interest in understanding the people and their culture; by the same token, indifference to Arabic characterizes those with less admirable motives. In the somewhat stratified economy of the novel, Arabic language competency on the part of European residents in Egypt is an index to their politics, so that no provision is made for Orientalists with superb language skills who serve as the agents of imperialism (although "good" Orientalists are prominent in the novel), or alternatively for those open-minded or progressive visitors to the country who do not know any Arabic.

This limitation in the discourse of the novel aside, the multidirectional linguistic and cultural translations among the protagonists of *The Map of Love* take place in the context of anti-imperial struggles and of multiple forms of love (romantic, sisterly, brotherly, maternal, paternal, philanthropic, patriotic, and even incestuous—a point emphasized by the little treatise on some Arabic words for love and their connotations quoted in the epigraph to this chapter [386–87]). In this way, the novel articulates both formally and thematically the relationship between ethics, love, and translation as pondered by Irigaray and Spivak, and at the same time draws attention to the epistemological limits of translation. In the discourse of the novel, ethical translation is not so much a matter of strategy (fluent or foreignizing) but of attention to context, liberatory impulse, and loving "surrender" to the experience of alterity (Spivak 1993, 183); by contrast, hegemonic translation (again, no matter the strategy) is expressed in metaphors of forgery and the desecration of the dead.

Linguistically, in both Arabic and English, translation takes place between different linguistic registers: from the distinctive spoken Arabic of Upper Egyptian peasants (rendered in literal translation of their idiomatic expressions and turns of phrase), to middle-class Cairene speech (translated into standard English peppered with literally translated expressions), to classical *belle-lettristic* and Modern Standard Arabics; and from Anna's Victorian style to Isabel's American English to the clipped syntax of Internet communications, all of which is interspersed with French and Italian. Examples of foreignizing translation also abound throughout the novel: proverbs that convey a worldview and an ethics, turns of phrase that reveal the relationship between rhetoric and logic, bits of dialogue that identify characters' regional and class affiliation, and Arabic words and phrases explained within the text or in the glossary. These stylistic elements function at once to maintain the theme of translation consistently before the readers, who are never allowed to forget the complexity of cultural and linguistic mediation, and to offer insights into the workings of the Arabic language. Some of the most salient examples of this strategy are scenes depicting acts of translation and language learning. Here is Amal explaining to Isabel, who has just learned the Arabic alphabet, how to build her vocabulary:

> Everything stems from a root. And the root is mostly made up of three consonants—or two. And then the word takes different forms . . . Take the root q-l-b, qalb. . . . Qalb: the heart, the heart that beats, the heart at the heart of things. . . . Then there's a set number of forms—a template almost—that any root can take. So in the case of "qalb" you get "qalab": to overturn, overthrow, turn upside down, make into the opposite; hence "maqlab": a dirty trick, a turning of the tables and also a rubbish dump. "Maqloub": upside-down; "mutaqallib": changeable; and "inqilab": a coup . . .
>
> So at the heart of all things is the germ of their overthrow; the closer you are to the heart, the closer to the reversal. . . . Every time you use a word, it brings with it all the other forms that come from the same root. (Soueif 1999, 81–82)

While derivation rules generate the forms, a semantic logic informed by a distinctive worldview gives them their meanings and connotations. Not only does a passage such as this explain something about a cultural-linguistic worldview, but (true to the logic of reversal it explains) it also confronts readers with the epistemological limits of translation—the untranslatable—and with "what [they]'re missing" (Clifford 39). Foreignizing translation may communicate some shades of meaning that domesticating translation obscures, but it ultimately remains incapable of conveying a sense of the cluster of cognates and connotations of a particular word, or the worldview it encodes. Hence the emphasis in the novel on the necessity of learning a foreign language, something that at once relies on translation, reveals its limits, and (paradoxically) seeks to circumvent it. The last comment about translation in the novel expresses Amal's (and Soueif's) near despair: "she has translated novels—or done her best to translate them. It is so difficult to truly translate from one language into another, from one culture into another; almost impossible really. Take that concept of 'tarab,' for example; a paragraph of explanation for something as simple as a breath, a lifting of the heart, tarab, mutrib, shabb tereb, tarabattatta tarabattattee, Taroob, Jamal wa Taroob" (Soueif 1999, 515); (earlier on: "How do I translate 'tarab'? How do I, *without sounding weird or exotic*, describe to Isabel that particular emotional, spiritual, even physical condition into which one enters when the soul is penetrated by good Oriental [*sic*] music? A condition so specific it has a root all to itself: t/r/b. Anyone can be a singer—a 'mughani'—but to be a 'mutrib' takes an extra quality" [332, my emphasis]).

Amal here suggests that the risks of foreignizing translation range from undue estrangement to (self-)exoticism. Anna Winterbourne spells out the political implications of those risks as she reflects on the conditions under which Egypt's case can be presented persuasively to British public opinion:

> I have come to believe that the fact that it falls to [anti-imperialist] Englishmen to speak for Egypt is itself perceived as a weakness; for how can the Egyptians govern themselves, people ask, when they cannot even speak for themselves? They cannot speak because there is no platform for

> them to speak from and because of the difficulties with language. By that I mean not just the ability to translate Arabic speech into English but to speak as the English themselves would speak, for only then will the justice of what they say—divested of its disguising cloak of foreign idiom—be truly apparent to those who hear it. (399)

Whether "the subaltern [could] speak" (Spivak 1988) depends in this context on *fluent* translation that does not so much domesticate the original as strategically downplay cultural difference in the interest of expedient political action, for what is at stake in this case is not so much the preservation of cultural or linguistic specificity as the construction of a political narrative within a universal framework of "justice" that foreignizing strategies risk undermining. Fluency here no longer equals domestication, nor, as Marilyn Booth cautions, does foreignizing guarantee "ethically aware translation practice" (Booth 51). In fact, through the trope of forgery, Soueif illustrates how foreignizing strategies can domesticate when they are put in the service of colonial discourse.

The Map of Love undermines colonial discourse by repeatedly confounding the expectations it creates for readers accustomed to several genres of Orientalist writing: fiction, romance, tourist guide, and imperial historiography. Soueif's narrative strategy here is to depict Anna as a principal first-person narrator whose diary evidences her gradual shift from a Eurocentric to a sympathetic observer of, and participant in, Egypt's struggle for independence.[8] At the outset, she is the wife of an officer in Kitchener's army, which conquered Sudan in 1898, and the daughter-in-law of Sir Charles Winterbourne, who participated in the 1882 bombardment of Alexandria that inaugurated the British occupation of the country. Sir Charles, to whom she is close, has since become a vehement critic of the British Empire, which he believes to have "done so much harm to so many people that it deserved to perish" (Soueif 1999, 13). He detests "the spirit of Empire, for he is angered equally by the doings of Kitchener in South Africa, the King of the Belgians in the Congo, the Americans in the Filipines and all the nations of Europe in China" (39). Edward Winterbourne, Anna's husband and Sir Charles's son, goes to Sudan searching for adventure, but returns to England haunted by the atrocities committed against the "fanatical dervishes," as they had been represented in the British press, who "transformed themselves in front of his eyes into men . . . impassioned by an idea of freedom and justice in their own land" (35). Unlike Joseph Conrad's Marlow in "Heart of Darkness," the complicit, albeit indignant, observer who seeks redemption through story-telling, Edward's disillusionment and guilt lead to his withdrawal into silence, deteriorating health, and death. His narrative remains unspoken, neither legitimizing nor unmasking the civilizing mission; literally and metaphorically, his silence becomes his death. Yet the novel goes on to dispose of Conrad's ambivalence about colonialism in the blunt words of George Wyndham, the Under-Secretary of War at the time, that "it is agreed by the Powers that the aim of African operations is to civilize Africa in the interests of Europe and that to gain that end all means are good" (32). As if to illustrate how this Machiavellian logic translates into action, this passage is followed by a report on

Kitchener's desecration of the tomb of the Mahdi, who was by then revered as a saint, and the use of his skull as an inkwell—reminiscent of the severed African heads adorning Kurtz's hut, but also resonating with the ecclesiastical taboo on improper "translation" of a saint's remains.[9] The skull qua inkwell becomes a powerful symbol for the conjunction of colonial barbarism and translation.

From this initial evocation of *Heart of Darkness*, Anna's story unfolds as a woman's travel narrative. Sir Charles's experience in Egypt, her dead husband's in Sudan, and the Oriental paintings of John Frederick Lewis all draw her to Egypt. The "luminous beauty" (27) of Lewis's famous harem paintings and "the wondrous colours, the tranquility, the contentment with which they are infused" (46) attract her to Egypt, much as the serpentine river on the map of Africa casts a spell on Marlow. Yet the contrast between the effect of the paintings and the river, associated, respectively, with vivid images of light and darkness, tranquility and anxiety, beauty and "horror," serves both to evoke and contradict Marlow's narrative. Nevertheless, the Orientalist character of the paintings and the whole romance of the East, with its harems and deserts, are later put into question as Anna's journey takes her into actual Egyptian harems and across the Sinai desert, where she discovers the rift between Orientalist discourse and the world it mediates for Europeans.[10]

Anna's own narration begins much like those of other European travelers to the East. Reading Anna's first letters and diary entries from Egypt ninety years later, Amal finds them

> a little self-conscious . . . a little aware of the genre—*Letters from Egypt, A Nile Voyage, More Letters from Egypt*. . . . Perhaps she was thinking of future publication. In any case, I forgive her . . . What else does she know—yet? And I am glad that she has broken away—that the brown leather journal is put aside gently. She did not draw a thick line under the last entry. She did not tear out and use any of the remaining pages. . . . She simply left them blank. (58)

Soueif inserts Anna within a tradition of women's writing about the East that begins with Lady Mary Wortly Montagu, women who, as Billie Melman shows in *Women's Orients*, "openly criticize male representations" of the East (75). Anna's abandonment of the discursive conventions of male travel writing comes about with her discovery of the narrow confines of colonial discourse. Her subsequent transgressions of it transform her understanding of Egypt, inform what she writes about it in her diary and letters, and motivate her translations of political tracts and intelligence memoranda into and from English and Arabic. But this transformation in her position from European tourist to an agent of transculturation is signaled in the text of her first Egyptian diary book not by an assertive discursive rupture, a thick line or torn paper, which would have placed her gesture on a par with Marlow's ripping of the infamous postscript to Kurtz's report on "savage customs" (Conrad 51). Rather, Anna's "gentle" abandonment of the notebook allows Orientalism simply to trail off into silence. Unlike Edward's withheld speech and Marlow's ambivalent lies, her text will henceforth construct an alternative discourse.

By contrast, the British residents in Egypt are insulated within the discourse of empire. They keep to themselves, aloof toward the only Egyptians they admit among themselves, the servants, while dismissing educated Egyptians as "the talking classes." The British residents are indifferent to the culture surrounding them and smug in their sense of superiority and knowledge of the "native character" (Soueif 1999, 98–99, 239). As Anna puts it, "there is a living world which . . . [they] are refusing to see or even hear about" (240).[11] Curious about that world, she ventures out of the closed circuit of the British Agency and on a trip to Sinai, disguised as an Englishman and accompanied by a single Egyptian attendant. Even before leaving Cairo, she finds herself in a situation that is the stuff of Oriental romance: she is mistaken for a British officer and kidnapped by two young nationalists who want to negotiate the release of a political prisoner. When they discover her identity, they panic and take her to the villa of an Egyptian pasha. There she is ushered into the women's quarter, which immediately evokes the well-known discourse on the harem—from Montesquieu to Ingres—and recalls Lewis's paintings, which drew her to Egypt in the first place. But here the Oriental romance ends, without a hint of eunuchs, opium pipes, or slave women. Instead, a dignified Egyptian woman greets Anna in perfect French. Layla al-Barudi reassures Anna and sends for her brother, Sharif Pasha al-Barudi, who reprimands the young kidnappers severely, apologizes to Anna, and offers to escort her back to her hotel. When she insists on continuing her journey, he arranges to accompany her to ensure her safety. A complicated game of disguise and cross-dressing follows, as Anna becomes, in turn, an Englishman, an Egyptian woman, then a Frenchman, as she and her Egyptian companions make their way into Sinai.

Like her transgression of colonial boundaries, Anna's cross-dressing gives her access to experience outside the bounds of Orientalist discourse. The transformative potential of the intertwining acts of cross-dressing, translation, and transgressing social boundaries is captured by Anna in a half-translated sentence in her diary: "Dépêchez-vous alors, if you are going to transform yourself," says Sharif, urging her to take a new disguise at one juncture in the trip (195). Anna's retention of part of the sentence in its "original" French while translating the rest brings cross-dressing into focus as a metaphor for self-transformation and for transformative translation. The bilingual sentence signals Anna's increasing awareness of this as she drifts farther and farther away from the epistemic universe of empire. Anna's transgression is empowering, but it comes at the price of surrendering her privileged subject position as a member of the European elite and losing herself (literally being kidnapped, held captive, and falling in love). Such acts of transgression and surrender illustrate Spivak's theory of translation; they initiate Anna into a fluid and multilingual episteme that stages the encounter with the other not as a threatening or violent event, but as an occasion for transculturation. Significantly, while she does not speak Arabic at first, Sharif does not speak English, so that they are forced to communicate in a language foreign to both of them: "'does it trouble you that you cannot speak to me in Arabic?' He replies, 'No, it makes foreigners of us both. It's good that I should have to come some way to meet you'" (157).[12] Their *amour trilingue* at that halfway meeting point, and their happy domestic life, contrast with the worsening conditions of Egypt under the British occupation and the mounting political tension. They pay a price for carving out this transgressive, translational space within the ideologically stratified world of empire: her compatriots shun her, and his suspect him of collaborating with the occupation, leading to his assassination.

The politically overdetermined love story is Soueif's answer to the genre of Oriental romance. Mystery, intrigue, harems, veiled women, deserts, camels, not to mention a highly melodramatic love affair—all the ingredients of lurid tales are present in the story, but in ways that subvert the ideology of the genre. Anna's diary and letters quickly become a historical record of bitter struggle against colonial policies and of dynamic social change that is often hampered, not accelerated as imperial historiography claims, by colonial policies (248, 257, 275–6, 367, 370, 379–80, 383–4, 397, 409, 412). Once Anna's transgression leads her into the midst of upper-class Egyptian society, the timelessness and mystery of the East turn out to be the effect of Orientalist discourse. As in Leila Ahmed's memoir, the harem is revealed here to be the space within which educated women live more or less independent lives. Likewise the veil, perennially represented in Europe and North America as the unequivocal sign of Muslim women's oppression and voicelessness, becomes the guarantor of freedom of movement. For example, it allows Anna to travel on the train in a second-class carriage among Egyptians, which would have been unthinkable for an Englishman—let alone an English woman—who would have traveled in first-class with other Europeans, with no access to the kind of transgressive knowledge that becomes available to Anna. Echoing Gérard de Nerval, she writes, "it is a most liberating thing, this veil. While I was wearing it, I could look wherever I wanted and nobody could look back at me. Nobody could find out who I was. I was one of many black-clad harem in the station and on the train and could have traded places with several of them and no one been the wiser" (195).[13] Moreover, the veil gives her a new perspective on the British. While at the train station, a group of her English friends walk past her. She writes:

> It was a most curious sensation; they passed so close that I could smell Lady Owsald's cologne and if I had put out my hand I could have plucked at the sleeve of her brown traveling coat. I felt at once the fear of being discovered and the strangeness of their sweeping by me without acknowledgement—but the oddest thing of all was that I suddenly saw them as bright, exotic creatures, walking in a kind of magical space, oblivious to all around them; at ease, chattering to each other as though they were out for a stroll in the park, while the people, pushed aside, watched and waited for them to pass. (194–5)

This unexpected reversal of the gaze, directed from the normalized perspective of the "natives" toward those who now appear as picturesque exotic creatures, turns the classic scene of travel literature inside out: the European traveler, erstwhile owner of the gaze and interpreter of the Orient, not only becomes the object of the natives' gaze, but his or her very ability to see, record, and narrate the East is radically questioned. By the same token, seen as the sign of Muslim women's invisibility and voicelessness, the veil becomes an authorizing subject position for Anna and a condition of seeing and speaking.

In putting into question the intuitive association in Euro-American epistemology of visibility with presence, voice, and subjectivity, the veil here functions as the horizon of translatability. The untranslatable beyond the veil becomes the test of ethics, demanding of the ethical agent an acknowledgment of the limits of knowledge and a refusal to submit the untranslatable to the discursive conditions of Orientalism. Anna exemplifies this position when, further along in her journey into Sinai and now dressed as a Frenchman, she and Sharif are entertained by a Bedouin tribal chief. During the festivities held in their honor, she observes the veiled Bedouin women, then writes:

> my only regret tonight is that I could not spend any time in the company of the women but perforce saw them only as a man would: slight figures in long, embroidered gowns, flitting about as they handed the food to the men who served us, their movements light, their sequined veils glittering in the firelight, their black eyes above them darting at me with curious looks which added piquancy to my situation. And although they took no part in the fantasia, they joined in the drumming and clapping and their voices rose so that I thrilled to that ululating joy-cry which I had read about but never heard. (209)

The tables are turned once again in this scene, with Anna now as the gendered exotic object of the native female gaze. Anna's masculine subject position confers on her a certain privilege—that of a European male—yet it also sets limits on what she can know. Once more, veiled women hold the authorizing gaze, except that it is now inaccessible. Their voices rise in the idiomatic cries of joy, but are untranslatable. Anna's text withholds translation precisely at the moment when the untranslatable seems to lend itself readily to domestication and exoticism; instead, her text preserves the space of the untranslatable that undermines any illusion of discursive mastery, neither in the mournful notes of modernist alienation nor in foreignizing translation that exoticizes and domesticates, but in a shared experience of joy.

This citing of the untranslatable at the limits of knowledge, as a gesture toward what is missing, and in affirmation of shared humanity, contrasts with the imposition of ethnocentric knowledge in domesticating translation, which risks negating shared humanity. Such translation takes several forms in the novel—from Anna's Thomas Cook tourist guide that translates the Bedouins of Sinai in the terms of anti-Black racism (approvingly quoting one Reverend T.W. Chambers who describes them as "a cheerful, contented race, very much like the American Negroes in their simplicity, thoughtlessness and good humor" [*Cook's* 304; Soueif 1999, 209]); to British attitudes toward Egyptians translated into Cromer's detrimental policies in Egypt; to the indifference of British colonial administrators to the Arabic language and its culture; to outright forgery. Cromer ruled Egypt for twenty-five years and believed himself to be a "friend of the fellaheen" (peasants) (Soueif 1999, 412), yet his ignorance of their language was notorious enough for

Egyptians to joke sardonically that he knew only two words of Arabic: "baksheesh" (gratuity or tip) and "imshi" (go away) (71). As for educated, polyglot Egyptians, he dismisses them as the "talking classes" (67)—the derogatory stereotype of "Westernized Oriental Gentlemen," or wogs—inauthentic Egyptians. Harry Boyle, his Oriental Secretary and close advisor, valued by Cromer for his knowledge of the language, in fact spoke only a smattering of the vernacular and was ignorant of written Arabic.

Within the economy of the novel, Boyle is the translator-forger, author of the most striking example in it of foreignizing translation that reinforces Orientalist stereotype: a letter allegedly written in Arabic about a planned uprising, intercepted by the British, translated by Boyle, and sent to the Foreign Office in London in a last-ditch effort to support Cromer's unsuccessful bid for military reinforcements in Egypt. Composed in bizarre language that supposedly reflects the irrationality of the "Oriental mind" while hinting obliquely at the plotted uprising, the letter begins,

> To the Branch of the Fair Tree, the Light Rain of the Generous Cloud, the Son and Daughter of the Prophet, the Drawn Sword of the Straight Way . . . May he always be under the protection of the divine eye—fullest greeting and most perfect benediction. May all the odor of these greetings be upon you and may the blessing of God cover you . . .(417)

A copy of this "sexed up evidence" (in the words of the late David Kelly on the manufactured evidence for Iraqi WMDs used to justify the 2003 invasion) is sent to Anna from London by her friend James Barrington who, knowing Arabic himself, suspects a forgery; Anna translates it into French for Sharif, who passes it on to his friend Ya'qub Artin who translates it from English into Arabic. In all three languages, the letter is found to be absurd, leading them to conclude that it "'could not have been written by an Arab. . . . It makes no sense.' 'This is the work of . . . an ignorant Englishman who imagines he knows how Arabs think'" (419). In her memoir, *Boyle of Cairo*, published almost sixty years later, Clara Boyle confirms this suspicion, revealing that her husband had indeed been the author of the letter, which she cites in full. Unapologetically, she claims that although her husband "invented the 'translation,' he did not invent the spirit of it" (Boyle 63; Soueif 1999, 494), for "there is all the picturesque, flowery language of the East, transposed into equally picturesque English" (Boyle 62; Soueif 1999, 493).

Spivak asks that translation create a model of the relationship between rhetoric and logic in the original rather than search for simple equivalences and local color; Harry Boyle invented a translation for which there was no original, so his forgery relied on Orientalist representations of the Arabic language as hyperbolic rhetoric devoid of logic—stereotypes that the narrative has debunked by now through the insights it has given into the language. Boyle employed the sort of radical literalism or foreignizing sometimes valorized in current translation theory as a safeguard against recuperating the text to the dominant ideology of the translating culture, but here foreignizing functions to reinforce the Orientalist sense of "unbridgeable otherness" (Booth 51). Yet Boyle does not only foreignize in order to recuperate or domesticate; the "original" of his forged translation exists not in Arabic, but in Orientalism's invented Orient and in pseudo-scholarship purporting to describe the "Arab mind." Despite its evident stupidity, the letter serves its desired purpose: "the Foreign Office [in London] . . . will read 'camels' and 'God is generous' and 'odors of blessings' and they will say 'fanatical Arabs' and send the troops" (Soueif 1999, 419). Like the "evidence" of Iraqi WMDs, the forgery functions to justify military violence, testifying to the conjunction of the discourse and the practice of imperial dominance. In its egregious ethical violation, the forged letter rounds off the theme of desecration by recalling at the end of the novel the early report on Kitchener's "translation" of the Mahdi's remains.

As an exemplary translational text, the novel maps the field of ethics from loving translation to translation as forgery. It unmasks the illusion of transparency and fluency while at the same time demonstrating that the opposite strategies of foreignizing and literalism are in themselves no guarantee of ethical agency in translation if they do not aim at "reform[ing] cultural identities that occupy dominant positions in the domestic culture" (Venuti 1998, 83). The novel also subverts the genres of the Oriental romance and travelogue, and rewrites British imperial history, represented in the novel by Cromer's memoir of his rule in Egypt, from the transgressive, collaborative, and collaborationist perspectives of Egyptian and British men and women who join in the cause of anticolonial resistance. Guided by an ethics of difference, love of the other, and hostility to essentialist notions of identity, their alliance depends on translation acts that transgress colonial and gender boundaries and surrender to the transformative experience of the foreign. The novel also stretches the three characteristics of minority literature described by Deleuze and Guattari beyond the confines of their theory: in its translational aspects, the deterritorialization of language is pushed to the limit by being both staged and thematized, while the themes, characters and plot demonstrate the extent to which the private is always political, and the personal collective, not only for members of a given minority, but also in the case of all those who are caught in sweeping historical circumstances that determine the course of their lives and, sometimes, their death.

8

Muslim Immigrant Fiction

> I look up and see the minaret of Regent's Park mosque visible above the trees. I have never seen it so early in the morning in this vulnerable light. London is at its most beautiful in autumn. In summer it is seedy and swollen, in winter it is overwhelmed by Christmas lights and in spring, the season of birth, there is always disappointment. Now it is at its best, now it is poised like a mature woman whose beauty is no longer fresh but still surprisingly potent.
>
> —LEILA ABOULELA

A Minor Literature Within a Minor Literature

In the two previous chapters, we have seen two new developments in Arab immigrant writing in the U.S. and Britain: Leila Ahmed's memoir and scholarly work on women and gender in Islam announce the emergence of an Islamic perspective, and Ahdaf Soueif formulates a translational poetics revolving around the problem of cross-cultural communication that has preoccupied Arab immigrant writers since Ameen Rihani. Those two trends converge in the fiction of Leila Aboulela (b. 1964), a Sudanese economist and Scottish immigrant. Like Soueif's *The Map of Love*, Abouelela's *The Translator* is a translational novel, while her fiction as a whole depicts the experience of practicing Muslims in Scotland and England, from a narrative perspective committed to an Islamic worldview that is shaped in part by the immigrant and minority status of British Muslims. Fiction inspired by Islam is not only highly unusual in a tradition in which, as we have seen so far, religious expression has been mystical, Christian, or secular; it is also very rare in modern Arabic literature, which has been predominantly secular. Thus if Anglophone Arab immigrant literature is a minor tradition in relation to Arabic, American, and British literatures, Aboulela's Muslim fiction represents a minor literature within a minor literature.

Aboulela also represents a new dimension to Scottish identity, as evidenced by her essay, "Barbie in the Mosque," which appears at the head of one hundred contributions to the anthology, *Being Scottish: Personal Reflections on Scottish Identity Today* (2002). The title and the author's photograph in Muslim headscarf are perhaps the least surprising part of Aboulela's answer to a question that, according to the editors, "continues to perplex many Scots today," namely "'who are we?'" (Devine and Logue, ix). More provocative is the testimonial narrative itself, which, contrary to expectations, does not narrate Aboulela's experience. Instead, Aboulela focuses on her friend Aisha, a native-born Scot, child beauty queen, former Catholic, Muslim convert, mother, and forceful presence at the Glasgow mosque. In effect, the essay presents the reader with two figures, Aisha and Aboulela herself, whose modulation of Scottish identity unhinges the naturalized triad of race, religion, and nation. The immigrant's experience of Scotland is defined equally by the North/South opposition that structures the work of the father of modern Sudanese fiction, Tayeb Salih, and by these minority enclaves within Britain where Turks, Bengalis, Lebanese, and Sudanese congregate, their children "speaking in the Scottish accent of Froghall and Tillydrone," in addition to Scottish Muslim converts like Aisha, who "has never been outside Britain, not once, yet she is closer to the world than those who go abroad On Holiday every year" (Aboulela, "Barbie" 2).

Aboulela's fiction depicts those unsuspected spaces in Britain that did not exist in the 1950s and 1960s when Salih penned his early short stories and his celebrated novel, *Season of Migration to the North* (1966). Indeed, whereas Salih's London is the colonial metropolis metonymically represented by Victoria Station as the gateway of empire, the focal point of Aboulela's London is its Central Mosque, whose minaret towers over the trees in Regent's Park (Aboulela 2005, 1). Her work represents two historical developments since the 1970s: the Islamic resurgence that has attempted to fill the void left by the failure of Arab secular ideologies of modernity (something that Salih's fiction as a whole dramatizes), and the growth of immigrant Muslim minorities in Europe and the United States. Her novel *The Translator* (1999), short story collection *Colored Lights* (2001), and to a lesser degree her second novel *Minaret* (2005), explicitly evoke Salih's fiction, model themselves after it, yet depart from it in significant ways. Both writers are Sudanese immigrants in Britain, but whereas Salih wrote in Arabic, Aboulela writes in English. Like Salih, Aboulela is preoccupied with migration between Sudan and Britain, cultural perceptions and stereotypes, and the possibilities of building bridges between former colonizer and colonized. Salih's last fictions express the failure of his generation to find adequate answers to the challenges of postcolonial nationhood and (as part of his powerful critique of patriarchal norms in Sudan) suggest that it may fall specifically to women of a younger generation to articulate an alternative vision (Waïl Hassan 179). Aboulela seems to take on that challenge, although she repudiates some of the fundamental tenets of Salih's ideological project, especially with regard to questions of gender and political agency. In this chapter, I analyze the ideological worldview that informs Aboulela's fiction, first by elaborating on *The Translator*'s allusions to *Season*, before tracing, in *Colored Lights* and *Minaret*, her divergent approach to the common problems that define their work, such as cultural misconceptions and stereotypes, the possibilities of cultural translation, the relationship between the sacred and the secular, and the status of women in male-dominated societies. I want to assess the possibilities and limitations of her contribution to what has been called "Muslim immigrant literature" (Aboulela 2007), a literature that seeks to articulate an alternative episteme derived from Islam but shaped specifically by immigrant perspectives. Ultimately, I argue that while it seeks to displace the Orientalist dichotomy between East and West (recast here, as in Salih, in Africanist terms as North and South) by way of clearing a space for Islam in the "West" (or "North"), this ideology maintains an investment in that dichotomy insofar as it necessarily defines itself against another "West" (a code word for secularism, Orientalism, and Islamophobia). This "West," in the discourse of Aboulela's fiction, overlaps with, but is not identical to, the "West" of Orientalism. In contrast to Orientalism's culturalist, racialist, and geographical determinations, Aboulela's "West" is ideological and attitudinal: it is defined by hostility to Islam and Muslims, wherever and in whomever such hostility may be found, regardless of race, ethnicity, culture, nationality, or geography.

One aspect of the novelty of this brand of Anglophone fiction is that it moves away from the reactive position of "writing back," which has so far served as a primary paradigm of postcolonial literature. If Salih's *Season*, as Edward Said argued, rewrites Joseph Conrad's *Heart of Darkness* (Said 1993, 30, 211–12), Aboulela is less concerned with reversing, rewriting, or answering back to colonial discourse than with attempting an epistemological break with it. Some readers who have noticed some of those parallels between *Season* and *The Translator* see the latter as a counter-narrative to the former. In her review of Aboulela's first two books, Ferial Ghazoul quotes Jamal Mohamed Ibrahim, the Sudanese ambassador in London, who described *The Translator* as "'a dialogue of civilizations,' in contrast to Tayeb Salih's novel . . . which depicts 'the clash of civilizations.'" Ghazoul adds that Aboulela's fiction envisions the possibility "to join South to North under the emblem of a universal quest, that of Islamic humanism" (Ghazoul). Multiple forms of colonial violence lie at the heart of Mustafa Sa'eed's failed rebellion against the British empire, which puts into sharp relief the crisis of British-educated (post)colonial intellectuals of Salih's generation who reject imperialism but remain imprisoned within its epistemic universe. The alternative Islamic discourse introduces a new narrative logic into Anglophone Arab and African fiction that finds its inspiration not so much in the European novel, as was the case with writers of an earlier generation, but in Islamic literature (the Qur'an, *hadith,* Sufi poetry, allegory, parable, and so forth).

This trend is actually discernible in Salih's rarely discussed later works, *Bandarshah* (1971–76) and "Yawm Mubarak 'ala shati' Umm Bab" (1993, A Blessed Day on the Coast of Umm Bab), in which Salih turns to Sufism in an attempt to grapple with the crisis of secular Arab ideology in the late 1960s–70s (Waïl Hassan 129–80). In its Islamic turn, therefore, Aboulela's fiction does not contradict Salih's, unless *Season* is taken out of both its historical context, written as it was at the height of the decolonization movement in the early 1960s, and the larger narrative cycle of which the novel is an episode, something that would discount the heavy influence of mysticism on Salih's works written before and after that novel. But if we consider the trajectory of Salih's fiction in its entirety, we would see that Aboulela takes up where Salih leaves off in *Bandarshah* and "Yawm mubarak." In fact, at times she seems to replicate the paradigm of *Season*: in "The Museum," the only story that focuses on colonial history, the psychological chasm between former colonizer and colonized remains as unbridgeable as it was in *Season* or, earlier still, in E. M. Forster's *A Passage to India*, and, like Mustafa Sa'eed, the cruelty, rudeness, and condescension of Aboulela's protagonist mask the humiliation of the weak and foreclose any possibility of mutual understanding. At other times, some of Aboulela's short stories take the dream visions of Salih's later work to strange new heights. Moreover, her direct and indirect quotations from Salih's writing constitute acts of literary homage to a revered predecessor: the two parts of *The Translator* are prefaced, respectively, by verses by the tenth century Arab poet Abu Nuwas that Salih uses as an epigraph in *Bandarshah*,[1] and by a key passage from *Season*; the title of her short story collection also recalls Mustafa Sa'eed's description of his bedroom in London, which was outfitted with "colored lights in the corners" (Salih 1969, 146); Mustafa Sa'eed's identification of his lovers with the city of London and with Queen Victoria and her empire (which in his warped logic justifies his sexual exploitation of English women), is unproblematically reproduced in the passage quoted in the epigraph to this chapter (Aboulela 2005, 1); and, in *Minaret*, Aboulela inserts into the dialogue Salih's famous exclamation about the military junta that overthrew the democratically elected government of Sudan in 1989, "Where did these people come from?" (Aboulela 2005, 138; Salih 1991, 94). In effect, Aboulela's fiction completes the project of Salih's: whereas his are narratives of failure (of the national project, of the colonial bourgeoisie, of postcolonial intellectuals, of secular Arab ideologies of modernity), hers are narratives of redemption and fulfillment through Islam. While Salih's work reflects the disappointments of the 1960s, Aboulela's embodies the slogan of the Islamist movement that emerged in the mid-1970s: "Islam is the solution."

Unlike *Season*, *The Translator* is a North–South romance with a happy ending. Both novels involve journeys by young Sudanese to the North. Sammar is born in Scotland to Sudanese parents who study there and return home when their daughter is seven years old—a significant number both for its mystical associations and because it is the number of years Salih's narrator, who would be roughly the age of her parents, spent in England. In that sense, one generation separates Sammar from the narrator in *Season*, and two from Mustafa Sa'eed. Sammar makes three journeys to Britain as an adult: with her first husband, then alone after his death, and finally back again with her four-year-old son (also born in Scotland) and her second husband at the end of the novel. Only the first two northward journeys are described in the novel, which focuses mainly on the protagonist's second interval in Scotland (the subject of Part One) and her return to Sudan after her estrangement from Rae (Part Two). The first journey is reported in flashbacks, the third remains in the future at the close of the narrative, but the continuous travel and return clearly gives the movement of the plot a cyclical quality that reproduces the dynamic described in the title of Salih's novel, a pattern that is likely to be repeated with her son in the future. In the discourse of Salih's and Aboulela's novels, Britain and Sudan are represented as opposites in terms of weather, culture, and customs, but they define each other, and movement between them is recurrent and inevitable, from one generation to the next.

The opening passages of both novels emphasize the contrast between North and South: the narrator of *Season* speaks of the deadly cold climate of the North versus the "life warmth of the tribe" (1), and of his entire experience in England as an isolating and dreary one that could not have ended too soon. Likewise, Sammar's life alone in Scotland is characterized by confinement—within her cold, drab room where she is often trapped by the weather; within her lonely existence that she escapes in sleep; and within her memories of the past and dreams of an uncertain future. Significantly, therefore, the novel opens with a dream in which she sees herself trapped at home by the elements:

> She dreamt that it rained and she could not go out to meet him as planned. She could not walk through the hostile water, risk blurring the ink on the pages he had asked her to translate. . . . She was afraid of rain, afraid of the fog and the snow which came to this country, afraid of the wind even. At such times she would stay indoors and wait, watching from her window people doing what she couldn't do: children walking to school though the swirling leaves, the elderly smashing ice on the pavement with their walking sticks. They were superhuman, giants who would not let the elements stand in their way. Last year when the city had been dark with fog, she hid indoors for four days, eating her way through the last packet of pasta, drinking tea without milk. On the fifth day when the fog lifted she went out famished, rummaging the shops for food, dizzy with the effort. (Aboulela 1999, 3)

North and South are defined, both in Salih and in Aboulela, by extreme weather. The cold of the north and the heat of the south are equally deadly, but both Sammar and Salih's narrator prefer Sudan. Northern winters accentuate Sammar's sense of alienation, for in contrast to her physical helplessness, even children and elderly people appear "superhuman." The point is that Aboulela here uses Salih's opening strategy, his frame of reference, and indeed some of his motifs. The fog and the wind appear in the first paragraphs of *The Translator* and *Season*. In fact, the fog is the first image in an extract from the opening paragraph of *Season* that Aboulela uses as an epigraph to Part Two of her novel, the part in which Sammar returns to Sudan:

> . . . the fog cleared and I awoke, on the second day of my arrival, in my familiar bed in the room whose walls had witnessed the trivial incidents of my life in childhood and the onset of adolescence . . . I heard the cooing of the turtle-dove, and I looked through the window at the palm tree standing in the courtyard of our house . . . I looked at its strong straight trunk, at its roots that strike down to the ground, at the green branches hanging down loosely over its top, and I experienced a feeling of assurance. I felt not like a storm-swept feather but like that palm tree, a being with a background, with roots . . . (Salih 1969, 1–2; Aboulela 1999, 121)

Aboulela leaves no doubt here about her literary sources; just in case readers have missed the allusions to *Season* at the start of Part One, the direct quotation in Part

Two establishes an unquestionable frame of reference for the scene of Sammar's return to Sudan. These intertextual links do not parody Salih, in the Bakhtinian sense of parody as double-voiced discourse that undermines the authority of the first text in a "hidden polemic" (Bakhtin 195). Rather, Aboulela's quotations "stylize" *Season*'s rhetorical strategies. Bakhtin makes an important distinction between stylization and parody. In stylization, "the author's thought, once having penetrated someone else's discourse and made its home in it, does not collide with the other's thought, but rather follows after it in the same direction, merely making that direction conventional" (193). By contrast, in parody, "every statement about the object is constructed in such a way that, apart from its referential meaning, a polemical blow is struck at the other's discourse on the same theme, at the other's statement about the same object" (195). Aboulela's allusions to *Season* in Part One and her direct quotation from it in Part Two do not contain any such "polemical blows" against that text, but rather "stylize" it and establish it as an authoritative frame of reference.

Nevertheless, Aboulela's quotation from *Season* contains a revealing omission, marked by the ellipsis dots at the end of the epigraph. Three important words are strategically left out: " . . . with a purpose" (Salih 1969, 2). Sammar's fear of the wind makes her feel "like a storm swept feather" in Scotland; back in Sudan, she is "a being with a background, with roots," but not "with a purpose." The quiet omission of that phrase complicates what seems like a straightforward borrowing from Salih's text, for she stops short of equating the experience of her protagonist with that of his narrator. Sammar, in effect, does not yet have a purpose—at least not one that fits with the trajectory of the novel and its ideological project. Salih's narrator *feels* that he is "a being with a background, with roots, with a purpose"—a purpose tied to the national project of the newly independent state, although that feeling begins to unravel gradually from the moment he articulates it and until he throws himself at the mercy of the waves in the final scene of the novel. Thus while the narrator's story in *Season* progresses from contentedness, at-homeness, and a seemingly clear sense of purpose to bitter disillusionment, suicidal despair, and helplessness (his last words in the novel are a cry for help [Salih 1969, 169]), *The Translator* follows the opposite trajectory: from disillusionment and despair (after the death of Sammar's first husband), to helplessness (in the opening paragraph), to misconstrued purpose (her attempt to force Rae to convert so that they could get married), to discovery of true purpose (when she recognizes her selfishness and prays for his salvation for his own sake). This discovery comes about two-thirds of the way through Part Two, significantly enough during the sacred month of Ramadan, when she has been fasting and praying:

> There were people who drew others to Islam. People with deep faith, the type who slept little at night, had an energy in them. They did it for no personal gain, no worldly reason. They did it for Allah's sake. She had heard stories of people changing: prisoners in Brixton, a German diplomat, an American with ancestors from Greece. Someone influencing someone, with no ego involved. And she, when she spoke to Rae, wanting

> this and that, full of it; wanting to drive him to Stirling, to cook for him, to be settled, to be someone's wife.
>
> She had never, not once, prayed that he would become a Muslim for his own sake, for his own good. It had always been for herself, her need to get married again, not to be alone. If she could rise above that, if she would clean her intentions. (Aboulela 1999, 160)

Within days of that resolution, the "miracle" of his conversion happens (171). *The Translator*, then, is a story of spiritual growth, with its central conflict being not, as in *Season*, between colonizer and colonized, or between traditional norms and the violent intrusion of modernity, or between oppressive patriarchy and a feminist, libratory impulse—major themes of postcolonial fiction in general. Rather, the conflict in *The Translator* is between worldly desires and spiritual discipline, an internal struggle that is an important theme in religious literature of all traditions. Salih's "A Handful of Dates," "The Cypriot Man," and *Meryoud* (the second part of *Bandarshah*) revolve around it, as do Aboulela's texts. But whereas in Salih's fiction this spiritual struggle is situated within a larger historical framework in which individual dilemmas reflect, and sometimes allegorize, political and ideological struggles, in Aboulela, history is ever present, but only as a backdrop for spiritual struggles that are rarely seen, within her narrative discourse, as having political implications. This rift between politics and spirituality characterizes the particular brand of Islam informing the ideological worldview of Aboulela's fiction.

Translation and Conversion

The rift between politics and spirituality parallels the distinction made in this translational novel between translation and conversion. It is a distinction that charts the horizon of the novel's translational function. Without a doubt, like *The Translator*, Salih's *Season* also has a translational dimension in that it seeks to change the terms of cultural understanding both for its Arab readers and for those who read it in translation.[2] The novel demonstrates the failure of cultural translation under the auspices of Orientalism and nativism. Mustafa Sa'eed plans his sexual revenge on empire by playing up its stereotypes of Arabs and Africans. When his masquerades fail, he returns to Sudan to live according to another discursive fiction, that of cultural authenticity. The contradictions of his life in England and in Sudan are premised on total untranslatablity. It is precisely his inability to conceive of a dialogic alternative that prompts him to disappear, having saddled his double, the narrator, with a dilemma that the latter tries to ignore when he constructs the fantasy of unproblematic return to the past announced in the opening scene. The failure of both characters to engage in positive and transformative cultural dialogue is behind the unfolding of the tragic events of the novel.

Aboulela responds to the crisis of translation depicted in *Season* by writing a translational novel. *The Translator* enacts a poetics of translation on several interrelated levels—plot, theme, language, and discourse. The novel announces its subject matter immediately in the title, foregrounding translation both as agency and as metaphor: Sammar, the protagonist, is a Sudanese woman working as a translator in a Scottish university, translating theological texts, newspaper articles, and fundamentalist tracts for Rae, a leftist scholar of Middle East history and politics who is a frequent target of hate mail because of his criticism of prejudicial views and policies toward the Arab world. Thus, as a plot device, the profession of translator is the formal connection between the two protagonists of a love story who are united at the end through mutual compromises and negotiations that transform each of them: he abandons what appears to her as the incongruous secular humanist stance of defending Islam without being a Muslim himself, and she learns to rise above her selfish demand for his conversion so that they could be married. The novel is, therefore, about the possibilities and limits of translation as an avenue to cultural communication. Translation here has two components: linguistic transfer, which is the subject of frequent and open reflection by the characters, and cultural mediation between disparate political discourses and ideological worldviews, often the more complicated part of the two. Those translational aspects of the novel coalesce around the question of the relationship between translation and conversion, which defines the novel's ideological project.

Frequently, passages that focus on translation emphasize the untranslatable and the impossibility of full communication because of cultural and linguistic incompatibility. For instance, although translation is an overriding concern for her, featured in the above-cited dream with which the novel begins, Sammar is hyper-conscious of the effects on others of the rendition not just of alien texts but of alien experiences, too: "she went on, wondering what part of the narrative to soften, to omit. How much of the truth could he take, without a look of surprise crossing his eyes? . . . In this country, when she spoke to people, they seemed wary, on their guard as if any minute she would say something out of place, embarrassing" (Aboulela 1999, 6). Along the same lines, she describes her work as translator in ways that emphasize the difficulty, even the impossibility of the task. For instance, at the beginning of the novel, she is in the process of translating a manifesto issued by a radical fundamentalist group in southern Egypt:

> The document was handwritten, badly photocopied and full of spelling mistakes. It was stained with tea and what she guessed to be beans mashed with oil. Last night she had stayed up late transforming Arabic rhetoric into English, imagining she could smell beans cooked in the way she had known long ago, with cumin and olive oil. (5)

Apart from rhetorical aspects that are language-bound and impossible to translate, the physical characteristics of the manuscript, the manner of its writing, the quality of the duplication, the orthographic errors, and the stains are all extra-linguistic but highly significant semiotic elements that speak to the heart of the problem that translation, in this case, is intended to penetrate: the motives, ideology, and threat level of a group suspected of terrorist activities. Yet such characteristics, laden as they are with cultural associations which Sammar could almost literally smell, cannot possibly be rendered in another language. This text is then translatable only at the risk of radical "transformation" that will likely be caught up in the rhetoric while obscuring the nonverbal signs that undercut it, contradictions that render the whole document "pathetic" rather than threatening (24). Later on, when interpreting for interrogators of terrorism suspects, she "worked hard pushing Arabic into English, English into Arabic" (143). Translation now is a violent process of forcing meaning expressed in one language—meaning tied to a particular worldview and the rhetorical modes of a specific language—into another language, in which that meaning conjures up a different worldview and discourse, incompatible with, and sometimes unintelligible from, the standpoint of the other.

This sense of linguistic and cultural incommunicability is dramatized throughout the novel: in the fixed ideas that Scots have of Muslims and that Sudanese have of Europeans; in the incompatibility of social customs and attitudes that continue to shock or surprise Sammar after so many years in Scotland; and even in the choice of protagonists' names. "Rae" is a near homonym to the Arabic noun "Rai'" [*sic*]("ra'y" means "opinion"), rendering Rae "opinionated" to Sammar as she tries to come to terms with what to her is his incomprehensible mix of secularism and sympathy to Islam (141). "Sammar," which means "conversations with friends, late at night," is pronounced like "summer," the homonymy working to disguise orthographic and semantic differences that escape translation (5). Moreover, the meaning of her name clashes with her isolated and alienated condition in Scotland. As such, the name functions to demarcate Sammar's public persona in Scotland as a veiled, dark-skinned Muslim woman and her conflicted private life. The difference between the symbolic geography, climate, and social customs of North and South in Salih's fiction is recoded in Aboulela as a separation of the public and the private in Sudan and Scotland, respectively: whereas for Sammar, the public and the private in Sudan are fluidly integrated, especially in the sphere of the extended family where siblings, cousins, parents, grandparents, uncles and aunts live together and share each other's concerns, in Scotland social life is fragmented and atomized in a way that is perhaps best captured by the title of a short story, "Make Your Own Way Home," from *Colored Lights*, in which a young woman lies alone in an abortion clinic while her family goes on vacation. What for Sammar is a rigid separation between the public and the private in Scotland is, of course, reinforced by her own position there as a cultural, racial, and religious Other.

Paradoxically, despite this overwhelming emphasis on untranslatability, the novel effectively translates the gendered worldview and religious logic by which a practicing, immigrant Muslim grapples with her love for a non-Muslim man, outside of multiculturalism's secular logic of accommodating religious difference. For Sammar, this logic is untenable, much like the semantic gap between her name and that of a season eludes English speakers. The novel, in effect, offers a critique not only of racism and Islamophobia, but also of nativism, liberalism, multiculturalism, and leftist politics. The nativist position is exemplified by Yasmeen, Sammar's British-born and raised Pakistani friend, who "had a habit of making general statements starting with 'we,' where 'we' meant the whole of the Third World and its people. So she would say, 'We are not like them, or 'We have close family ties, not like them'" (10). She advises Sammar to "go home and may be you'll meet someone normal, someone Sudanese like yourself. Mixed couples just don't look right, they irritate everyone" (83). Most of her convictions are proven wrong in the resolution of the plot.

Ugly incidents of racism and harassment of Muslims, particularly Muslim women wearing *hijab*, are depicted in most of Aboulela's texts, but so is the unconscious racism of liberals and multiculturalists. For example, during the 1991 Gulf War, Jennifer, the head of the Languages Department, for which Sammar does some work, calls her in "unexpectedly and abruptly" to say that her "boyfriend is Nigerian" and that she "has no problem at all with the way you dress" (88–89). The paradox here, of course, is that even an academic whose work is cross-cultural and who may be progressive on some issues, remains prejudiced when it comes to Islam and Muslims. For Sammar, the condescension of Jennifer's affected liberalism is typical of the academic attitude of researchers, including Rae, who deliberately try to avoid "being Eurocentric" by "tak[ing] what each culture says about itself. So they could study all sorts of sacred texts and be detached. They could have their own religious views or be atheists" (83). Obviously, this attitude is far more enlightened than the stance of religious or cultural chauvinists, and appears to be more suited to grapple with cultural complexity than that of leftists like Frantz Fanon, who "had no insight into the religious feelings of the North Africans he wrote about" and "never made the link between Islam and anti-colonialism" (97), despite the plain fact that for many Algerians the anticolonial war was a *jihad*. Nevertheless, for Sammar, the academic attitude is condescendingly detached. Rae tells her, for instance,

> "I studied Islam for the politics of the Middle East. I did not study it for myself. I was not searching for something spiritual. . . . I believed the best I could do, what I owed a place and people who had deep meaning for me, was to be objective, detached. In the middle of all the prejudice and hypocrisy, I wanted to be one of the few who was saying what was reasonable and right." . . .
>
> She said, "Don't you realize how much you hurt me saying objective and detached, like you are above all this, above me, looking down . . ." (113–14)

From Sammar's religious standpoint, there is only one truth, and consequently truth-claims of different religious and nonreligious ideologies cannot all be valid. The multiculturalist sense of superiority is incompatible with the humility at the core of religious belief. After his conversion, Rae says, "What I regret most . . . is that I used to write things like 'Islam gives dignity to those who otherwise would not have dignity in their lives,' as if I didn't need dignity myself" (Aboulela, *The Translator* 180). The statement he now regrets begs the question of why such people would be without dignity but for Islam, and one cannot help but think that their supposed lack of dignity derives from their being non-Western, non-white, from underdeveloped countries, and so on. If imperialism defines as civilized those who adopt (or convert to) European modes of thought, notions of modernity, secularism, and so forth, Aboulela rejects this definition (she satirizes it directly in

"The Ostrich") and reverses it: it is not enough for Rae, if he is to marry Sammar, to be open-minded or anti-imperialist, or even to defend Islam while remaining secular in outlook. He must convert.

Rae does not merely represent a political and academic position; he also looks Arab (5–6, 54) and he believes in God (84), apparently necessary qualifications! He knows some Arabic, but not enough to conduct research in the language, and, unlike Orientalists for whom, as Edward Said argued, linguistic expertise sanctions unexamined methodology, he is theoretically fluent, with Marxist revolutionary leanings that he developed during the 1960s, partly as a result of reading Fanon and Malcolm X (46–47). When Sammar's friend Yasmeen calls him "an Orientalist," Sammar is silently puzzled and bemused, a reaction that betrays the level of her awareness of the politics of knowledge: "Sammar did not like the word Orientalist. Orientalists were bad people who distorted the image of the Arabs and Islam. Something from school history or literature, she could not remember. Maybe modern Orientalists were different" (19). Working to undo Orientalist knowledge, Rae depends on a translator who is thus technically in the position of a native informant. However, since she precipitates his conversion, the power differential between metropolitan scholar and native informant is canceled in the resolution of the plot.

While Sammar's apolitical religiosity gravitates toward the private sphere, Rae's secular approach to Islam belongs squarely in the public arena of his profession as a teacher and author to whom the media refers as "an Islamic expert" (5). That he does not convert (initially) despite his extensive knowledge of Islam is a source of puzzlement to his Muslim friends and to Sammar, for whom to know Islam is to embrace it. Before his conversion, their attitude "annoys him" (20); afterwards, he says, "I found out at the end that it didn't have anything to do with how much I've read or how many facts I've learned about Islam. Knowledge is necessary, that's true. But faith, it comes directly from Allah." Translating knowledge into action is the hallmark of his public career, but translating knowledge into faith is possible only by a *deus ex machina*—"a miracle," as Sammar puts it (180). There is, then, a crucial distinction between human forms of translation (linguistic transfer, putting knowledge into practice, cultural mediation, and so on), which are "necessary," and divine translation (conversion, the transfer of saints to heaven without death). There is a doubleness in human translation that necessitates constant movement back and forth between source and target languages and which explains the need to keep retranslating literary and philosophical texts.[3] This movement embodies the work of interpretation, which is always historical, situated, and ever incomplete, limited as it is by linguistic, cultural, and ideological horizons. By contrast, divine translation negates human agency, interrupts history, and supersedes all worldly affiliations—the very definition of miracle. Conversion does not acknowledge doubleness, for it posits a clean break with the past, or with the original, and claims to transport the convert to a realm beyond history. The convert begins life anew, with a clean slate, all previous sins wiped out, and acquires a new identity—which is why many converts assume new names: Aisha in "Barbie in the Mosque," Ruqiyya in "Majed," and Ali in *Minaret*. This distinction is key to understanding Aboulela's fictional project—what it seeks to accomplish and its limits. The novels and short stories seek to extend the knowledge through cultural translation (and also by indicating the limits of translation), but not the faith. They do not aim to convert because from their own ideological standpoint that would be impossible.

In that sense, Aboulela's fiction is not missionary literature, which is perhaps one way of glossing J. M. Coetzee's praise for *The Translator* as a "story of love and faith all the more moving for the restraint with which it is written" (*Minaret*, flyleaf). Given the crucial distinction in the novel between translation as a discursive strategy aimed at influencing ideological worldviews in the secular realm, and conversion as a manifestation of God's will over and beyond human agency, "restraint" appears to be the wrong word to describe Aboulela's writing. That is, such restraint is conceivable only from the standpoint of a reader whose expectations are based on the identity of the author as a practicing Muslim woman. Since it becomes quickly apparent that the novel does not conform to the stereotype privileged by many in the publishing industry of the Arab and/or Muslim woman who escapes from the oppressive patriarchy of her native culture to freedom and independence in Europe or the U.S., Coetzee seems to have expected the novel to be preachy, or to put it more crudely, a piece of Islamic propaganda, and was relieved to find that it is not. This welcome disappointment on the part of some readers signals the success of the novel's translational project: it has broken through a prejudicial barrier and conveyed (translated) a complex experience that cannot be contained within the dominant stereotypes. Translation here works as a paradigm for cross-cultural encounters that anticipates and preempts the confirmation of stereotype, exposes the structures of racism and Islamophobia, and posits consensual relationships as an alternative to the deception, violence, and rape that prevail in Salih's *Season* and the colonial texts to which it responds. By the same token, for other readers, the practicing Muslims living in non-Muslim countries, Aboulela's fiction indeed preaches to the converted by depicting models of community and individual behavior that sustain the faithful.[4]

Displaced Dichotomies

The cultural divide in Salih, which in colonial discourse is a split between civilization and barbarism, becomes in Aboulela a split between the public and the private, secularism and religiosity, translation and conversion, and as far as the reception of the novel is concerned, Muslim and non-Muslim readers. The realm of the public is that of the secular and of translation for non-Muslim readers, while the private sphere is that of faith and conversion within the Muslim minority. Rae's conversion in *The Translator* is a crossing over from the one to the other, a condition for the fulfillment of the cross-cultural romance. This is a romance in which love as a private sentiment is not a paramount value, but rather one that is subordinated to religious principles. *Minaret* drives this point home: the lovers are both practicing Muslims but Najwa is twice Tamer's age. The novel violates the rules of romance by not uniting the lovers at the end while still depicting them in a state of contentment akin to a happy ending—one that results from their spiritual growth. This is the only guarantee of a happy ending in Aboulela's Muslim fiction.

The narrative logic, intertextual references, translational strategies, and ideological horizons of this fiction express a religious worldview that does not normally inform modern literature. That worldview consists, as with other religious ideologies, of a particular mythology that explains the origin of the world and of human beings, and determines their relationship to it (theology). In addition, there is a set of laws and regulations (*shari'a*), and rituals that set the rhythm of the religious way of life. At this structural level, Islam is not unique; as in other religions, those aspects of it are disseminated through the usual institutions of the family, schools, religious organizations, the media, and sometimes the state. Modern imaginative literature is usually not among them. In fact, in Arab societies where religious culture is powerful and pervasive, there is no need for fiction to offer such explanations; indeed, much Arabic fiction is secular and often oppositional toward the dominant religious outlook (Salih's narrative cycle is an exception here).[5] Thus, written in English and committed to an Islamic worldview, Aboulela's fiction represents a linguistic and ideological departure from Arabic fiction, and a new dimension in Anglophone immigrant and postcolonial literature—a minor literature in relation to both traditions. Aboulela has stated in an interview that she is

> interested in writing about Islam not as an identity but going deeper and showing the state of mind and feelings of a Muslim who has faith. I want also to write fiction that follows Islamic logic. This is different than writing 'Islamically correct' literature—I do not do that. My characters do not behave necessarily as a 'good Muslim' should. They are not ideals or role models. They are, as I see them to be, ordinary Muslims trying to practice their faith in difficult circumstances and in a society which is unsympathetic to religion. (Aboulela 2005)

Her works undertake to explain Islamic theology, *shari'a*, and rituals to Muslim and non-Muslim readers who have no access to the Islamic tradition in its original language and who live in predominantly secular or non-Muslim societies. The conflicts facing her characters almost always have to do with how to harmonize their desires and actions with the dictates of Islamic belief, law, and ritual; how to find their way to God or strengthen their faith; and how to do so while living in a society that views them and their religion with various degrees of suspicion and hostility.

Thus the numerous descriptions of ritual throughout Aboulela's texts dwell on their effects on the faithful; when, in *The Translator*, Sammar breaks her fast with dates and water at sunset during Ramadan, she "*felt herself to be simple*, someone with a simple need, easily fulfilled, easily granted. The dates and the water made her heart feel big, with no hankering or tanginess or grief" (1999, 32, emphasis added). At another point, upon entering a makeshift mosque on campus, "she felt eerily alone in the spacious room with its high ceiling," but as soon as she recites the first verses of her prayers "the certainty of the words brought unexpected tears, something deeper than happiness, *all the splinters inside her coming together*" (66, emphasis added). The first of these quotes recalls the narrator's contentment in the opening scene of Salih's *Season*, an ironic scene in that his state of mind begins to unravel almost immediately afterwards, as the rest of the novel demonstrates just how complicated his predicament is and how false his sense of wholeness. By contrast, in Aboulela's episteme of faith, there is neither room nor use for irony. In matters of faith, the faithful lack a sense of irony, since irony identifies a discrepancy or a lack that diminishes the status of its object; by contrast, faith elevates and exalts. As such, it makes simple that which is complicated, and provides a sense of wholeness to splintered lives. Such wholeness may seem illusory from a nonreligious perspective, but it is the *sense* of wholeness and its becalming effect that matters. As the image of fragmentation in the second quote implies, brokenness cannot be reversed, but it can be mended. For the protagonist, prelapsarian wholeness cannot be restored in this world, but faith glues the splinters together and encloses their sharp edges within a protective frame. Yet their danger remains very much real and threatening if faith were to be compromised. The emphasis on wholeness and peace, repeatedly described in Aboulela's other works as well, is in stark contrast to the alienation and fragmentation which are the hallmarks of Salih's fictional world and of modernist and postmodernist sensibility, while the attributes of peace and harmony fly in the face of Islamophobic charges that Islam is an oppressive, fanatical religion, charges that invite acts of bigotry depicted throughout Aboulela's fiction.

In the same vein, Islamic law, which is often described by non-Muslims as oppressive and outdated, is represented as contributing to individual and social well-being. For instance,

> Sammar had not worn make-up or perfume since Tarig [her husband] died four years ago. Four months and ten days, was the *sharia* [sic] mourning period for a widow, the time that was for her alone, time that must pass before she could get married again, beautify herself again. Four months and ten days. Sammar thought, of the four months and ten days, such a specifically laid out time, not too short and not too long. She thought of how Allah's *sharia* was kinder and more balanced than the rules people set up for themselves. (1999, 60–61)

Elsewhere: "Nothing that Allah forbids His servants is good. It will only diminish them, ultimately or soon, in this life or the next" (103). Several of Aboulela's characters illustrate this principle: the alcoholic mother in "The Boy from the Kebab Shop," the schoolgirl who is tempted to eat pork in "Tuesday Lunch," the women at the abortion clinic in "Make Your Own Way Home," the drunken father who urinates in his son's cot in "Majed," the jailed, drug-addicted brother of the narrator in *Minaret*. They offset practicing Muslims, born-again Muslims ("reverts" as they are called in one short story [2001, 64]), and European converts to Islam, who appear in several narratives.

The latter group is especially important to Aboulela because they demonstrate the universality of Islam.[6] In *The Translator*, Scottish Rae says, "Ours is not a religion . . . tied to a particular place" (1999, 179). Supra-national and multi-ethnic Islamic identity is emphasized in *Minaret* when Tamer, whose father is Sudanese, says, "My mother is Egyptian. I've lived everywhere except in Sudan: Oman, Cairo, here [London]. My education is Western and that makes me feel that I am Western. My English is stronger than my Arabic. So I guess, no, I don't feel very Sudanese though I would like to be. I guess being a Muslim is my identity"; by contrast, his non-practicing sister "considers herself Arab" (2005, 110). Islamic identity here takes precedence over cultural, ethnic, and national identities, and in fact renders them irrelevant. Later on in the same novel, an explicit contrast is drawn between Anwar, a Sudanese Marxist who "believed it was backward to have faith in anything supernatural" and "despise[d] those who needed God, needed Paradise and the fear of Hell," and Ali, a fundamentalist English convert who left Christianity because "the Church was not strict enough for him" (241).[7] Likewise, prejudice and harassment by total strangers against practicing Muslims, identifiable by their beards and headscarves, comes both from Islamophobic Britons and from secular Arabs; for some among the latter group, the *hijab* is either "irritating" (134) or "a fancy dress" (223). The point is driven home in "The Boy from the Kebab Shop," in which a secular Arab Scot feels "pity" for practicing Muslims, and a practicing Muslim feels the same way for non-practicing ones (2001, 66, 68). Having lived a "Westernized" lifestyle in Khartoum, Najwa, the protagonist of *Minaret*, leads a devout life in London, where she feels much more at home with the multiethnic group of Muslim women at the mosque than with secular Sudanese and other Arabs. As for Scottish converts, they are often better Muslims than casual or non-practicing born Muslims because the converts have made a conscious choice and because they have more to lose. In the opinion of one character, conversion for a Middle East expert like Rae would be "professional suicide" (1999, 20).

Anwar, whose views are dismissed but not refuted, explains Najwa's fascination with converts this way: "as Muslims our self-esteem is so low that we're desperate for approval. And what greater stamp of approval can there be than a white man's?" (2005, 159) Yet the white men who convert are flawed. Practicing Muslim males in general, whether converts or reverts, are always somehow lacking: Scottish Rae is physically weak and emotionally dependent on Sammar (she makes him feel "safe" [1999, 45], and in his dreams she offers him a glass of milk and cooks for him [85]). In "Majed," Sudanese Hamid is literally and metaphorically shortsighted, frivolous, mediocre, and incapable of resisting alcohol outside of the stern gaze of Ruqiyyah, his converted Scottish wife. Tamer is "sensitive but not particularly bright, not quick and sharp" (2005, 3). English Ali is "not very bright," either (241). Female characters do not fare much better, except for Ruqiyyah, who is strong and devout (much like Aboulela's real-life friend, Aisha). Most of Aboulela's Muslim-born female characters are weak, vain, self-involved, and with limited intelligence, few choices, and average to mediocre abilities. Even reverts like Sammar and Najwa often have serious weaknesses. Sammar is lethargic, escapist, self-absorbed, and even spiteful at times (1999, 116). Najwa is dim-witted, inarticulate, and often incapable of analyzing her views. Many female characters in the short stories are vain, conceited, classist, or rude. But those characters are often more content at the end than they are at the beginning of the stories, thanks to their religious awakening and spiritual growth. Their strength comes not from personal qualities, but from their faith and their struggle to live according to its dictates. Indeed, the point seems to be that average people who have no special talents or ambition can find direction, purpose, and strength in Islam. They illustrate the belief that Islam "will make you stronger" (Aboulela 1999, 79).

Yet the "strength" that those characters derive from their religiosity seems to consist merely in not collapsing under the pressure of living with their faith in a hostile environment, and in resiliency in the face of existential adversity (poverty, loss, aging, mortality, and so on). And it comes at a hefty price. The version of Islam propagated in Aboulela's fiction involves a complete disavowal of personal liberty as incompatible with Islam, of feminism as a secular and godless ideology, of individual agency in favor of an all-encompassing notion of predetermination, and consequently of political agency as well. For example, in *The Translator*, Sammar is not troubled by her lack of understanding of the role she plays within the networks of power and knowledge production she inhabits, since all the circumstances of her life, including her choices, can be explained by God's will:

> She had been lucky. There was a demand for translating Arabic into English, not much competition. Her fate was etched out by a law that gave her a British passport, at a point in time when the demand for people to translate Arabic into English was bigger than the supply. "No," she reminded herself, "that is not the real truth. My fate was etched out by Allah Almighty, if and who I will marry, what I eat, the work I find, my health, the day I will die are as He alone wants them to be." To think otherwise was to slip down, to feel the world narrowing, dreary and tight. (64–65)

Call it luck, fate, God's will, or the logic of social history, there are, of course, historical reasons why her parents were studying in Britain when she was born, why Arabic translators were in demand in the late 1990s, and so forth—reasons in which she is not interested. Islamic theology does not bar the investigation of such reasons.[8] Sammar's brand of religiosity restricts human agency in the world to the narrow sphere of personal conduct and worship, thereby encouraging complacency with regard to political responsibility. Sammar describes the radical fundamentalists who seek political change, such as the ones who write the tracts she translates and the detainees in whose interrogation she participates, as semiliterate, poor, and "pathetic . . . in spite of the bravado . . . overwhelmed by thinking that nothing should be what it is now" (1999, 24). Sammar's own supposedly more enlightened religiosity is turned inwards, toward the private world of the individual and the close circle of family; it even absolves her of responsibility for choices in food and marriage. It is no wonder then that the novel begins and ends with her dreams, or that she spends most of her non-working hours in Scotland sleeping so as to escape the dreariness of her life there. Despite her acute awareness of the pitfalls of translation, her notion of fate negates any sense of urgency or commitment to her role as an agent of cross-cultural communication, a role with political and ethical consequences. For her, it is no more than a means of earning a living. And lest we be tempted to see this as a gendered notion of agency, Aboulela generalizes it by having a male character echo the same belief in *Minaret* when he complains, "unless you're political, people think you're not a strong Muslim" (2005, 117). This wholesale embrace of a fatalistic notion of predetermination that hearkens back to medieval debates over free will is a rejection of the existential concept of freedom as an ethical and political responsibility. This attitude relieves Aboulela's characters of the burden of grappling with complex questions and making tough choices, not only in their personal lives, in which they are often passive and reactive, but also in the public sphere, where they are remarkably apolitical.

Aboulela goes even further by repudiating "freedom," as such. While freedom has different meanings in different cultural contexts (meanings that may be incompatible with one another depending, for instance, on whether a given system places a premium on individualism or collectivity), no cultural or religious tradition has ever claimed that it is against freedom, *tout court*. On the contrary, all religions claim that they offer freedom, however they define it. Yet Aboulela rejects freedom wholesale, even though what she appears to be reacting against is a narrowly defined notion of personal freedom that she construes as Western (the operative ontology of Orientalist discourse remains intact here) and anti-religious. Significantly, the repudiation of freedom often occurs in narrative contexts dealing with women and gender. This is not the place to tackle the complex question of women's rights in Islam, or for that matter the subject of Islamic feminism.[9] Suffice it to say here that, while Muslim writers and activists have developed various forms of feminism, Aboulela's version of Islam reinscribes male supremacy. There are several instances in Aboulela's writing where feminism is rejected in favor of patriarchal gender roles. For instance, in the spiritual allegory "Days Rotate," a bizarre futuristic utopia, male superheroes representing "spiritual forces" live hundreds of years and change the color of their eyes at will—powers they acquired after defeating "technology, materialism, the nation state" (and with them poverty, disease, and guns), which all predominated when the world was ruled by so-called "Freedom Lovers," who are supposed to be evil, materialistic forces (Aboulela 2001, 134, 137–38). The superheroes of the "spiritual forces" practice polygamy and act as spiritual gurus to their many wives. The narrator, a pre-adolescent wife to one such superhero, falters in her ascent of a sort of mystical mountain toward heaven because of her attachment to material things, family, and country; her corporeality; and her sinful desire to be "free" from the spiritual struggle. "Freedom" here equals materialism, free-falling down the mountain, submission to gravity, destruction of the environment, and injury to oneself—the opposite of submitting to her husband's will and moving upwards toward heaven (135). As the title suggests, the evils of freedom will one day destroy the utopian order, and the struggle between spirituality and materialism is as inevitable as the rotation of night and day.

Back to reality (and realism), consider the reaction of Najwa, the protagonist in *Minaret*, to the Sudanese Marxist Anwar, the only character who comes close to expressing feminist views (never mind his treatment of her). He accuses her of being "brainwashed . . . Arab society is hypocritical . . . with double standards for men and women" (175). She can confirm that from her own experience, but her unspoken response would be that men and women are not equal. When he condemns religion as backwards and fundamentalism as responsible for the Sudanese civil war, human rights violations, the suppression of free speech, and terrorism, she is confused:

> But that is exactly where I got lost. I did not want to look at these big things because they overwhelmed me. I wanted me, my feelings and dreams, my fear of illness, old age and ugliness, my guilt when I was with him. It wasn't fundamentalists who killed my father, it wasn't fundamentalists who gave my brother drugs. . . . These men Anwar condemned as narrow-minded and bigoted, men like Ali, were tender and protective with their wives. Anwar was clever but he could never be tender and protective. Once I told him that Kamal [his roommate] had come up behind me in the kitchen, pressed against me quickly pretending it was an accident. All he said was, "You're sophisticated enough to deal with this, Najwa. Don't make a big thing out of it" (*Minaret* 241–42).

Gender equality is out of the question; men are supposed to be protective of women, and women want and expect to be protected by men. For that reason, Najwa, who later on is attracted to a man many years her junior, is rebuked by her friend: "When I think of a man I admire, he would have to know more than me, be older than me. Otherwise I wouldn't be able to look up to him. And you can't marry a man you don't look up to. Otherwise how can you listen to him or let him guide you?" Characteristically, Najwa cannot respond: "I don't have anything to say. I stare down at my hands, my warped self and distorted desires. I would like to be his family's concubine, like something out of *The Arabian Nights*, with life-long security and a sense of belonging. But I must settle for freedom in this modern time" (215).[10] This absurd preference for slavery, in an idealized fantasy of the past, over a reductive notion of freedom as a modern invention, can only be explained by her situation as a veiled Muslim woman in Britain, isolated and constantly bombarded by hostile representations of her religion as oppressive. Touted in Eurocentric discourse as an exclusive Western privilege, "freedom" and "modernity" come to represent to her an empty space devoid of the jealous and sometimes violent protectiveness of male relatives, which nonetheless guarantee precisely what she lacks in Britain, "life-long security and a sense of belonging." Her notion of freedom, then, is a mixture of wholesale rejection of "Western" modernity, which means to her little more than secularism and Islamophobia, and nostalgia for an idealized Arab past paradoxically and unreflectively conceived in Orientalist terms.

It is in this rejection of feminism, tied as it is to a total denial of freedom and agency, that Aboulela's ideological project parts ways with Salih's. An apt example drives this idea home. In *The Translator*, Sammar clings to gender roles sometimes considered outdated even back in Sudan. She is willing, shortly after the death of her husband, to be the third and youngest wife of Ahmad Ali Yasseen, a man nearly three times her age who seems to be a variation on Wad Rayyes, the aging womanizer in Salih's *Season*: "I want to get married again, I need a focus in my life"

(*The Translator* 26). Sammar's stance sharply contrasts with Salih's character Hosna bint Mahmoud, a fiercely independent woman who, when forced to marry Wad Rayyes, kills him and herself. Ironically, Sammar is prevented from marrying Yasseen by her aunt, the structural counterpart and opposite of Salih's Bint Majzoub, who rebukes Sammar: "An educated girl like you, you know English . . . you can support yourself and your son, you don't need marriage. . . . In the past, widows needed protection, life is different now" (12). Although she makes no secret of her ulterior motives (77, 155), the aunt's objection illuminates an aspect of Sammar's and other immigrants' brand of conservatism. In her desperate attempt to find a new anchor for her life (and such an anchor for her can only be another husband), a British-educated woman, out of synch with evolving norms at home, clings to a notion of tradition that is made up of immigrant nostalgia (as family members keep reminding her [131, 135]), an uncritically reactive embrace of Orientalist stereotypes, and the rejection of British norms with which she cannot identify. In the process, Salih's powerful critique of traditional patriarchy in the story of Hosna Bint Mahmoud is turned inside out in the Ahmad Ali Yasseen episode.

Aboulela's Islamism and the fiction that embodies it ultimately remain reactive and in many ways regressive. In attempting to bypass the dead end of the postcolonial project of nationhood—a project that was ideologically progressive but conceptually flawed in its futile pursuit of a Eurocentric notion of modernity and its adoption of European models of development—this Islamism succumbs to the fiction of authenticity. The content of this fiction of authenticity is a reverse-Eurocentrism held hostage by what it perceives as a threat. In its conservatism, its rejection of existential freedom and political responsibility, and its unreflective (or desperate) embrace of an idealized past, this ideology has all the elements of the fundamentalist rejection of a "West" defined by its hostility to Islam. What distinguishes this fundamentalism from its "radical" twin is its apolitical nature, for what is often described as "radical fundamentalism" is also a religiosity under siege that rejects certain (mainly cultural if not scientific and technological) aspects of "Western" modernity and embraces a fiction of authenticity based on an idealized past, but with a strong sense of political mission that is grounded in a theological preference for free will over predetermination. In *The Translator*, Sammar describes terrorism suspects as "overwhelmed by thinking that nothing should be what it is now" (24); the difference between her and them is that they act on their beliefs in the public arena, while she withdraws within a rigidly demarcated private sphere.

Needless to say, there are other forms of Islamic religiosity within Muslim immigrant literature. In fact, read alongside the work of other writers of Muslim background (Arabs and non-Arabs), Aboulela's fiction adds nuance and complexity to the representation of Islam and Muslims, especially Muslim minorities in Britain and North America. From a literary historical viewpoint, Muslim immigrant literature in general represents a significant new departure from the predominantly secular orientation of Arabic, Arab American, and Arab British fiction, in which Islam is often seen as a problem or as part of a crisis, rather than as one of many possible modes of identification and living.

9

Queering Orientalism

> It seemed to him that he had been so preoccupied with stressing cultural differences . . . that he had not wanted to see any similarities.
>
> —RAMZI SALTI
>
> The story of who you are is never about you.
>
> —RABIH ALAMEDDINE

Ramzi Salti's Scholarly Fiction

As a minor literature within a minor tradition, Arab Muslim immigrant literature finds an unlikely bedfellow in Arab immigrant queer fiction. Both minorities-within-a-minority shift the attention from Orientalism's ontological opposition between East and West which, regardless of their ideological orientation, most Arab immigrant writers considered in this book have felt compelled to utilize or to contest in any number of ways. We have seen in the previous chapter that Leila Aboulela displaces that dichotomy with another one that sustains its sense of embattled religious identity: Muslim (universalist, multiracial, and multiethnic) vs. secular (Arab and European alike). Rabih Alameddine (b. 1960) also displaces the East/West dichotomy, but in a radically different way by stressing what the Arab world and the U.S. have in common, namely their shared heteronormativity and homophobia, justified and sustained by the same religious (Abrahamic) tradition. In their demonization of homosexuality, Kipling's infamous twain meet at last. That queering of Orientalism is coupled with a satire of the sectarianism and ethno-religious nationalism that fueled Lebanon's civil war (1975–90) and the ongoing Arab–Israeli conflict, all leading to a critique of identity politics.[1] In Ramzi Salti (b. 1966), condemnation of homophobia, patriarchy, and hypocrisy extends to Arab countries as well, and is intertwined with a critique of Orientalism and anti-Arab racism. While obviously overlapping with other Arab American and Arab British writers' treatment of the problems of Orientalism and cultural translation, Salti's and Alameddine's approaches share a unique perspective that sets them apart.

By the same token, they diverge in emphases, methods, and aesthetic projects. For one thing, Alameddine's critique mainly targets the representation of gays in the U.S., while Salti attacks it in Jordan. Like Ahdaf Soueif, Salti comes up against the problematic of social critique that would not lend itself to anti-Arab racism and propaganda, which his realistic stories written in the manner of Arabic-language authors such as Alifa Rifaat, Yusuf Idris, and Nawal el Saadawi could easily invite. Billed on the cover of his collection as "six stories of defiance from the Arab world" and targeting with their criticism everything from homophobia to domestic violence and even rituals for mourning the dead, most of the stories come across as an all-out attack on Arab culture and society, even the ones which highlight British colonial attitudes and anti-Arab racism in the U.S. By contrast, Alameddine's latest novel has been aptly described as "a tender love letter to Arab culture" for its exuberant celebration of "the oud, Umm Kalthoum and the poetry of Abu Nawas and Al-Mutanabbi" (Wilson-Goldie), and in it Alameddine appreciatively explains, of all things, the same mourning rites that Salti condemns (Alameddine 2008, 460; Salti 1994, 1–3). In Alameddine's experimental, formally innovative, and syncretic fiction, fusing together elements from numerous literary and philosophical traditions, form embodies the ideological project. Alameddine's fiction queers Orientalism by, first, laying bare the discriminatory and often violent processes by which all identities (sexual, social, national, cultural, religious, and so forth) are formed; second, staging storytelling as an epistemology that reveals the ideological constructedness of all cultural knowledge; and third, demonstrating the limits as well as the potentials of cultural translation as both impossible and inevitable.

While his collection has more modest goals, Salti articulates the project of two-way cultural translation that I have been describing and its objectives more explicitly than any other writer. Lebanese by birth and Jordanian by upbringing, Salti came to the U.S. in 1983, studied English and French literature at Santa Clara University, then went on to earn a Ph.D. in comparative literature from the University of California at Riverside, with a concentration in postcolonial studies and a dissertation on marginalized sexualities in Arabic literature. Since then he has taught Arabic at Stanford University. This academic background has left its imprint on his collection, *"The Native Informant" and Other Stories* (1994), although not so much in the stories themselves as in the scholarly introduction and the somewhat didactic synopses appended at the end. This metafictional commentary not only states the thematic concerns of the stories, but also how they ought, in the author's view, to be read. One reason for this explicit attempt to control the interpretation may be that the stories themselves do not support the full meaning that the author wishes them to convey. But more importantly, that commentary represents an attempt to preempt certain readings that will readily suggest themselves to readers of English. Salti, in other words, is fully conscious of the fact that his subject matter is not only controversial in the Arab world, but is also and differently so in the U.S. and Britain, where it runs the risk of reinforcing hostile stereotypes of Arabs. As we have seen earlier, Soueif came to the same conclusion after the publication of her first book, the reception of which prompted her to modify her fictional project. No doubt because of the focus of his academic studies, Salti's fiction is informed by his knowledge of the dynamics of literary reception from the outset. As a result, his fictional-critical project tries to meet the seemingly irreconcilable demands of two minoritarian positions: that of a sexual minority in the patriarchal, heteronormative context of Arab world, and that of an Arab minority in the U.S., where hostile representations of Arabs are prevalent. Those two conditions are sometimes exploited by writers more interested in selling books than in combating anti-Arab racism. For Salti, as is the case also with Leila Ahmed and Soueif, it becomes a matter of fighting two distinct battles, each on a different front. Salti, therefore, tries to connect the question of marginalization due to gender and sexual orientation to the politics of imperialism, so that his critique of social inequality in the Arab world is linked to the critique of racism and neocolonialism. The complexity of this undertaking, which is the focus of this section, explains his felt need for metafictional commentary.

Salti begins by clearly defining one arena of struggle in the Introduction:

> *The Native Informant and Other Stories* is a collection of six short stories dealing with "unmentionable" aspects of Arab life in parts of the Arab world and in the West. Inspired by such modern writers as Alifa Rifaat, Nawal al-Sa'dawi, and Youssef Idris—authors who have, despite immeasurable odds, managed to emphasize subjects ranging from feminism to homosexuality in their works—these short stories attempt to further engage various social and political issues that remain, for the most part, largely ignored or silenced in modern Arabic literature. (Salti vii)

The unmistakable scholarly tone, the identification of major themes, the naming of literary predecessors, and the statement of a critical project are all highly unusual elements in a work of fiction—even when one knows that at the time the book was published, Salti was writing a doctoral dissertation on "marginalized sexualities" in classical and modern Arabic literature, with one chapter devoted to two of the three writers he mentions (Salti 1997). Of course, the very fact that inspiration to write the stories came from prominent predecessors belies the claim that the topic is "unmentionable" in Arabic literature, although it is indeed the case that feminism remains an embattled cause and homosexuality is socially stigmatized and, in many Arab countries, criminalized. Hence the sense of urgency and mission in Ramzi's words, although it must also be noted that writing his "tales of defiance" in English rather than in Arabic, as his literary models had done, takes his work out of the arena of struggle for the rights of women and gays in the Arab world and situates it squarely within the Anglo-American discursive field. Salti's recognition that, despite his use of English, his stories are written *as though* they were part of modern Arabic literature prompts him to preface them with critical remarks that spell out the stakes in the Arab and American contexts:

> Recent developments in the international political arena, accompanied by an anti-Arab sentiment that has surged as a result of the [1991] war in the Gulf, make *The Native Informant and Other Stories* more relevant today than ever. Yet the sense of urgency with which the stories were written is not meant to overshadow the basic assumption that any kind of binary

> thinking must be rejected if the seemingly eternal gap between East and West is to be bridged. The aim of these stories is thus far removed from simplistic notions of privileging the West over the Arabs, or vice versa. Rather, these stories attempt to fuel and maintain a dialogue centering on the marginalization of certain social elements in parts of the Arab world and to highlight the ways in which some Arabs view themselves. (1994, viii)

To avoid "binary thinking," Salti instructs his readers to keep in mind that

> [m]ost of the stories . . . operate on a dual level by addressing not only issues related to women, homosexuals, and victims of violence in southwest Asia, but also by examining the seemingly conflictual relationship between notions of Arabness, Islam, and the West. The collection thus aims at highlighting the plight of marginalized groups in Arab countries by broaching various issues on the social spectrum, ranging from religious intolerance, to the subjugation of women, to homophobia, to domestic violence, to Western and Eastern concepts of "terrorism" or neo/post-coloniality, to the ethnic experience of being Arab in the United States at a time when the media seems to be promulgating the negative stereotype of the Arab. (vii)

That list of themes roughly corresponds, in inexact order, to the six stories, which, however, are much more heavily weighted toward the Arab, especially Jordanian, context. Only one of the stories, "Checkpoint," takes place partially in the U.S. and addresses the last theme in that list, and only "The Native Informant" draws on the theme of British colonialism, which created the Hashemite Kingdom of Jordan out of the region formerly known as Syria (or Greater Syria). The four other stories present a scathing condemnation of religious intolerance ("Antara and Juliet," which makes explicit reference to Shakespeare's play), the subjugation of women and domestic violence ("Wedding Song"), and homophobia ("Vivian and Her Son" and "The Taxi Driver"). Straightforward and unambiguous, those stories do, indeed, evoke the Arabic fiction of Rifaat, el Saadawi, and Idris.

Yet unlike those writers, Salti writes in English, so his social critique paradoxically is not addressed to those for whom it is intended. And lest his work serve to justify anti-Arab racism, Salti proposes in the synopses that the oppression of women and gays in Arab societies is symptomatic of a "universal" injustice, and that the "Arab" case is an exemplary rather than a unique predicament. For example, the synopsis of one story goes as follows:

> "Wedding Song" is the story of Su'ad, an Arab woman who is battered and abused by her husband. In her attempt to seek refuge in her parents' house, she faces up to the harsh realities of being a woman in a society where many women are turned over from the father's "care" to that of their husbands. *Su'ad's story is thus universal in that it serves to underline women's subjugation by patriarchal societies.* (98, emphasis added)

While the first two sentences describe the plot, nothing in the story itself gestures toward a universal predicament, as the third sentence claims. Indeed, the very use of a refrain from a popular wedding song serves instead to *localize*, not universalize, the protagonist's experience. Here as elsewhere in the collection, the author's awareness of this discrepancy between his aspiration for the stories and what they actually accomplish is likely behind his decision to sandwich them between an introduction that explains his intention and a synopsis that serves no other purpose than to state the moral of each story, leaving almost nothing to the reader, who cannot be trusted not to read them as a condemnation of Arab culture, rather than as constructive social critique. This attempt to control the interpretation is the author's way of crowding out such a possibility. As such, the collection clearly illustrates the immigrant writer's attempt to walk the fine line between progressive critique of cultural politics in the Arab world and feeding grist to the mill of anti-Arab racism—the same fine line treaded by predecessors like Ameen Rihani and Abraham Rihbany, and contemporaries like Fawaz Turki, Leila Ahmed, and Ahdaf Soueif, each in his or her own very different way.

The dual level of meaning claimed in the Introduction occupies a relatively limited space in the collection, operating in only two stories. "Checkpoint," the only story referencing the U.S., recounts the experience of Sami, a Jordanian student returning home after four years of university study. During his first two years in the U.S., he feels besieged by hostile stereotypes. Withdrawn and defensive, he fails to make American friends, while at the same time feeling alienated from other Arab students. During his third year, he changes his name to Sam, leaves the Arab student club, joins a fraternity (which he later leaves because "fraternities were exclusionary organizations that promoted racism and bigotry" [15]), and highlights his hair as a sign of Americanization, all of which, apparently, enable him to acquire a number of male American friends, each of whom teaches "him a little more about his own self" (15). One day in a park, he decides to share with one of them a dream that has plagued him since puberty about an attractive snake that causes him to be ashamed, obviously a symbol of his repressed homosexuality (13). His friend opines that "it's the cross that each of us has to bear. You probably don't have that expression in your religion, since it comes from the Bible, but that's exactly what your snake is. It represents everything from guilt to hating oneself. The reason you wanted to protect it is that you knew in your heart that it wasn't evil" (15). The snake also represents the temptation to open himself up to another culture:

> George had also verbalized something that Sami had previously been afraid to face. He said that some things were the same in all cultures, and that simple observation had overwhelmed Sami's mind. It seemed to him that he had been so preoccupied with stressing cultural differences for three years that he had not wanted to see any similarities. . . . The idea that George could understand things in him that his own culture had denied him throughout his life made Sami uneasy. He felt that by accepting George's words, he had betrayed his culture and his home. That very same night, the snake visited him again after a long absence. (15)

Whereas earlier in Jordan Sami had to repress his homosexuality, in the U.S. he felt compelled to erect psychic defenses against a society that demonized his culture; he becomes hyperconscious and proud of his Arabness, which he used to bring up in every conversation. The pivotal moment in his personal development occurs when he is made to see that the dualistic worldview in which he had sought refuge was itself repressive; consequently, as Salti puts it in the synopsis of the story, Sami "begins to reject his former binary mode of thinking" (97). This revelation is possible only through his friendship with an American who adds another dimension to Sami's heretofore monolithic understanding of the U.S. He returns home with this enlightened perspective, although it is not clear whether it will survive the symbolically charged checkpoint at the airport, which, as Salti explains in the synopsis, "comes to represent the final point of separation between East and West, between what he leaves behind and what lies ahead" (97). Manned by a megalomaniac soldier who presumably stands for ignorance, arrogance, and parochialism, Sami has no rosy hopes for the future: "His new situation . . . exemplifies the quest for an identity that many Arab students face upon their return home with high hopes and aspirations, only to discover that the alienation they felt in the West may well be duplicated in their home country" (97).

While in "Checkpoint" the cross-cultural experience takes place in the U.S., in "The Native Informant" that encounter happens in Jordan and involves a young Jordanian man and a middle-aged British woman. Salti summarizes the story in this way:

> "The Native Informant" is set in a neo-colonial society where adoration of the West has come to take precedence over local justice. A mediocre and seemingly apolitical Arab civil servant named Majid is set up with a British reporter, Ms. Penn, who wishes to record "authentic" aspects of Arab life while seeming to have already decided what these aspects will be. The relationship between Majid and Ms. Penn thus develops in a way that parallels the colonial encounter. Yet as the story progresses, Majid finds himself entangled in a complex plot that will eventually lead him not only to reexamine his own subject position but also to understand the lingering effects of colonization and negative stereotyping as promulgated by Western media and literature. (98–99)

This "synopsis" actually leaves out the crucial details of the story, offering instead an interpretation of it. Majid is chosen by his boss to escort Ms. Penn because of his university education and knowledge of English; he is charged with the task of "giving these people a good image of the Arabs" (74). The plot begins to unfold when he meets Ms. Penn at the airport. She asks to be taken to Palestinian refugee camps and other locations not frequented by tourists because, as she puts it, "I am writing a book on Jordan and I want to get to know the real natives, not the government officials and the rich" (81), "the *real* Jordan. Not the Westernized one. After all, I am not here as a colonizer" (92). Majid is not only "apolitical," he does not have any understanding of the historical determinations of his position toward Ms. Penn—the British reporter writing a book about her country's former colony without having once visited it before, yet already confident in her knowledge of what is authentic about it and what is not, what she will find, how the "real natives" feel, and (what proves disastrous for Majid) how native males act toward European females. Further, his role is not simply that of a tour guide; she wants him to translate for her as she interviews Palestinian refugees. Without any awareness of the implications, he steps into the role of translator and native informant. He quickly realizes what he needs to do to make her happy and to render the task easier for himself. Once inside the home of one Palestinian family, he finds out that she is not satisfied with the answers they give her. For example, when she asks the family, through him, what life is like in the camp, the following dialogue ensues:

> "She can see how we live by looking around her. We are eleven people living in this shack; we have no electricity and we have access to water on some days only. My brothers and sisters go to school every day, and I work most of the time since I am still not married. Is that what she wants to know?"
>
> Majid translated Sabir's statement but she still did not seem to be content. "Did he use any adjectives to describe the place?" she wanted to know; "you know, *dirty*, *overcrowded*, things like that? I want to quote his exact words, not substitute my own as most foreign reporters do."
>
> "No," replied Majid.
>
> "Well ask him to."
>
> Majid turned to Sabir and asked him to use adjectives to describe the place. Sabir looked at him suspiciously and said in an annoyed tone, "Adjectives? She wants me to use adjectives? Tell her I don't know any adjectives and that if she wants them, to go read a book."
>
> Majid thought about the answer for a moment, then he said to the woman, "He says that this place is unsanitary, miserable, and alienating."
>
> The woman seemed pleased at that reply and jotted down the words in her notebook. (84)

From this and similar exchanges, Majid realizes that for all her eagerness to know the "real natives," Ms. Penn will only be satisfied with answers that confirm her already formed opinions, and that

> the best way to please [her], and the only for him way to get food in his stomach soon [he had not had any breakfast yet], lay in altering the answers to suit her questions. He thus began to feel around for what response the woman wanted, then he tailored the answers accordingly. The method must have worked, because the conversation flowed quickly and by the time they had left the camp half an hour later, the woman's notebook was half full. (85–86)

In this way, the story dramatizes some of the ways in which Orientalist discourse perpetuates itself, even in the very act of disavowing neocolonial hegemony, and the role that translation can play in this process when undertaken by complicit native informants, whether out of apathy and political naïveté (as in

Majid's case) or out of cynical and unscrupulous opportunism (as in the case of Norma Khouri's forgery). Here, Majid is cunning enough to realize the benefits of falsifying the answers just enough to fit the expectations of his smug patroness. Yet he begins to understand the power of stereotype at the end of the story when an ambiguous situation leads to an attempted rape accusation reminiscent of the Adela Quested and Dr. Aziz debacle in E. M. Forster's *A Passage to India*, except that here Majid is arrested, tortured, and possibly (it is not clear whether he is hallucinating in his jail cell) extradited for trial in England. The stereotypes he has perpetuated ultimately destroy him, and the story thus becomes a parable about the pitfalls of complicit translation that caters to Orientalist expectations.

War and AIDS in Rabih Alameddine

Like Salti's, Alameddine's treatment of homosexuality interlocks with other themes, particularly the Lebanese Civil War and Arab American identity. His novel *Koolaids: The Art of War* (1998), short story collection *The Perv* (1999), *I, the Divine: A Novel in First Chapters* (2001), and his latest novel *The Hakawati* (2008; published in Britain as *The Storyteller*) are also brilliant experiments in storytelling that contemplate the physical and psychological damages of war, a theme that unites Alameddine's work. While Salti stresses homophobia in Jordan, Alameddine focuses on the AIDS epidemic, which was seen, especially in its first decade in the U.S., as anything from a local problem afflicting the gay community to divine punishment for what the religious right considered an abomination. In *Koolaids* and *The Perv*, homophobia and AIDS are seen as problems ravaging the U.S. to a similar extent that sectarianism and the civil war are destroying Lebanon. In the face of so much senseless death in both countries, the banalities of religion, philosophy, conventional morality, and discourses of identity (whether racial, ethnic, cultural, or religious) are no more than "Koolaids"—a pun on the brand name of the artificially flavored powdered drink that serves as a symbol for superficiality and hypocrisy: the nutrient-deficient concoction claims to "kool" but does nothing to alleviate, let alone heal, the deadly disease whose acronym completes the brand name.

The critique of identity politics becomes stronger in Alameddine's later works, but is nevertheless direct in the portrayal, in *Koolaids*, of incidents of anti-Arab racism (47–48, 53–54), arguments and counter-arguments about whether Lebanon is Phoenician or Arab (57–60, 69–72), and the differences between Lebanese Francophiles and fundamentalists (28–29). *Koolaids* also dismantles religious pieties sanctioning homophobia and violence and sustaining a heteronormative culture, as, for example, in the appalling treatment of a gay man dying of AIDS at the hands of his devout Christian family (108–12), the insensitivity of media representations of the epidemic (29–30), and the tokenism characterizing the culture industry's treatment of gays (54–55). One unnamed narrator comments on the story of Sodom and Gomorrah in the Bible and Qur'an, which he says has always fascinated him for its "straight" logic:

> God tells us men fucking men is a terrible thing, but a father offering his two daughters, vestal virgins no less, to a horde of horny buggers is heroic. Now that's straight. . . . God destroys the faggots with fire and brimstone. He turns a disobedient wife into salt. But he asks us to idolize drunks who sleep with their daughters or offer them to a horny, unruly mob. (64)

The novel also ridicules the elaborate justifications for war and fratricidal violence found in *The Bhagavad Gita*. In a scene from a play that Mohammad, one of the characters, keeps trying to write—draft after draft punctuating the novel at more or less regular intervals (37, 83, 135, and 168)—Arjuna fails to understand Krishna's explanations of the purpose of life or why he (Arjuna) should fight his cousins. In response, a nihilistic, Shakespeare-quoting Krishna tells him that "life has no unity. It is a series of nonlinear vignettes leading nowhere, a tale told by an idiot, full of sound and fury, signifying nothing. It makes no sense, enjoy it" (38, punctuation modified), advice later repeated by Mame Dennis (168). In this way, the philosophical discourse on the meaning of *dharma* in Hinduism is treated in the same way as the "straight" Abrahamic religions: reduced to absurdity.

The novel itself seems to embody that absurdity, both in terms of its philosophical outlook and its bricolage form comprising fragmentary narration, multiple narrators, intertwining plots, a motley cast of characters (including Eleanor Roosevelt, Krishnamurti, Julio Cortázar, and Tom Cruise), and intermingling of history and fiction, tragedy and farce. The novel consists of a string of first-person narrative fragments by several narrators (male and female, Lebanese and American, gay and straight) some of whom are either dying of AIDS or tending to friends who are, or both at various points of their lives, while others witness the violent and often random death of family members or friends during the shelling of Beirut by foreign invaders—Americans, Israelis, Syrians—or domestic militias—Phalangist, Shiite, Palestinian, and others. The senselessness of death, which is arguably the overarching theme of the novel, is captured in scenes such as the one that conveys a child's horror at seeing his father, who a moment earlier was joking with him while shaving in front of the bathroom mirror, suddenly collapse in a pool of blood, his throat slit by shrapnel flying through the window; or the one in which a San Francisco teenager who has just come out is taken to an orgy where he is drugged and raped by a series of anonymous men, contracting HIV in the process and later dying of AIDS—the irony being that it was his physician lover who gave him the deadly initiation.

The main narrator of the novel, Mohammad, is an autobiographical character. Born in the same year as Alameddine, he comes to the U.S., like him, at the age of fifteen (8), then, also like the author, becomes a painter. Mohammad, however, is in a hospital bed dying of AIDS in the opening scene of the novel. He wishes for death, as his recurrent dream indicates—and apparently dies in the final scene, or at least imagines his death. In this polyphonic novel, his voice frames those of other characters. A successful painter, Mohammad is a failed writer: "I wish I could write better. I have never been able to write anything because I don't trust my writing" (18). Among his abortive book projects are "a book about Jesus meeting Mohammad" (18); a play based on *The Bhagavad Gita*; a novel about a gay, HIV-infected Jesus figure who returns to Lebanon only to be handed over by his father to killers who crucify and stab him to death (169–71); and another about AIDS. This last unfinished book provides another recurring scene that punctuates the novel at roughly 50–60 page intervals (1, 53, 98, 244; with a variation on p. 166); it is not clear whether these are drafts of the opening scene or Mohammad's recurring dreams, or both. It begins with this axiomatic pronouncement: "Death comes in many shapes and sizes, but it always comes. No one escapes the little tag on the big toe" (1). This is followed by the appearance of four horsemen (an obvious allusion to the biblical Apocalypse) coming to escort him to the afterlife. Three riders on red, black, and pale horses proclaim, "This good and faithful servant is ready. He Knoweth war [the Lebanese Civil War] . . . plague [AIDS] . . . death [from both causes]." In each of the dream variations but the last, the fourth rider on a white horse denies him the comfort of death: "Fuck this good and faithful servant. He is a non-Christian homosexual, for God's sake. You brought me all the way out here for a fucking fag, a heathen. I didn't die for this dingbat's sins" (1); at the end, however, the same horseman accepts him: "'I love you, Mohammad.' . . . I die" (245).

There are at least two remarkable things about this scene, in its multiple versions. First, it is the opening salvo in what becomes, over the course of this and subsequent works by Alameddine, an ongoing parody of religious traditions that justify prejudice and violence. Second, like the truncated form, fragmentary narration, cacophony of intermingling voices, and admixture of genres (dream narratives, diary entries, letters, fiction, drama, poetry, journalism, email, web posts), the theme of the failure of writing gestures toward the impossibility to communicate fully—to translate—the horrific effects of war and AIDS, as well as the tragicomic absurdities they reveal. There is, on the one hand, the urgent desire to communicate, and on the other, the inevitable descent into either farce or sentimentality:

> When I first started seeing my friends die, I wanted to write a book where all the characters died in the beginning. . . . I never went beyond the incipit, which I thought was a damn good one. *Death comes in many shapes and sizes, but it always comes.* I thought it was great. I wanted to make sure death and sex were associated. Look at the words *shapes*, *sizes*, and *it always comes*. Sexual allusions galore.
>
> I showed it to Scott. He said I should stick to painting. I guess he thought my incipit was insipid. He did not like the idea of the book. He said one could rarely write a book about death without being sentimental. He thought only Danielle Steel could write a book about the ravages of the AIDS epidemic and get away with it. (18)

Mohammad's failed attempts to write are echoed by his friend Ben's dismal paintings, which earn him the title of "the worst painter of all time" (8), even though he spends his final months before dying of AIDS totally absorbed in the activity—just as Mohammad apparently dies while trying to rework the opening scene of his novel about death. Even good art fails to communicate: Mohammad's paintings of stylized Lebanese villages are interpreted by their American admirers as abstract art (100–1). The creative act has no healing, but only sedative, power. It promises neither redemption nor immortality nor penetrating insight, but makes it easier to cope with disaster. It administers a sobering dose of nihilism in the face of absurdity, a better alternative to the vacuous Koolaids of religion and philosophy. Unlike Ramzi Salti's prefatory and synoptic interpretations of his own fiction, Alameddine's metafictional commentary on the expressive limits of fiction are woven into the fabric of the novel itself. One of the main thematic concerns of Alameddine's first three books is that the failure to communicate is a failure to translate, as Mohammad puts it: "I have had many ideas which I could not translate well into painting. I wanted to write them down. I never really did. I just did not have a good command of the written word" (18).

This failure also becomes a structural principle in *I, the Divine: A Novel in First Chapters*, which consists of the protagonist Sarah Nour el-Din's interminable attempts to write her life story. Like Mohammad in *Koolaids*, she discards draft after draft of the first chapter and starts anew at a different point in her life or the lives of family members and friends. Her restless abandonment of each draft is matched by her determination to start again, alternating between first-and third-person narration, novel and memoir, English and French. The "novel" as such consists of a string of repudiated versions of the first chapter, although the aggregate effect of the whole is no less successful than any linear novel at painting a lively picture of the protagonist from childhood to middle age and of those around her.[2]

Born to a Lebanese father and an American mother, Sarah was named by her grandfather after the "Divine" Sarah Bernhardt, whom he idolized, and who gives the novel its title. The name had a shaping influence on Sarah's life (2001, 78–80). Growing up in the shadow of the "Divine" Sarah, the protagonist becomes cripplingly perfectionist as she strives to live up to the example of her legendary namesake. Though a failed writer, Sarah's persistent re-starts eventually make her a successful painter. Her success and failure at creative self-expression are far from gratuitous: she is much more at ease with abstract painting than she is with words. It eventually becomes clear that her difficulty with narration is the result of a horrifically violent episode in her life that she struggles to confront in at least three chapters, one of which is written in French: her abduction and gang rape during the total breakdown of law and order in war-torn Beirut. It is not until two-thirds of the way through the novel, and only in a fictionalized third-person, rather than the autobiographical first-person voice, that she manages to narrate this event. At that point, things begin to fall into place and make sense: her chronic depression, her broken relationships, her inability to help the dying AIDS patients whom she volunteers to counsel, her restless wanderings from San Francisco to New York to Beirut and back again, and her obsession with storytelling coupled with total rejection of canonical narrative genres, from fairy tales to realistic fiction ("Count Leo Nikolayevitch Tolstoy lied" [63]), to popular romance (a shelf of first edition Danielle Steel novels is ripped by a ricocheting sniper's bullet in Beirut [234–35]). For Sarah, these narrative genres, with their ideological assumptions about order and final resolution, cannot possibly contain her experience. Nor can the memoir or the *Bildungsroman* (title pages interspersed throughout advertise her projected work alternately as "a memoir" and "a novel"), genres that apparently cannot accommodate the kind of knowledge she acquires—namely, that she is not an autonomous individual, but the product of her family history and the sum of her relationships.

This critique of individualism is set in the context of Sarah's ongoing effort to define herself. The child of a Lebanese father and an American mother, Sarah is born and raised in Lebanon, then moves to the U.S. She struggles to reconcile competing value systems—the American creed of rugged individualism and the Lebanese (and Arab) valorization of family and society over the individual. For Sarah, the U.S. and Lebanon are a study in contrasts insofar as identity is concerned: "I moved from a country that ostracized its nonconformists to one more tolerant and more hypocritical. I moved from Lebanon to the United States" (227). This is a far cry from the celebration by earlier writers discussed in this book of their coming to America as a sort of salvation. Rather, each country is seen here as fulfilling some needs while frustrating others. As Sarah puts it in another chapter (where she speaks of herself in the third person), "whenever she is in Beirut, home is New York. Whenever she is in New York, home is Beirut. Home is never where she is, but where she is not" (99)—which echoes Mohammad's complaint in *Koolaids*, "In America, I fit, but I do not belong. In Lebanon, I belong, but I do not fit" (1998, 40). In Lebanon, both characters (like the protagonist of *The Hakawati*), relish the warm, close-knit family atmosphere. And yet, Sarah cannot simply return to Lebanon for good: "My life is there [in the U.S.]. I have nothing here anymore" (2001, 272). She lives the paradox expressed in the first sentence of this passage:

> I have been blessed with many curses in my life, not the least of which was being born half Lebanese and half American. Throughout my life, these contradictory parts battled endlessly, clashed, never coming to a satisfactory conclusion. I shuffled ad nauseam between the need to assert my individuality and the need to belong to my clan, being terrified of loneliness and terrorized of losing myself in relationships. I was the black sheep of my family, yet an essential part of it. (299)

A nostalgia that grows with age complicates matters further:

> I hated Umm Kalthoum. I wanted to identify with only my American half. I wanted to be special. I could not envision how to be Lebanese and keep any sense of individuality. Lebanese culture was all consuming. Only recently have I begun to realize that like my city [Beirut], my American patina covers an Arab soul. These days I avoid Umm Kalthoum, but not because I hate her. I avoid her because every time I hear that Egyptian bitch, I cry hysterically. (299)

Consequently, neither country is entirely satisfactory or acceptable on its own. She describes the glorification of rugged individualism as hypocritical ("the rigorous practice of rugged individualism usually leads to poverty, ostracism and disgrace" [228]). In the final chapter, provocatively yet appropriately titled "Introduction," she has an epiphany while watching a PBS program about lions. Sarah is horrified when a young male, after ousting the aging head of the pride and taking possession of his females, proceeds to kill his predecessor's cubs; but then she decides that the pride as a collective outlasts each member, and that this is perhaps the way to think about identity. The deification of the individual implied in the title of the novel (I=Divine) is thus contradicted and subverted by the closing allegory of the lions. Indeed, Alameddine's next novel goes on to affirm that "the story of who you are is never about you" (2008, 90). Yet in allegorizing the behavior of lions, *I, the Divine* naturalizes patriarchal violence, an ironic and surely unintended consequence for a rape victim, albeit in line with Krishna's nihilism in *Koolaids*. This solution is philosophically and ethically problematic, though psychologically understandable as a trauma victim's repression of painful experience. The lion story provides a convenient closure to the narrative, insofar as any can be envisioned, by allowing Sarah to rationalize her crisis of authorship, which encodes her crisis of identity. However, the implicit acceptance of patriarchal violence as a fact of nature deepens instead of resolves the problem. Consequently, this resolution remains yet another draft that may well be discarded like those that preceded it, an "introduction" to further efforts.

Queering Orientalism

Even though it offers no satisfactory resolution, *I, the Divine* critiques dominant discourses, ideologies, and sanctioned narratives that have prevailed in Orientalist as well as in some immigrant and Arab American fiction and autobiography—teleological narratives of progress and development; of self-confident knowledge of, and discursive mastery over, other cultures; and of individualistic becoming and self-realization. Alameddine's next novel, *The Hakawati*, his first since the terrorist attacks of September 11, 2001, continues that effort while bringing his preoccupation with homosexuality, storytelling, and narrative form to bear on the question of Orientalism. The novel is also the boldest satirical subversion to date of American Orientalism ever attempted by an Arab American novelist. Reclaiming and reworking the two texts that served, according to Fu'ad Sha'ban, as the pillars of nineteenth-century American Orientalism, the Bible and *The Arabian Nights*, *The Hakawati* queers Orientalism by exposing and undermining the homophobic bent of the Abrahamic tradition earlier attacked in *Koolaids*, and by reappropriating the sourcebooks of Orientalist stereotypes in a counter-narrative that de-anthropologizes (de-Orientalizes) the *Nights*, returning it to its original realm of pure, and often subversive, storytelling.

As indicated earlier in this book, the highly syncretic origins of the *Nights* (a heterogeneous compilation of Indian, Persian, and Arabic folktales), the setting of the frame story in a mythic past and a remote land (Indochina), and the Persian names of the main characters in the frame story (Shahrazad, Shahrayar, Shahzaman, Dinazad) all indicate that, for its Arab audiences over the centuries, the tales were about exotic, faraway peoples and places. The irony—or rather the comedy of errors—involved in *The Thousand and One Nights'* reception history is that when the work was translated into European languages, and acquired the title *The Arabian Nights*, it was read by many in Europe as, among other things, a source of sociological and anthropological information about Arabs.[3] Because American Orientalism interpreted the medieval work in that way as a more or less direct reflection of Arab life, early Arab American writers used the *Nights* in crafting their discourses. We have seen, for instance, how Abraham Rihbany divided his autobiography into two memoirs, one drawing upon the Bible and the other on the *Nights*, and how Salom Rizk depicted his grandmother Kbashy as a Shahrazad figure, a wise and crafty storyteller. In so doing, both writers invoked the authority of American Orientalism to make their subjects more accessible to their readers than they would have presumably been without such mediation—a form of domesticating translation. Numerous Arab American novelists, memoirists, poets, and scholars not considered in this book have also made use of the *Nights* in a wide range of discursive maneuvers—Diana Abu-Jaber (2003), Mohja Kahf (2003), Susan Muaddi Darraj (2004), Khaled Mattawa and Pauline Kaldas (2004), among others. In fact, Abu-Jaber's novel *Crescent* may have provided the model for Alameddine's *The Hakawati*, with its structure of alternating chapters narrating the story of the protagonist and the fantastic tales of her hakawati uncle. Appearing at a rapid pace after the September 11, 2001 terrorist attacks, when the demonization of Arabs reached heights unattained since the 1967 Arab–Israeli war, such formal, thematic, and metaphoric appropriations of the *Nights* have been qualitatively different from those of early Arab American writers in that the purpose has now shifted from invoking to contesting the authority of American Orientalism, taking charge of the representation of Arabs, and changing the terms of cultural discourse. *The Hakawati* is the latest and the most extensive effort in this vein.

The title means "The Storyteller," from the Arabic verb "*haka*" (to relate or to tell); in the Lebanese dialect, "*haki*" is also "speech," so that "to speak" is synonymous with telling a story. In that sense, storytelling is the condition of language and of all human knowledge—religion, philosophy, science, ideology, and so on. Thus, if reality is socially constructed in language, then storytelling is the mode of its apprehension and also of its endless deconstruction and reconstruction. Indeed, Alameddine proposes storytelling as an inherently subversive epistemology in that it constantly transgresses discursive boundaries and surpasses ideological horizons, just as language itself is unbounded by such strictures. As Mohammad, Sarah, and the protagonist of "The Perv" (who assumes a false identity in his correspondence with adolescent boys while dying of AIDS) realize, identities are invented and reinvented in language, that is, in narrative acts that remain open-ended and unfinished. This idea becomes the organizing principle in *The Hakawati*, the culmination of Alameddine's fictional project so far.

The novel consists of two frame narratives, intertwined in narration, one told in the first and one in the third person. Each of these narratives branches off into numerous other plots and subplots, much like the tales of the *Nights*. The overall effect is that of two large compendia of tales, each grouped within a frame story, that have been shuffled together like two decks of cards. If there is one common thread running through the whole, it is that of storytelling and the pleasure taken in telling and listening to stories. Rather than trying to disentangle the numerous narrative threads and to reweave them into a comprehensive interpretation of the novel—a task that would lead into directions beyond the scope of this book—I will focus in the remaining pages on Alameddine's queering of Orientalism through the theme of storytelling.

The first-person narrative is, like Ameen Rihani's *The Book of Khalid*, a narrative of a Lebanese immigrant's return. A Lebanese American narrator called Osama returns to postwar Lebanon to visit his dying father. He reminisces about the past, encounters numerous family members, and recalls the tales of his legendary storytelling and pigeoneering grandfather Ismail al-Kharrat. Osama also recalls the tales of his late, beloved gay uncle Jihad, who was a peerless hakawati himself. Like Jihad, Osama is gay, although their sexuality is only hinted at and never discussed in the novel (it is in the other main narrative that sexuality plays a significant part). Osama's life for twenty-six years in Los Angeles is not part of the narrative, except for the story of his first arrival there with his father and uncle to enroll in UCLA. As for Jihad, he is not openly gay, either, but lives a celibate life in the family-owned apartment building, which is also inhabited by his siblings and their families—a social context where it would be unthinkable to lead an openly gay life. In fact, there are hints that some of his siblings may not even realize his sexual orientation, despite his anomalous marital status (418).

Jihad's and Osama's sexuality is, thus, more or less unmentionable—and all the more conspicuous for it—a function of the fact that homosexuality remains, as Ramzi Salti points out, a social taboo. Yet, unlike Salti, Alameddine is not interested in the status of homosexuality in Lebanon, similar to many other Arab, African, and Asian countries. On the contrary, his portrayal of Jihad's closetedness is mitigated by explicit references to such classics of Arabic literature that celebrate homosexual love as Abu Nuwas's (c. 755–c. 813 C.E.) poetry, Ibn Hazm's (994–1064) *Tawq al-hamamah* (*The Ring of the Dove*), and Ahmad al-Tifashi's (1184–1253) *Surur al-nafs bi madarik al-hawas al-khams* (*The Delight of the Hearts*), and by the unrestrained depictions of homosexuality in the novel's other main narrative. The effect is to project an image of an Arab cultural tradition that is much more tolerant of homosexuality than Salti claims, despite the stigma attached to it in public, religious, and even legal discourse. *Tolerant* is probably how the novel seeks to portray Arab culture's attitude toward homosexuality, and that is precisely how one reviewer read the book, as revealed in her characterization of Jihad as "a fabulous gay man whose homosexuality is apparent to and relished by all but never discussed and altogether not so much an issue" (Wilson-Goldie 10). In fact, homosexuality is "not so much an issue" precisely because it is never discussed. It can be tolerated, even relished, only when it is *not* openly acknowledged (don't ask, don't tell, don't show), or when it is clothed in poetic or belle-lettristic forms and enshrined among the literary classics. And indeed the novel indicates as much, albeit obliquely, in two scenes. In the first, Osama discovers Jihad dead of a heart attack in the bathroom of his hotel room in Los Angeles, his pajama pants around his ankles, and the bathroom smelling foul. After the initial shock and flurry,

Osama closes his nose and flushes the toilet. He then wipes Jihad's soiled bottom and pulls his pants on (Alameddine 2008, 291–92) before moving the body to the bedroom. The indignity of Jihad's death and the prevention of his indecent exposure parallel another scene that takes place later on in Jihad's Beirut apartment, where his brother finds a "movie wall" covered with clippings from film magazines, one of Jihad's passions (365). When the brother finds, hidden in a corner of the wall, a picture of Alan Bates and Oliver Reed kissing, he laboriously scrapes it off, ostensibly to protect his late brother's reputation. In a single oblique reference to his own sexuality, Osama kisses the disfigured image (366). In both instances, Jihad's close family members must hide his shame.

Those scenes complicate the representation of Jihad's social position: the most likeable character in the novel and the most popular member of the family, he is more vulnerable to scandal than his openly womanizing brother. Nonetheless, Alameddine places Jihad at the center of the novel's thematization of storytelling, for as Wilson-Goldie observes, Jihad serves as "the narrative compass" (Wilson-Goldie 10). He is also Osama's mentor, telling him bedtime stories in childhood and teaching him lessons about identity ("The story of who you are is never about you" [Alameddine 2008, 90]) and about the function of narration as the only access to reality ("What happens is of little importance compared with the stories we tell ourselves about what happens. Events matter little, only stories of those events affect us" [450]). Those statements seamlessly tie in with Alameddine's narrative philosophy as expressed in his previous novels and in the numerous epigraphs prefacing each of *The Hakawati*'s four parts. For example, the explicit refutation of the autonomy of the individual (and hence of individualism) in Jihad's assertion that "the story of who you are is never about you" echoes similar statements in *I, the Divine* (2001, 228), a novel formally and thematically structured around a central character who fails repeatedly to tell her story except through elaborate portraits of those surrounding her, and whose final epiphany bespeaks her rejection of individualism. Jihad likewise articulates the current theoretical consensus on the inaccessibility, indeed the unintelligibility, of reality outside of language (and narrative), which lies at the heart of the preoccupation with narrative in psychoanalysis, postcolonial studies, trauma and memory studies, historiography, and anthropology, among other fields. Yet in their counter-intuitiveness, Jihad's metafictional pronouncements retain for the nonacademic reader the force of original insights that could trigger a reassessment of common assumptions. As the foregoing chapters have demonstrated, such reassessment is the shared objective of much Arab American and Arab British writing.

Other tenets of Alameddine's fictional project are expressed in the twelve epigraphs that, in threes, preface each of the novel's four parts. The sources are varied, but all quotations express functions of storytelling in the novel, among which are intellectual exercise and entertainment, as in al-Tifashi's "Praise to God, Who has so disposed matters that pleasant literary anecdotes may serve as an instrument for the polishing of wits and the cleansing of rust from our hearts" (quoted 3); "ignoring life" in "the most agreeable way" (Fernando Pesso, quoted 403); coping with sorrow, according to Hannah Arendt who quotes Isak Dinesen's assertion that "all sorrows can be borne if you put them into a story or tell a story about them" (quoted 137); the "search for a purpose, a cause, an ideal, a mission and the like," which are "largely a search for a plot and a pattern in the development of his [man's] life story—a story that is basically without meaning or pattern" (Eric Hoffer, quoted 403); self-expression: "What Hells and Purgatories and Heavens I have inside of me! But who sees me do anything that disagrees with life—me, so calm and peaceful?" (Fernando Pessoa, quoted 3); satire: "Please tell me a story. It is surely as weird as the story of Moses's staff, the resurrection of Jesus, and the election of the husband of a lady bird to the presidency of the United States" (Emile Habibi, quoted 137); connecting to one's past, as in the proverb "If you cannot climb a tree that your father has climbed, at least place your hands upon its trunk" (Ahmadou Kourouma, quoted 265); spirituality: "A life in which the gods are not invited is not worth living" (Roberto Calasso, quoted 265); and subversiveness, as the Qur'an warns in its denunciation of poets, "And as to poets, those who go astray follow them" (quoted 265), and its refutation of the same charge when leveled against Muhammad by Mecca's pagans: "Nay, say they, these are but muddled dreams; nay, he hath but invented it [the Qur'an]; nay, he is but a poet" (quoted 403). Two more quotations from Javier Marías echo Alameddine's conviction that "everything can be told. It's just a matter of starting, one word follows another" (quoted 3), and this:

> Stories do not belong only to those who were present or to those who invent them, once a story has been told, it's anyone's, it becomes common currency, it gets twisted and distorted, no story is told the same way twice or in quite the same words, not even if the same person tells the story twice, not even if there is only ever one storyteller. (quoted 137)

This last quote is particularly important because it points to the syncretism at the heart of Alameddine's conception of cultural identity, and hence of his critique of Orientalism. For if storytelling is humanity's predominant characteristic and the embodiment of values, purpose, mission, and meaning (Eric Hoffer), and if, according to Marías, stories belong to all those who tell, hear, distort, and reshape them, then it would be folly to claim that any one culture is autonomous, self-identical, uncontaminated by outside influences, or has a monopoly on knowledge or truth. The supposed ontological distinction between "East" and "West" that Edward Said identified as the basis of Orientalism is exposed as an ideological fiction.

This idea is also embedded in other aspects of the novel, such as Osama's genealogy: Lebanese by birth and American by immigration, he has "English, Armenian, and Druze blood . . . and Albanian, too" (511). His hakawati grandfather, Ismail al-Kharrat, grew up listening to the biblical stories of his own father, the English missionary Simon Twinning, as well as those of Turkish, Armenian, and Kurdish hakawatis. That syncretism is also explicitly stated in the acknowledgments page in each of Alameddine's novels; in *The Hakawati*, that list is longer, more varied, and interlaced with metafictional commentary:

> By nature, a storyteller is a plagiarist. Everything one comes across—each incident, book, novel, life episode, story, person, news clip—is a coffee bean that will be crushed, ground up, mixed with a touch of cardamom, sometimes a tiny pinch of salt, boiled thrice with sugar, and served as a piping-hot tale. A brief list of sources that provided the most beans: *A Thousand and One Nights* (uncensored), Ovid's *Metamorphoses*, the Old Testament, the Koran, W.A. Clouston's *Flowers from a Persian Garden*, Italo Calvino's *Italian Folktales*, *Kalila wa Dimna* (uncensored), Ahmad al-Tifashi's *The Delight of Hearts*, Ibn Hazm's *The Ring of the Dove*, Mahmoud Khalil Saab's *Stories and Scenes from Mount Lebanon*, Homer's *Iliad*, Jim Crace's *The Devil's Larder*, *The Letters of Abelard and Heloise*, Ida Alamuddin's *Maktoob*, Shakespeare's plays, numerous Internet folktale sites, and quite a few books of Syrian and Lebanese folktales bought for pennies from street vendors. (515)

The list of sources that, like coffee grounds, are impossible to sort goes on to include stories from "almost every Lebanese I know, even those I don't know so well" (516). Alameddine also insists on the fictitiousness of his tales: "This is a work of fiction. It might seem redundant, stating the obvious, but it does bear repeating. Nothing herein should be considered fact of biography." Even when a historical figure is in question, legend is preferred to history: "The character of Baybars has little to do with the historical one. . . . The tale of Baybars is based on oral stories as well as an actual hakawati book. . . .[4] Readers who wish to study the history of Baybars might consider *The Lion of Egypt: Sultan Baybars I and the Near East in the Thirteenth Century* by Peter Thorau." That Baybars was the Turkish Mamluk sultan of Egypt and Syria who fought against the Mongols and the Crusader states in Palestine is itself significant for the ways in which legend is born of a long, tangled history of cultural contact, conflict, and hybridization, something that endures in the narrativization, or fictionalization, of all identities. Not even religion escapes fictionalization and syncretization, as in the playful merger of Muslim and Catholic saints' cults: "the religion in the piece was invented to fit a better narrative (to the best of my knowledge, Zainab [the Prophet Muhammad's daughter] doesn't appear at shrines, nor does anyone worship a Lady Zainab in blue" (515).

Such views turn storytelling into an antidogmatic epistemology that resists any fixed categories of identity. "Belief is the enemy of storytelling," explains Ismail al-Kharrat, who found Simon Twinning's favorite stories from the Bible to be dull: "Stories with obvious moral lessons are like eels in a wooden crate. They slither over and under each other, but never leave the tub. . . . No imagination. And heaven forbid, if he should forget something, his wife was right there to correct him" (61). Alameddine cheekily merges the sacred and the profane in order to undermine that regime of truth. Biblical and Qur'anic stories, especially that of Abraham and his two sons, are reworked in the tone, style, narrative mode, and all the vernacular bawdiness of the *Nights*. Alameddine uses the framework of the biblical story of Abraham and his two sons, Ismail (or Ishmael) and Isaac, who are the mythical progenitors of Arabs and Jews, respectively, and the conventions of the *Nights*, to weave a story that undermines the authority of the three monotheistic religions and, by extension, of American Orientalism, while at the same time satirizing the competing ethno-religious nationalisms at the heart of the modern conflict over Palestine. The effect of such mixture is to de-sacralize the scriptural stories, revealing them to be no more than variations on common narrative patterns that permeate all mythology and folktales—allegories of conflicts, family relations, prohibitions, taboos, tyrannies, and feuds—many of which serve to consolidate discriminatory identities.

The novel opens with an unnamed hakawati (the speaker in the third-person, Shahrazad-like narrative) who tells the story of an emir who lived "a long, long time ago . . . in a distant land" (5), and whose wife, much to his chagrin, bore him twelve daughters and no son. His vizier reasons, in the first of a series of allusions, "Sarah offered her Egyptian slave to her husband to produce a boy. If it was good enough for our prophet, it can be good enough for us" (6), and so an Egyptian maidservant named Fatima is called upon to play Hagar's role. However, the story takes numerous arabesque turns away from the plotline found in the Bible and the Qur'an, so that Fatima goes on a journey to her native Alexandria to enlist the aid of a famous magician descended from Cleopatra's healer, and along the way fights off a band of horny bandits (tricking them into killing each other, with only the homosexual among them being spared), descends into Hell (in a scene that recalls the myth of Innana), and becomes the lover of Afreet Jehanam (Hell's demon, or Satan), who seduces her after lobbing off her hand, before eventually returning her to her masters to give birth to a boy, at the same time that the emir's wife does the same (297). The newborns, an Ishmael-and-Isaac pair, are christened Shams (Sun) and Layl (Night) because one of them is white and the other black. The boys are switched at birth, but they grow up inseparable as brothers and lovers at the same time. Predictably, next comes the wife's banishment of the maid and her son, but also with a twist: when the emir's wife catches the two boys engaged in oral sex, she calls upon another wizard to arrange the kidnapping and dismemberment of Layl, her misrecognized son. The rest of the story follows the quest by Fatima and Shams to retrieve the captive with the help of Satan and his troupe of demon servants who bear the names of prophets mentioned in the Bible and the Qur'an (Adam, Noah, Izra, Jacob, Job, Elijah), including a gay imp couple named Ishmael and Isaac. At the end of the story, the scattered limbs of Layl (like those of Osiris) are gathered together, bringing him back to life in Hell, before the eyes of his biological mother, with whom he copulates before expiring again for good.

The story of Abraham is also woven into Osama's first-person narrative, narrated by Osama upon his return to Beirut in 2003. He recalls, among other things, the tales of his grandfather, who is, unsurprisingly, called Ismail. Born to an alcoholic English doctor and his wife's Armenian maid in the city of Urfa, the supposed birthplace of Abraham, his first name "was predetermined. What would you call a son of your maid if you lived in Urfa?" (36). Moreover, Ismail was born while his mother was listening to his father tell the biblical story of Abraham to the assembled members of his household (37). Needless to say, Ismail was later banished by his stepmother. Eventually, he settled in Lebanon and, for his penchant for spinning fantastic tales, acquired the nickname al-Kharrat ("'exaggerator,' 'teller of tall tales,' 'liar'" [9], "fibster" [36]), which became his surname. In turn, he retold the same story, among many other tales, though much embellished and transformed, to his grandson Osama (47–48). At one point, Ismail points to a map and says to Osama, "This is . . . the tomb of the Patriarchs in Hebron . . . where the sons of Sarah are still trying to cast out the sons of Hagar" (62). Asked by his grandson to tell him the story of Abraham sacrificing Ismail (in the Islamic version of the story, God commands Abraham to sacrifice Ismail, not Isaac), Ismail al-Kharrat replies, "No, I already told you that one. It's common, too common. Boring, even. It was the doctor's favorite story, and he told it so badly. It's so hackneyed and clichéd. A story needs to be entertaining" (62). Instead, he tells a story in which a son turns into a lamb that is slaughtered by his father (62–65)—an unmistakable allusion to the Christian representation of Christ as both the lamb and the son of God, sacrificed for humanity's sake. Highly troubled, Osama asks his mother, "'If God asks you, would you kill me?' I felt her shudder" (40). He goes on: "What if God told someone to kill another person—would that be okay? . . . What if God told someone to kill a lot of people? . . . God tells a man to kill all the French, and he goes out and shoots all the Frenchmen he sees. Bang, bang, bang. Is that okay? Does he get blamed?" Speaking for Alameddine and articulating the moral of all this retelling and reshaping of scriptural narratives, Osama's mother, who does not believe in God, confides: "God doesn't talk to people. . . . God doesn't tell anybody to do anything. God doesn't do anything." The child objects, saying, "But people believe God talks to them," to which she responds, "Stupid people, only stupid people" (41).

The irrationality of the sacred narratives and of the violence perpetrated in the name of God is exposed through the shock and fear of the child, who inherits his grandfather's skill as a storyteller along with his mother's atheism. The exchange cited above clearly alludes to mass murder masterminded by another Osama and to the zealotry of his antagonist, a U.S. president who spoke with God everyday. In a bold reappropriation of the two most notorious Arabic words in the U.S. in the months and years following the terrorist attacks of September 11, 2001, Alameddine names his main narrator Osama, and gives the novel's most likeable character and "narrative compass" the name Jihad. Depicting the two as gay further intensifies the parody of anti-Arab racism and Islamophobia, but also of al-Qa'ida's bigoted fanaticism. At the same time, the first and last words of novel, "Listen," seem to be addressed not only to the fictional hakawati's audience, but also to Alameddine's readers who, by such a gesture, are placed in the position of Shahrazad's audience, the tyrannical Shahrayar, who is tamed, educated, and humanized through storytelling. Storytelling is, therefore, liberating as a means of subverting oppressive religious and political authority, and of queering Orientalism. Yet, ultimately, Alameddine does not ascribe a moral purpose to storytelling; it is for entertainment, or as Fernando Pessoa puts it in one of the epigraphs, "the most agreeable way of ignoring life" (403). Or perhaps more accurately, in Alameddine's fiction, storytelling is a mode of coping with the consciousness of death, especially given the death of most of the heroes of the novel's longer narratives, including hakawatis like Ismail and Jihad, as well as the impending death of Osama's father, who is regaled with stories on his deathbed by his son—similar to the function of painting and writing for dying AIDS victims in *Koolaids*.

If by "sexual identity" is understood an overarching or exclusive preoccupation with homosexuality, then such is not the case in queer Arab American fiction so far, even though the representation of homosexuality and its status in the dominant social and religious discourses is a central concern for Alameddine and Salti. Instead, fighting homophobia is inseparable from the projects of fighting anti-Arab racism and dismantling Orientalist discourse. Indeed, as we have seen, Alameddine is suspicious of the very category of identity and of the ideology of individualism that sustains it. Witness Mohammed's declaration, "I do not want to be considered Lebanese. But that is not up to me. Would people think of me as a painter or a Lebanese painter? That is not up to me" (1998, 244); or Jihad's admonition to Osama in *The Hakawati*, "the story of who you are is never about you" (2008, 90); or, for that matter, Sarah's rejection of individualism in favor of collectivity—not so much collective *identity*, per se, but the *survival* of the collective, something that is dramatized in the epiphany she gains from the animal world, lacking as it is in language, discourse, ideology, and hence identity. This is a rejection of identity as a burden and of identity politics as inherently discriminatory. What is offered instead is a vision of cultural syncretism, expressed, for example, in Osama's multinational, multiethnic, multiconfessional family tree, and in the emphasis on the multicultural genealogy of the tales woven into the novel. Almost exactly one century after the publication of the first Arab American novel, Rihani's *The Book of Khalid* (1911), which attempted to fuse two literary traditions, the Arabic and the European, Alameddine attempts to fuse all of world literature into a novel about the inadequacy of all fictions of identity that depend on discriminatory or exclusionary practices.

Conclusion

The story of Arab immigrant literature recounted in this book begins with positivist conceptions of identity along Orientalist lines and ends with Alameddine's affirmation of Edward Said's idea of the self as "a cluster of flowing currents" rather than "a solid self" (Said 1999, 295), and the notion that "no one today is purely *one* thing" (1993, 336). These reflections on identity represent some of the consequences of Said's critique of Orientalist discourse. The fluid and open-ended conception of subjectivity he proposes undermines discourses of unitary identity, which are always constructed through mechanisms of differentiation, opposition, and discrimination, and frequently manifested in myriad forms of racism, culturalism, and nationalism.

However, while I have tried to chart a sort of history of ideas, if not a literary history, my intention has not been to write a narrative of progress or evolution. Minority and postcolonial studies have often succumbed to the desire to construct narratives of triumphant resistance that overlook complicity, melancholy, defeat, reactionism, and failure. The preceding critical readings have not shied away from underscoring the latter tendencies at every stage of the traditions's history. Rather than reading the tradition as a heroic or revolutionary narrative of resistance, this book has instead sought to locate strategies of resistance as well as currents of complicity within the complex matrix of cultural, ideological, commercial, religious, and political forces that have shaped Arab immigrant writing in the U.S. and Britain since the early twentieth century. I have also shown how the critiques of identity elaborated by Rihani, Said, Soueif, and Alameddine coexist with powerful identitarian positions, whether entrenched in the dominant discourse, such as those of Rihbany, Rizk, and Ihab Hassan, or resistant to it, like Ahmed's and Aboulela's. And while the rejection of unitary notions of identity is in line with the current consensus in Anglo-American cultural theory among secular intellectuals and academics, Aboulela's critique of secularism and multiculturalism reflects the resurgence of fundamentalism in many religious traditions as a result of the failures of development and national projects in many postcolonial states, intensified migration and the backlash against it, the Middle East and other regional conflicts, globalization, and post-9/11 geopolitics.

I have also tried to show how the ideologies expressed in Arab immigrant literature are channeled through modulations of genre, experiments in narrative technique, and stylistic innovations that constitute rich formal dimensions of the tradition. We have seen, for example, how Rihani reinvents the novel by hybridizing it linguistically and intertextually through the use of the Arabic language and the *maqama* genre; how Gibran amalgamates Hindu ideas, biblical style, and Nietzschean aphorisms into his latter-day prophetic parables; how Rihbany splits his life story along generic lines; how Turki blurs the distinction between memoir and journal and all but erases the autobiographical subject; how Ihab Hassan fragments the autobiography through postmodern aesthetics; how Soeuif subverts several genres of Orientalist writing and develops a poetics of translation that can illuminate the work of bilingual writers everywhere; how Aboulela reconfigures the romance along Islamic lines; and how Alameddine blends sacred and profane narratives and proposes storytelling as an epistemology in its own right. Despite their differences, many of those writers carry out their projects of cultural translation by violating the rules of genre.

However, such violation does not always aim at a critique of Orientalism. We have seen that writers such as Abraham Rihbany and Salom Rizk, who use conventional linear narration, follow the same discursive procedures found in coming-to-America stories as Ihab Hassan, and that all three invoke the authority of American Orientalism. By the same token, Ahmed's formally conventional memoir subverts dominant representations of Islam and Muslim women. Another case in point is the formal contrast between Salti's realistic and Alameddine's experimental fiction, despite the convergence of their ideological projects. In other words, while formal innovation and experimentation may give shape to a critique of the dominant discourse and its conventional narratives, such is not always or necessarily the case. What matters is how a writer uses form to articulate his or her ideological project at a given historical moment (and as we have seen in the case of Gibran, Rihbany, Turki, and Soueif, the ideological project can shift and evolve over the course of a writer's career). The interplay between the writer's aesthetic choices and political vision is thus one of the richest areas of inquiry in Arab American and Arab British literature.

The foregoing study of Arab immigrant literature also has implications for the fields of American, Arabic, and British studies and for humanities education that I would like briefly to outline. Above all, the implications of Said's critique of Orientalism remain to be fully implemented in college curricula that still divide the field of humanistic education into "Western" and "non-Western" traditions, reflected in the distribution of general education requirements and civilization survey courses, which in turn spur the production of textbooks and anthologies. Here, the Manichean dichotomy of East/West is replaced by an opposition between A and non-A, a catch-all negation that serves as a sort of epistemological black hole. Meanwhile, the primary category in that Aristotelian formulation continues to be posited as self-evident and autonomous, over and against a seemingly innocuous substitute for the now embarrassing term "Orient." Literary history has begun to recognize the validity of this theoretical insight, but curricular thinking and pedagogical practice in many cases still lag behind.

One can speak volumes about literary history's validation of Alameddine's insistence on the irrevocable hybridity of all cultures: Homer was first written down in Alexandria, a melting pot of cultures and traditions; Augustine was North African (from present-day Tunisia), with intellectual roots extending to Persia; much of the energy of medieval European literature derives from the construction of the enemy "Saracens" (Tolan); the courtly love tradition from Provençal to medieval French and Italian to Renaissance England was a continuation of the Arabic, Mozarabic, and Hebrew love poetry of Muslim Spain, which in turn descended from a tradition going back to pre-Islamic Arabic poetry (Menocal); Cervantes's claim that his novel, the first European specimen of the genre, is based on an Arabic manuscript testifies, if anything, to the powerful impact of Arabic literature; translations of Sanskrit, Persian, and Arabic works into European languages from the eighteenth century on had enormous implications for European and North and South American literatures; European literature, in turn, has had a lasting impact on literature around the world in the past two centuries; the literatures of colonialism, slavery, and postcolonial states in African, Asian, European, and Native American languages put to rest any claim of cultural autonomy. It was by a considerable *tour de force* that the "Western canon" was constructed by abstraction from this always-already globalized context, in opposition to so-called "Oriental" or "non-Western" traditions. The point is emphatically not to belittle or to deny the validity of studying the literary traditions of Europe and North America (which would be silly), but to avoid doing so in ways that reinforce the ideology of Western exceptionalism by denying formative Asian and African influences. Instead, reading all traditions comparatively, or as Said would say, contrapuntally, would safeguard against the passive reinforcement of any kind of exceptionalism.

If the "Western canon" is the expression of a unitary identity vis-à-vis what is constituted as civilizational Others, national canons are conceived in the same fashion as the embodiment of a cohesive, discriminatory identity in opposition to other nations. This is nowhere clearer than in the case of English literature, which, as Gauri Viswanathan has shown in *Masks of Conquest: Literary Study and British Rule in India* (1989), was first curricularized in nineteenth-century India in order to project an idealized English identity that would serve to consolidate British power, before being imported "back," so to speak, and made into the core of humanistic education in England. The same imperial logic was projected into the hierarchical relationship between English literature and other Anglophone literatures in the construct of "Commonwealth literature," which survived well into the 1980s, and by which English literature was held up as the model and touchstone of quality and taste (Moore-Gilbert 22–33). Since then, British literature and Englishness itself have had to confront the challenge of postcolonial studies, in part because of the Naipauls and the Rushdies, the Soueifs and the Aboulelas—new British minorities from the former colonies—but also because postcolonial studies has rendered it nearly impossible to speak of Victorian or Modernist literature without reference to empire and to African, Asian, and Caribbean writing. In fact, serious arguments have been made about the postcolonial Middle Ages (Cohen) and postcolonial Shakespeare (Cartelli, Loomba). In the meantime, Irish and Scottish literatures have claimed postcolonial status vis-à-vis the English canon. Empire spurred the consolidation of a notion of Englishness and a national literary canon that can function pedagogically to sustain imperial power, but in so doing empire also ultimately laid the grounds for undoing precisely what it had sought to construct.[1]

Across the pond, Wai Chee Dimock's call to study American literature comparatively is based on the recognition of the relationship between a hermetically sealed national canon and imperial aspirations. That is why she begins her book, *Through Other Continents: American Literature Across Deep Time* (2006), by referring to the U.S.'s latest imperial misadventure in Iraq, and specifically to the destruction of the Iraqi National Library. She calls for American literature to be studied "across deep time," so that American identity can be reconceived in relation to, rather than in isolation from (and hence in implicit opposition to) the heritage of the world, beginning in this case with the very Mesopotamia whose cultural legacy the Marines and their Pentagon commanders failed to protect. Her point, I think, is not that Americanists should abandon Thoreau, Emerson, Fuller, James, Pound, and Lowell, or even the idea of an American tradition, but rather to read those canonical figures—indeed to read the tradition itself—in relation to other figures and other traditions; that is to say, to read American literature from a comparative perspective. In successive chapters, she reads the above-mentioned writers in relation to *Gilgamesh*, the Egyptian *Book of the Dead*, Latin literature, Hafez, the traditions of Islam, Dante's *Commedia*, and Chinese and Caribbean authors. Rather than discarding the national tradition and becoming Egyptologists and Sinologists, Dimock calls upon Americanists to abandon the creeds of American exceptionalism, isolationism, and Manifest Destiny on which the field of American literary studies has been predicated, and to proceed instead from the premise that American literature, like other traditions—all porous and contaminated with one another—belongs within, and is shaped by, the entire world's cultural heritage.

Dimock's is only the latest effort to internationalize American literary studies. Similar arguments have been made, for instance, by John Shields in his book *The American Aeneas: Classical Origins of the American Self* (2001), and differently by Werner Sollors in his work on multilingual American literature (1998). While Dimock and Shields argue for comparative approaches to American literature that place it in the context of the literatures of the world, Sollors has demonstrated that ethnic literatures of the United States demand an expanded sense of "American literature" that also necessitates comparative approaches. Arab American literature is a case in point: since the late nineteenth century, it has been written in three languages—Arabic, English, and French. Moreover, the fact that some of the earliest slave narratives, such as that by Omar ibn Said, were written in Arabic calls for African American literature to be studied comparatively, and not only in the sense that Henry Louis Gates meant when he argued, in the *The Signifying Monkey* (1988), that "anyone who analyzes black literature must do so as a comparativist, by definition, because our canonical texts have complex double formal antecedents, the Western and the black" (xxiv); it is also multilingual. Indeed, Marc Shell and Werner Sollors's anthology of multilingual American literature includes works written in eighteen languages. The national, in other words, is always already multiple and polyglot, and American literature, if by that we understand not the restricted canon of old but the totality of American literature in all its ethnic and multilingual diversity, is a prime example of that.

As for Arabic literature, it is a pre-national as well as a supranational tradition reaching back to the sixth century, including Arabic-language works by writers hailing from any of the territories that were part of the Arab empires in the past, such as Arabic-language works by Medieval Persian and Spanish authors, to the twenty-two Arabic-speaking countries of today. Here, the national paradigm obviously falters, and the canon is defined primarily in linguistic terms that encompass many geographical coordinates, not to mention an unparalleled historical spread. Yet despite this generous scope, scholars of Arabic literature have not taken notice of the work of Arab writers in other languages, even, curiously, in the case of bilingual writers such as Rihani and Gibran. Their Arabic works are regarded as an important contribution to the development of modern Arabic literature, yet their English-language texts are familiar to very few specialists and rarely translated into Arabic. More curious still is the case of Maghrebian writers: those who write in Arabic are discussed in Arabic literary circles, while their compatriots who write in French are studied as part of francophone literature, neither group being referenced by students of the other. Smaller traditions still of Arab writers in Dutch, German, and Italian go completely unnoticed, often not considered part of the national canons of their adopted countries and outside of the Arabic. The same can be said about Arab Latin American writing in Portuguese and Spanish. Even though for methodological reasons deriving entirely from my chosen sociopolitical context and the theoretical perspective suited to it, I have focused in this book on Anglophone Arab American and Arab British works, I hope to have shown that immigrant and minor literatures make visible some of the cross-cultural and interlinguistic ties that undergird all literature.

Therefore, immigrant and minor literatures have a role to play in reconceptualizing literary studies beyond the restrictive paradigm of the national canon. Whether the minor literature is written in the major (national) language or in another language altogether, it straddles the imaginary borderlines and serves as a reminder that no literature, no language, no nation, no culture, and no civilization is an island. Indeed, minor American literatures in Arabic, German, Polish, Spanish, Yiddish, and so on, just like the writing of Arab authors in English, Dutch, French, German, Hebrew, Italian, Portuguese, and Spanish can do more than that. If taken seriously in pedagogical and critical practice, as they should be, they could help expose the nationalist and culturalist roots of the institutional configuration of literary studies.

NOTES

Preface

1. See Layla Al Maleh's "Anglophone Arab Literature: An Overview" for a comprehensive survey of worldwide Arab writing in English. In addition to the bulk of Arab American poetry, not discussed here are U.S.- and British-born Arab novelists, Arab Canadians, Arab Australians, and Anglophone Arab writers who live in Arab countries. On Arab Canadian literature, see Dahab; on Arab British writers, see Nash 1998 and 2007; on Arab American literature, see Salaita 2006 and 2011.

Introduction

1. On the history of the term "Middle East," see Adelson, 22–26. As Magda al-Nowaihi points out, "the very appellation is a creation of colonialism, for the region is 'Middle' simply because the point of reference is . . . Europe. People who live in these countries understand themselves to be 'Middle Eastern' only in relation to the West, and use the term primarily within the context of discussion of geopolitical considerations and configurations of world power. Their own self-designated parameters of identity would not include this category. No one would say: 'As a Middle Easterner, I . . . ,' while people would say, 'As an Arab,' 'an Egyptian,' 'a Muslim,' in addition to 'as a woman,' 'a physician,' 'a Marxist,' etc. If people of the region want a more encompassing designation that transcends national, linguistic, or religious classifications, they tend to use the term 'peoples of the Third World'" (al-Nowaihi 283).

2. For an overview of those debates, see Bart Moore-Gilbert (34–61).

3. See Raymond Savage, *Allenby of Armageddon*, which contains numerous passages animated by the romance and sentimentalism of the title. For example, the arrival of the British army at Jerusalem is described thus: "Dawn was approaching with no sound from the ancient city where Abraham made the covenant with Abimelech—the southern gateway to the Holy Land before which the silent hosts were closing in, 907 years after the destruction of Charlemagne's Christian Protectorate first roused the Crusaders' challenge, '*Deus vult!*' for the Wars of the Cross. Resurgent when Saladin conquered Galilee, the Crescent had dominated the cradle of Christianity in unbroken sway for its destined span from that sanguinary October to October, 1917, exactly seven hundred and thirty years" (217). Less given to sentimentalism than Savage, Archibald Wavell, another biographer of Allenby, invokes the same kind of logic to suggest, even more audaciously than Savage, that the defeat of "Turks" by "Englishmen" seems to be a historical destiny fulfilled over and over again: on September 18, 1918, the British army "passed over a battlefield where an English commander had won a notable victory more than seven hundred years previously. At the battle of Arsuf (September 7, 1191) Richard Cœur de Lion . . . had outmanœuvered and outfought a worthy opponent in Saladin. Saladin's host had included a considerable force of Turkish bowmen, while Richard's international force of Crusaders contained an English

contingent of horse and foot. So that it was not the first time that the ground over which the cavalry now rode had felt the victorious rush of English cavalry in pursuit of Turks" (Wavell 274). On the reaction of British and U.S. media to the invasion of Palestine, see Lawrence James 144.

4. The controversy that swirled around the book is reminiscent of that occasioned by Said's *Orientalism*. See, for example, Berlinerblau 2001.

5. According to the 2001 census, the U.K. immigrants represent about 7.9 percent of the population, or 4.6 million. Three-quarters of them are Asian and African (including Caribbean), the rest are from European Union countries. Most of the minority ethnic population comes from (in this order) India, Pakistan, Bangladesh, and Somalia. There are no separate figures for Arabs. Source: http://www.statistics.gov.uk/CCI/nugget.asp?ID=764&Pos=4&ColRank=1&Rank=176

6. On the ambiguities and contradictions of the idea of America as a "nation of immigrants," see Ali Behdad's perceptive book, *A Forgetful Nation*, especially 1–22.

7. On Arabs in the New World before the first major wave of immigration in the late nineteenth century, see Beverlee Turner Mehdi, 1–5.

8. According to the 2000 U.S. Census, which does not have a separate category for Arab Americans and defines peoples from the Middle East and North Africa as white, Arab Americans number around 1.25 million; however, the Arab-American Institute estimates that figure to be around 3.5 million. Source: http://www.aaiusa.org/arab-americans/22/demographics. The most comprehensive and up-to-date history of Arab Americans is Gregory Orfalea's *The Arab Americans: A History*. For a concise history of Arab immigration, with a focus on Muslim immigrants, see Yvonne Yazbeck Haddad (2004). Other important studies of Arab immigration and Arab communities include those by Philip Hitti, Adele Younis, Albert Hourani and Nadim Shehadi, Alixa Naff (1985), Eric Hooglund, Baha Abu-Laban and Michael Suleiman, Ernest McCarus, Michael Suleiman (1999), Sameer and Nabil Abraham, Elain Hagopian and Ann Paden, Barbara Aswad, Nabeel Abraham and Andrew Shryock, Kathleen Benson and Philip Kayal, and Elizabeth Boosahda. On Arab Muslims in the U.S., see Abdo Elkholy, Barbara Aswad and Barbara Bligé, Yvonne Yazbeck Haddad and Jane Idleman Smith, and Haddad (1991, 1994). On Arab Christians, see Philip Kayal and Joseph Kayal.

9. See chapters 5, 6, and 7 of Geoffrey Nash's *The Arab Writer in English* and his *The Anglo-Arab Encounter*, which together offer the most detailed study to date of Arab British literature.

10. On the Arabic language press in the U.S., see Alixa Naff.

11. "For instance, in a 1929 Florida incident involving the lynching of a Syrian man after a car accident . . . the Syrian immigrant community responded not only with outrage, but also with a defensive attempt to assert their 'whiteness.' A letter published in a Syrian immigrant journal declaimed, 'The Syrian is not a Negro whom Southerners feel they are justified in lynching when he is suspected of an attack on a white woman. The Syrian is a civilized white man who has excellent traditions and a glorious historical background' ('Has the Syrian Become a Negro' 42)" (Majaj 2000, 325).

12. For a detailed study of the subject, see Gualtieri.

13. As of this writing, it is still too early to tell whether President Barack Obama's conciliatory discourse toward Arabs and Muslims will represent a temporary lull in this hostility or usher in a new era of lasting sensitivity. If anything, the backlash against him on this account does not augur well. One example is the infamous John McCain town hall meeting

held in Lakeville, Minnesota on October 10, 2008, in which a woman said that Obama was an Arab. Indignant, the Republican presidential nominee said, "No, ma'am. He's a decent family man [and] citizen that I just happen to have disagreements with on fundamental issues and that's what this campaign's all about. He's not [an Arab]" (Martin and Parnes). McCain's rebuttal endorsed and the idea that to be "decent" is incompatible with being "Arab."

14. This is the subject of former Congressman Paul Findley's *They Dare to Speak Out: People and Institutions Confront Israel's Lobby*. See also former U.S. Senator James Abourezk's *Advise & Dissent* (167–91).

15. On the rise of Christian Zionism, see Sha'ban 2005 (151–209) and Salaita 2006 (167–88).

16. See, for example, Tejaswini Niranjana's *Siting Translation*, which examines the ways in which translations of Indian texts by William Jones and others produced India and the "Indian character."

17. The work of Talal Asad and John Dickson on translation in the field of anthropology has been groundbreaking in this regard (1985, 1986).

18. See also Marilyn Booth on the marketability of translated Arabic literature in the U.S. The relative dearth, until very recently, of English translations from Arabic explains the lack of critical reflection on Arabic-English translation. Apart from a handful of critiques of particular cases, neither a theory nor a systematic study of Arabic-English literary translation has yet been published. For specific case studies, see Fatma Mousa and Tarek Shamma on translations of *The Thousand and One Nights*, Amal Amireh on el Saadawi, Mohja Kahf on Huda Sha'rawi, Edward Said (2000) on Mahfouz, and Nirvana Tanoukhi on Muhammad Choukri.

19. I use the words "Arabizing" and "Arabized English" after the manner of what Braj Kachru calls the "Indianization" of English in the work of Raja Rao and other Anglo-Indian writers (Kachru, *The Indianization of English*), and of Eyamba Bokamba's discussion of the "Africanization" of English.

20. On "fluency," see Venuti's introduction to *Rethinking Translation*; on intelligibility in domesticating vs. foreignizing translation, see his *The Translator's Invisibility* 17–39.

21. Needless to say, not all texts containing foreign words, phrases, expressions, or even passages are translational, in the ways I have been describing. Countless authors from around the world have participated in a long tradition of bilingual writing by inserting foreignisms in their texts for various literary effects, but "translational literature," as I use the term, refers to those texts which focus on the process of translation within formal, thematic, linguistic, and/or discursive registers.

22. See the debates about the use of English in African literature (Achebe, Ngugi). On Francophone North African writing, see Armitage and Mehrez.

23. Lital Levy raises similar questions in reference to Arabophone Iraqi Israeli novelist Samir Naqqash.

24. Abdelfattah Kilito's metaphor for bilingualism as mortal combat sharply contrasts with the language of love used by Khatibi, Shammas, and (as I explaine in chapter 7) Ahdaf Soueif: for Kilito, "bilingualism does not evoke the image of two gladiators advancing upon each other armed with nets and tridents; rather it suggests that one of the two combatants is already sprawled in the dust awaiting the fatal blow" (2001, 108). Used in the context of classical Arabic literature, the image projects the attitude of many Francophone writers from North Africa on whom the colonizer's language has been imposed forcibly, to the

detriment of Arabic. A case in point is Assia Djebar's moving struggle with linguistic exile, in *Fantasia* and elsewhere, as Nada Elia explains. Emily Apter's theorization of "translation zones" as "war zones" parallels Kilito's (see Apter chapters 8–12).

25. *Webster's New World Dictionary*, 3d ed., gives this definition: "**trans.late** ***vt.*** [ME *translaten* < ML & L: ML *translatare* < L *translatus*, transferred, used as pp. of *transferre*: see TRANSFER] **1** to move from one place or condition to another; transfer, specif., (a) *Theol.* to convey directly to heaven without death (b) *Eccles.* to transfer (a bishop) from one see to another; also, to move (a saint's body or remains) from one place of interment to another **2** to put into the words of a different language **3** to change into another medium or form [to *translate* ideas into action] **4** to put into different words; rephrase or paraphrase in explanation **5** to transmit (a telegraphic message) again by means of automatic relay **6** [Archaic] to enrapture; entrance **7** *Mech.* to impart translation to—***vi.*** **1** to make a translation into another language **2** to be capable of being translated—**trans.lat'able** ***adj.***"

26. As do to a lesser degree other kinds of texts that stage moments of negotiation between gendered, racialized, and/or class-based linguistic and cultural codes. Among such texts, Spivak lists J. M. Coetzee's *Foe*, Wilson Harris's *The Guyana Quartet*, and Toni Morrison's *Beloved* (Spivak, "The Politics" 194–97). Other examples of translational texts include Mario Vargas Llosa's *El Hablador* (1989) and Milorad Pavic's *Dictionary of the Khazars* (1989).

27. On the experiences of several such writers, see Shalal-Esa.

Chapter 1

1. For a complete list of Rihani's published and still unpublished works in Arabic and English, see www.ameenrihani.org.

2. See Hourani (1967) 51–102.

3. See Hourani (1991) 315–19.

4. On Rihani's Arabism, see Nash (1998) 46–78. On his relationship with the Saudi monarch, see Shahid (1988).

5. The symposium was sponsored by the Ameen Rihani Institute (Washington, D.C.) and the American University Center for Global Peace, Washington, D.C., April 19–20, 2002.

6. Rihani and Rihbany attended college briefly in the U.S. but did not finish their degrees. Although his Arabic seems to have been good, Rihbany did not write in that language. Rihani struggled to master literary Arabic early on in his career, while Gibran's Arabic works were often criticized for their stylistic weakness and even for being ungrammatical. Naimy argues that Rihani's "break with 'classic formulas' and 'authoritative grammarians' . . . seems not to represent a genuine new development, being in reality more of a necessity for him than a deliberate artistic choice" (20). This is true of Gibran as well, but it is also the case that the revolutionary fervor of Romanticism, which required less elaborate style, very much suited their temperament and their sociopolitical agenda.

7. On the influence of the *Mahjar* writers on Arabic literature in the early twentieth century, see Badawi 41–47.

8. See Dunnavent's study of Rihani and American transcendentalism.

9. Albert Rihani compiled a list of Arabic and English reviews of his brother Ameen's works; see *Where to Find Ameen Rihani*, pp. 68–103 of the English section. Ameen Rihani's books on Arabia were much better received in the U.S. than his creative works.

10. An immensely popular narrative genre that emerged in the tenth century and continued till the beginning of the twentieth, involving the adventures of a wandering rogue

who lives by his wits. For a brief introduction to the genre, see Roger Allen (1998) 268–78; Abdelfattah Kilito's *Les séances* is the most thorough study of the genre in a European language.

11. See Wolfgang Iser's article on this aspect of Carlyle's novel. On the influence of *Sartor Resartus* on *The Book of Khalid*, see Nash 1994.

12. Rihani here anticipates the tradition in Arabic fiction of "East–West romance," the best-known example of which is Tayeb Salih's *Season of Migration to the North* (see chapters 1 and 3 of my *Tayeb Salih*).

13. Nash does not escape that binarism, despite his avowed indebtedness to Edward Said, nor do the contributors to the Funk and Sitka collection, nor for that matter those scholars who have written about Rihani in Arabic, notable among them Rihani's nephew, biographer, editor, and namesake Ameen Albert Rihani, author of an important book, *Faylasuf al-Freike* (The Philosopher of Freike). The categories of "East" and "West," which have no analytical validity whatsoever, continue to govern much of the discussion.

Chapter 2

1. On Orientalist attitudes to Arabic language and literature, see Said's *Orientalism* (128, 142–45, 320) and Kilito (10–15).

2. For a detailed study of the development of modern Arabic poetry and the role of each one of the *Mahjar* poets in it, see Jayyusi, esp. vol. 1, 85–138.

3. See Arthur Christy's *The Orient in American Transcendentalism: A Study of Emerson, Thoreau and Alcott* and Wendell Thomas's *Hinduism Invades America*.

4. Gibran met Tagore and painted his portrait (Hawi 112).

5. Other than "Al-Mawakib" and *Irama dhat al-'imad*, after 1918 Gibran published compilations of brief articles and previously written pieces: *Al-Bada'i' wa al-tara'if* (Best Things and Masterpieces, 1923), *Al-'Awasif* (Storms, 1920), which contained prose poems and narratives written between 1912 and 1918, and then *Al-sanabil* (Spikes of Grain, 1929). Many of those pieces are translated in *A Treasury of Kahlil Gibran*.

6. For a detailed exposition of Gibran's religious and philosophical beliefs as expounded in his Arabic and English works, see Hawi.

7. See also "Huffar al-qubur wa al-ahya'" ("Grave Diggers and the Living"), a 1916 essay in which he argued that Britain could play that constructive role in Syria as it had, allegedly, done in Egypt (60–65).

8. See Nassar's chapter "On the Posture of Exultant Dualism" in his *Essays* (52–64).

9. Claude Bragdon's blurb, printed on the dust jacket of *The Prophet*, is characteristic: "His power came from some great reservoir of spiritual life else it could have not been so universal and potent . . ."

10. Both underlined sentences are quoted from *The Prophet* (17).

11. Allusions to *The Prophet* (15).

Chapter 3

1. In the U.S., one of the earliest such studies is Roy Pascal's *Design and Truth in Autobiography*. Other important books include Elizabeth Bruss, *Autobiographical Acts: The Changing Situation of a Literary Genre*; James Olney, ed., *Autobiography: Essays*

Theoretical and Critical, which includes an important bibliographical essay by Olney, 3–27; William Spenglemann, *The Forms of Autobiography: Episodes in the History of a Literary Genre*, which also includes an excellent bibliographical essay; and Sidonie Smith, *A Poetics of Women's Autobiography: Marginality and the Fictions of Self-Representation*. In France, Philippe Lejeune has produced several important books on the subject, notably *Le pacte autobiographique*, which has exerted considerable influence on subsequent work both in France and in the U.S.

2. On the development of Arabic autobiography, see Dwight Reynolds.

3. See Reynolds 7–8 and 56–59. Allen Austin's *African Muslims in Antebellum America* examines many such narratives in detail; Ronald Judy discusses their implication in *(Dis) Forming the American Canon: African-Arabic Slave Narratives and the Vernacular*.

4. Lejeune has advanced a controversial definition of autobiography ("*Récit rétrospectif en prose qu'une personne réelle fait de sa propre existence, lorsqu'elle met l'accent sur sa vie individuelle, en particulier sur l'histoire de sa personalité*" [14, Lejeune's emphasis]), which has been challenged on several counts, as Brunner points out (41–42, 46, 48). In another vein, John Sturrock has explored at length the vexed relationship between theory and autobiography, since, unlike novelists, for example, autobiographers do not tend to write, nor are they usually read, within a separate literary tradition.

5. In light of recent research on the brain and memory in cognitive and social psychology, psychiatry, and neurobiology, Paul John Eakin states that "[t]he notion that autobiographical memory is socially and culturally constructed may at first seem counterintuitive. From Rousseau's *Confessions* on down, readers have been conditioned by the ideology of individualism to think of autobiography as a theater in which the self's uniqueness, privacy, and interiority are on display." Instead, Eakin invokes the concept of "social constructivism" advocated by developmental psychologists like Kenneth Gergen, Katherine Nelson, Robyn Fivush, Peggy Miller, Catherine Snow, and Dennie Palmer Wolf, who have researched the ways in which children, for example, assimilate narrative patterns from their parents and environment, then use those patterns in describing their own experiences (Eakin 295). Thus according to Gergen, "To report on one's memories is not so much a matter of consulting mental images as it is engaging in a sanctioned form of telling" (Gergen 90). All of this lends weight to Mikhail Bakhtin's concept of the "dialogic imagination," which "displaces the essentialist ideology of individualism that makes of the 'self' an atomized privacy, a unified and unique core isolable from society and 'representable' in autobiography" (Smith 48).

6. Some of the most salient examples include the titles of pioneering anthologies of Arab American writing such as Gregory Orfalea and Sharif Elmusa's *Grape Leaves: A Century of Arab American Poetry* and Joanna Kadi's *Food for Our Grandmothers: Writings of Arab-American and Arab-Canadian Feminists*. Diana Abu-Jaber's novel *Crescent* uses Arabic food as a central metaphor, as does her "food memoir," *The Language of Baklava*.

7. Burton claimed that the tales show "the Arab at his best and his worst. In glancing over the myriad pictures of this panorama, those who can discern the soul of goodness in things evil will note the true nobility of the Moslem's mind in the Moyen Age, and the cleanliness of his life from cradle to grave . . . nor is the shady side of the picture less notable. Our Arab at his worst is a mere barbarian who has not forgotten the savage" (Burton 1934, 3653–55).

8. It is worth recalling here that Rihani's vision of civilizational synthesis was secular and Hegelian, achievable in this world.

Chapter 4

1. Evelyn Shakir finds that the depiction of Arab women as strong and influential in many of those autobiographies challenges Orientalist stereotypes. "According to popular belief [in the U.S.], all Arab women can be divided into two categories. Either they are shadowy nonentities, swathed in black from head to foot, or they are belly dancers—seductive, provocative, and privy to exotic secrets of lovemaking. The two images, of course, are finally identical, adding up to a statement that all Arab women are, in one sense or another, men's instruments or slaves." Shakir goes on to argue that in Rihbany's and Rizk's autobiographies "we have, at last, an unjaundiced portrayal of the Arab woman or at least of the Christian Arab woman in the Levant" (Shakir 1988, 39). In two articles on the subject, Shakir points out that Rihbany's mother and Rizk's two grandmothers, among other women in Arab American autobiographies, are formidable women who occupy unchallenged leadership positions (Shakir 1988 and 1991–92). However, the potentially subversive implications of this figuration of the strong Arab woman are not pursued in any of those texts, which go on to confirm Orientalist representations of other aspects of Arab culture. In Rizk's case, even strong women are represented within the twin registers of American Orientalism, the Bible and *The Arabian Nights*.

2. In 2000, a certain Rev. Harold Schmidt published a revised and enlarged version of *Syrian Yankee* under the title, *America, More Than a Country* (Beverly Hills: Laredo Publishing Co.). Rizk had dedicated *Syrian Yankee* "to the Rev. Harold E. Schmidt without whose inspiring friendship, constant encouragement, and help there could have been no *Syrian Yankee*." Schmidt added some seventy pages to the book in the form of new and expanded chapters. The copyright page of Schmidt's edition states, "Out of love for America and his long time friendship with Salom Rizk, Rev. Schmidt has revised his autobiography, capturing the essence of the original, and added thoughts about his personal experience. Every effort has been made by Rev. Schmidt to locate the rightful heirs of Mr. Rizk." My own efforts to locate Rev. Schmidt failed, and in September 2010, the publisher of Laredo informed me that he had died three or four years earlier. When I pressed him for more details, the publisher said that his records were lost when the press relocated from California to Englewood, New Jersey, and that he had no recollection of the circumstances surrounding the publication of the new edition, which has since gone out of print.

Chapter 5

1. Given the large number of Palestinian autobiographies available in English, I concentrate here on English-language texts by three Palestinian Americans who were exiled in 1948. Other Palestinian memoirs available in English include Hisham Sharabi's *Embers and Ashes: Memoirs of An Arab Intellectual* (originally written in Arabic in 1978, English translation 2008), Bassam Abu-Sharif's *Tried by Fire* (1995), Ghada Karmi's *In Search of Fatima: A Palestinian Story* (2002), Mourid Barghouti's *I Saw Ramallah* (in Arabic 1997, English translation 2003), Jean Makdisi's *Teta, Mother and Me: Three Generations of Arab Women* (2006), Sari Nusseibeh's *Once Upon a Country: A Palestinian Life* (2007), and Ibtisam Barakat's *Tasting the Sky: A Palestinian Childhood* (2007).

2. The celebrated Palestinian novelist Ghassan Kanafani, who wrote in Arabic, based his novella, "Returning to Haifa," on this phenomenon.

3. See the 1998 BBC documentary, *In Search of Palestine*, which follows Said's journey to Jerusalem and the West Bank.

4. *Orientalism* (1978) was closely followed by *The Question of Palestine* (1979), which applied his critique of the epistemology of Oriental studies to Zionist ideology and the political discourse on Palestine in the United States. Said subsequently authored and collaborated on several books on the Palestinian–Israeli conflict: *After the Last Sky* (1986), *Blaming the Victims: Spurious Scholarship and the Palestinian Question* (1988), *The Politics of Dispossession: The Struggle for Palestinian Self-Determination 1969–1994* (1994), *Peace and Its Discontents* (1996), *The End of the Peace Process: Oslo and After* (2000). He also commented on Palestine in most of his other books on literary and cultural criticism.

5. Before Said's memoir appeared in bookstores, the right-wing Zionist New York magazine *Commentary*, which had viciously attacked Said before, ran a story (in its September 1999 issue) by Israeli researcher Justus Wiener who accused Said of lying about his birth in Jerusalem, the ownership of a family house there in which he spent part of his childhood, and other details about Said's life in Palestine. The libelous article was quickly excerpted in London's *Daily Telegraph* and New York's *Wall Street Journal*, both known for pro-Israeli leanings. Many newspapers subsequently published articles defending Said, but the affair as a whole illustrates, among other things, the embattled status of Palestinian American writing.

6. The equivalent, in Said's work, of this ongoing effort to chronicle the Palestinian struggle for survival is his journalistic writing, collected in several of the volumes referenced above.

7. Douglass argued that slavery brutalizes both slave and slave master (Douglass 81–82), and Césaire likewise contended that colonialism dehumanizes colonizer and colonized (Césaire 19–20).

Chapter 6

1. On Pharaonism and Egyptian, as distinct from, Arab, nationalism, see Hourani 1991 (308–10, 340–45). One of the clearest illustrations of this discourse is Taha Husayn's argument, in *Mustaqbal al-thaqafa fi misr* (1938, "The Future of Culture in Egypt"), that Egypt has stronger cultural and historical ties with Europe than with Asia and should, therefore, see itself as part of European civilization (Husayn 7).

2. Elsewhere, she explains, "in British English 'Black' meant all . . . non-Europeans" (207).

Chapter 7

1. For a detailed discussion of Atiyah's views on culture and politics, see also Nash 1998, 94–119.

2. Soueif has translated Murid Barghuti's *I Saw Ramallah* into English and co-translated her own short stories and *The Map of Love* into Arabic (Soueif 1996, 1998). Many of her articles in English, written between 1981 and 2004, are collected in *Mezzaterra: Fragments from the Common Ground* (2005).

3. See chapter 2 of my book on Salih. An immigrant in England since the early 1950s, Salih has exerted an immeasurable influence on the Arabic novel and, naturally, on Anglophone Arab writers in Britain, as the next chapter on Leila Aboulela demonstrates. On Idris, see Roger Allen (1994) and Mona Mikhail.

4. She adds, "I operate in Arabic perfectly well. I write essays and criticism and letters and reports and so on, but I simply cannot write fiction in Arabic. It's as if I'm not good enough. It becomes a blunt instrument in my hand. It won't do what I want" (Soueif 2000, 99–100). In another interview she says, "I think in both English and Arabic. And I dream in both. But I only write [fiction] in English. All the narratives come to me in English; I can't do narrative in Arabic. The dialogue, I can hear it in Arabic and I produce it in English" (Pakravan 280; see also Massad 87).

5. In *The Map of Love*, only the two love stories and their protagonists, along with some of the other characters, are fictional. Soueif reports having "spent quite a while researching those years at the beginning of the century, and plotted them so I had a month by month schedule of events that took place. And then I hooked my story onto those events, so it was really as if these characters were alive at the time—attending the opening of this bridge, attending this ball at the palace, taking part in these demonstrations, and so on" (Soueif 2000, 101). The events of the 1990s are similarly set against the historical backdrop of the effects of globalization on the Egyptian economy, war in the Balkans, and the Oslo Accords and their aftermath.

6. See Andrea Shalal-Esa's "The Politics of Getting Published," which focuses on comparable experiences of Arab American writers.

7. In an article published in *The Guardian* on October 26, 1999, John Sutherland, a member of the jury for the 1999 Booker Prize, wrote that Soueif's novel "was, by general agreement, the 'best read,' of the shortlist. A romance of the desert, it had something of the oriental exotic about it, mixed with fashionable post-colonialism. But its anti-Zionist sentiments made some members of the committee slightly uneasy" (Sutherland 5).

8. Soueif has told an interviewer that Anna's narrative is inspired by "travel writing done by . . . English women, mostly Victorian, and of course they are very varied, from people with very set, very colonial attitudes, to people who were very broad-minded and opened themselves up to the culture they were coming to see, like Lucy Duff Gordon . . . You can see them changing as you go through the letters, you see a different character evolving" (Soueif 2000, 102–3).

9. See note 25 in the introduction.

10. On Lewis's paintings, see Yeazell 221–30.

11. In a letter to Sir Charles, Anna writes, "I certainly find it most difficult to speak of my Egyptian friends to my English ones here. . . . I have tried—since what they know they seem to know from hearsay only—to tell them about my experience. And they appear to listen but then resume their conversation as though I had not spoken" (247).

12. Compare this to the scene of Anna and Sharif's meeting with Cromer in his office to ratify their marriage certificate. Anna reports that "throughout the interview Lord Cromer spoke in English, I in French, and Sharif Basha in Arabic. No tea or coffee was offered, no pleasantries exchanged" (320–21). French would have been the lingua franca, but like Cromer's withholding of hospitality, his use of English insultingly excludes Sharif, who resorts to Arabic (and an interpreter) to return the favor, thereby excluding Anna.

13. " . . . is it not encouraging to see that in countries where women are believed to be prisoners, they can be seen by the thousands on the streets, in markets and gardens, walking aimlessly by themselves, in pairs, or accompanied by a child? Truly, European women do not enjoy as much freedom" (Nerval 1:149, my translation).

Chapter 8

1. The epigraph appears in the Arabic original of *Dau al-Beit*, the first part of *Bandarshah*, and is omitted in the English translation.

2. The translation of *Season* by Denys Johnson-Davies, with collaboration from Salih, was begun before the novel was finished. Salih said in an interview that while he was writing it in London between 1962 and 1966, he was hoping that it would induce Arab and European readers to reconsider their perception of themselves, of each other, and of the relationship between them (Salih 1976, 125; quoted in my *Tayeb Salih* 88).

3. In a similar vein, the untranslatability of the Qur'an, considered to be the literal word of God revealed in Arabic, is an article of faith—over and above the acknowledged difficulties and limitations of translating other works. Its "meanings can be translated but not reproduced" because its language itself constitutes a "miracle" (*The Translator* 112).

4. I am told that Aboulela's fiction is popular with teenage Muslim girls in Britain and the United States.

5. Aboulela says, "When I read books by Arab and Muslim authors I am often conscious of the absence of religion in the characters' lives. I find this unrealistic, as religion in Third World countries in general is strong in people's lives. Also in my personal experience, I have found religious people to be very interesting and positive—yet they are often depicted in novels as dull and harsh. I wanted to put my own experience in my fiction and pay tribute to the many religious people I know who have enhanced my life: my grandmother, Scottish friends who converted to Islam, the sisters at Aberdeen Mosque who supported me and became my new family away from home" (Aboulela 2005).

6. Incidentally, the figure of the convert also appears in Salih's *Season*: Mrs. Robinson's husband is an Orientalist who converts to Islam and is buried in a Muslim cemetery in Cairo (Salih 1969, 111), and the title character in *Dau al-Beit*, the first part of *Bandarshah* (1996, 60–80).

7. Conversely, in *The Translator*, another would-be convert finds that Calvinism is stricter than Islam (91).

8. In fact, the fourteenth-century Arab founder of modern sociology and historiography, Ibn Khaldun, constructed a theory of history on the basis of such investigation.

9. On Islamic feminism, see the work of Leila Ahmed, Asma Barlas, Miriam Cooke, Fatima Mernissi, and Amina Wadud listed in the bibliography.

10. The very title *Arabian Nights* is an Orientalist rendering of the original, *The Thousand and One Nights*. This mistranslation has contributed to the common misconception that the book depicts Arab life, whereas the Persian names of the main characters in the frame story (Shahrazad, Shahrayar, Shahzaman, Dinazad) and the setting of the narrative in a mythic past in "the lands of India and Indochina" indicate that, for its Arab audience, the tales are about exotic, faraway peoples and places. The irony here is that an immigrant Arab living in Europe comes to regard the book, in Orientalist fashion, as an authentic depiction of her culture's past.

Chapter 9

1. Indeed, the Civil War has been the single most important theme of Lebanese fiction written in Arabic, English, and French since the 1970s. See Miriam Cooke, Elise Salem, and Steven Salaita (2007).

2. In a sense, Sarah's repeated attempts to tell her story mirror Alameddine's output as a painter, which consists of over two hundred and seventy self-portraits.

3. See note 7 to chapter 3.

4. A professional storyteller's mnemonic aid.

Conclusion

1. On the construct of Englishness, see Robert Young.

WORKS CITED

Aboulela, Leila. *The Translator.* Edinburgh: Polygon, 1999.

———. *Colored Lights.* Edinburgh: Polygon, 2001.

———. "Barbie in the Mosque." In Devine and Logue, 1–3.

———. *Minaret.* New York: Black Cat, 2005.

———. Interview with Leila Aboulela. *The iWitness* July (2005), 13 January 2007. <http://www.iwitness.co.uk/features/0705fe03.htm>.

Abourezk, James G. *Advise & Dissent: Memoirs of South Dakota and the U.S. Senate.* Chicago: Lawrence Hill Books, 1989.

Abraham, Nabeel. "Anti-Arab Racism and Violence in the United States." In McCarus, 155–214.

———, and Andrew Shryock, eds. *Arab Detroit: From Margin to Mainstream.* Detroit: Wayne State U, 2000.

Abraham, Sameer, and Nabeel Abraham, eds. *Arabs in the New World: Studies on Arab-American Communities.* Detroit: Wayne State U, 1983.

Abu-Jaber, Diana. *Crescent.* New York: Norton, 2003.

———. *The Language of Baklava: A Memoir.* New York: Pantheon, 2005.

Abu-Laban, Baha, and Faith Zeadey, eds. *Arabs in America: Myths and Realities.* Wilmette, Ill.: Medina UP International, 1975.

———, and Michael Suleiman, eds. *Arab Americans: Continuity and Change.* Belmont, Mass.: Association of Arab-American University Graduates, 1989.

Abu-Laban, Sharon. "Stereotypes of Middle East People: An Analysis of Church School Curricula." In Abu-Laban and Zeadey, 149–69.

Abu-Sharif, Bassam, and Uzi Mahnaimi. *Tried by Fire: The Searing True Story of Two Men at the Heart of the Struggle Between the Arabs and the Jews.* London: Warner Books, 1995.

Achebe, Chinua. "The African Writer and the English Language" (1975). In Lucy Burke, et al., eds. *The Routledge Language and Cultural Theory Reader.* London: Routledge, 2000. 427–33.

Adelson, Roger. *London and the Invention of the Middle East: Money, Power, and War, 1902–1922.* New Haven and London: Yale UP, 1995.

Adnan, Etel. *Sitt Marie Rose.* Paris: Editions des Femmes, 1977. Trans. Georgina Kleege. Sausalito, Ca.: Post-Apollo Press, 1982.

———. *Paris, When It's Naked.* Sausalito, Ca.: Post-Apollo Press, 1993.

———. *Master of the Eclipse.* Northampton, Mass.: Interlink, 2009.

Ahmed, Leila. *Women and Gender in Islam: Historical Roots of a Modern Debate.* New Haven: Yale UP, 1992.

———. *A Border Passage: From Cairo to America—A Woman's Journey.* New York: Farrar, Straus and Giroux, 1999.

Akash, Munir, and Khalid Mattawa, eds. *Post-Gibran: Anthology of New Arab American Writing.* Bethesda: Kitab, Inc., 1999.

Alameddine, Rabih. *Koolaids: The Art of War.* New York: Picador, 1998.

———. *The Perv: Stories*. New York: Picador, 1999.

———. *I, the Divine: A Novel in First Chapters*. New York: Norton, 2001.

———. *The Hakawati*. New York: Knopf, 2008.

Allen, Roger, ed. *Critical Perspectives on Yusuf Idris*. Boulder, Co.: Lynne Rienner, 1994.

———. *The Arabic Literary Heritage: The Development of Its Genres and Criticism*. Cambridge: Cambridge UP, 1998.

———. "Translating Arabic Literature." *The Translation Review* 65 (2003): 1–5.

Al-Nowaihi, Magda. "The 'Middle East'? Or . . . /Arabic Literature and the Postcolonial Predicament." In *A Companion to Postcolonial Studies*, ed. Henry Schwarz and Sangeeta Ray. London: Blackwell, 2000. 282–303.

Al-Qazzar, Ayad. "Images of the Arab in American Social Science Textbooks." In Abu-Laban and Zeadey, 113–32.

Amin, Samir. *Eurocentrism*. Trans. Russell Moore. New York: Monthly Review Press, 1989.

Amireh, Amal. "Framing Nawal El-Saadawi: Arab Feminism in a Transnational World." In Majaj, et al., 33–67.

———, and Lisa Suhair Majaj, eds. *Going Global: The Transnational Reception of Third World Women Writers*. New York: Garland, 2000.

Apter, Emily. *The Translation Zone: A New Comparative Literature*. Princeton: Princeton UP, 2006.

Armitage, Anne. "The Debate over Literary Writing in a Foreign Language: An Overview of Francophonie in the Maghreb." *Alif: Journal of Comparative Poetics* 20 (2000): 39–67.

Asad, Talal. "The Concept of Cultural Translation in British Social Anthropology." *Writing Culture: The Poetics and Politics of Ethnography*. Ed. James Clifford and James Marcus. Berkeley: U of California P, 1986. 141–64.

———, and John Dickson. "Translating Europe's Others." *Europe and Its Others*. Ed. Frances Barker, et al. Clochester: U of Sussex P, 1985.

Aswad, Barbara, ed. *Arabic Speaking Communities in American Cities*. New York: Center for Migration Studies, 1974.

———, and Barbara Bligé, eds. *Family & Gender Among American Muslims: Issues Facing Middle Eastern Immigrants and their Descendants*. Philadelphia: Temple UP, 1996.

Atiyah, Edward. *An Arab Tells His Story: A Study in Loyalties*. London: John Murray, 1946.

———. *The Palestine Question*. London: Diplomatic Press and Publishing Co., 1948.

———. *The Thin Line*. New York: Harper, 1951.

———. *The Black Vanguard*. London: Peter Davies, 1952.

———. *Lebanon Paradise*. London: Peter Davies, 1953.

———. *What Is Imperialism?* London: The Batchworth Press, 1954.

———. *The Arabs*. London: Penguin, 1955.

———. *The Crime of Julian Masters*. London: Robert Hale, 1959.

———. *The Eagle Flies from England*. London: Robert Hale, 1960.

———. *Donkey from the Mountains*. London: Robert Hale, 1961. Published in the U.S. as *The Cruel Fire*. New York: Doubleday, 1962.

Austin, Allan D. *African Muslims in Antebellum America: A Sourcebook*. New York: Garland, 1984.

Badawi, M. M. *A Critical Introduction to Modern Arabic Poetry*. Cambridge: Cambridge UP, 1975.

———. *A Short History of Modern Arabic Literature*. Oxford: Clarendon, 1993.

Bakhtin, Mikhail. *The Dialogic Imagination: Four Essays.* Trans. Caryl Emerson and Michael Holquist. Austin: U of Texas P, 1981.

Barakat, Ibtisam. *Tasting the Sky: A Palestinian Childhood.* New York: Farrar, Straus and Giroux, 2007.

Barghouti, Mourid. *I Saw Ramallah.* Trans. Ahdaf Soueif. New York: Anchor Books, 2003.

Barlas, Asma. *"Believing Women" in Islam: Unreading Patriarchal Interpretations of the Qur'an.* Austin: U of Texas P, 2002.

Bayoumi, Moustafa. *How Does It Feel to Be a Problem? Being Young and Arab in America.* New York: Penguin, 2008.

Beard, Michael. "Royal Gossip and the Meaning of Fencing." *New York Times Book Review,* 1 February, 1987: 24.

Behdad, Ali. *A Forgetful Nation: On Immigration and Cultural Identity in the United States.* Durham: Duke UP, 2005.

Benson, Kathleen, and Philip Kayal, eds. *A Community of Many Worlds: Arab Americans in American Cities.* New York: Museum of the City of New York/Syracuse UP, 2002.

Berlinerblau, Jacques. *Heresy in the University: The Black Athena Controversy and the Responsibilities of American Intellectuals.* New Brunswick: Rutgers UP, 1999.

Berman, Antoine. *The Experience of the Foreign: Culture and Translation in Romantic Germany.* Trans. S. Heyvaert. Albany: SUNY P, 1992.

Bernal, Martin. *Black Athena: The Afroasiatic Roots of Classical Civilization,* 3 vols. New Brunswick: Rutgers UP: *The Fabrication of Ancient Greece 1785–1985, vol. 1* (1987). *The Archaeological and Documentary Evidence, vol. 2* (1991). *The Linguistic Evidence, vol. 3* (2006).

———. *Black Athena Writes Back: Martin Bernal Responds to His Critics.* Ed. David Chioni Moore. Durham: Duke UP, 2001.

Blaut, J. M. *The Colonizer's Model of the World: Geographical Diffusionism and Eurocentric History.* New York: Guilford, 1993.

Bokamba, Eyamba. "Thc Africanization of English." In Kachru (1992), 125–47.

Boosahda, Elizabeth. *Arab-American Faces and Voices: The Origins of an Immigrant Community.* Austin: U of Texas P, 2003.

Booth, Marilyn. "On Translation and Madness." *Translation Review* 65 (2003): 47–53.

Bosman, Julie. "Carter Book Stirs Furor With Its View of Israelis' 'Apartheid.'" *The New York Times* December 14, 2006. <http://www.nytimes.com/2006/12/14/books/14cart.html?_r=1>.

Boyle, Clara. *Boyle of Cairo.* Kendal: Titus Wilson, 1965.

Brunner, Jerome. "The Autobiographical Process." In Folkenflik, 38–56.

Bruss, Elizabeth. *Autobiographical Acts: The Changing Situation of a Literary Genre.* Baltimore: Johns Hopkins UP, 1976.

Buheiry, Marwan. *Intellectual Life in the Arab East, 1890–1939.* Beirut: American University of Beirut, 1981.

Burton, Richard. "Terminal Essay." *The Book of the Thousand and One Nights,* vol. 3. Trans. Richard Burton. New York: Heritage Press, 1934.

Bushrui, Suheil, and John Munro. Introduction. *A Chant of Mystics and Other Poems by Ameen Rihani.* Ed. Suheil Bushrui and John Munro. Beirut: The Rihani House, 1970.

Cainkar, Louise A. *Homeland Insecurity: The Arab American and Muslim American Experience After 9/11.* New York: Russell Sage Foundation, 2009.

Cartelli, Thomas. *Repositioning Shakespeare: National Formations, Postcolonial Appropriations.* London: Routledge, 1999.

Césaire, Aimé. *Discourse on Colonialism.* Trans. Joan Pinkham. New York: Monthly Review Press, 1972.

Christy, Arthur. *The Orient in American Transcendentalism: A Study of Emerson, Thoreau and Alcott.* New York: Columbia UP, 1932.

Clifford, James. *Routes: Travel and Translation in the Late Twentieth Century.* Cambridge: Harvard UP, 1997.

Coetzee, J. M. *Foe.* New York: Viking, 1987.

Cohen, Jeffrey Jerome. *The Postcolonial Middle Ages.* New York: St. Martin's, 2000.

Conrad, Joseph. *Heart of Darkness.* Ed. Robert Kimbrough. 3rd ed. New York: Norton, 1988.

Cook's Tourists' Handbook for Egypt, the Nile and the Desert. London: Thomas Cook & Son, 1897.

Cooke, Miriam. *War's Other Voices: Women Writers in the Lebanese Civil War.* New York: Cambridge UP, 1988.

———. *Women Claim Islam: Creating Islamic Feminism Through Literature.* New York: Routledge, 2001.

Cromer, Evelyn Baring. *Modern Egypt*, 2 vols. New York: Macmillan, 1908.

Dahab, Elizabeth. *Voices in Exile in Contemporary Canadian Francophone Literature.* Landham, Md.: Lexington Books, 2010.

Darraj, Susan Muaddi, ed. *Scheherazade's Legacy: Arab and Arab American Women on Writing.* Westport, Conn.: Praeger, 2004

Deleuze, Gilles, and Flix Guattari. *Kafka: Toward a Minor Literature.* Trans. Dana Polan. Minneapolis: U of Minnesota P, 1986.

Devine, Tom, and Paddy Logue, eds. *Being Scottish: Personal Reflections on Scottish Identity Today.* Edinburgh: Polygon, 2002.

Dimock, Wai Chee. *Through Other Continents: American Literature Across Deep Time.* Princeton: Princeton UP, 2006.

Dingwaney, Anuradha, and Carol Maier, eds. *Between Languages and Cultures: Translation and Cross-Cultural Texts.* Pittsburgh: U of Pittsburgh P, 1995.

Djebar, Assia. *L'amour, la fantasia.* Paris: Editions Jean-Claude Lattès, 1985. In English, *Fantasia: An Algerian Cavalcade.* Trans. Dorothy S. Blair. Portsmouth, N.H.: Heinemann, 1993.

Douglass, Frederick. *Narrative of the Life of Frederick Douglass, an American Slave.* New York: Penguin, 1982.

Du Bois, W. E. B. *The Souls of Black Folk.* New York: Penguin, 1989.

Dunnavent, Walter Edward III. "Ameen Rihani in America: Transcendentalism in an Arab-American Writer." Diss. Indiana U, 1991.

Durczak, Jerzy. *Selves Between Cultures: Contemporary American Bicultural Autobiography.* San Francisco: International Scholars Publications, 1999.

Eakin, Paul John. "Autobiography, Identity, and the Fictions of Memory." In Schacter and Scarry, 290–306.

Elaasar, Aladdin. *Silent Victims: The Plight of Arab & Muslim Americans in Post 9/11 America.* Bloomington, Ind.: AuthorHouse, 2004.

El-Enany, Rasheed. *Arab Representations of the Occident: East-West Encounters in Arabic Fiction.* London: Routledge, 2006.

Elia, Nada. "The Fourth Language: Subaltern Expression in Djebar's Fantasia." In Majaj,et al., 183–99.

Elkholy, Abdo. *The Arab Moslems in the United States*. New Haven: College and UP, 1966.

Elmusa, Sharif. "Dream on the Same Mattress." In *Orfalea and Elmusa*, 232–33.

Falcoff, Mark. Review of Ihab Hassan's *Out of Egypt*. *The American Spectator* 22:10 (October 1987): 48–49.

Fabian, Johannes. *Time and the Other: How Anthropology Makes its Object*. New York: Columbia UP, 1983.

Fanon, Frantz. *Black Skin, White Masks*. Trans. Charles Lam Markmann. New York: Grove Weidenfeld, 1967.

Findley, Paul. *They Dare To Speak Out: People and Institutions Confront Israel's Lobby*. Chicago: Lawrence Hill Books, 1989.

Folkenflik, Robert, ed. *The Culture of Autobiography: Constructions of Self-Representation*. Stanford: Stanford UP, 1993.

Frank, Andre Gunder. *ReOrient: Global Economy in the Asian Age*. Berkeley: U of California P, 1998.

Funk, Nathan C., and Betty J. Sitka. *Ameen Rihani: Bridging East and West, a Pioneering Call for Arab-American Understanding*. Lanham, Md.: UP of America, 2004.

Gabriel, Judith. "'Seducing America: Selling the Middle Eastern Mystique': Orientalist Ephemera Collection at UCLA on Its Way to Online Database, Book." *Aljadid: A Review & Record of Arab Culture and Arts* 11:52 (Summer 2005): 18–20.

Gates, Henry Louis, Jr. *The Signifying Monkey: A Theory of African American Literary Criticism*. New York: Oxford UP, 1988.

Gergen, Kenneth. "Mind, Text, and Society: Self-Memory in Social Context." In Neisser and Fivush, 78–104.

Ghali, Waguih. *Beer in the Snooker Club*. New York: Knopf, 1964.

Ghareeb, Edmund. *Split Vision: The Portrayal of Arabs in the American Media*. 2nd ed. Washington, D.C.: American-Arab Affairs Council, 1983.

Ghazoul, Ferial. "Halal Fiction." *Al-Ahram Weekly Online* 12–18 July 2001, no. 542, 13 January 2007. <http://weekly.ahram.org.eg/2001/542/b04.htm>.

Gibran, Kahlil. "Khalil al-kafir." *Al-arwah al-mutamarridah*. New York: Al-Mohajer, 1908. 66–125.

———. *Kitab Dam'a wa ibtisamah*. New York: Atlantic, 1914.

———. *The Madman: His Parables and Poems*. New York: Knopf, 1918.

———. *The Forerunner: His Parables and Poems*. New York: Knopf, 1920.

———. *Al-'awasif*. Cairo: Al-Hilal, 1920.

———. *Al-bada'i' wa al-tara'if*. Cairo: Yusuf al-Bustani, 1923.

———. *The Prophet*. New York: Knopf, 1923.

———. "To Young Americans of Syrian Origin." *The Syrian World* 1:1 (July 1926): 4–5.

———. *Jesus, the Son of Man*. New York: Knopf, 1928.

———. *Al-sanabil*. New York: As-Sa'ih, 1929.

———. *The Earth Gods*. New York: Knopf, 1931.

———. *The Garden of the Prophet*. New York: Knopf, 1933.

———. *A Treasury of Kahlil Gibran*. Ed. Martin L. Wolf. Trans. Anthony Rizkallah Ferris. New York: Citadel Press, 1951.

———. *Al-Mawakib*. Beirut: Mu'assasat Nawfal, 1981.

———. *Nusus kharij al-majmu‘*. Ed. Antoine al-Qawwal. Beirut: Dar Amwaj, 1993.

Gibran, Jean, and Kahlil Gibran. *Kahlil Gibran: His Life and World*. Boston: New York Graphic Society, 1974.

Gilmore, Leigh. *Autobiographics: A Feminist Theory of Female Self-Representation*. Ithaca: Cornell UP, 1994.

Gleason, Philip. "American Identity and Americanization." In Petersen, Novak, and Gleason, 57–143.

Gollomb, Joseph. "An Arabian Poet in New York." *The New York Evening Post* (March 29, 1919): Book section 1, 10.

Griswald, William J. *The Image of the Middle East in Secondary School Textbooks*. New York: Middle East Association of North America, 1975.

Gualtieri, Sarah. *Between Arab and White: Race and Ethnicity in the Early Syrian American Diaspora*. Berkeley: U of California P, 2009.

Haddad, George. *Mt. Lebanon to Vermont*. Rutland, Vt.: The Tuttle Co., 1916.

Haddad, Yvonne Yazbeck, ed. *The Muslims of America*. New York: Oxford UP, 1991.

———. *Not Quite American? The Shaping of Arab and Muslim Identity in the United States*. Waco: Baylor UP, 2004.

———, and Jane Idleman Smith, eds. *Muslim Communities in North America*. Albany: SUNY P, 1994.

Hagopian, Elain, and Ann Paden, eds. *The Arab-Americans: Studies in Assimilation*. Wilmette, Ill.: Medina UP International, 1969.

Halaby, Raouf J. "Dr. Michael Shadid and the Debate over Identity in the Syrian World." In Hooglund, 55–65.

Hamid, George A. *Circus*. New York: Sterling, 1950.

Harris, Wilson. *The Guyana Quartet*. London: Faber, 1975.

"Has the Syrian Become a Negro." *As-Shaab*, New York, May 24, 1929. Reprinted in *The Syrian World* 3:12 (June 1929): 42.

Hassan, Ihab. *The Right Promethean Fire: Imagination, Science, and Cultural Change*. Urbana: U of Illinois P, 1980.

———. *Out of Egypt: Scenes and Arguments of an Autobiography*. Carbondale and Edwardsville: Southern Illinois UP, 1986.

———. *The Postmodern Turn: Essays in Postmodern Theory and Culture*. Columbus: Ohio State UP, 1987.

———. *Selves at Risk: Patterns of Quest in Contemporary American Letters*. Madison: U of Wisconsin P, 1990.

———. *Rumors of Change: Essays of Five Decades*. Tuscaloosa: U of Alabama P, 1995.

Hassan, Waïl S. *Tayeb Salih: Ideology and the Craft of Fiction*. Syracuse: Syracuse UP, 2003.

Hawi, Khalil. *Kahlil Gibran: His Background, Character and Works*. Beirut: American University of Beirut, 1963.

Herzl, Theodor. *The Jewish State*. New York: American Zionist Emergency Council, 1946.

Hite, Molly. Foreword. In Morgan and Hall, xiii–xvi.

Hitti, Philip K. *The Syrians in America*. New York: George H. Doran Co., 1924.

Hooglund, Eric, ed. *Crossing the Waters: Arabic-Speaking Immigrants to the United States Before 1940*. Washington, D.C.: Smithsonian Institute Press, 1987.

Hornung, Alfred, and Ernstpeter Ruhe, eds. *Autobiographie & Avant-garde*. Tübingen: Gunter Narr Verlag, 1992.

Hourani, Albert. *Arabic Thought in the Liberal Age 1789–1939*. London: Oxford UP, 1970.

———. *A History of the Arab Peoples*. Cambridge, Mass.: Belknap, 1991.

———, and Nadim Shehadi, eds. *The Lebanese in the World: A Century of Immigration*. London: Center for Lebanese Studies/I.B. Tauris, 1992.

Husayn, Taha. *Mustaqbal al-thaqafa fi misr*. Cairo: Matba'at al-ma'arif, 1938.

Iser, Wolfgang. "The Emergence of a Cross-Cultural Discourse: Thomas Carlyle's Sartor Resartus." *The Translatability of Cultures*. Ed. Sanford Budick and Wolfgang Iser. Stanford: Stanford UP, 1996. 245–64.

Jabra, Jabra Ibrahim. *Hunters in a Narrow Street*. Washington, D.C.: Three Continents Press, 1990.

Jamal, Amaney, and Nadine Naber, eds. *Race and Arab Americans Before and After 9/11: From Invisible Citizens to Visible Subjects*. Syracuse: Syracuse UP, 2008.

James, Lawrence. *Imperial Warrior: The Life and Times of Field-Marshal Viscount Allenby 1861-1936*. London: Weidenfeld and Nicolson, 1993.

Jarrar, Samir Ahmad. "The Treatment of Arabs in U.S. Social Studies Textbooks." In Ghareeb, 381–90.

Jayyusi, Salma Khadra. *Trends and Movements in Modern Arabic Poetry*. 2 vols. Leiden: Brill, 1977.

Judy, Ronald A.T. *(Dis)Forming the American Canon: African-Arabic Slave Narratives and the Vernacular*. Minneapolis: U of Minnesota P, 1993.

Kachru, Braj. *The Indianization of English*. New Delhi: Oxford UP, 1983.

———, ed. *The Other Tongue: English Across Cultures*, 2nd ed. Urbana: U of Illinois P, 1992.

Kadi, Joanna, ed. *Food for Our Grandmothers: Writings of Arab-American and Arab-Canadian Feminists*. Boston: South End Press, 1994.

Kahf, Mohja. "Packaging 'Huda': Sha'rawi's Memoirs in the United States Reception Environment." In Amireh and Majaj, 148–72.

———. *Emails from Sheherazad*. Gainesville: UP of Florida, 2003.

———. *The Girl in the Tangerine Scarf*. New York: Carroll & Graf, 2006.

Kaldas, Pauline, and Khaled Mattawa, eds. *Dinarzad's Children: An Anthology of Contemporary Arab American Fiction*. Fayetteville: U of Arkansas P, 2004.

Kanafani, Ghassan. *Palestine's Children: "Returning to Haifa" and Other Stories*. Trans. Barbara Harlow and Karen Riley. Boulder: Lynne Rienner, 2000.

Karim, Karim H. *Islamic Peril: Media and Global Violence*. Montreal: Black Rose Books, 2000.

Karmi, Ghada. *In Search of Fatima: A Palestinian Story*. London: Verso, 2002.

Katibah, Habib I. "What Is Americanism?" *The Syrian World* 1:3 (September 1926): 16–20.

Kayal, Philip, and Joseph Kayal. *The Syrian-Lebanese in America: A Study in Religion and Assimilation*. Boston: Twayne Publishers, 1975.

Kayat, Assaad Y. *A Voice from Lebanon*. London: Madden & Co., 1847.

Kenny, L.M. "The Middle East in Canadian Social Science Textbooks." In Abu-Laban and Zeadey, 133–47.

Khalidi, Rashid. *Resurrecting Empire: Western Footprints and America's Perilous Path in the Middle East*. Boston: Beacon, 2004.

Khatibi, Abdelkébir. *L'amour bilingue*. Paris: Fata Morgana, 1983. In English, *Love in Two Languages*. Trans. Richard Howard. Minneapolis: U of Minnesota P, 1990.

Khouri, Norma. *Honor Lost: Love and Death in Modern-Day Jordan*. New York: Atria, 2003.

Kilito, Abdelfattah. *Les séances: Récits et codes culturels chez Hamadhanî et Harîrî.* Paris: Sindbad, 1983.

———. *The Author and His Doubles: Essays on Classical Arabic Culture.* Trans. Michael Cooperson. Syracuse: Syracuse UP, 2001.

———. *Thou Shalt Not Speak My Language.* Trans. Waïl S. Hassan. Syracuse: Syracuse UP, 2008.

King, Bruce. Review of Ahdaf Soueif's *The Map of Love. World Literature Today* 74:2 (Spring 2000): 453.

Klinkowitz, Jerome. *Rosenberg, Barthes, Hassan: The Postmodern Habit of Thought.* Athens: U of Georgia P, 1988.

Knippling, Aplana Sharma, ed. *New Immigrant Literatures in the United States: A Sourcebook to Our Multicultural Literary Heritage.* Westport, Conn.: Greenwood, 1996.

Lejeune, Philippe. *Le pacte autobiographique.* Paris: Éditions du Seuil, 1975.

Levy, Lital. "Exchanging Words: Thematizations of Translation in Arabic Writing from Israel." *Comparative Studies of South Asia, Africa and the Middle East* 23: 1–2 (2003): 106–27.

Loomba, Ania, and Martin Orkin. *Post-Colonial Shakespeares.* London: Routledge, 1998.

Macaulay, Thomas Babington. "Indian Education: Minute of the 2nd of February, 1835." *Macaulay: Prose and Poetry.* Ed. G. M. Young. London: Rupert Hart-Davis, 1952. 719–30.

Maier, Carol. "Toward a Theoretical Practice for Cross-Cultural Translation." In Dingwaney and Maier, 21–38.

Majaj, Lisa Suhair. "Arab American Literature and the Politics of Memory." In *Memory and Cultural Politics: New Approaches to American Ethnic Literatures.* Ed. Amritjit Singh, Joseph Skerrett, Jr., and Robert Hogan. Boston: Northeastern UP, 1996. 266–90.

———. "New Directions: Arab-American Writing at Century's End." In Mattawa and Akash, 67–77.

———. "Arab-Americans and the Meaning of Race." In Singh and Schmidt, 320–37.

———, and Amal Amireh, eds. *Etel Adnan: Critical Essays on the Arab-American Writer and Artist.* Jefferson, N. C.: McFarland, 2002.

———, Paula W. Sunderman, and Therese Saliba, eds. *Intersections: Gender, Nation, and Community in Arab Women's Novels.* Syracuse: Syracuse UP, 2002.

Makdisi, Jean Said. *Teta, Mother, and Me: Three Generations of Arab Women.* New York: Norton, 2006.

Maleh, Layla Al. "Anglophone Arab Literature: An Overview." In *Arab Voices in Diaspora: Critical Perspectives on Anglophone Arab Literature.* Ed. Layla Al Maleh. Amsterdam: Rodopi, 2009. 1–63.

Malek, Abbas. *News Media and Foreign Relations: A Multi-faceted Perspective.* Norwood, N.J.: Ablex Publishing, 1996.

Martin, Jonathan, and Amie Parnes. "McCain: Obama Not an Arab, Crowd Boos." *Politico* 10/10/2008. http://www.politico.com/news/stories/1008/14479.html

Massad, Joseph. "The Politics of Desire in the Writings of Ahdaf Soueif." *Journal of Palestine Studies* 28:4 (Summer 1999): 74–90.

Mattawa, Khaled, and Munir Akash, eds. *Post-Gibran: Anthology of New Arab-American Writing.* Bethesda: Jusoor, 1999.

McCarus, Ernest. *The Development of Arab-American Identity.* Ann Arbor: U of Michigan P, 1994.

Mehdi, Beverlee Turner, ed. *The Arabs in America 1492–1977: A Chronology & Fact Book.* Dobbs Ferry, N.Y.: Oceana Publications, 1978.

Mehrez, Samia. "Translation and the Postcolonial Experience: The Francophone North African Text." In Venuti (1992), 120–38.

Melman, Billie. *Women's Orients: English Women and the Middle East, 1718–1918.* Ann Arbor: U of Michigan P, 1992.

Menocal, María Rosa. *The Arabic Role in Medieval Literary History: A Forgotten Heritage.* Philadelphia: U of Pennsylvania P, 1987.

———. *The Ornament of the World: How Muslims, Jews, and Christians Created a Culture of Tolerance in Medieval Spain.* New York: Little, Brown and Co., 2002.

———, Jerrilynn Dodds, and Abigail Krasner Balbale. *The Arts of Intimacy: Christians, Jews, and Muslims in the Making of Castilian Culture.* New Haven: Yale UP, 2008.

Mernissi, Fatima. *The veil and the male elite: a feminist interpretation of women's rights in Islam.* Trans. Mary Jo Lakeland. Reading, Mass.: Addison-Wesley, 1991.

Mikhail, Mona. *Studies in the Short Fiction of Mahfouz and Idris.* New York: New York UP, 1992.

Miller, Sally M. *The Ethnic Press in the United States: A Historical Analysis and Handbook.* New York: Greenwood, 1987.

Mokarzel, Salloum. Foreword. *The Syrian World* 1:1 (July 1926): 1–3.

Moore-Gilbert, Bart. *Postcolonial Theory: Contexts, Practices, Politics.* London: Verso, 1997.

Morgan, Janice. "Subject to Subject/Voice to Voice: Twentieth Century Autobiographical Fiction by Women Writers." In Morgan and Hall, 3–19.

———, and Colette Hall, eds. *Redefining Autobiography in Twentieth-Century Women's Fiction.* New York: Garland, 1991.

Morrison, Toni. *Beloved.* New York: Plume, 1987.

———. *Playing in the Dark: Whiteness and the Literary Imagination.* Cambridge: Harvard UP, 1992.

Mousa, Fatma. "Alf layla wa layla wa kutub al-rahalat fil-qarn at-tasi' 'ashar." *Fusul* 13:2 (Summer 1994): 229–46.

Naff, Alixa. *Becoming American: The Early Arab Immigrant Experience.* Carbondale: Southern Illinois UP, 1985.

———. "The Arabic-Language Press." In Miller, 1–14.

Naimy, Nadeem. *The Lebanese Prophets of New York.* Beirut: American U of Beirut P, 1985.

Nash, Geoffrey P. "Ameen Rihani's *The Book of Khalid* and the Voice of Thomas Carlyle." *New Comparison* 17 (1994): 35–49.

———. *The Arab Writer in English: Arab Themes in a Metropolitan Language, 1908–1958.* Brighton: Sussex Academic P, 1998.

———. *The Anglo-Arab Encounter: Fiction and Autobiography by Arab Writers in English.* Bern: Peter Lang, 2007.

Nassar, Eugene Paul. *Wind of the Land: Two Prose Poems.* Belmont, Mass.: Association of Arab American University Graduates, 1979.

———. *Essays Critical and Metacritical.* East Brunswick, N.J.: Associated UP, 1983. 84–102.

Neisser, Ulric, and Robyn Fivush, eds. *The Remembering Self: Construction and Accuracy in the Self-Narrative.* New York: Cambridge UP, 1994.

Nerval, Gérard de. *Voyage en Orient,* 2 vols. Paris: Garnier-Flammarion, 1980.

Ngugi wa Thiong'o. *Decolonising the Mind: The Politics of Language in African Literature.* Portsmouth, N.H.: Heinemann, 1986.

Niranjana, Tejaswini. *Siting Translation: History, Poststructuralism, and the Colonial Context*. Berkeley: U of California P, 1992.

Nusseibeh, Sari, with Anthony David. *Once Upon a Country: A Palestinian Life*. New York: Farrar, Straus and Giroux, 2007.

Olney, James, ed. *Autobiography: Essays Theoretical and Critical*. Princeton: Princeton UP, 1980.

Orfalea, Gregory. "Literary Devolution: The Arab in the Post-World War II Novel in English." *Journal of Palestine Studies* 17:2 (Winter 1988): 109–28.

———. *The Arab-Americans: A History*. Northampton, Mass.: Olive Branch Press, 2008.

———. *Angeleno Days: An Arab American Writer on Family, Place, and Politics*. Tucson: U of Arizona P, 2009.

———, and Sharif Elmusa, eds. *Grape Leaves: A Century of Arab American Poetry*. Salt Lake City: U of Utah P, 1988.

Pakravan, Saïdeh. "An Interview with Ahdaf Soueif." *Edebiyât* 6 (1995): 275–86.

Pascal, Roy. *Design and Truth in Autobiography*. Cambridge: Harvard UP, 1960.

Perry, Glenn. "The Treatment of the Middle East in American High School Textbooks." *Journal of Palestine Studies* 4:3 (1975): 46–58.

Petersen, William, Michael Novak, and Philip Gleason. *Concepts of Ethnicity*. Cambridge: Belknap, 1982.

Pratt, Mary Louise. *Imperial Eyes: Travel Writing and Transculturation*. New York: Routledge, 1992.

Pynchon, Thomas. *The Crying of Lot 49*. New York: Harper & Row, 1990.

Reynolds, Dwight F., ed. *Interpreting the Self: Autobiography in the Arabic Literary Tradition*. Berkeley: U of California P, 2001.

Rihani, Albert. *Where to Find Ameen Rihani: Bibliography*. Beirut: The Arab Institute for Research and Publishing, 1979.

Rihani, Ameen, trans. *The Quatrains of Abu'l-Ala*. New York: Doubleday, Page & Company, 1903.

———. *Myrtle and Myrrh*. Boston: The Gorham Press, 1905.

———. *The Book of Khalid*. New York: Dodd, Mead, and Company, 1911.

———. *The Luzumiyat of Abu'l-Ala*, trans. New York: James T. White & Co., 1918.

———. *The Descent of Bolshevism*. Boston: The Alpine Press, 1920.

———. *A Chant of Mystics and Other Poems*. New York: James T. White & Co., 1921.

———. *The Path of Vision: Essays of East and West*. New York: James T. White Co., 1921.

———. "Where East and West Meet." *The Syrian World* 1:12 (June 1927): 8–11.

———. *The Maker of Modern Arabia*. Boston: Houghton Mifflin, 1928.

———. *Around the Coasts of Arabia*. London: Constable and Co., 1930. Boston: Houghton Mifflin, 1931.

———. *Arabian Peak and Desert*. London: Constable and Co., 1931. Boston: Houghton Mifflin, 1931.

———. *The Fate of Palestine: A Series of Lectures, Articles, and Documents about the Palestinian Problem and Zionism*. Beirut: The Rihani Printing and Publishing House, 1967.

———. *Al-A'mal al-'arabiyyah al-kamilah*. 12 vols. Ed. Ameen Albert Rihani. Beirut: Al-mu'assassah al-'arabiyyah li al-dirasat wa al-nashr, 1980–86.

———. *Wajdah: A Play in Four Acts*. Washington, D.C.: Platform International, 2001.

———. *The Lore of the Arabian Nights*. Washington, D.C.: Platform International, 2002.

Rihani, Ameen Albert. *Faylasuf al-Freike, sahib al-madinah al-'udhma*. Beirut: Dar al-Jil, 1987.

Rihbany, Abraham Mitrie. *A Far Journey*. Boston: Houghton Mifflin, 1914.

———. *The Syrian Christ*. Boston: Houghton Mifflin, 1916.

———. *Militant America and Jesus Christ*. Boston: Houghton Mifflin, 1917.

———. *America Save the Near East*. Boston: Beacon, 1918.

———. *The Hidden Treasure of Rasmola*. Boston: Houghton Mifflin, 1920.

———. *Wise Men from the East and from the West*. Boston: Houghton Mifflin, 1922.

———. *The Christ Story for Boys and Girls*. Boston: Houghton Mifflin, 1923.

———. *Seven Days with God*. Boston: Houghton Mifflin, 1926.

———. *The Five Interpretations of Jesus*. Boston: Houghton Mifflin, 1940.

Rizk, Salom. *Syrian Yankee*. New York: Doubleday, 1943.

Robinson, Douglas. *Translation & Taboo*. DeKalb: Northern Illinois UP, 1996.

Ross, Edward. *The Old World in the New: The Significance of Past and Present Immigration to the American People*. New York: The Century Co., 1914.

Said, Edward W. *Orientalism*. New York: Penguin, 1978.

———. *The Question of Palestine*. New York: Times Books, 1979.

———. "Orientalism Reconsidered." *Race and Class* 27:2 (1985): 1–15.

———, with Jean Mohr. *After the Last Sky*. New York: Pantheon, 1986.

———, and Christopher Hitchens, eds. *Blaming the Victims: Spurious Scholarship and the Palestinian Question*. London: Verso, 1987.

———. "Embargoed Literature." *The Nation* 251:8 (September 17, 1990): 278–80.

———. "The Anglo-Arab Encounter." *Times Literary Supplement* (June 19, 1992): 9. Reprinted in *Reflections on Exile* 405–10.

———. *Culture and Imperialism*. New York: Knopf, 1993.

———. *The Politics of Dispossession: The Struggle for Palestinian Self-Determination 1969–1994*. New York: Pantheon, 1994.

———. *Peace and Its Discontents: Essays on Palestine in the Middle East Peace Process*. New York: Vintage, 1996.

———. *Covering Islam: How the Media and the Experts Determine How We See the Rest of the World*. 2nd ed. New York: Vintage, 1997.

———. *Out of Place: A Memoir*. New York: Alfred Knopf, 1999.

———. *Reflections on Exile and Other Essays*. Cambridge, Mass.: Harvard UP, 2000.

———. "The Cruelty of Memory." *The New York Review of Books* 47:19 (November 30, 2000): 46–50.

———. *The End of the Peace Process: Oslo and After*. New York: Pantheon, 2000.

———. *In Search of Palestine: Edward Said's Return Home*. Directed by Charles Bruce. Princeton: Films for the Humanities and Sciences, 2005.

Salaita, Steven. *Anti-Arab Racism in the USA: Where It Comes From and What It Means for Politics Today*. London: Pluto, 2006.

———. *Arab American Literary Fictions, Cultures, and Politics*. New York: Palgrave, 2007.

———. *Modern Arab-American Fiction: A Reader's Guide*. Syracuse: Syracuse UP, 2011.

Salem, Elise. *Constructing Lebanon: A Century of Literary Narratives*. Gainesville: UP of Florida, 2003.

Salem, Lori Ann. "Far-Off and Fascinating Things: Wadeeha Atiyeh and Images of Arabs in the American Popular Theater, 1930–1950." In Suleiman (1999), 272–83.

Salih, Tayeb. *Season of Migration to the North.* Trans. Denys Johnson-Davies. London: Heinemann, 1969.

———. "Al-Tayyib Salih riwa'iyyan wa naqidan." Al-Tayyib Salih: 'Abqari al-riwaya al-'arabiyya. Ahmad Sa'id Muhamadiyya, et al., eds. Beirut: Dar al-'awda, 1976. 118–36.

———. "Nahwa ufuqin ba'id, 144." *Al-Majallah* 612 (October 30–November 5, 1991): 94.

———. *Bandarshah.* Trans. Denys Johnson-Davies. London: Kegan Paul, 1996.

———. "Yawm mubarak 'ala shati' Umm Bab." *Mukhtarat min al-qisas al-qasira fi 18 baladan 'arabiyyan.* Ed. al-Tahir Ahmad Makki. Cairo: Markaz al-Ahram li al-tarjama wa al-nashr, 1993.

Salti, Ramzi. *The Native Informant: Six Tales of Defiance from the Arab World.* Colorado Springs: Three Continents Press, 1994.

———. *Exploring Arab Concepts of Homosexuality.* Diss., University of California-Riverside, 1997.

Samhan, Helen Hatab. "Politics and Exclusion: The Arab American Experience." *Journal of Palestine Studies* 16:2 (Winter 1987): 11–28.

———. "Not Quite White: Race Classification and the Arab-American Experience." In Suleiman (1999), 209–26.

Sam'o, Elias. "The Arab-Israeli Conflict as Reported by the Kalb Brothers." In Abu-Laban and Zeadey, 45–52.

Sartre, Jean-Paul. "Orphée noir." In *Anthologie de la nouvelle poésie nègre et malgache.* Ed. Léopold Sédar Senghor. Paris: Presses Universitaires de France, 1948. ix–xliv.

Savage, Raymond. *Allenby of Armageddon.* Indianapolis: Bobbs-Merrill, 1926.

Schacter, Daniel, and Elaine Scarry, eds. *Memory, Brain, and Belief.* Cambridge, Mass.: Harvard UP, 2000.

Schueller, Malini Johar. *U.S. Orientalisms: Race, Nation, and Gender in Literature, 1790–1890.* Ann Arbor: U of Michigan P, 1998.

Semmerling, Tim Jon. *"Evil" Arabs in American Popular Film: Orientalist Fear.* Austin: U of Texas P, 2006.

Sengupta, Mahasweta. "Translation as Manipulation: The Power of Images and Images of Power." In Dingwaney and Maier, 159–74.

Sha'ban, Fuad. *Islam and Arabs in Early American Thought: The Roots of Orientalism in America.* Durham: Acorn, 1991.

———. *For Zion's Sake: The Judeo-Christian Tradition in American Culture.* London: Pluto, 2005.

Shaheen, Jack. *The TV Arab.* Bowling Green: Bowling Green State UP, 1984.

———. *Arab and Muslim Stereotyping in American Popular Culture.* Washington, D.C.: Center for Muslim Christian Understanding, 1997.

———. *Reel Bad Arabs: How Hollywood Vilifies a People.* Northampton, Mass.: Olive Branch Press, 2001.

———. *Guilty: Hollywood's Verdict on Arabs after 9/11.* Northampton, Mass.: Olive Branch Press, 2008.

Shahid, Irfan. "Amin al-Rihani and King 'Abdul-'Aziz Ibn Sa'ud." *Arab Civilization: Challenges and Responses.* Ed. George N. Atiyeh and Ibrahim M. Oweiss. Albany: SUNY P, 1988.

———. "Gibran and the American Literary Canon: The Problem of The Prophet." *Tradition, Modernity, and Postmodernity in Arabic Literature.* Ed. Kamal Abdel-Malek and Wael Hallaq. Leiden: Brill, 2000. 321–34.

Shakir, Evelyn. "Pretending to Be Arab: Role-Playing in Vance Bourjaily's 'The Fractional Man.'" *MELUS* 9:1 (Spring 1982): 7–21.

———. "Mother's Milk: Women in Arab-American Autobiography." *MELUS* 15:4 (Winter 1988): 39–50.

———. "Arab Mothers, American Sons: Women in Arab-American Autobiographies." *MELUS* 17:3 (Fall 1991): 5–15.

———. "Arab-American Literature." In Knippling, 3–18.

———. *Bint Arab: Arab and Arab American Women in the United States*. Westport, Conn.: Praeger, 1997.

Shalal-Esa, Andrea. "The Politics of Getting Published: The Continuing Struggle of Arab-American Writers." *Al-Jadid: A Review & Record of Arab Culture and Arts* 15:61 (2009). http://www.aljadid.com/essays_and_features/ArabAmericanWriters.html

Shamma, Tarek. "The Exotic Dimension of Foreignizing Strategies: Burton's Translation of the Arabian Nights." *The Translator* 11:1 (2005): 51–67.

Shammas, Anton. *Arabesques*. Trans. Vivian Eden. New York: Harper & Row, 1988.

Sharabi, Hisham. *Neopatriarchy: A Theory of Distorted Change in Arab Society*. New York: Oxford UP, 1988.

———. *Embers and Ashes: Memoirs of An Arab Intellectual*. Trans. Issa J. Boullata. Northampton, Mass.: Olive Branch Press, 2008.

Shell, Marc, and Werner Sollors, eds. *The Multilingual Anthology of American Literature*. New York: New York UP, 2000.

Shields, John C. *The American Aeneas: Classical Origins of the American Self*. Knoxville: U of Tennessee P, 2001.

Shihab, Aziz. *Does the Land Remember Me? A Memoir of Palestine*. Syracuse: Syracuse UP, 2007.

Siddiq, Muhammad. "Al-kitaba bi al-'ibriyya al-fusha: Taqdim riwayat 'arabisk wa hiwar ma'a Anton Shammas." *Alif: Journal of Comparative Poetics* 20 (2000): 155–67.

Simon, Reeva. *The Middle East in Crime Fiction: Mysteries, Spy Novels, and Thrillers from 1916 to the 1980s*. New York: Lilian Barber, 1989.

Singh, Amritjit, and Peter Schmidt, eds. *Postcolonial Theory and the United States: Race, Ethnicity, and Literature*. Jackson: U of Mississippi P, 2000.

Smith, Sidonie. *A Poetics of Women's Autobiography: Marginality and Self-Representation*. Bloomington: Indiana UP, 1987.

Sollors, Werner, ed. *Multilingual America: Transnationalism, Ethnicity, and the Languages of American Literature*. New York: New York UP, 1998.

Soueif, Ahdaf. *Aisha*. London: Jonathan Cape, 1983.

———. *In the Eye of the Sun*. New York: Pantheon, 1993.

———. *Sandpiper*. London: Bloomsbury, 1996.

———. *Zinat al-hayah*. Cairo: Dar al-Hilal, 1996.

———. *Mukhtarat min a'mal Ahdaf Soueif*. Cairo: General Egyptian Book Organization, 1998.

———. *The Map of Love* (1999). New York: Anchor, 2000.

———. "Ahdaf Soueif: Talking about *The Map of Love*." *EnterText* 1:3 (2000): 97–112.

———. *Mezzaterra: Fragments from the Common Ground*. New York: Anchor, 2005.

———. *I Think of You: Stories*. New York: Anchor Books, 2007.

Spenglemann, William. *The Forms of Autobiography: Episodes in the History of a Literary Genre*. New Haven: Yale UP, 1980.

Spivak, Gayatri Chakravorty. "Can the Subaltern Speak?" *Marxism and the Interpretation of Culture*. Ed. Cary Nelson and Lawrence Grossberg. Urbana: U of Illinois P, 1988. 271–313.

———. "The Politics of Translation." *Outside in the Teaching Machine*. New York: Routledge, 1993.

Starr, Deborah. "Drinking, Gambling, and Making Merry: Waguih Ghali's Search for Cosmopolitan Agency." *Middle Eastern Literatures* 9:3 (December 2006): 271–85.

Steet, Linda. *Veils and Daggers: A Century of National Geographic's Representation of the Arab World*. Philadelphia: Temple UP, 2000.

Sturrock, John. "Theory vs. Autobiography." In Folkenflik, 21–37.

Suleiman, Michael. "Perceptions of the Middle East in American News Magazines." In Abu-Laban and Zeadey, 28–44.

———. *Arabs in the Mind of America*. Brattleboro, Vt.: Amana Books, 1988.

———. "Early Arab-Americans: The Search for Identity." In Hooglund, 37–54.

———. "Arab-Americans and the Political Process." In McCarus, 37–60.

———, ed. *Arabs in America: Building a New Future*. Philadelphia: Temple UP, 1999.

Stockton, Ronald. "Ethnic Stereotypes and the Arab Image." In McCarus, 119–53.

Sutherland, John. "The Booker Turns a New Leaf." *The Guardian* October 26, 1999. 5.

Tanoukhi, Nirvana. "Rewriting Political Commitment for an International Canon: Paul Bowles's *For Bread Alone* as Translation of Mohamed Choukri's *Al-khubz al-hafi*." *Research in African Literatures* 34:2 (Summer 2003): 127–44.

Terry, Janice. *Mistaken Identity: Arab Stereotypes in Popular Writing*. Washington, D.C.: American-Arab Affairs Council, 1985.

Tolan, John V. *Saracens: Islam and the Medieval European Imagination*. New York: Columbia UP, 2002.

Toubbeh, Jamil I. *Day of the Long Night: A Palestinian Refugee Remembers the Nakba*. Jefferson, N.C.: McFarland, 1998.

Trafton, Scott. *Egypt Land: Race and Nineteenth-Century American Egyptomania*. Durham: Duke UP, 2004.

Turki, Fawaz. *The Disinherited: Journal of a Palestinian Exile, With an Epilogue 1974*. New York: Monthly Review Press, 1974.

———. *Poems from Exile*. Washington, D.C.: Free Palestine Press, 1975.

———. *Tel Zaatar Was the Hill of Thyme: Poems from Palestine*. Washington, D.C.: Free Palestine Press, 1978.

———. *Soul in Exile: Lives of a Palestinian Revolutionary*. New York: Monthly Review Press, 1988.

———. *Exile's Return: The Making of a Palestinian American*. New York: Free Press, 1994.

Venuti, Lawrence, ed. *Rethinking Translation: Discourse, Subjectivity, Ideology*. London: Routledge, 1992. 1–17.

———. *The Translator's Invisibility: A History of Translation*. London: Routledge, 1995.

———. *Scandals of Translation: Towards an Ethics of Difference*. London: Routledge, 1998.

Vishwanathan, Gauri. *Masks of Conquest: Literary Study and British Rule in India*. New York: Columbia UP, 1989.

Wadud, Amina. *Qur'an and Woman: Rereading the Sacred Text from a Woman's Perspective*. 2nd ed. New York: Oxford UP, 1999.

———. *Inside the Gender Jihad: Women's Reform in Islam*. Oxford: Oneworld, 2006.

Waterfield, Robin. *Prophet: The Life and Times of Kahlil Gibran*. New York: St. Martin's, 1998.

Wavell, Archibald. *Allenby: A Study in Greatness*. New York: Oxford UP, 1941.

Webster's New World Dictionary of American English. Third College Ed. New York: Simon & Schuster, 1988.

Wendell, Thomas. *Hinduism Invades America*. New York: Beacon, 1930.

Wilson-Goldie, Kaelen. "Living to Tell the Tale." *The Review at The National* June 27, 2008. 10. http://www.thenational.ae/apps/pbcs.dll/article?AID=/20080627/REVIEW/708930937

Winant, Howard. *Racial Conditions*. Minneapolis: U of Minnesota P, 1994.

Woods, Robert A., ed. *The City Wilderness: A Settlement Study*. Boston: Houghton Mifflin, 1898.

Young, Barbara. *This Man from Lebanon*. New York: Knopf, 1945.

Young, Robert J.C. *The Idea of English Ethnicity*. Oxford: Blackwell, 2008.

Younis, Adele L. *The Coming of the Arabic-Speaking People to the United States*. Ed. Philip M. Kayal. New York: Center for Migration Studies, 1995.

Yeazell, Ruth Bernard. *Harems of the Mind: Passages of Western Art and Literature*. New Haven: Yale UP, 2000.

INDEX

CPSIA information can be obtained at www.ICGtesting.com
Printed in the USA
BVOW01s0851210514

354034BV00002B/7/P